FREEPORTS AND FREE ZONES

MARITIME AND TRANSPORT LAW LIBRARY

MARITIME AND TRANSPORT LAW LIBRARY

Ship Building, Sale and Finance
Edited by Bariş Soyer and Andrew Tettenborn

The Modern Law of Marine Insurance
Volume 4
Edited by D. Rhidian Thomas

Air Cargo Insurance
Malcom A. Clarke and George Leloudas

Offshore Oil and Gas Installations Security
An International Perspective
Mikhail Kashubsky

International Trade and Carriage of Goods
Edited by Bariş Soyer and Andrew Tettenborn

Maritime Law and Practice in China
Liang Zhao and Lianjun Li

Maritime Cross-Border Insolvency
Lia Athanassiou

The Law of Yachts and Yachting
Second Edition
Edited by Filippo Lorenzon and Richard Coles

Maritime Liabilities in a Global and Regional Context
Edited by Bariş Soyer and Andrew Tettenborn

New Technologies, Artificial Intelligence and Shipping Law in the 21st Century
Edited by Bariş Soyer and Andrew Tettenborn

The Law of Wreck
Nicholas Gaskell and Craig Forrest

Codification of Maritime Law
Challenges, Possibilities and Experience
Edited by Zuzanna Pepłowska-Dąbrowska and Justyna Nawrot

Transport Documents in Carriage of Goods by Sea
International Law and Practice
By Caslav Pejovic

Maritime Law
Fifth Edition
Edited by Yvonne Baatz

Ship Operations: New Risks, Liabilities and Technologies in the Maritime Sector
Edited by Bariş Soyer and Andrew Tettenborn

Maritime Safety in Europe
Edited by Justyna Nawrot and Zuzanna Pepłowska-Dąbrowska

Fresh Produce Shipping
Damages and Compensation
Rex C. Tester

Freeports and Free Zones
Operations and Regulation in the Global Economy
Mark Rowbotham

Disruptive Technologies, Climate Change and Shipping
Edited by Bariş Soyer and Andrew Tettenborn

For more information about this series, please visit:
www.routledge.com/Maritime-and-Transport-Law-Library/book-series/MTLL

FREEPORTS AND FREE ZONES

OPERATIONS AND REGULATION IN THE GLOBAL ECONOMY

MARK ROWBOTHAM

informa law
from Routledge

First published 2022
by Informa Law from Routledge
2 Park Square, Milton Park, Abingdon, Oxon OX14 4RN

and by Routledge
605 Third Avenue, New York, NY 10158

Informa Law from Routledge is an imprint of the Taylor & Francis Group, an informa business

British Library Cataloguing-in-Publication Data
A catalogue record for this book is available from the British Library

Library of Congress Cataloging-in-Publication Data
A catalog record has been requested for this book

ISBN: 978-1-032-14025-4 (hbk)
ISBN: 978-1-032-14029-2 (pbk)
ISBN: 978-1-003-23202-5 (ebk)

DOI: 10.4324/9781003232025

CONTENTS

ABOUT THE AUTHOR

Mark Rowbotham is an international consultant, trainer and writer in Customs and VAT Compliance and Risk issues, as well as other areas including International Trade, Excise, Import and Export Controls, Oil & Gas/Renewables Offshore and Marine issues. He has spent a considerable length of time working in both the Government, Commercial and Academic sectors. He deals primarily with Compliance, Control and Procedural issues in Customs, Excise, VAT and Logistics, and is a trainer in these issues as well as International Trade, the Supply Chain, Finance and Risk Management courses.

He was originally an officer in HM Customs & Excise, dealing with Import and Export Controls on maritime freight traffic into and out of UK ports, and became an independent consultant and trainer in 2000, dealing primarily with Customs compliances, procedures and documentation. He advises on these issues, and undertakes training, advisory and consultancy work in these areas.

He gained a Master's Degree in International Relations and Political Economy in 1995, as well as a graduate qualification with the Institute of Export, and is a Chartered Fellow of the Chartered Institute of Logistics and Transport (UK).

He has written extensively on the subjects of Customs, International Supply Chain and Marine Compliance issues for a wide variety of International Trade and Logistics publications and journals, and has had two books published. The first, in 2008, was entitled *Introduction to Marine Cargo Management*, with the second edition published 2015. The second, published in 2021, is called *Cybernetic Synergy*, concerning the use of cybernetics in business, and a third, on the subject of Freeports and Free Zones, is due to be published later in 2021. He also advises several Chambers of Commerce in the UK on Customs, VAT and International Trade issues, including Freeports and Free Zones, frequently delivering advice, training courses and seminars on these subjects, as well as presenting papers on Freeports and Free Zones to symposiums. To this extent, he wrote and presented a paper on the comparisons between the Prestwick Freeport and the Montréal Mirabel Free-Trade Zone for a symposium at Glasgow University in 2004, as well as previously advising the Québec Investment Authority on the merits of the Montréal Free-Trade Zone. He is an accredited trainer in Customs & International Trade for the British Chambers of Commerce, and is also an adviser to the Department of International Trade on Customs and VAT Procedures pertaining to international trade.

FOREWORD

Mark Rowbotham is a nationally and internationally recognised expert in the detail and operational practice of Freeports and Free Zones and his book comes at a time when the UK is on the point of launching into the highly competitive world in which Freeports and Free Zones operate.

I have known and worked with Mark for many years and I respect his uncompromising views and the clarity of his vision. His book is a pragmatic, detailed account of the history, context and crucial modern relevance of Freeports and Free Zones. It speaks openly about their benefits, their regenerative capacity, their flexibility. It also addresses areas of risk and potential abuse and details strategies for mitigation.

The timeliness of this publication coincides with a dearth of knowledge on the subject matter amongst logistics providers, shippers, governments (both national and local) and national media. Indeed this lack of knowledge has demonstrated the capacity to spark quite unreasonable alarm amongst some political parties and newspapers when a calm analysis of the subject should have allayed fears and suspicions.

Mark uses his experience and expertise in this book to provide that calm analysis.

It would be naïve to suggest that understanding Freeports and Free Zones is a small undertaking but this book works exceptionally well as a detailed guide for those perhaps approaching the matter for this first time and, indeed, for those who are in need of refreshment.

Through case studies and worked examples, the technical examples of operation within these Zones are laid bare and confront, with clarity, the many misconceptions that are held. Freeports and Free Zones around the world are relatively common but unfortunately they are commonly misunderstood.

Freeports and Free Zones are specific tools for economic development, and at a time when recovery of our national and global economies is of paramount importance, they are tools which need capable and knowing practitioners. The UK is undergoing enormous change in its national economics and in its practice of international trade. Its government has committed to an unprecedented project in its history, with the creation of eight Freeports. The ambition is to use these Freeports as one of the tools to 'level up' the economy as recovery and regeneration happen and it is essential that this is done at pace and with confidence.

I commend this book to the reader and to Freeport and Free Zone operators around the world. Along with publications like Incoterms© 2020, it should be kept close to hand.

Tony Walford FCILT
Somerset
2021

PREFACE

There are more than 5000 Special Economic Zones worldwide, and, according to the World Free Zones Organization (WFZO), the trend is rising. According to the Organization for Economic Co-Operation and Development (OECD), global Free Zones are responsible for exports worth at least 3,500 billion a year, equivalent to around 20% of global trade in goods. Despite their importance for the global economy, little is known about economic activity in Free Zones.

Special Economic Zones, or Free Zones, are defined areas in which companies are subject to special rules that differ from those in the rest of the country, especially fiscal rules and regimes. Investors are often granted tax breaks, Import Duty suspensions and other financial incentives. In addition, they often benefit from simplified administrative procedures and high-quality infrastructure. SEZs are a widely-used economic policy instrument, especially in emerging and developing countries, aiming at creating attractive investment conditions for companies and thus compensating for weaknesses in the national business environment. They usually aim to attract Foreign Direct Investment, increase and diversify exports and create jobs. Additionally, governments expect their domestic economies to benefit from knowledge and technology overspills in the long term.

Special Economic Zones are particularly widespread in Asia, where they are regarded as a key driver of export-oriented growth in recent decades. However, there are also Free Zones in industrialised countries. The United States, for example, host more than 250 Foreign-Trade Zones. The number of Special Economic Zones worldwide is currently estimated at more than 5000, according to UN Conference on Trade and Development's (UNCTAD) World Investment Report 2019. In the 1980s, this figure was still below 200. However, despite the substantial boom in Free Zones, surprisingly little is known about economic activity in Special Economic Zones.

In 1984, the UK Government passed the Finance Act, which paved the way for the introduction of a Customs-controlled Freeport regime in the UK. Several Freeports were opened, in locations as diverse as Tilbury, Birmingham, Liverpool and Prestwick in Scotland, as well as a Free Zone at Ballasalla on the Isle of Man, adjacent to the island's airport, which was in reality created by a similar act of legislation passed by the Isle of Man government at the same time. The Ballasalla Free Zone was not part of the UK initiative, but was a separate venture sanctioned by the Isle of Man government, given its Customs Union with the United Kingdom. Some Freeports were more successful than others in their years of operation, with Liverpool Freeport the most successful of all the UK's Freeports. A year later, in 1985, the Jebel Ali Free Zone was opened, adjacent to the port of Jebel Ali, close to the city of Dubai, United Arab Emirates (UAE).

The main difference between the UK and UAE Free Zones was that the UK Freeports were Customs-controlled storage areas, whereas the Jebel Ali Free Zone was a combined Customs-controlled storage and manufacturing area, which also embraced tax incentives for its users. Thirty years later, the Jebel Ali Free Zone was still expanding and enjoying unprecedented levels of success, while the UK Freeport initiative was terminated in 2012, with most of the UK's Freeports having already closed prior to this date. In 2020, as part of its policy for withdrawal from the European Union, the UK Government decided to revive the Freeport concept in the UK and to pave the way for a new set of UK Freeports, all destined to open in 2021 as part of the government's post-Brexit economic policy of growth and development. Ironically, this is in direct contrast to EU Free Zone policy, which seeks to clamp down on and restrict the operation of the 82 EU Free Zones, which the EU authorities claim have given rise to money laundering, contraband and other illicit activities.

This text has been written as a guide to and explanation of the concept and function of Freeports and Free Zones, past and present. It is the result of many years of experience working with Free Zone authorities, governments and advisory organisations, and is a consolidation of existing knowledge and experience in these areas.

The study of Free Zones and Freeports is at best fragmented and at worst dysfunctional. Several books have been written about Special Economic Zones and the Mexican Maquiladora sector, but there is very little substantive literature about the generic subject of Free Zones and Freeports. This study seeks to redress that balance, especially given the decision by the UK Government to revisit the Freeport concept that existed between 1984 and 2012 and revive it once the UK has formally left the EU Single Market at the end of 2020.

The text comprises two parts. The first part is an overall definition and analysis of the concept of Free Zones and Freeports, explaining the function of each type of Free Zone, as well as highlighting the benefits of such facilities as well as some of the critiques of the Free Zone system.

The types of Free Zone covered are:

- Freeports;
- Free Zones & Free-Trade Zones;
- Export Processing Zones;
- Special Economic Zones; and
- Financial Free-Trade Zones.

The text also explains the legal, economic and political elements that influence Free Zones and their overall contribution to the international economy. The second part deals with an analysis of several global Free Zones, their location and their function, and how they have benefitted the areas where they are located. Free Zones on most continents are covered, along with the various benefits that can be found in each zone. It is designed for those who have never heard of the Free Zone concept, as well as those who may have heard of the concept but have never had the opportunity to understand the benefit of such facilities. It is also intended as a supplementary guide to existing literature covering fiscal and economic management.

The second part provides case studies of various worldwide Free Zone concepts, and covers most continents, including North America, Latin America, Africa and the Middle

East, as well as Turkey, Mauritius, the European Union, South-East Asia and China. It provides details of specific Free Zone projects, the types of businesses located in the Free Zones covered, and the requirements and benefits associated with operating within such Free Zones.

It should be noted that this text does not cover Free Trade Areas, which are mistakenly referred to by many economists as Free-Trade Zones. Free Trade Areas have nothing to do with Free-Trade Zones. These are collections of Free Trade Agreements between several nations, where each nation agrees to trade with its neighbours or other specific countries on the basis of the economic and political independence of each country, but allowing for the free movement of goods, capital and services, with the origin of the goods concerned being one of the primary conditions of the Free Trade Agreement. Free-Trade Zones are designated enclaves within a specific country which exist to employ Customs-controlled duty and tax suspension facilities, as well as domestic tax incentives, to encourage international trade and regional economic benefit by the use of these specific facilities.

LITERARY ANALYSIS

It is essential that the reader understands not only the basic principles and elements of Free Zones and Export Processing Zones, but also is able to refer to literary sources of material on the subject where deemed appropriate. Although the concept of Free Zones is not hugely difficult to understand, each type of Free Zone has different characteristics depending upon its function. Because of the various types of Free Zone in operation around the world, it is therefore necessary to understand these differences prior to making any informed decisions concerning how and where such Zones can and should operate and also what type of zone is most beneficial for a specific economy, be it national or international.

The subject of Free Zones is somewhat sparse, despite its importance. Although specific books and academic papers have been written on the subject of Free Zones, they are very specific in their nature and refer to specific cases of Free Zone development, especially in the developing world. The Internet has a wide range of articles about Free Zones in various parts of the world, and indeed these Internet sites have been used in compiling Part Two of this text. They can be easily accessed by reference to the particular country involved, and contain useful material about Free Zone legislation for each country concerned, as well as specific details about each country's Free Zone regime. The US government has produced a Guide to US Foreign-Trade Zones, setting out the conditions and regulations governing the function and operation of all US Foreign-Trade Zones (FTZs), and other governments have also produced guides to national Free-Trade Zone legislation. There are also many economic reports about national Free Zone regimes, particularly in the case of China, which is covered by the *Asia Briefing* website. The World Export Processing Zones Association (WEPZA) website, including research work carried out by its erstwhile division the Flagstaff Institute, has also published a series of papers and articles about the merits and benefits of the global network of EPZs, which have proven to be a valuable asset and instrument in the economic development of many nations worldwide. Similarly, the Emirate of Dubai's websites also contain a large amount of data and overall information about the Free Zones in the Emirate, including guides to investing in such Zones.

Specific academic papers have also been published in pdf format, usually as contributions to other journals or for university reference purposes, but they have tended to be very specific and only applicable to specific national economic development cases.

The author produced a paper on the comparisons between the Glasgow Prestwick Freeport and the Montréal Mirabel Free-Trade Zone which was delivered as part of a symposium on comparisons between Montréal and Glasgow held in 2004 at Glasgow

University, and much of this study is included in this text, particularly concerning the section on the Montréal Mirabel Free-Trade Zone.

Some books have been published on Free Zones, but these concentrate on specific national Free Zone initiatives, particularly the Mexican Maquiladora sector and global SEZs. To date, there has been no specific book published on the generic subject of Free Zones, given the variety of types of Free Zone in the present-day world.

The books that are (or were) available are:

- *Problems and Opportunities of the Mexican Maquiladora Industry* (K. Gehring, University of Paderborn, 2001);
- *The Maquiladora Industry: Economic Solution or Problem?* (Ed. K. Fatemi, Praeger, 1990);
- *Special Economic Zones* (Eds T. Farole and G. Akinci, The World Bank, 2011);
- *The Political Economy of Special Economic Zones* (L. Moberg, Routledge, 2017);
- *Special Economic Zones: Issues, Laws and Procedures* (Ed. K.R. Gupta, Atlantic, 2008).

Other papers have been written on behalf of the World Bank on the subject of Export Processing Zones and Special Economic Zones, and these are available in pdf format through the SEZ Knowledge Bank, also accessible through the website www.wepza.com. A report written in 2019 on behalf of UNCTAD by François Bost of the University of Reims, France, on the subject of Special Economic Zones, their methodology and definition, also gives a comprehensive insight into the concept of Special Economic Zones and their impact on the global economy.

Another useful paper written for the World Bank is *A Review of the Role and Impact of Export Processing Zones* by Dorsati Madani (presently on the WEPZA Advisory Board), written in 1999, at the time that EPZs were being developed, and which concentrates on the African Export Processing Zones. It deals primarily with economic advantages and disadvantages, and also discusses administrative and regulatory issues, exemplifying the Free Zones of Mauritius and Senegal, against the background of trade initiatives implemented by the Uruguay Round of trade negotiations. Although slightly outdated, the paper still provides an excellent insight into EPZ regimes of the period and lessons to be learned from such Free Zone operations.

The books and papers quoted explain the background and structure of Export Processing Zones and Special Economic Zones, depending upon the country where they are located, their functions and their contribution and benefits to the global economy. They should be read by anyone wishing to gain an overall knowledge of Export Processing Zones, as they give a substantial insight into the whole concept of such Zones and how they are used. However, they should also be read with an open mind, and should be closely analysed in terms of balance and application given the differing views held by their respective authors.

Further papers were published through the Flagstaff Institute, the literary and information division of WEPZA and these were written between the period 1999 and 2004. Titles contained within the *Flagstaff Journal* include:

- 'Why Export Processing Zones are necessary' (Richard L. Bolin, Director, WEPZA, 2004);

- 'Economic Realities and Free Zones' (Robert C. Haywood, Director, WEPZA, 2004);
- 'Developing Trade Capacity through Free Zones' (Robert C. Haywood);
- 'Economic Processing Zone Incentives and the WTO Agreement on Subsidies and Countervailing Measures' (Robert C. Haywood);
- 'Free Zones in the Modern World' (Robert C. Haywood);
- 'A Critique of Cost-Benefit Analysis in the Evaluation of Export Processing Zones' (Claude Baissac, WEPZA Round Table on Export Processing Zones, Vienna, 15 April 1996).

All these papers are available in pdf format through the website www.wepza.org. Although they date back some years, they nevertheless provide a sound basis for the study and analysis of global Free Zones and Export Processing Zones, and explain the complexities and details of the function of such Zones and their importance and even necessity to the global economy. In essence, the principle of EPZs has never changed, and therefore these papers still hold weight and validity concerning their explanation and exposition of the EPZ concept and function. The rationale behind such papers was based on the work carried out by WEPZA in promoting and overseeing the establishment and operation of the global Export Processing Zone system and network, including the arrangement of global conferences and symposiums dealing with the various subjects surrounding the function and operation of Export Processing Zones, and in ensuring that not only were such Zones established according to the guidelines of both UNIDO (United Nations International Development Organization) and UNCTAD but also in accordance with national rules and guidelines established by national law.

Each of the above titles covers the justification for and critique of EPZs and Free Zones in general, and provides significant detail on the whole raison d'être of Free Zones and EPZs. These papers were written in the era of the development of Export Processing Zones and have in many ways become a benchmark for the establishment, function and operation of Free Zones and Export Processing Zones. The World Bank reports originated from the same period, but the books presently available on Special Economic Zones were written in a later period, and tend to have a view more influenced by present political and social considerations, as well as a more politically correct view of the subject, rather than a purely objective view of the concept.

These books are specific to particular types of Zones and the countries operating them, and much centres around the focus on economic development, essentially relating to the contribution of such types of zone to economic development in several countries. For example, the book on Special Economic Zones by K.R. Gupta concentrates mainly on India's SEZ regime, although certain elements of the book deal with the Chinese SEZ regime. The book on Special Economic Zones published by the World Bank also deals with the SEZ and EPZ regimes of developing countries throughout the world, including the Chinese SEZs, Free Zones in Central America and Africa, and the Caribbean, but also analyses the effects of SEZs on other developing countries, including social and environmental issues which have become increasingly prevalent in recent years. This text has included certain aspects of the analysis of such Zones by the World Bank, but seeks not to dwell on major social, employment and environmental concerns, as these are not major elements of this text. However, such subjects are worthy of reference by readers who wish to analyse more wider approaches to the overall subject of Free Zones.

The book, *The Political Economy of Special Economic Zones* (Lotta Moberg), deals with the political approach to the economy of such SEZ regimes. It deals with many political aspects of national SEZ policy, as well as the role of SEZs in driving political and economic reforms in various countries, as well as determining national SEZ policy as part of national politico-economic strategy. To this extent, it compares the function and roles of different countries, including India, China and the Dominican Republic, and compares the use and operation of SEZs in these national economies as case studies. In this respect, this book more closely concentrates on the political and economic aspects of SEZ policy, rather than examining social and environmental aspects of the impact of SEZs on the national economy.

It should be pointed out that although national SEZ policy may be an instrument of national political reform, it is not as such intended to be an instrument of national political policy; the author maintains that the primary driving force of any form of Free Zone is for economic reform and development, especially concerning the fostering of international trade through fiscal reform and incentive. What is not fully recognised in these books is the whole issue of national and indeed international fiscal policy in the encouragement of international trade, especially concerning the influence of Customs Duties and Sales Tax as major contributing factors in the global economy. It is widely accepted that taxes stifle international trade. The Laffer Curve, expounded by the US economist Arthur Laffer, shows that as the national tax rate rises, the incentive for corporate productivity falls once the tax rate hits 50% of corporate revenue. The main principle of any tax policy relating to international trade is that when Customs (Import) Duties are reduced or suspended, international trade increases. Although loosely referred to in various publications, this is not a major factor in the analyses of many EPZ or SEZ regimes as detailed by the various books available.

The publication on the Maquiladora industry by K. Gehring, which was a paper in support of a University Diploma, and the book on the Maquiladora industry by K. Fatemi, concentrate on the advantages and drawbacks of the Mexican Maquiladora sector, about which there is a section in Part Two of this study. Although much of these publications deal with many of the economic benefits and advantages of the Mexican maquila system, much space has also been devoted to the drawbacks and disadvantages of the regime, including environmental, social and infrastructural issues, which detract from the whole reason that the Maquiladora program (The Border Industrialisation Program) was introduced in the first place.

One common thread that pervades much of the literature on Free Zones is the issue of labour and how the developing world has used the Free Zone concept, especially in Special Economic Zones and Export Processing Zones, to encourage the use of unskilled labour, predominantly female labour force, and also a policy of low wage levels. Sheba Tejani, in Chapter 11 of the book *Special Economic Zones* (World Bank, eds T. Farole and G. Akinci), highlights the issue of the use of female labour and gender inequality in many of these Zones throughout the world, although it is pointed out that as time has progressed, an increasing level of employment has shifted from female to male (Chapter 11, Special Economic Zones).

Another common thread is that of environmental sustainability. Chapter 12 in the same book (H-K. Yeo and G. Akinci) deals with environmental sustainability and the development of Green SEZs, a policy which is becoming increasingly prevalent given global initiatives on environmental sustainability and protection. The concept of the Green SEZ encompasses pollution control and environmental compliance, including centralised services for sewage and wastewater treatment, hazardous waste collection and disposal, and environmental training programs for zone managers and company operations. The chapter then states that the implementation of environmental management tools and benchmarks such as the International Standards Organisation (ISO) 14001 Environmental Management System (EMS) may be one of the systematic programs to consider in these Zones. The concept of Eco-Industrial Zones takes this systematic management approach further, and looks at the whole subject of environmental sustainability. This approach, according to the authors, takes in the management of the whole resource, energy and environmental impact in an integrated manner. The World Bank publications *Eco-Industrial Park Handbook* (2019) and *A Practitioner's Handbook for Eco-Industrial Parks* (2018) concentrate on the measures necessary to create, develop and run Eco-Industrial parks in line with the requirements for global environmental sustainability. The 2019 Handbook, developed by the Asian Development Bank, states that 'an Eco-Industrial Park is a community of manufacturing and service businesses located together on a common property. Members seek enhanced environmental, economic and social performance through collaboration in managing environmental and resource issues' (Yeo and Akinci, Ch. 12, Special Economic Zones). However, the concentration of study on SEZs cannot simply apply to this concept alone, or even to EPZs as an associated concept of SEZs; it must apply to the whole global regime of Free Zones as a generic global concept. The US Foreign-Trade Zones (FTZs), Mexican Maquiladoras and other Free Zones also come into the same category and must therefore apply the same principles.

It is understandable that books written on the subject must be balanced in their approach, especially concerning discussions on the relative merits and drawbacks of such regimes, but one of the primary areas of Free Zone, SEZ and EPZ initiatives has always been the economic and fiscal incentives of such regimes, especially concerning the promotion and encouragement of international trade. Ultimately, all Free Zones are driven by the encouragement of international trade, and this policy must ultimately shape the future of such initiatives. The economic and fiscal approach still dominates the whole raison d'être of the Free Zone concept, and therefore prevails over all other considerations. The fact that economics also overlap with social and environmental issues is an indicator that fiscal and economic strategy comes at a price; social and environmental issues must be taken into consideration as key elements in determining the viability of the whole Free Zone concept, be it Freeports, Free Zones, EPZs or SEZs. The publications available do not necessarily cover this whole generic approach. If a consideration applies to one specific element of a concept, it must apply to all elements. Since the concept of Free Zones embraces all types of government-approved zone, especially where specific fiscal rules apply, this concept must include all the elements of economic, social and environmental issues in all cases.

Given that the Internet provides the majority of the information available on Free Zone, Export Processing Zone and Special Economic Zone activities and operations, the purchase of the books mentioned is only recommended if readers wish to engage in more in-depth study of the subject. In many cases, pdf articles published on various elements of Free Zone practice have also been included or referred to in several books, although since the publication of these books, other articles have also been published, bringing a more updated approach to the Free Zone concept. Given the growing importance of such Zones in many economies, including that of the UK, it is necessary to understand the basics of the Free Zone concept prior to making important strategic decisions concerning the location, type and function of the specific Free Zone appropriate to the relevant economy.

PART ONE

FREEPORTS AND FREE ZONES

CHAPTER 1

Introduction

For a number of centuries, governments, emperors, kings, queens, rulers and presidents have been providing traders and investors with special sites offering respite and relief from normal import-export tax regimes and regulations in return for a steady stream of much-needed revenue for the national coffers. Before modern times, such places were concentrated in the Mediterranean basin, at Delos in Greco-Roman times, and in Venice, Genoa and Marseille during the Middle Ages, as well as many ports in the German Hanseatic League. By the 19th century, they had spread to Southeast Asia, especially Malaya. However, it was not until the latter half of the 20th century that so-called 'Free Zones' made their mark as deliberate tools of economic development, most notably in China in 1979 when one of the most famous Chinese Free Zones was established at Shenzhen, followed by the Free-Trade Zones at Shanghai. In 1985, the now-famous Jebel Ali Free Zone opened adjacent to the port of Jebel Ali, close to the city of Dubai, in the United Arab Emirates.

Today, there are several hundred Free Zones around the world, from the Americas to the Far East, and the MENA (Middle East/North Africa) region has its fair share of successes, from Dubai's Jebel Ali Free Zone and the Media and Internet cities that caught the early wave of the electronic economy, through the Gulf of Suez Free Zones at Aqaba and in Egypt, all the way to the Tangier Free Zone in North Morocco. In the Americas, there are the Foreign-Trade Zones in the US, the Maquiladora system in northern Mexico, close to the border with the US, and the Manaus Free Zone at Manaus, in the Amazonia region of Brazil.

The UNCTAD reports

The generic term 'Free Zone' can be defined as an area of variable size, in which authorised companies are exempt from the normal regime applicable in the host country, in particular with regard to Customs Duties (or even taxation where the country so authorises). In return for this concession and other benefits, countries expect these companies to create large numbers of jobs, stimulate exports and help to diversify the economy by introducing new sectors of activity into it, as quoted by F. Bost in his article on Special Economic Zones (2010).

The use of the term SEZs relegates the term 'Free Zones' to a subtype, with the specific characteristic of being separate Customs territories, as defined by UNCTAD (2019), along with EPZs. Indeed, a Free Zone offers its users reduced or no Customs Duties for goods that are manufactured, assembled or are simply in transit. This makes it possible to differentiate them from other types of SEZs.

DOI: 10.4324/9781003232025-2

The growth of Special Economic Zones (5,383 SEZs across 147 economies in 2019) worldwide (UNCTAD Report 2019), particularly in developing countries, is one of the major features of contemporary globalisation. However, the use of SEZs as a generic term is very recent, as it coincides with the publication of UNCTAD's *World Investment Report 2019* (WIR 2019), which defines such Zones as 'geographically delimited areas within which governments facilitate industrial activity through fiscal and regulatory incentives and infrastructure support' (UNCTAD 2019, p. 128). Before the WIR 2019 was published, it was more common to use the term 'Free Zones' and 'Export Processing Zones' in most academic work and publications, although several publications had already begun to popularise the term SEZ, as detailed by T. Farole and G. Akinci in their 2011 publication on Special Economic Zones (OECD) and referred to in the literary analysis.

According to F. Bost, Free Zones are still the most prevalent subset within the vast group of SEZs: 2,296 Free Zones, or 42.6% of the world total of SEZs in 2019. In reality, Free Zones and SEZs are all grouped within the overall generic definition of Special Economic Zones; the function of each type of zone may vary from zone to zone, but the overall concept, as defined by the Revised Kyoto Convention, is a commercial zone separated from the domestic economy by way of fiscal, financial and economic incentives, usually in the form of tax and duty reductions and exemptions.

Free Zones are still the most prevalent subset within the vast group of SEZs: 2,296 Free Zones, or 42.6% of the world total of SEZs in 2019, as shown by the table below. The table below, presented by F. Bost for UNCTAD (2019), shows the number of global Free Zones and Special Economic Zones and their distribution throughout the world. Figures may differ from other data quoted, but the number of recorded Free Zones varies as some Free Zones may have opened or ceased to function from time to time, and thus the data may change accordingly.

	NUMBER OF FREE ZONES	*PERCENTAGE OF TOTAL*	*NUMBER OF SEZS (UNCTAD)*	*PERCENTAGE OF TOTAL*
Global	**2,296**	**100**	**5,383**	**100**
Developed Economies	295	12.9	374	7
United States	191	8.3	262	4.7
Europe	85	3.7	105	2
Developing Economies	**1,869**	**81.4**	**4,772**	**88.6**
Africa	215	9.4	237	4.4
Asia	1,196	52	4,046	75
Philippines	385	16.8	528	9.8
China	135	5.9	2,543	47.2
Malaysia	45	2	45	0.83
India	231	10	373	7
United Arab Emirates	47	2	47	0.9
Oceania	1	0.04	3	0.05

	NUMBER OF FREE ZONES	*PERCENTAGE OF TOTAL*	*NUMBER OF SEZS (UNCTAD)*	*PERCENTAGE OF TOTAL*
Latin America and the Caribbean	457	19.9	486	9
Colombia	101	4.4	101	1.9
Dominican Republic	71	3.1	73	1.3
Transitional Economies	**132**	**5.7**	**237**	**4.4**
Russia	39	1.7	130	2.4

Source: Bost F., 2019, University of Reims and UNCTAD, World Investment Report 2019.

Note: This table includes single factory Free Zones but does not include individual free points, i.e. Customs Warehouses.

Free points are ignored by international institutions, even though their export activities can be important. This is partly because free points are much less visible in the landscape than Free Zones, especially since the countries concerned have given them very different names (e.g. enclave companies, export-oriented units, Free-Trade Zone points, Free Zone enterprises, Maquiladoras (as in Mexico), pioneer industries) and do not use the generic term 'free points'. It is suggested that in future, free points should be more widely recognised by institutions and included in their own right in the accounts, but in a dedicated section.

Finally, simple warehouses of goods (through which many sensitive goods such as cigarettes and alcohol pass) not integrated into Free Zones, as in the case of individual Customs Warehouses and Excise Bonded Warehouses, do not fall into the category of Free Zones, and are also not SEZs, even if they benefit from temporary tax exemptions for goods in transit (Figure 1.1). Warehouses are present in large numbers in almost all countries (in Switzerland, for example, there are 240) and are also not included in SEZ classification.

The report goes on to distinguish SEZs and Free Zones in the following manner according to the new UNCTAD classification.

Special Economic Zones	*Free Zones*
High-Tech Parks	Export Processing Zones
Science Parks	Free-Trade Zones
Science and Technology Zones	Freeports
Free Economic Zones	Single Factory Free Zones (SubZones in the US)
Services Parks	
Green Zones	
Safe Zones	
Tourism Development Zones	
Financial Free Zones	

The above tabular representation constitutes the UNCTAD Database.

The above table summarises the distribution of the different Zones according to the new UNCTAD classification. The SEZ group includes all the Zones that meet the definition given in the introduction to this chapter. Among them is the large subgroup of Free Zones (Export Processing Zones, Free-Trade Zones, Single Factory Free Zones) whose main characteristic is to benefit from Customs Imports advantages. The other SEZs, which benefit from other incentives, are mainly specialised in advanced technologies and services. Free points are not, strictly speaking, 'Zones' (which explains why they cannot be classified as SEZs), but they are quite comparable to single factory Free Zones, with the difference that the latter are officially declared as Free Zones.

However, because of the Customs advantages they offer, free points belong to the same category as SEZs, as explained by F. Bost. For the sake of clarification, single factory Free Zones ought to be officially reclassified as free points, but this is a matter that must be decided by the states concerned. Finally, Figure 1.1 shows that simple warehouses, industrial Zones and industrial estates do not belong to this group of SEZs.

Since a major objective of creating Free Zones is to increase exports as well as stimulate regional and national economic growth and development, most Free Zones around the world are either ring-fenced enclaves exempt from national import and export duties or formally operate outside the Customs area of their host country. Governments often add other benefits to the package, such as tax, regulatory, administrative and financial incentives.

Free Zone development differs from one country to another. Different countries use different types and concepts of Free Zones. In some countries, Free Zones are developed to stimulate incoming trade, as in the case of the US, while in others, such as developing countries, they exist to stimulate export-oriented trade. There is no one single raison d'être for the policy and operation of Free Zones; much depends upon the economic status of the country concerned, and its aspirations towards national economic growth.

In general, there are several types of Free Zone, namely the following:

- Freeports;
- Free Zones;
- Export Processing Zones (EPZs);
- Special Economic Zones.

Other Zones are essentially variations on these themes, and may incorporate different economic and fiscal incentives depending upon the function and purpose of the zone concerned. There is no one single panacea or solution to such Free Zone policy, as Zones vary globally according to demand and national requirement, as well as being established according to national law governing the operation and function of such Zones.

The World Bank, in the book Special Economic Zones, defines these types of zone as follows:

Type of zone	*Development objective*	*Typical size*	*Typical location*	*Activities*	*Markets*	*Examples*
Free-Trade Zone/ Freeport	Support Trade	<50 Hectares	Port of Entry	Entrepôt (Warehousing) and trade-related activity	Domestic, Re-Export	Colón Free Zone (Panama)

Type of zone	*Development objective*	*Typical size*	*Typical location*	*Activities*	*Markets*	*Examples*
Traditional EPZ	Export Manufacturing	<100 Hectares	None	Manufacturing or other Processing	Mostly Export	Bangladesh, Vietnam
Free Enterprises (Single Unit EPZs)	Export Manufacturing	No Minimum	Country-wide	Manufacturing or other Processing	Mostly Export	Mauritius, Mexico
Hybrid EPZ	Export Manufacturing	<100 Hectares; only part of area is EPZ	None	Manufacturing or other Processing	Export and Domestic	La Krabang, Thailand
SEZ	Integrated Development	>1,000 Hectares	None	Multi-use	Internal, Domestic, and Export	Aqaba (Jordan), Shenzhen (China)

UNCTAD define two main generic types of Free Zone.

1. **Free-Trade Zones** (FTZs) were the first type of Free Zones to have been developed. The World Bank uses the following definition: 'FTZs are fenced-in, duty-free areas, offering warehousing, storage, and distribution facilities for trade, transshipment, and re-export operations.' Five FTZs are hubs of international trade by the very nature of their activities: transshipment, re-export, international trade, and so on. They fulfil a vital role as trade facilitators in the process of globalisation. These areas are generally located in or in the immediate vicinity of seaports (known as 'free ports') and major airports. They are also present along the main transportation axes (maritime, rail and road), along the development corridors, or in border regions.
2. **Export Processing Zones** (EPZs) are the second kind of Free Zone. EPZs specialise in manufacturing (textiles and clothing, footwear, sports goods, consumer electronics, industrial components, etc.) and, increasingly, in the provision of services that can be supplied at a distance through digital networks (digital data processing, IT development, call centres, financial services, etc.). Their particularity is to export all or part of their production abroad, according to very precise rules set by the investment code of the country of origin (usually varying between 80% and 100% of their production). If manufactured products from the EPZs are transferred to the domestic market, companies must pay Customs Duties equivalent to those they would have had to pay if they had imported these products, in order to avoid a distortion of competition. This said, they also generate competition in the sense that, globally, they may compete against each other concerning location and national fiscal policy. Some of the best-known examples of EPZs include Shannon (Ireland, from 1959 to 2017); Kaohsiung (Taiwan, since 1966); Manaus (Brazil, since 1967); La Romana (Dominican

Republic, since 1968); Masan (South Korea, since 1970); Bayan Lepas (Malaysia, since 1972); Batam (Indonesia, since 1978). It should be noted that under new EU rules, Shannon lost its official Free Zone status. However, it is now a Special Economic Zone according to UNCTAD criteria, albeit without the main fiscal advantages offered by conventional Free Zones.

These EPZs have been and indeed still are very successful and have attracted a great many foreign and domestic investors. They continue to serve as models for the dissemination of the concept of industrial Free Zones and services throughout the world.

In the book, Freeports are grouped in the last category along with SEZs, but, in reality, they are separated from the other types of Free Zone, in that they are located close to or adjacent to seaports or airports, and are generally used in the same way as the above description for Free-Trade Zones. They are more limited in size, owing to their locations, and are more oriented towards import storage activities and re-export where appropriate.

It should also be noted that Bangladesh passed a new Economic Zones Act in 2010 that opened up the potential of Free Zone activities beyond the traditional EPZs. Vietnam has various forms of economic Zones, of which EPZs are one element. These overall concepts are addressed later in this text.

Background

Customs and Revenue Authorities in most countries have facilities that enable importers and exporters to avoid paying Import Duty and tax on materials which are either imported in bulk, for long-term storage, for manufacture under specific conditions, or for re-export. These facilities depend upon the process involved, and the ultimate destination of the goods concerned.

The main facilities are:

- Temporary Storage;
- Customs (Bonded) Warehousing;
- Inward Processing;
- Processing under Free Circulation (Tariff Inversion).

In different countries, these terms may have different names. For example, Inward Processing can also be referred to as processing for re-export, and can be authorised for either a single company or as an integral part of an EPZ, which is a Customs-controlled zone designed specifically for this type of activity. Customs (Bonded) Warehousing is a global facility allowing for the Duty-suspended storage of goods on a medium- to long-term basis. In many cases, Bonded warehousing is also associated with the storage of excisable goods such as alcohol or tobacco under Excise Duty Suspension, but in general these warehouses are separate from Customs Warehouses, as they deal with Excise Duty, not Customs (Import) Duty.

Temporary Storage

Prior to analysing the above definitions, it is pertinent to describe another form of Customs-controlled storage, namely that of Temporary Storage. Previously known as

Transit Sheds, Temporary Storage facilities were always areas within the confines of a seaport where goods could be held for a short period prior to clearance through Customs. Materials such as raw and basic commodities in bulk, and large items shipped on breakbulk cargo vessels were often held prior to Customs clearance, owing to a need for Customs officers to examine these cargoes prior to clearing them for Import Duty purposes. In a world of the increasing use of computer technology, Customs clearances are carried out electronically, but there is still the need for Temporary Storage as a means of avoiding congestion through the Customs clearance process. According to the rules set out by HMRC, goods and materials can be kept in Temporary Storage for a maximum of 90 days before Customs clearance, which is a mandatory requirement after this period. This gives time for shipping agents to check the materials to ensure that they are fit for purposes and can be released through Customs.

The term 'Temporary Storage' therefore means the Customs status on imported goods temporarily stored under Customs supervision between their presentation to Customs and their placement under a Customs procedure.

In the case of the UK, imported goods brought into the UK may be stored in Customs-approved premises for a period of up to 90 days until they are declared to a Customs procedure or re-exported. A Temporary Storage facility is a Customs-approved facility and is a place situated inside or outside the approved area of a sea or airport. Temporary Storage is a facility found in most countries, as it allows for the Temporary Storage of goods in designated storage facilities within or just outside the confines of a seaport for a limited period until they are either declared to Customs for removal to an inland premises, or are re-exported to another international destination.

These facilities are known as the following:

Internal Temporary Storage Facility (ITSF), an approved place situated within the appointed area of an approved port/airport where non-UK goods are held in Temporary Storage until they are assigned a Customs-approved treatment or use. Internal Temporary Storage Facilities may also be used for the storage of goods subject to export control.

External Temporary Storage Facility (ETSF), an approved place situated outside the appointed area of an approved port/airport where non-UK goods may be held until they are assigned to a Customs-approved treatment or use.

Internal Temporary Storage Facility Remote (ITSFR), an approved place situated within the boundaries of the appointed area of an approved port/airport but outside the Customs-approved area where non-UK goods may be held until they are assigned to a Customs-approved treatment or use. Temporary Storage facilities may also include bulk tanks and open-air areas such as container yards. Silos can be used for the storage of grains and other loose homogeneous commodities, and are generally located close to quaysides to facilitate the easy and smooth transfer of such commodities from and to bulk carriers.

A Temporary Storage area may, in certain circumstances, be allowed inside other Customs-approved premises. Where premises are multi-use, for example for storing warehouse goods, export freight, the Temporary Storage area must be clearly demarcated unless there is an economic need. This must be marked inside the premises as well as on the building plan.

The majority of these facilities (with the exception of Approved Depositories) are considered to be part of the UK Border and as a result must be approved for this purpose by the Border Force.

Goods are to be assigned to a Customs procedure or re-export within 90 days from the time goods have been declared to Temporary Storage. Once cleared through Customs, goods can be moved from Temporary Storage into either Free Circulation (duty paid), a Duty Relief Facility such as Inward Processing or Customs Warehousing, or into a Freeport/Free Zone. They can also be re-exported within the 90-days period without the need for a Customs declaration, as they are deemed to be in transit en route to another overseas destination.

Customs Warehousing

Customs Warehousing is used as a means of storing goods and materials that are imported in bulk in medium-term or long-term storage under Customs control, that is, duty and tax suspension. These goods are held under such conditions until required by the customer, at which point the individual consignments required by the customer are drawn off from the total stock held under Customs control and are released into Free Circulation by paying the Import Duty and tax at the point of release and declaration, but only on the consignment being released from the warehouse. The rest of the consignment remains under Customs control in the warehouse until required by the customer(s).

Customs Warehouses are also especially useful for the Customs-controlled storage of goods subject to import quotas, be these physical or tariff-based. It is often the case that imported goods are subject to quota limits, where only a limited quantity of goods can be imported per year subject to government-imposed quota controls. In cases where such quotas are in force, goods can still be imported, but cannot be cleared into Free Circulation because of the limits imposed. They are therefore held in a Customs warehouse until the quotas are relaxed and import of these goods into Free Circulation is allowed.

The use of Customs warehouses means that goods can be inspected and examined for quality or other reasons while still held under Customs control, in case there is need to reject elements of the consignment because of substandard quality or damage, without these items being subject to Import Duty and Tax liability.

Materials can also be re-exported from the Customs warehouse under duty suspension, with no duty or tax liable on the basis of re-export.

Such facilities are especially applicable to materials stored in bulk, whether finished products, components, sub-assemblies or raw materials such as steel, timber or other basic commodities. The finished products market such as the large retail groups use these facilities, as well as large industrial and productive sectors such as the automotive sectors, including companies such as BMW, Mercedes and Volkswagen, which use these facilities on a global scale.

Customs Warehousing therefore allows imported goods to be stored on suspension of Import Duty and VAT until they are to be released into Free Circulation to their respective buyers. It should be remembered that such goods are not duty-free, but are liable to Import Duty and VAT once they are released into Free Circulation. They are held in a Customs warehouse under Duty and VAT/Sales Tax suspension.

Customs Warehousing is an advantage if the importer:

- Wants to delay paying duty and/or VAT on stocks of imported goods; or
- Wants to delay having a Customs treatment, i.e. release into Free Circulation, applied to imported goods; or
- Wants to re-export goods under Customs control (Import Duty and/or VAT may not be payable at all); or
- Has difficulty at the time of import in meeting certain conditions or licence/certification requirements.

A Customs warehouse can be either a place or inventory system authorised by HMRC for storing non-EU goods which are:

- Chargeable with Import Duty and/or VAT; or
- Otherwise not in Free Circulation.

Goods can be warehoused in a Customs warehouse:

- Directly from import;
- On removal from a Free Zone (see Free Zones) or from another Customs warehouse in an EU State;
- On transfer from another Customs regime under which duty has been suspended.

Goods can be removed for:

- Free Circulation;
- Export to a third country;
- Shipment as stores;
- Transfer to another Customs warehouse;
- Transfer to a Free Zone.

A variety of goods and also basic commodities or raw materials can be warehoused, and usually HMRC will allow goods to be warehoused for an unlimited period. Such goods can also include Consignment Stock, which is the property of the exporter at the time of entry into the zone, and which will be kept in Customs-controlled storage until called/drawn off by the importer and paid for at the time of release into Free Circulation. Such facilities are necessary because, under Customs and Tax Law, Import VAT can only be reclaimed by the actual owner of the goods, and not necessarily the importer of record. Since Consignment Stock is still the property of the exporter at the time of import into the Free Zone, the importer cannot release the goods into Free Circulation and account for the Import Duty and VAT. This can only be done once the importer has paid for the consignment in question and therefore is liable for the Import Duty and VAT on the release of the consignment into Free Circulation.

Goods liable to Excise Duty and VAT may also be imported for warehousing. Excise warehousing takes place at premises specifically approved for this purpose and, unless the premises are also approved for Customs Warehousing, the goods must be in Free Circulation before they can enter the warehouse. Some traders use both Customs Warehousing and Excise (Tax) Warehousing regimes on the grounds that they not only trade in Excise goods, but they also import Excise goods from outside the UK.

The other issue concerns inventory control. In a Customs Warehousing or Freeport environment, it is imperative that the trader is able to identify and control all inventory stock, especially where there is a combination of Customs-controlled and Free Circulation stock. In a Customs warehouse, the trader must be able to ensure that they have full control over all stock records, the Customs status of the stock, inward deliveries of stock and releases of stock for onward shipment. These are conditions imposed by HMRC, and must be adhered to at all times. Indeed, HMRC require from the trader a set of warehouse and stock records showing how these activities are controlled and monitored on a frequent basis. In general, all records must be electronically maintained and controlled, so that spreadsheet records can be submitted to and monitored by HMRC, including the relationship between the company's Warehouse Management System (WMS) and Duty Management System (DMS).

The distinction between Customs Warehouses or CWs and FTZs, and the risks that they pose, also needs to be clearly understood and included in any Regulatory Governance review of FTZs. Customs Warehouses are effectively temporary goods storage centres established under the general supervision of Customs. The owners of the warehouse must be able to guarantee to the Customs Authority that they can store goods in the Customs Warehouse with complete safety and security, and these guarantees are assessed at the time of application for Customs Warehouse approval. Once approval has been granted by the Customs Authority, the goods stored in the Customs Warehouse are suspended from all Duty and VAT liability. Goods at the warehouse may be manipulated, or even repackaged, but their identity, description and Commodity Code is largely preserved for the purpose of tariff classification. This process is in contrast to activity within the adjacent FTZ, which may involve manufacturing and legitimate changes in tariff classification, value and country of origin, as long as approval has been given to the zone operators by the national Customs Authority. This additional facility generally falls under the generic function of Inward Processing Relief (IP).

Given that the UK Freeport concept automatically includes and embraces the facility of Customs Warehousing as a matter of course, the aforementioned conditions imposed by HMRC apply to all Freeport operators, albeit using Simplified Procedures as sanctioned by HMRC.

Inward Processing

Inward Processing is a facility where materials are imported under duty and tax suspension for the purpose of manufacturing into finished or semi-finished products. These products can then be imported into Free Circulation using the Commodity Code of the finished product, or re-exported as finished products. While the goods are under the Customs Inward Processing (IP) facility, they are under Import Duty and tax suspension, and only become liable for Import Duty and tax when they are released into domestic Free Circulation. If they are re-exported, there is no duty or tax liability.

The **Duty Suspension** principle works in such a way that all imported materials may be declared on the basis of Duty and VAT Suspension on the grounds that they are to be incorporated in a process where the finished product resulting from the incorporation of such materials will be re-exported in its entirety to a non-EU customer. The condition is that the process allows for a complete transformation from raw materials to finished product, that is, the implication being that there will be a transformation of the item concerned either by refining, processing or manufacture into another item which is completely different from the original imported components which constitute it. Thus, the Tariff Commodity Code of the Raw Material will be changed to that of the finished product.

In the case of the UK, it is necessary for the processor to apply to HM Revenue & Customs for a full IP authorisation in advance of any such activities being commenced. The application details all activities to be undertaken, as well as details of both raw materials to be imported and finished products to be processed.

What does IP cover?

Inward Processing Relief (IP) covers a wide range of activities, all of which relate in some way to manufacturing or processing work being undertaken on a specific **imported** item of non-EU origin for the purposes of **re-export** to another non-EU destination.

The implication for most forms of IP is that there will be a transformation of the item concerned either by refining, processing or manufacture into another item which is completely different from the original imported components which constitute it. Where Simplified Authorisation is concerned, the nature of the goods concerned may not change, but some process is applied to enhance the product in some way without altering its essential structure, nature or description.

Examples

IP activities cover the following processes:

- Manufacturing;
- Processing;
- Refining;
- Assembly;
- Preparing for distribution and sale;
- Sorting, repackaging and relabelling;
- Removal of defective items or parts;
- Repair;
- Maintenance;
- Modification.

The main reason for the use of Inward Processing Relief (IP) is so that the trader may be approved for suspension from Import Duty and VAT on all imported items used in a process for the purposes of re-export of the finished product on condition that they abide by the requirements imposed by HMRC. The trader must agree to abide by these requirements, and must ensure that appropriate records are kept for the purposes of monitoring and controlling such operations.

Case study 1

A company in the UK manufactures engine management assemblies for export to a variety of customers in the automotive industry, most of whose assembly plants are located outside the European Union. It imports a variety of items from various countries, most of which are not in the European Union. For example, it imports casings from the USA, circuit boards from China and other electronic items from South-East Asia. It exports the finished assemblies to the USA, Canada, Brazil, Argentina, Australia and South Africa. A small proportion of the items remain in the UK for use in British vehicles.

Imports

USA
China
SE Asia

Exports

USA
Canada
Brazil
Argentina
Australia
South Africa

If the company did not use the IP regime, it would have to pay Import Duty and VAT on all imported consignments, despite the fact that few of the items were to be retained in the UK or in the EU. It has the ability under the IP regime of importing everything under IP status, manufacturing the finished product and then exporting the vast bulk of the production to the overseas country under IP conditions. Under the new regime, the company may also declare the UK-destined materials into Free Circulation by paying the appropriate amount of Import Duty and VAT on that element being released into Free Circulation.

Case study 2

A company based in the North-East of England manufactures equipment for the offshore oil industry. It imports a variety of items from the USA and Australia for incorporation in the equipment, which is then sent to the North Sea Oilfields and Norway as well as Brazil and the South American offshore oilfields.

In this case, the company may use not only the IP regime but also the End Use/Continental Shelf relief regime, as it supplies the North Sea Continental Shelf. It re-exports its finished products to other areas of the world as well as the North Sea, so it is engaged in import and export activities.

Imports

Australia
USA

Exports

North Sea
Norway (Offshore)
Brazil (Offshore)
West Africa (Offshore)

As with Case Study 1, IP is a necessary regime, as in this case no items are retained in UK national territory. Everything is re-exported owing to the nature of the business. However, the items shipped to offshore locations may be entered into the company's despatch records under the new regime of EIDR (Entry in Declarant's Records).

The Processor MUST quote their IP Authorisation Number as issued by HM Revenue & Customs (e.g. **IP/0907/514/19**) in Box 44 of the Import and Export Declarations.

Processing under Free Circulation (PFC)

Originally a separate Import Duty relief, this facility has become part of the overall IP facility under the EU's Union Customs Code. It uses the principle of **Tariff Inversion**, where the Commodity Code on the finished product yields an Import Duty rate lower than those on its components. For example, a computer has an Import Duty rate of 0%, whereas the components of that computer may have Import Duty rates ranging from 2% up to 6.5%. The components are therefore imported under Import Duty suspension using the PFC/IP facility, manufactured into the finished product, which is then either released into Free Circulation at the Commodity Code and Import Duty rate of the finished product, but using the value of the imported components. The finished product can also be re-exported under Import Duty and tax suspension.

All these facilities can therefore be incorporated into the Freeport/Free Zone facility, although in general a Freeport, in its true sense, is an extension of the port facilities, where goods can be stored in the zone on a short-, medium- and long-term basis under Customs control until required by the customer, when they are either released into Free Circulation or re-exported.

Basis of Free Zone use

Whereas the above facilities are generally used by individual companies, they are also incorporated into the concept of Free Zones and Freeports, where several companies can be located to carry out such Customs-controlled activities within the designated confines of an integrated zone, which, in its entirety, is controlled and monitored by the national Customs and Revenue Authority.

The basis of the use of Freeports and Free Zones is therefore:

- Customs-controlled storage of goods for release into Free Circulation in smaller batches at a later stage;
- Customs-controlled manufacturing for release of the finished product into Free Circulation using the Tariff Inversion method;
- Re-export of finished products or materials stored in the zone.

It should be noted and understood that while the materials or goods are stored in the zone, they are under Import Duty and Tax (i.e. VAT or Sales Tax) **SUSPENSION**, NOT EXEMPTION. There is no such thing as duty exemption, as all suspension of duty is conditional upon the terms of usage of the Customs facility and complete compliance with Customs requirements.

A simple diagram illustrates the principle of the Free Zone with relation to frontier controls and the flow of trade.

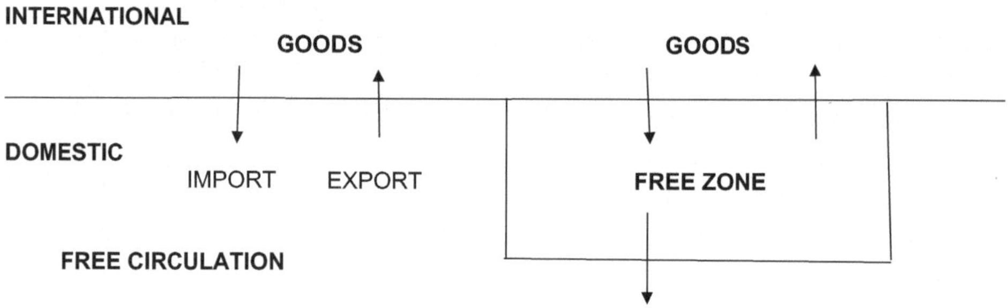

As can be seen from the diagram, goods passing through an international frontier must be declared at the point of import into the country, and Import Duty and VAT paid outright (or on deferment) at the point of import. With a Free Zone, the goods are imported into the Free Zone under Customs control and hence under Duty and VAT Suspension, for the purpose of storage or manufacturing. They are then released from the zone into Free Circulation or are re-exported. In the case of import into Free Circulation, Import Duty and VAT is paid on the individual consignment of goods being released at the time of release from the Free Zone. The Free Zone allows goods to be held for an indefinite period under Customs control until a decision is made to remove a specific quantity of these goods and either release them into Free Circulation, or to another Customs-controlled environment such as an individual Customs Warehouse or Inward Processing Relief for Customs-controlled processing by an individual company, or for re-export to another country. In reality, such processing could be carried out within the zone if the individual company is authorised by Customs for such duty-suspended operations.

CHAPTER 2

Free Zone history and overview

The Freeport/Free Zone application

The world's first documented Free-Trade Zone was established on the Greek Island of Delos in 166 BCE, and lasted until about 69 BCE when the island was overrun by pirates. The Romans had many *Civitas Libera*, or free cities, some of which could create their own money, establish their own laws, and not pay an annual tribute to the Roman Emperor. These continued through at least the first millennium CE. Historians also believe that Ephesus in modern-day Turkey may have been one of the world's first Free-Trade Zones. It was apparently established some 2,000 years ago when the city's Greek and Roman rulers opened its port to traders in a bid to fuel higher growth. This initiative helped Ephesus to grow rapidly into the second largest city in the Roman Empire, behind only Rome. It was also mentioned in the Bible as a place visited by the Apostle St. Paul, who wrote an entire letter to the church in Ephesus.

In the 12th century, the Hanseatic League began operating in Northern Europe and established trading colonies throughout Europe. These Free-Trade Zones included Hamburg and the Steelyard in London. The Steelyard, like other Hansa Free Zone locations, was a separate walled community with its own warehouses, weighing house, chapel, counting houses, and residential quarters. In 1988, remains of the former Hanseatic trading house, once the largest medieval trading complex in Britain, were uncovered by archaeologists during maintenance work on London's Cannon Street Railway Station.

Modern Free-Trade Zones, sometimes called Foreign-Trade Zones and Special Economic Zones, have replicated that success throughout modern history. So much so that almost every country seeking a growth thrust, including the United States, has chosen this path at one time or another. The Shannon Free Zone at Shannon, Western Ireland, established in 1959, has claimed to be the first 'modern' Free-Trade Zone. The Shannon Zone was established to help the adjacent international airport adjust to a radical change in aircraft technology that permitted longer range aircraft to skip previously-required refuelling stops in Shannon. It was seen as an attempt by the Irish government to maintain employment around the airport so that the airport would continue to generate revenue for the Irish economy. It was hugely successful and is still in operation today. Other Free Zones to note are the Kandla Free Zone in India, which started in about 1960, and the Kaohsiung Export Processing Zone in Taiwan, which started in 1967. The number of worldwide Free-Trade Zones proliferated in the late 20th century, including the Shanghai Export Processing Zones and the world-famous Jebel Ali Free Zone just outside Dubai, UAE.

DOI: 10.4324/9781003232025-3

Within the EU, there are currently 80 Free Zones located across 21 EU Member States, according to a list for the EU Member States provided by the Directorate General for Taxation and Customs Union (DG TAXUD). These pertain to **'Control Type I Free Zones'**, which are enclosed defined and demarcated geographical areas (with a perimeter fence), with a cluster of storage units instead of a single building or premises, and where goods placed within the area are checked by the Customs Authorities upon entry and exit. Some of these are inland within the country concerned, while others are located adjacent to seaports and international airports.

In the EU, there were also originally **'Control Type II Free Zones'**, where physical control of goods placed within the zone was done on the basis of stocktaking (rather than at entry and exit points to the zone) and additional physical inspections. However, as of 1 May 2016, these were reclassified as Customs Warehouses due to the application of the Modernised Customs Code in the EU (see Article 288(2) of the Union Customs Code), more generally known as the Union Customs Code, and which replaced the Community Customs Code of 1993.

UK Free Zones were in operation from 1984 – when areas of Birmingham, Belfast, Cardiff, Liverpool, Prestwick and Southampton were designated to become the UK's first Free Zones (Freeports) – until July 2012, when the UK stopped renewing the licences for Free Zones. Prior to 2012, there were five Free Zones in the UK, located in Liverpool, Prestwick, Sheerness, Southampton and Tilbury, which were classed as 'Control Type II Free Zones', i.e. Freeports. Technically not part of either the UK or the EU, a Free Zone was also in operation on the Isle of Man, adjacent to the Isle of Man Airport at Ballasalla. However, with the termination of the UK Freeport licences in 2012, the Isle of Man Freeport licence was also terminated, given the Customs Union between the Isle of Man and the UK.

Corporations establishing operations within a zone may be given a number of regulatory and fiscal incentives, such as the right to establish a business, the right to import parts and equipment without duty, the right to keep and use foreign exchange earnings, and sometimes income or property tax breaks. There may also be other incentives relating the methods of Customs control and filing requirements. The rationale is that the Zones will attract investment, create employment and thus reduce poverty and unemployment, stimulating the area's economy. These Zones are often used by multinational corporations to set up factories to produce goods (such as clothing, shoes, and electronics).

Free-Trade Zones should be distinguished from Free Trade Areas. A Free-Trade Zone is normally established in a single country as a designated area under Customs control where goods can be kept under Import Duty and Tax suspension while they are in the zone, although there are a few exceptions where a Free Zone may cross a national border, such as the Syrian/Jordanian Free-Trade Zone. Free-Trade Zones are therefore designated industrial Zones within a national territory which are controlled by the national Customs and Revenue Authority for the specific purpose of storing and manufacturing goods under Customs control, for either release into Free Circulation or for re-export to another country.

Free Trade Areas are international blocs of countries brought together by Free Trade Agreements (FTAs) concerning the free movement of goods, services and capital between these specific countries within the bloc, based on the origin of the goods concerned being established within the Free-Trade bloc. This means that only goods originating within the Free-Trade bloc can move between countries within the bloc on a preferential duty-free basis. For example, the Latin America Free Trade Association (LAFTA) was created in the 1960 Treaty of Montevideo by Argentina, Brazil, Chile, Mexico, Paraguay, Peru and Uruguay (of which Argentina, Brazil, Paraguay and Uruguay were later to create the MERCOSUR (Common Market of the South) Free Trade Area in the 1990s). Similarly, the North American Free Trade Agreement (NAFTA) was established between Mexico, the United States, and Canada in 1993. This was replaced in 2020 by the USMCA (US-Mexico-Canada) Free Trade Agreement, which in reality is composed of three separate Free Trade Agreements between each of the three member countries. In Free Trade Areas, tariffs are only lowered or eliminated between member countries on the basis of the Rules of Origin pertaining to the specific FTA. They should also be distinguished from Customs Unions, such as the former European Economic Community, or even the Customs Union between the EU and Turkey, where several countries agree to unify Customs regulations and eliminate Customs controls between the union members, as well as having a Common External Tariff with the same Commodity Codes and Import Duty rates for all members of the Customs Union.

Free-Trade Zones have more recently been also called SEZs in some countries. SEZs have been established in many countries as testing grounds for the implementation of liberal market economy principles, as well as specific fiscal incentive regimes. SEZs are viewed as instruments to enhance the acceptability and the credibility of the transformation policies and to attract domestic and foreign investment. The change in terminology has been driven by the formation of the WTO, which prohibits members from offering certain types of fiscal incentives to promote the exports of goods, thus why the term EPZ is no longer used with newer Zones. For example, India converted all of its EPZs to SEZs in 2000.

In 1999, there were 43 million people working in about 3,000 FTZs spanning 116 countries and producing clothes, shoes, electronics, engineered goods, consumer goods and toys. The basic objectives of economic Zones are to enhance foreign exchange earnings, develop export-oriented industries and generate employment opportunities. Indeed, the standard PESTEL factors apply to the function of Free Zones, namely:

Political;
Economic;
Social;
Technological;
Environmental;
Legal.

The **political** element of Free Zones is that they are sanctioned by government legislation or decree, and therefore have a degree of political influence or control about them, especially how they are governed within the State framework. This area is covered later in the study.

The **economic** element of Free Zones is that they are established to bolster the national and regional economy, and exist to foster economic growth and wellbeing, in terms of the generation of commerce, revenue and employment.

The **social** element of Free Zones is that they are designed to generate employment in terms of in-zone activities, be they administrative, logistics, manufacturing and storage. They are seen in most cases as focuses for employment in the area where they are located, as well as proving ancillary employment in companies that may be associated with the Zones, equally in terms of manufacturing, logistics and storage, as well as the transport sector.

The technological aspect of Free Zones lies in the fact that they use technological means of control and operation, as well as, in many cases, the manufacture of technological items related to the IT industry, as well as electronic goods in general.

The **environmental** aspect of Free Zones lies in the need to maintain a degree of sustainability and the protection of the regional environment by the use of legislation and governance. The UNCTAD is placing increasing emphasis on the need for Export Processing Zones to become more enhanced in order to achieve greater levels of sustainability and environmental harmony.

The **legal** element of Free Zones is that they are established by government statute, and are therefore classed as legal entities in their own right, especially through the establishment of Free Zone authorities to control and manage them. Because of their very nature, they are subject to specific laws and regulations concerning fiscal management and compliance, and as a consequence, all companies operating within Free Zones are equally governed by these regulations and compliances.

CHAPTER 3

Overall definition and purpose

According to the 1999 Revised Kyoto Convention, a '"Free Zone" means a part of the territory of a contracting party where any goods introduced are generally regarded, insofar as import duties and taxes are concerned, as being outside the [national] Customs territory'. The main principle of any form of Free Zone is that materials are stored and/or manufactured within the zone on a Customs-controlled basis, that is, under duty and tax suspension. The goods are not deemed to be tax-exempt or duty-free. They are only suspended from Import Duty and Sales Tax or VAT (Value Added Tax), while they are in the zone. This means that they are deemed to be outside Customs jurisdiction, as they are technically under international conditions. They can be released from the zone in two ways, namely by declaration to Customs for entry into Free Circulation on the basis of duty and tax liability, or for re-export out of the country. However, Free Zones have come to account for many more activities than purely manufacture and processing; they now encompass a much wider range of activities, including the service sector, including logistics, financial and IT services. However, they still have one major element in common, that is, tax reductions and other fiscal and economic benefits, such a specific assistance for start-ups and business development through fiscal incentives, especially where the emphasis is on international trading and the encouragement of inward Foreign Direct Investment from overseas-based companies. However, such development also allows for the export of such services, and in this respect the Free Zone concept also enables the development and expansion of local companies, especially in the international sphere. There are some views that such a policy could be seen as an unfair subsidy, but when a country is engaged in international economic development, any form of policy which fosters domestic and international growth must be seen as beneficial to the regional and national economy, especially where it not only benefits the local economy in terms of productivity and economic generation, but also stimulates an increase in employment and social Standards.

In many ways, businesses are often hampered by strict and oppressive fiscal regimes, along with high levels of bureaucracy and red tape. Developing businesses do not need such restrictions; they require incentives for growth. In this respect, Free Zones of whatever kind stimulate this by significantly reducing such levels of taxation and bureaucracy. Indeed, one of the main advantages of any Free Zone is the facility for significant simplification of procedures, practices, regulations and requirements, be they legal or fiscal. The Free Zones of the developing world have succeeded greatly in providing these incentives, as well as fostering economic growth for a variety of economic and commercial sectors, based on a significant reduction in barriers and

DOI: 10.4324/9781003232025-4

impediments to economic and commercial growth. The variety of these incentives, be they direct or indirect tax, economic assistance and other benefits, have shown that the purpose of the Free Zone is to develop the regional and national economy, not to stifle it or impede it through unnecessary protectionist or bureaucratic measures. Governments which impede the development of Free Zones induce economic stagnation, while governments encouraging the creation and operation of Free Zones encourage economic growth and development. In the developed world, countries such as the US have encouraged such growth and development, especially in times of economic adversity, while others, such as the European Union, have actively discouraged the development of Free Zones, resulting in their present economic woes, owing to inflexibility and high levels of bureaucracy, as well as seemingly-oppressive tax and overall fiscal regimes, which in fact pose major barriers to international trade, largely on the basis of increasing levels of protectionism. The Vinerian principles of Trade Creation within the bloc and Trade Diversion away from non-bloc countries is especially prevalent within the EU, and can be clearly seen concerning the EU's stance towards the UK since the exit for the UK from the European Union at the end of 2020. The very fact that the UK has decided to engage in a Freeport policy flies in the face of European protectionism and the stifling of certain incentives towards fiscal and trade liberalisation, and shows that the UK now has a much more independent policy, free from the constraints of EU membership. The policy of the European Union is to work towards an integrated taxation policy throughout the bloc, where a common tax system would prevail in the same way that the Common External Tariff exists, that is, the raising of all European taxes, be they VAT or Direct Tax, to the levels of the highest tax rates of any individual Member State of the EU. This was the policy of the original Customs Unions in Europe and the introduction of the Common External Tariff as part of the European Common Market initiative resulting from the 1957 Treaty of Rome, which established the European Economic Communities (EEC), as they were then known.

Furthermore, the introduction of the Union Customs Code in the EU in 2016 to replace the Community Customs Code imposed punitive Customs Comprehensive Financial Guarantees on businesses applying to operate any form of Special Economic Procedures as defined by the EU Customs Authorities, namely Customs Warehousing and Inward Processing Relief (IP). These guarantees stand at 100% of potential Import Duty and VAT applicable to any imported consignments subject to such Special Economic Procedures. The only reductions in these bank guarantees, which are designed to cover such Import Duty and VAT liability in the event of a breach of the use of these Special Economic Procedures such as non-compliance, are available to companies holding Authorised Economic Operator (AEO) status, where such guarantees are reduced to between 10% and 30% of the potential Import Duty and VAT liability. This imposition of Customs Guarantees means that there is little advantage in any trader operating a facility such as a Customs Warehouse, as the Customs Comprehensive Guarantee (CCG) would apply to all goods held in the warehouse at any time under Duty and VAT Suspension. The inference is that only the large traders with a large amount of disposable capital would tend to use such facilities, thus making the facility much less advantageous and accessible to other smaller traders. Indeed, in the EU, even a deferment account covers Import Duty and VAT, and is also subject to bank guarantees covering the Import Duty and VAT on all imports carried out using the company's deferment account. In the UK, however, HM Revenue & Customs took the step of largely abandoning the need for such Customs Guarantees, especially on the use of Special Economic Procedures which include Customs Warehousing and IP facilities, instead opting for the Guarantee Waiver scheme, as well as removing any guarantee from the Import VAT element of the deferment account, given that in the UK, Import VAT is now taken care of through the Postponed VAT Accounting (PVA) scheme, where Import VAT is not paid outright at the time of import, but is accounted for on the subsequent VAT Return submitted electronically by the importer to HMRC. The PVA system will also fit in well with the principle of the Freeport, as goods released from the Freeport into UK Free Circulation by any importer will be subject to the use of both the deferment account and the PVA system. Indeed, it is more than likely that one of the conditions of the release of goods from the Freeport into UK Free Circulation will be the automatic required use of both deferment accounts and the PVA facility, as well as the use of CFSP (Customs Freight Simplified Procedures) electronic declaration facilities, which are in any case used for all Customs Warehousing (CW) operations in the UK. In short, the purpose of the Freeport is not only to facilitate the Customs-controlled storage and processing of goods, but also to facilitate the use of simplified Customs clearance and Duty/VAT accounting procedures, thus resulting in significant cashflow and procedural advantages to the importer. In turn, this stimulates a smoother and more efficient flow of goods from the Freeport into Free Circulation, thus facilitating a more simplified and efficient supply chain.

The implication of the Freeport initiative as defined by HMRC is that there will be no bank guarantees required for Customs-controlled activities, although conditions will still exist for the use of duty deferment accounts as operate at present under the Guarantee Waiver scheme. This, along with other Customs simplifications, means that the function of the Freeport becomes much more advantageous to importers because of the relaxation and simplification in Customs requirements for Freeport operations. It also flies in the face of the more oppressive, inflexible and bureaucratic EU Customs regimes.

Business and trade laws differ between countries, therefore the exact definition and the operating models of Free Zones will be different for different countries. Free Zones (alternatively free ports or Free-Trade Zones) are designated areas of a country, which are inside the geographic boundary of that country but are considered to be outside of that country for the purposes of the import duties. Free Zones facilitate trading procedures by allowing fewer Customs formalities for goods from the rest of the world. Goods that are imported into the Free Zones do not incur the usual conventional import procedures on entry and re-exit, and import duties are not payable until these goods are released for Free Circulation in the domestic economy (or used or consumed within the Free Zone).

Businesses operating in Free Zones are therefore offered the following benefits:

- **Simplified Customs procedures**;
- **Relief on Customs Imports Duties** relating to transshipment, handling and processing of goods destined for re-export;
- **Cash flow benefits of duty deferral** until goods are released for Free Circulation in the domestic economy (or used or consumed within the Free Zone);
- **Added security** from the perimeter fence enclosing the Free Zone;

- **Tariff Inversion**: some finished goods incur lower tariffs than intermediate goods; this means that intermediate goods can be imported to Free Zone tariff-free, processed and sold as a final product, incurring lower tariff rates.

Free Zones are one type of **'Special Economic Zones'**, which are designated geographical areas within a country where business activity is subject to different rules from those prevailing in the rest of the country.

Therefore, three possible outcomes may occur:

- The goods are released at some stage, usually in lesser quantities, into Free Circulation, and Import Duty and Sales Tax are liable and paid at the point of declaration to Customs and release into Free Circulation;
- The goods are transferred to a company authorised for and operating Customs-controlled procedures;
- The goods are re-exported out of the country, and therefore all potential Import Duty and tax is zero-rated.

These are the only criteria which can apply. However, there are various kinds of Free Zone, depending upon the activities carried out therein, and this is where more detailed explanations are required.

Free Zones generally fall into one of five categories: Freeports; Free-Trade Zones, Export Processing Zones, Special Economic Zones, or Industrial Zones/Parks. **Freeports**, located adjacent to seaports and airports, have been traditionally created to act as Customs-controlled storage Zones, where goods can be stored by a variety of companies located within the zone for release into Free Circulation or re-export. **Free-Trade Zones**, typically located near seaports or airports, mainly offer suspensions from national import duties on goods that are re-exported or released into national Free Circulation. Local services, such as storage and logistics, gain significant benefits, although there is little, if any, value-added to the goods traded, other than light processes such as repackaging, sorting, consolidation or breaking bulk. **Export Processing Zones (EPZs)** go a step further by focusing on exports with a significant value-added, for example processing or manufacture, rather than only on re-exports of existing goods or commodities. **Special Economic Zones (SEZs)** apply a multi-sectoral development approach and focus on both domestic and foreign markets. They offer an array of incentives including infrastructure, tax and custom exemptions and simpler administrative procedures. **Industrial Zones** are targeted at specific economic activities, for example media, IT, electronics or textiles, with infrastructure adapted accordingly. In this respect, Industrial Zones/Parks may be more specialist, covering specific industrial sectors, whereas the other types of Free Zone may serve a wider variety of industrial and commercial sectors. There are specific Zones in Dubai, UAE, which cover the electronic sector, the media sector and the financial services sector. These Zones are not necessarily production Zones, but are concentrated more on the services sector, particularly on an international basis.

Freeports should not be confused with the actual seaports themselves. Although Freeports are located adjacent to and outside seaports themselves, but are linked to the seaports by way of controlled access and IT security systems. Freeports can, however, contain internal integrated areas defined as Primary Customs Zones, which can also be part of the port facilities themselves.

Primary Zones are defined as areas delimited and defined by the appropriate Customs Authority:

1. Land or water area, continuous or discontinuous, in the Customs ports;
2. The land area, at the Customs airports; and
3. The land area, which includes the Customs points.

Therefore, the Primary Zones are defined by ports, airports and Customs border points. It should not be forgotten that not all airports or ports have a border point, although under the international ISPS (International Ship and Port Security) Code, all international seaports must have security controls, including fences and gatehouses. In this respect, Primary Zones are considered to be Customs-controlled areas of seaports, where goods and cargoes may be stored under Customs control while in the confines of the port zone. Such storage facilities normally include Transit Sheds (known as Temporary Storage) and open-air storage facilities. Freeports, however, have the facility to store goods on a longer-term basis, dependent on the needs of the various customers, and linked with a variety of Customs-controlled processing and manufacturing facilities where deemed permissible.

Zone programs should target a wide assortment of economic sectors, including commercial and manufacturing activities and professional services, such as warehousing and transshipment. But then, this being the standard aspiration of any Free-Trade Zone, the general function of most Free Zones is precisely this, as the main purpose of the exercise is to ensure that the whole economy of the region or country benefits from such concepts.

To reduce the burden placed on public resources and increase the efficiency of Zones, the private sector should be encouraged to help develop them and be allowed to operate under market mechanisms. It has been seen that several governments have developed and managed Zones that have been less effective than those of their private counterparts, although government-sponsored initiatives that have led to the development of private Free Zones, governed by private corporate authorities, have succeeded in their aims and objectives.

Moreover, though Free Zones operate as offshore locations, with major tax incentives, or at very least locations close to or adjacent to seaports, they are geared to international activity. To avoid unfair competition, preferential duties on sales to the rest of the host economy and other discriminatory practices should be resisted, although the use of Free Zones does mean much more effective use of import tariffs, especially on goods produced inside Free Zones for admission to domestic territory, especially where techniques such as Tariff Inversion or reversed cascading, where the Import Duty on the finished product is significantly lower than the import duties on its components, if not 0% Import Duty rate altogether. The technique and objective in this case is to import the materials on a duty-suspended basis into the Free Zone and then manufacture these components into the finished products. These resulting finished products can then be imported out of the Zone into Free Circulation domestic territory using the Import Duty rate of the finished product but at the value of the imported components. If the 0% Import Duty rate applies, this equals zero Import Duty, with only Import VAT or Sales Tax to be accounted for. In all cases where Import VAT applies, the Import VAT is reclaimed by the trader in any case, generally through the VAT Return. Of course, much of the production of finished goods can also be re-exported without any duty and tax liability at all, thus reducing the overall tax liability on all products manufactured in the zone. This strategy is used by many companies in the United States, where Foreign-Trade Zones (Subzones) are used significantly for this purpose, as allowed and encouraged by the US Foreign-Trade Zones Act.

Free Zones have many merits and have boosted investment and economic growth in many MENA countries and other countries elsewhere in the world, including South-East Asia and China, as well as simplifying and rendering more efficient the international supply chain process. More Zones are in the process of development and implementation, and still more will emerge in the years ahead. However, encouraging investment is only one, albeit vital, step in a long journey. The ultimate goal must be to make those investments work to the benefit of the wider economy, both nationally and internationally. Not all Zones succeed immediately; some have taken several years to develop and provide economic benefits, while others have not been successful and have ultimately closed down or are limited in their use, as in the case of the Free Zone at Subic Bay, Philippines. In the case of the original UK Freeports, these met with limited success during their lifetimes, and some fared better than others. The most successful of these was Liverpool Freeport, while others, such as Prestwick, never achieved their potential and were closed sooner than others. Much of this success or failure relates to national government policy. If a national Free Zone policy is more flexible and ambitious, then it is more likely that a national Free Zone policy will succeed. If a national Free Zone policy is more limiting and restrictive, then it is likely that Free Zones will not enjoy long-term prosperity and will ultimately fail or decline into obscurity.

CHAPTER 4

Fiscal and legal status

Fiscal status

Certain organisations, including political parties, have claimed that Free Zones are a source of Import Duty exemption. This is false information, as there is no such thing as Import Duty exemption. The World Customs Organization (WCO) and the WTO state clearly that global tariffs are designed in such a way that duty exemptions of any kind do not exist, and that all imported goods into any country must be declared on import for Customs Imports Duty liability purposes. In other words, Import Duty is payable on all imported goods at the time of import, and therefore cannot be avoided. The main elements where either Customs Imports Duty or Excise Duties may not apply are the following:

IMPORT (CUSTOMS)

- Zero-rated Tariffs (where the ad valorem Import Duty rate is Zero (0%));
- Duty-Free Preference (where a Free Trade Agreement exists);
- Import Duty Reliefs, such as Inward Processing, Processing for Free Circulation, Customs Warehousing, Outward Processing Relief, End-Use Relief (Prescribed use, e.g. Military, Shipwork, Aviation);
- Re-export of products out of Customs control;
- Tariff Inversion/Reversed Cascading (the Import Duty rate pertaining to the finished product is lower than on its imported components).

EXCISE

- Tied Oils Relief (specific products processed from hydrocarbon oils which are not used as combustible fuels or their derivatives);
- Alcohol conversion or denaturing, and alcoholic beverage ingredients;
- Re-export of excisable products.

These are the only circumstances where duty reliefs may be used, and even then these facilities are conditional, with duty being relieved under suspension conditions, that is, non-payment on condition that all Customs compliances are adhered to. However, the only other time where Import Duty does not apply is where it is classified as zero in the national tariff, for example computers (HS Commodity Code 8471).

DOI: 10.4324/9781003232025-5

The European Union defines the issue of duty liability for Free Zones as follows:

> Member States may designate parts of the Customs territory of the Union as 'Free Zones'; these Free Zones must be communicated to the European Commission.
>
> 'Free Zones' are enclosed areas within the Customs territory of the Union where non-Union goods can be introduced free of Import Duty, other charges (i.e. taxes) and commercial policy measures.
>
> Such goods may, following the period in the Free Zones, be released for Free Circulation (subject to payment of Import Duty and other charges), or be placed under another special procedure (e.g. Inward Processing, temporary admission or end-use procedures – under the conditions laid down for these procedures) or re-exported.
>
> Union goods may also be entered into or stored, moved, used, processed or consumed in Free Zones. Such goods may afterwards be exported or brought into other parts of the Customs territory of the Union.

In terms of the benefits of Free Zones for duty management purposes, the main two factors which provide benefits are:

- Bulk storage of goods and materials under Customs control;
- Progressive release of goods into Free Circulation from bulk consignments stored in a Free zone;
- Reversed Cascading/Tariff Inversion;
- Re-export of products.

Indeed, goods held in a Free zone are located in the zone for two purposes:

- Storage;
- Processing/Manufacture.

When they leave the zone, they are subject to any one of five procedures. They are either:

- Re-exported out of national territory;
- Shipped to an offshore destination for Oil & Gas operations;
- Imported into Free Circulation duty and tax paid;
- Transferred to a company authorised for Customs Warehousing (CW) facilities;
- Transferred to a company authorised for IP Relief facilities.

If the goods are re-exported to another country or are shipped to an offshore Oil & Gas field, they are completely suspended from all import duties and taxes. In the case of re-exports, the goods are declared to Customs for export purposes, and, once cleared, are exported to another country.

Where offshore activities are involved, these are mainly conducted in a specific kind of Customs-controlled Free Zone called an Offshore Supply Base, generally located adjacent to the seaport, where materials destined for offshore operational purposes, such as drilling and oil/gas extraction operations, are imported through the port and into the Supply Base. They are then stored inside the base on a duty and tax-suspended basis until they are to be shipped offshore. Examples of this can be found at Luanda, Angola, and the combined Supply Base/Free Zone at Onne, located in the Niger Delta in Nigeria.

If the goods are cleared out of the zone into national Free Circulation, Import Duty and Tax (VAT/Sales Tax) is paid on the consignment being cleared out of the zone. The other goods remain in the zone on a duty and tax suspension basis until they too are cleared through Customs formalities out of the zone, either for export, shipment to an offshore location or for entry into domestic Free Circulation.

Where goods or commodities are stored in bulk in a Free Zone, they will be held in the zone until required by the customer(s), often under Consignment Stock or draw-off/ call-off basis. Once the customer issues a request to draw off specific quantities of goods or commodities, these requests will be applied to the schedules for draw off and release from the zone, and simplified release instructions will be issued by the zone operator in a manner similar to releases from Customs Warehouses, Import Duty and VAT is paid on the specific release of the commodity concerned, while the rest of the consignment remains under Customs control in the Free Zone.

If the goods are transferred to a company authorised by Customs for Customs Warehousing or Inward Processing Relief facilities, Import Duty and VAT is suspended on the goods concerned until the goods are released from the Customs Warehouse or from IP processing. Again, the goods can either be cleared into Free Circulation from the Customs facility on a duty and tax-paid basis, or can be re-exported or shipped offshore. Free Zone tenants will have to apply separately for Inward Processing authorisation, although the application process is to be streamlined for Free Zone operators.

Inward Processing and Tariff Inversion

Inward Processing Relief (IP) suspends Import Duty and VAT on goods that are imported from outside the EU to be processed into final goods and then exported outside the EU. IP also allows for **Tariff Inversion** if the final goods are released for Free Circulation in the EU, or, beyond 1 January 2021, in the UK. From that date, shipments to the EU will be classed as UK exports.

In this case, a manufacturer can base Customs Imports Duty and Import VAT on the value of imported goods or final manufactured or processed goods, depending on whichever has a lower *ad valorem* (value-based) Import Duty rate. Data is not available on the uptake or use of Inward Processing Relief by UK companies, and therefore the costs to HM Treasury (in terms of foregone revenues) and benefits to business (in duties avoided) cannot be accurately estimated. The IP application form and self-assessment questionnaire requires businesses to provide details on the throughput period (how long it takes to convert imported goods into exported goods), the rate of yield (the ratio of imported goods to exported goods) and, for some agricultural products, an economic test explaining why EU produced goods cannot be used. Businesses are required to maintain records for four years.

The Reversed Cascading/Tariff Inversion concept works for products manufactured from a variety of components, where the finished product has a rate of Import Duty which is lower than the duty rates of its components. This means that the components are imported duty-suspended into the Free Zone, where they are manufactured into the finished product, using a Customs facility called processing for Free Circulation (PFC). The finished products are declared into Free Circulation at the Import Duty rate of the finished product, but at the value of the imported components. This tool is used in the following examples.

Example 1

As a variation to the principle described earlier in this text, a company manufacturing computers uses a Free Zone to manufacture these computers. It uses some components sourced locally, mainly electronic components, while it imports casings and other materials made of plastic from overseas. Normally, these items would attract an ad valorem Import Duty rate of 6.5%, so in order to reduce the duty liability, they are imported into the Free Zone under Import Duty suspension using the facility known in the UK as PFC. They are then manufactured under duty suspension into the computers, which have an Import Duty rate of 0% (Zero duty). The finished computers are then declared into Free Circulation with no Import Duty liability. They can also be re-exported with no duty liability, and it is possible the countries of destination also use a tariff where the Import Duty rate is 0% as well.

Example 2

The automotive company BMW uses a subzone facility in the US State of South Carolina, at its plant at Greenville-Spartanburg. It manufactures cars for both North America and re-export to the EU. The US tariff duty rate for many of the imported components is between 3.5% and 6.5%, whereas the Import Duty rate for finished cars is only 2.5%. The components are imported under duty suspension into the zone, along with components sourced locally and regionally, and are manufactured into the finished cars. Import Duty is paid on the value of the imported components but at the duty rate of the finished product, that is, 2.5%, thus incurring huge savings on import duties and taxes. For the re-exported cars, Import Duty and Sales Tax is totally suspended.

The third element of fiscal savings is on commodities or goods re-exported from the Free Zone. Where goods are re-exported, there is no duty or tax liability, as the goods concerned are not entering Free Circulation but are leaving the country concerned. They will only attract duty and tax liability once they arrive at the country of ultimate import, thus relieving significant levels of duty and tax form the supply chain.

Legal status

All Free Zones, Freeports, Export Processing Zones and Special Economic Zones can only be established by national legal decree or legislation. The establishment of a Free Zone regime in a country requires national legislation to implement it.

For example, Turkish National Free Zone Law encompasses matters related to the following issues:

- The establishment of Free Zones;
- The determination of their location and boundaries;
- Their management;
- The scope of their activities;
- Their operation;
- The establishment of installations and facilities within the zone;
- The objective of increasing export-oriented investment and production in the country concerned;

- Accelerating the entry of foreign capital and technology;
- Procuring inputs of the economy in an economic and orderly fashion; and
- Increasing the utilisation of external finance and trade possibilities and opportunities.

Every piece of national legislation implementing national Free Zone regimes encompasses most, or all, of the above elements. Given that Free Zones operate outside national Customs and, in general, tax jurisdiction, they must all have authorisation from the national Customs and Revenue Authority to operate, subject to terms and conditions laid down by the national Customs & Revenue Authorities.

An example of Free Zone Law is as follows, taken from Turkish Free Zone Law:

Free Zones Law

Explanation

The Directorate General of Free Zones was founded in 1983 within the organisation of the Prime Ministry on the basis of Statutory Decree Nr. 151. Later in 1984 it was included into the organisation of the State Planning Organization as the Directorate of Free Zones on the basis of Statutory Decree Nr. 223 and in 1991 it was included into the organisation of the Undersecretariat of Treasury and Foreign Trade of the Prime Ministry as the Directorate General of Free Zones on the basis of Statutory Decree Nr. 438. In 1994, the Directorate General of Free Zones was included into the organisation of the Undersecretariat of Foreign Trade of the Prime Ministry since the Undersecretariat of Treasury and Foreign Trade was divided into two on the basis of Statutory Decree Nr. 534. However, this decree was cancelled. Thereafter, as the result of the reorganisation of two Undersecretariats as the Undersecretariat of Foreign Trade and the Undersecretariat of Treasury, with Law No. 4059, in 1994, the Directorate General of Free Zones began to carry out its activities within the structure of the Undersecretariat of Foreign Trade.

FOR CONTACT

Republic Of Turkey
The Prime Ministry
The Undersecretariat of Foreign Trade Directorate General of Free Zones
06510 Emek Ankara Turkey
Tel: (312) 212 58 87–212 89 06–212 82 58 Fax: (312) 212 89 06
Free Zones Law
Law No. 3218 Approved: June 6, 1985 Issued: June 15, 1985

Section one
General provisions
Objectives and scope

Article 1 – This Law covers issues on establishment of Free Zones, determination of areas and borders and the scope of activities of the Free Zones, management and operation of

Free Zones, establishment of buildings and facilities in the Zones, with the aim of promoting export-oriented investment and production, accelerating Foreign Direct Investment and technology entry, directing enterprises towards export and developing international trade.

Authority Article 2 – The Council of Ministers has the authority to determine the location and boundaries of the Free Zones.

The Council of Ministers grants permission for the establishment and operation of Free Zones to public institutions and agencies, resident or non-resident real persons or legal entities.

Definitions

Article 3 – In the implementation of this Law:

- **Operator** signifies the public institution and agency; the resident and non-resident real persons or legal entities operating the Free Zone.
- **User** signifies the real and legal person bearing an operating license and having a specific place of business within the Free Zone.
- **Foreign exchange** refers to all currencies, or all types of accounts or bills, considered as being convertible by the Central Bank of the Republic of Turkey.

Activities

Article 4 – Any kind of industrial, commercial and service activities approved by the Supreme Coordination Council of Economic Affairs can be carried out within Free Zones.

Except the demands from the manufacturer enterprises, any authority regarding prices, quality and Standards granted to public institutions and agencies by laws or by other legislation is not valid in the Free Zones.

Free Zones Coordination Board is formed to evaluate the Free Zone activities, to determine the strategies and to offer recommendations for improving the Free Zones and for resolving occurring problems, The structure, working procedures and principles of the Board shall be determined in the Governing Regulation.

Section two
Organisation of Free Zones
Principles related to the organisation of the zone

Article 5 – Land and facilities needed within the declared Free Zones may be acquired pursuant to the provisions of the Expropriation Law.

Domestic or foreign real persons or legal entities may operate in the Free Zones provided that Undersecretariat of Foreign Trade grants them an operating license. The land, building plots and buildings exclusively Treasury owned can be leased or granted easement for 49 years to the investor users of Free Zones. On the places under State dictum and disposition, right of usage can be given for the same period.

All other permits and licenses regarding the use of land as well as the design, construction and utilisation of buildings and installations within the Free Zone are issued and supervised by the zone directorate.

Security services for Free Zones are provided by the police.

Exceptions and incentives

Article 6 – Free Zones, although being parts of the Customs Territory of Turkey, for the goods provided that they are not released for Free Circulation or placed under another Customs procedure or used or consumed under conditions other than those provided for in Customs regulations are deemed as being out side of the Customs territory for the purposes of import duties, commercial policy measures and exchange legislation; and are places where the goods in Free Circulation can benefit from provisions normally attaching to the export of goods by virtue of being placed in a Free Zone.

Legislative provisions pertaining to Customs and foreign exchange obligations are not applicable in these Zones.

Regarding the account books the users must keep and documents they draw up, Ministry of Finance is authorised to make necessary arrangements independent from the provisions of the Tax Procedures Law No. 213 dated 4.1.1961.

During the investment and production stages of their activities, operators and users may qualify for incentives other than tax incentives, determined by the Council of Ministers.

Revenues and expenditure of the Free Zones

Article 7 – From the revenues obtained from the Free Zones;

- Fees to be collected for operating licenses and permits,
- Fees to be paid in advance amount to 0.5 percent of the Cost Insurance Freight (CIF) value of goods entering the zone from abroad and fees to be paid in advance amount to 0.5 percent of the Free On Board (FOB) value of goods leaving the zone towards Turkey,
- Payments specified in the contracts made with real persons and legal entities operating the Free Zones,
- Other revenues obtained from the zone activities are deposited in the Special Account to be opened with the Central Bank of the Republic of Turkey, after deducting the income share transfers specified in the contracts made with the legal entities by the interested administration. After reducing the rejections and returns, the rest of the amount collected in this account is deposited in the account of the Main Treasurers Office which is in charge of the payments of the Undersecretariat for Foreign Trade. The amount deposited in the account of the Main Treasurers Office is registered as revenue to the budget.

Goods utilised during the investment and construction stages, goods brought into the zone for renovation and capacity building purposes, as well as goods, which are not owned by the users brought into the zone for maintenance and repairing purposes, temporarily brought instruments, tools and equipment, and goods brought for the purpose of outsourced material processing, goods brought into the zone from abroad and/or sent to Turkey by the non-producer users who obtained the operating license after 06/02/2004 are not subject to the payments specified in sub-paragraph (b) of paragraph 1 of this Article. However, a fee is charged on the value-added created during the maintenance, repairing, and outsourced material processing and on the goods brought into the zone from abroad and sold within the zone by the non-producer users who obtained the operating license after 06/02/2004.

Procedures and principles concerning the management of the Special Account opened with the Central Bank of the Republic of Turkey are determined by a regulation of the Undersecretariat for Foreign Trade upon the approval of the Ministry of Finance. Revenues not deposited in due course, are subject to the provisions of the Law No. 6183 on the Procedures on the Collection of Public Receivables.

Section three
Goods and services
Goods in Free Zones

Article 8 – Trade conducted between a Free Zone and other regions of Turkey is subject to the foreign trade regime.

Upon request goods of Turkish origin in value less than 5,000 US $ or its equivalent in Turkish Lira can be exempted from export procedures.

Foreign exchange and services

Article 9 – All payments related to Free Zone activities are made in the form of foreign exchange. The Council of Ministers may decide that payments be also made in the form of Turkish Lira.

Shipping and port services in Free Zones are provided either by the operator or assigned to public institutions and agencies or to real persons or legal entities.

Section four
Labour and social security, repealed and inapplicable provisions, and regulations
Labour and social security provisions

Article 10 – Foreign managers and qualified personnel may be employed by firms operating in a Free Zone. Related principles are specified by governing statutes.

Provisions of the Social Security Regulations of the Republic of Turkey are applied in Free Zones.

Repealed provisions

Article 11 – The Free Zones Law No. 6209 dated December 21, 1953, is hereby repealed.

Inapplicable provisions

Article 12 – In the Free Zones, Law No. 4817 on Working Permits of Foreigners, Law No. 4875 on Foreign Direct Investment, provisions of Municipality Law No. 5393 except provisions on death and fire, building and maintenance of sewerage, procurement of drinking, potable and industrial water, inspection of gas, water and electric consumption, Passport Law No. 5682; Law No. 5683 for Foreigners Traveling and Residing in Turkey and provisions of other laws contrary to this Law are not applicable. Furthermore, the transactions in second paragraph of Article 5 are not subject to the provisions of Public Procurement Law No. 2886.

Free Zone Governing Regulation

Article 13 – Where the arrangement of matters in this Law are left to governing regulations, concerning any organisation, duties, authority and/or responsibilities of operators who are active in Free Zones, or granting and cancellation of any Operating Licenses provided to such operators and/or users; concerning the maintenance of their industry and commercial registers; concerning any payments they make to the Special Account; concerning principles governing conduct of activities in a Free Zone; concerning zone entry permits and identity cards; residence permits; and concerning work principles and other matters pertaining to the operation of Free Zones are determined by governing regulations.

Interim Article 1 – (Abolished by Law No. 4771)

Interim Article 2 – This Law is effective for each Free Zone upon the commencement of operations in that Free Zone.

The date of commencement of operations is the date when the construction of the perimeter fence, tower and gate are completed and the zone directorate, police and Customs units assume their duties.

Interim Article 3 – By the date this article comes into effect, the taxpayers, who obtained licence to operate in the Free Zones that were established according to this Law, are

- Excepted from income or corporate taxes on the earnings generated through their activities in these Zones, within the limits of the period specified in their operating licences as of the date this article comes into effect. This exception does not affect the deduction carried out within the scope of sub clause (b) of sub paragraph 6 under the first paragraph of the article 94 of the Income Tax Law No. 193 dated 31.12.1960.
- Excepted from the income tax on the wages they pay to their workers until 31.12.2008. However, if the validity period of their operating licence ends before 31.12.2008, the date of completion of the operating licence period is taken into consideration regarding this exception.
- Excepted from all taxes, levies and duties on their activities related to their Free Zone operations until 31.12.2008.

*Until the end of the taxation year including the date Turkey becomes a full member of the European Union;

a) The earnings of the manufacturer taxpayers, generated through the sales of the goods they produced in the Free Zones, are excepted from the income or corporate taxes. This exception has no effect on the withholding carried out according to within the scope of sub clause (b) of sub paragraph 6 under the first paragraph of the article 94 of the Income Tax Law No. 193 dated 31.12.1960 and, Article 15 and Article 30 of the Corporate Tax Law No. 5520.
b) The wages of the workers employed by the taxpayers that export at least 85 percent of the FOB value of the goods they produce in the Free Zones are excepted from income tax. Council of Ministers is authorised to reduce the rate to 50% or to increase up to its statutory level. The taxes that are not collected in time from the taxpayers, whose annual sales remains below this rate, shall be collected including the delinquent tax-due without penalties.
c) The transactions and arranged documents related to the activities carried out in the Zones are except from stamp duties and fees.

The Ministry of Finance is authorised to determine the procedures and principles concerning the implementation of this Article.

Interim Article 4 – Since goods brought into the zone and/or sent to Turkey by the non-producer users who obtained an operating license after 06/02/2004 are not subject to payments specified in sub-paragraph (b) of paragraph 1 of Article 7 of this Law, to compensate the revenue allocation loss of the founder and operator companies stemming from the exception of the payments specified in this Law in the Free Zones where the revenue allocation is regulated by the founder and operator companies' operation contracts, a modification will be made in the Governing Regulation.

Interim Article 5 – The Operating Licence period and the lease period of users that obtained an operating licence before the date this Law comes in to effect that rented the Treasury-owned land, building plot and buildings can be extended up to 49 years by Undersecretariat for Foreign Trade. The issues regarding the implementation of this Article shall be determined in the Governing Regulation.

Interim Article 6 – Free Zones, until the date Turkey becomes a full member of the European Union, are deemed to be outside of the Customs Territory of Turkey for the purposes of Customs procedures, and are deemed to be parts of the Customs Territory of Turkey for the purposes of Rules of Origin.

Entry into force

Article 14 – This Law goes into effect on the date of its publication.*

Execution

Article 15 – The provisions of this Law are enforced by the Council of Ministers.

***The second paragraph of Interim Article 3 shall come into effect on 1/1/2009.**

Important notice

By the Law No: 5810, the Interim Article below is added to the Customs Law No. 4458 dated 27/10/1999.

'INTERIM ARTICLE 7: The provisions that are contrary to Free Zones Law No:3218 in Article 152, Article 157 except sub paragraph (a) of the first paragraph, Article 158 and Article 185 of this Law are not applicable until the date Turkey becomes a full member of the European Union. On the other hand, for the purposes of Excise Duties Law No: 4760, the provisions of Article 158 and Article 185 shall be applied.

For the periods before this Law comes into effect, any tax shall not be imposed according to Law No: 4760, the taxes imposed before shall be renounced, the accrued amounts shall be cancelled. The amounts collected shall not be refused and refunded.'

Please note that the English version is an unofficial translation. Only the Turkish version is legally binding.

It should be noted that the above example is precisely that; an example. Other national Free Zone legislation can and does differ depending upon the national requirements and the terms and conditions imposed upon Free Zone legislation. However, the gist is the same throughout the world, as all Free Zone activities must be precisely detailed and defined according to the function of the individual Free Zones, and must be maintained and monitored at all times by the national Customs & Revenue Authority.

The Revised Kyoto Convention (RKC)

The Revised Kyoto Convention of 1999 was implemented by the WCO to more closely define global Customs procedures and practices, as well as to define legislation concerning specific concepts and regimes. This included Free Zones and their functions. The following table specifically defines the provisions of Chapter 2, Specific Annex D (SAD) concerning Free Zone provisions.

Chapter 2 (Free Zone) of Specific Annex D to the RKC defines a Free Zone as 'a part of the territory of a Contracting Party where any goods introduced are generally regarded, insofar as import duties and taxes are concerned, as being outside the Customs territory'.

Although their scope, size, institutional structure and set-up, locations and incentives for investors vary significantly, the Special Customs Zone/Free Zone (SCZ) concept's general aim is to provide a wide range of economic incentives to attract foreign investment, foster economic activities led mainly by export-oriented activities, and boost employment.

Revised Kyoto convention (chapter 2 (Free Zones) of Specific Annex D)

According to the World Customs Organisation, Chapter 2 of Specific Annex D is the only international agreement for Free Zones. Customs policy in relation to SCZs is outlined in Chapter 2 of Specific Annex D to the RKC, and the RKC Guidelines on Free Zones provide technical specifications regarding this Chapter. Chapter 2 contains 21 Standards covering a wide range of Customs procedures and controls related to SCZs, and these can be found below. To date, the RKC is the only international agreement which includes provisions on this subject.

Based on the RKC, except of for revenue collection, all other Customs functions such as procedures' facilitation and border control (including inspections and seizures) should be applied and enforced in SCZs. For example, Standard 4 is essential in that it stipulates that Customs 'shall have the right to carry out checks at any time on the goods stored in a Free Zone'.

However, despite these Standards, Customs controls in SCZs are generally more flexible than those exercised in other contexts. Furthermore, some countries interpret these Zones as 'being outside the Customs territory' altogether, leading to a denial of Customs' jurisdiction over goods in SCZs, and opening the way for illegal trade.

Category	*Article number*	*Text of provisions*
	Definition	'Free Zone' is 'a part of the territory of a Contracting Party where any goods introduced are generally regarded, insofar as import duties and taxes are concerned, as being outside the Customs territory'.

Category	*Article number*	*Text of provisions*
Principle	Standard 1	The Customs regulations applicable to Free Zones shall be governed by the provisions of this chapter and, insofar as applicable, by the provisions of the General Annex.
Establishment and Control	Standard 2	National legislation shall specify the requirements relating to the establishment of Free Zones, the kinds of goods admissible to such Zones and the nature of the operations to which goods may be subjected in them.
	Standard 3	The Customs shall lay down the arrangements for Customs control including appropriate requirements as regards the suitability, construction and layout of Free Zones.
	Standard 4	The Customs Authority shall have the right to carry out checks at any time of the goods stored in a Free Zone.
Admission of Goods	Standard 5	Admission to a Free Zone shall be authorised not only for goods imported directly from abroad but also for goods brought from the Customs territory of the Contracting Party concerned.
	Recommended Practice 6	Admission to a Free Zone of goods brought from abroad should not be refused solely on the grounds that the goods are liable to prohibitions or restrictions other than those imposed on grounds of: – public morality or order, public security, public hygiene or health, or for veterinary or phytosanitary considerations; or – the protection of patents, trade marks and copyrights, irrespective of country of origin, country from which arrived or country of destination. Goods which constitute a hazard, which are likely to affect other goods or which require special installations should be admitted only to Free Zones specially designed to receive them.
	Standard 7	Goods admissible to a Free Zone which are entitled to exemption from or repayment of import duties and taxes when exported shall qualify for such exemption or repayment immediately after they have been introduced into the Free Zone.
	Standard 8	Goods admissible to a Free Zone which are entitled to exemption from or repayment of internal duties and taxes when exported shall qualify for such exemption or repayment after they have been introduced into the Free Zone.
	Recommended Practice 9	No Goods declaration should be required by the Customs in respect of goods introduced into a Free Zone directly from abroad if the information is already available on the documents accompanying the goods.
Security	Recommended Practice 10	The Customs Authority should not require security for the admission of goods to a Free Zone.

Category	*Article number*	*Text of provisions*
Authorised Operations	Standard 11	Goods admitted to a Free Zone shall be allowed to undergo operations necessary for their preservation and usual forms of handling to improve their packaging or marketable quality or to prepare them for shipment, such as breaking bulk, grouping of packages, sorting and grading, and repacking.
	Standard 12	Where the competent authorities allow processing or manufacturing operations in a Free Zone, they shall specify the processing or manufacturing operations to which goods may be subjected in general terms and/or in detail in a regulation applicable throughout the Free Zone or in the authority granted to the enterprise carrying out these operations.
Goods Consumed Within The Free Zones	Standard 13	National legislation shall enumerate the cases in which goods to be consumed inside the Free Zone may be admitted free of duties and taxes and shall lay down the requirements which must be met.
Duration of Stay	Standard 14	Only in exceptional circumstances shall a time limit be imposed on the duration of the stay of goods in a Free Zone.
Transfer of Ownership	Standard 15	The transfer of ownership of goods admitted to a Free Zone shall be allowed.
Removal of Goods	Standard 16	Goods admitted to or produced in a Free Zone shall be permitted to be removed in part or in full to another Free Zone or placed under a Customs procedure, subject to compliance with the conditions and formalities applicable in each case.
	Standard 17	The only declaration required for goods on removal from a Free Zone shall be the Goods declaration normally required for the Customs procedure to which those goods are assigned.
	Recommended Practice 18	Where a document must be produced to the Customs in respect of goods which on removal from a Free Zone are sent directly abroad, the Customs should not require more information than already available on the documents accompanying the goods.
Assessment of Goods	Standard 19	National legislation shall specify the point in time to be taken into consideration for the purpose of determining the value and quantity of goods which may be taken into home use on removal from a Free Zone and the rates of the import duties and taxes or internal duties and taxes, as the case may be, applicable to them.
	Standard 20	National legislation shall specify the rules applicable for determining the amount of the import duties and taxes or internal duties and taxes, as the case may be, chargeable on goods taken into home use after processing or manufacturing in a Free Zone.
Closure of Free Zone	Standard 21	In the event of the closure of a Free Zone, the persons concerned shall be given sufficient time to remove their goods to another Free Zone or to place them under a Customs procedure, subject to compliance with the conditions and formalities applicable in each case.

The provisions detailed in Annex 2 apply to all Free Zones throughout the world, regardless of the country where these Zones are located. They are global Standards, given their definition by the World Customs Organization as part of the Revised Kyoto Convention, and are designed to account for all issues relating to the management and function of Free Zones as a generic function. They predominantly deal with Customs and Fiscal provisions, but may be adapted and applied according to the national fiscal rules and regulations of each country implementing and operating a Free Zones initiative and policy. Indeed, the provisions of Annex 2 generally prevail over national legislation, although national legislation provides specific details concerning individual national Free Zone law as determined by national fiscal policy. This implies that individual countries may impose specific regulations depending upon the function of Free Zones in their national territory.

CHAPTER 5

Specific zone definitions, locations and comparisons

Specific zone definitions Freeport

A **Freeport** is a Customs-controlled area adjacent to either a seaport or an international airport. It differs from a Temporary Storage area in that goods can be held under Customs control, that is, under Import Duty and VAT/Sales Tax suspension, for an unlimited period, whereas with a Temporary Storage facility, for example a Transit Shed, goods can only be held under such conditions for a limited finite period, usually up to 90 days, before being cleared through Customs or being re-exported on a transit basis out of the country. To this extent, a Freeport acts as an overall area populated by Customs Warehouses (**Note**: this does not include Excise warehouses, which must be approved by the national Revenue Authority on a separate basis). However, although a Customs warehouse may be a stand-alone warehouse at an inland destination, a Freeport is, as its name suggests, a Free Zone adjacent to a port or airport used for the storage of a wide range of materials under Duty and VAT Suspension by different companies located within the zone. It can be part of a seaport. But it still requires a separate designation from a Customs approval aspect, as ports are for the transit of goods between maritime and land-based transportation, whereas a Freeport/Free Zone is a Customs-controlled storage and processing area, and therefore must be kept separate from port-related handling activities.

However, Freeport activities can be limited. Freeports do not necessarily allow for the processing of materials under Duty and VAT Suspension other than light activities such as the following:

- Warehousing and storage;
- Breaking bulk;
- Sorting, grading, cleaning and mixing;
- Labelling, packing and repacking;
- Minor processing;
- Transshipment;
- Export-oriented port-based activities;
- Export-oriented airport-based activities;
- Import-oriented port and airport-based activities;
- Simple and light assembly;
- Reshipment;
- Quality control and inspection services.

DOI: 10.4324/9781003232025-6

In the EU, Freeports are limited to Customs-controlled areas within port facilities, where goods can be stored in longer-term Customs-controlled storage facilities away from conventional transit/Temporary Storage sheds, where storage time is more limited.

For more complex assembly, manufacturing and processing activities, other specific Customs approvals, such as Inward Processing, may be sought. These are especially useful where finished products resulting from manufacturing facilities are to be re-exported without any Customs Duty or VAT liabilities, a facility also found in Export Processing Zones (EPZs).

Certain industries, such as the automotive or FMCG sectors, can benefit hugely from Freeport activities, as the Freeport can be used for the storage of large quantities of materials prior to being released in smaller amounts for delivery to plants or distribution centres located further inland. In this respect, they can also be used for the onward shipment of materials to other regional international locations on a hub-and-spoke basis.

UK Free Zones were established with the implementation of the 1984 Finance Act, which provided for the creation of a Freeport regime in the UK, and which led to the creation of several Freeports in the UK, including Birmingham, close to the international airport, Prestwick, adjacent to Glasgow Prestwick International Airport, and Liverpool Freeport, part of the Port of Liverpool, as well as the Isle of Man Free Zone at Ballasalla, located just outside Ronaldsway Airport. In reality, the Liverpool Freeport proved the most successful of all the Zones, and effectively was the only zone operating on a successful commercial and economic basis until its demise in 2012, when all Freeport licences were terminated by the UK Government.

Under the new UK Government Freeport initiative of 2020 following the exit of the UK from the European Union, a new set of Freeports in the UK has been sanctioned by the 2021 Finance Act. This has resulted in the bids for eight new Freeports in England, at Teesport, Humber (Hull/Immingham), Harwich/Felixstowe, Thames (Tilbury/London Gateway), Solent (Southampton), Plymouth, Liverpool and East Midlands Airport. These are detailed later in this book, as they are designed to be an enhanced form of Freeport, allowing for storage and manufacturing facilities within the confines of each zone. However, the Freeport model is still maintained, as these facilities are still to be located adjacent to the main seaports, and, in the case of the East Midlands Freeport, the East Midlands Airport close to Castle Donington, owing to its large international air freight facility. These new Freeports are intended to commence activities in late 2021, although much preparatory work is required to facilitate these Freeports in advance of this schedule. Of these new Freeports, Tilbury, Southampton and Liverpool are essentially the renaissance of the original Freeports created as a result of the 1984 Finance Act, but with much-extended facilities and activities.

Free-Trade zone

Not to be confused with a Free Trade Area, which is a Free Trade Agreement between two or more countries, for example the USMCA (US-Mexico-Canada Free Trade Agreement), the MERCOSUR (Common Market of the Southern Cone of South America) or the ASEAN (Association of South-East Asian Nations) Free Trade Agreement, a **Free-Trade Zone** is a specific type of Special Economic Zone located in a specific location within a country, usually close to a seaport, international airport, or as an industrial zone close to a conurbation. These are a defined geographic area, generally close to or adjacent to seaports or airports, where goods may be landed, handled, manufactured, processed or reconfigured, and re-exported without the intervention of the national Customs Authorities. To this extent, they are outside Customs jurisdiction and are therefore not considered as being part of domestic national Free Circulation territory. However, they are still Customs-controlled, as goods need to be declared to Customs when entering or leaving the zone, as the goods located in a Free-Trade Zone is under Customs control and is Import Duty and tax-suspended while in the zone. In short, it is a geographic area where goods may be landed, stored, handled, manufactured, or reconfigured and re-exported under specific Customs regulation and generally not subject to Customs Duty. Free-Trade Zones are generally organised around major seaports, international airports, and national frontiers, areas with many geographic advantages for international trade. They contain clusters of companies involved in Free Zone activities, especially storage, distribution and manufacturing, either for domestic distribution using Tariff Inversion advantages, or for re-export.

Only when the goods are moved to consumers within the country in which the zone is located do they become subject to the prevailing Customs Duties. Free-Trade Zones are organised around major seaports, international airports and national frontiers – areas with many geographic advantages for trade.

The World Bank defines Free-Trade Zones as 'duty-free areas, offering warehousing, storage, and distribution facilities for trade, transshipment, and re-export operations'. Free-Trade Zones can also be defined as labour-intensive manufacturing centres that involve the import of raw materials or components and the export of factory products, especially in the cases of the Mexican Maquiladoras which were established in the 1960s, but this is a dated definition as an increasing number of Free-Trade Zones focus on service industries such as software, back-office operations, research, and financial services, especially those services involving international operations which also attract large-scale foreign investment. Free-Trade Zones may also incorporate other fiscal incentives concerning the elimination or reduction in Corporation Tax, Income Taxes and Property Taxes, but these depend upon national government policy and equally the overall political and economic reasons for establishing the particular Free-Trade Zone in the first instance.

Corporations setting up in a zone may be given a number of regulatory and fiscal incentives, such as the right to establish a business, the right to import parts and equipment without duty, the right to keep and use foreign exchange earnings, and sometimes income or property tax breaks. There may also be other incentives relating the methods of Customs control and filing requirements. The rationale is that the Zones will attract investment, create employment, and thus reduce poverty and unemployment, stimulating the area's economy. These Zones are often used by multinational corporations to set up factories to produce goods (such as clothing, shoes, and electronics).

Free zone facilities include:

- Customs-controlled storage of goods and materials;
- Storage facilities close or adjacent to seaports and airports;
- Import Duty and VAT/Sales Tax Suspension on goods and materials stored within the zone;
- Unlimited time for goods stored in Zones;
- Easy access to local markets.

In the United States, Free-Trade Zones are referred to as 'Foreign-Trade Zones', and were originally established by the Foreign-Trade Zones Act of 1934. In the United States, FTZs provide Customs-related advantages as well as exemptions from State and local inventory taxes. In other countries, they are called 'Special Economic Zones' or 'Free Zones' and were previously called 'free ports' or 'Export Processing Zones'. Free Zones range from specific-purpose manufacturing facilities to areas where legal systems and economic regulation vary from the normal provisions of the country concerned. Free Zones may reduce taxes, Customs Duties, and regulatory requirements for registration of business. Zones around the world often provide special exemptions from normal immigration procedures and foreign investment restrictions as well as other features. Free Zones are intended to foster economic activity and employment that could occur elsewhere (Farole and Akinci, 'Special Economic Zones: Progress, Challenges and Future Directions', World Bank, 2011).

Export Processing Zone

An **Export Processing Zone** (EPZ) is one of many export promotion tools, including Customs-controlled warehouses, manufacture and temporary admission schemes. According to the World Bank, Export Processing Zones are primarily established to foster national economic growth by way of the encouragement of inward foreign investment, manufacturing of imported materials for re-export and the use of local employment in the process. Indeed, EPZs are primarily established to serve export markets based on low wage rates, the availability of local employment, relaxed environmental rules and generous fiscal incentives to encourage zone-based commercial activity by overseas-based multinational companies. Today's Export Processing Zones have evolved from their original definition as 'an industrial estate, usually a fenced-in area of 10–300 hectares, that specialise in manufacturing for export' (World Bank, Special Report on Export Processing Zones, 1992, p. 7). Many companies, called export processing firms, now benefit from the incentives offered in the Zones without being physically fenced in. In addition, countries have liberalised domestic sales; Mexico, for example, allows 20–40% of its maquila Zones' output to be sold domestically.

Export Processing Zones have three main goals. They exist to provide a country with foreign exchange earnings by promoting non-traditional exports. They facilitate the creation of jobs and the generation of income. They also exist to attract Foreign Direct Investment, engendering technology transfer, knowledge development, economic development, demonstration effects and catalysts of regional and national economic growth, backward linkages between zone-based companies and domestic Suppliers and overall regional and national prosperity. However, they are generally discouraged from supplying finished goods to the local or national economy of the country where they are based, given that their primary objective is export-led economic growth.

Cost-benefit analysis

In terms of cost-benefit analysis, EPZs may yield different results depending upon their effectiveness, viability and overall efficiency, as well as their net contribution to the national economy and the profitability of the companies operating within them. A paper on the Cost-Benefit Analysis of Export Processing Zones presented in April 1996 at a

WEPZA symposium in Vienna by C. Baissac states that a problem with the view that EPZs are primarily economic instruments and, therefore, submitted to the necessity of financial efficiency, lies in the definition of the financial efficiency or profitability of Export Processing Zones. Indeed, most EPZs that, at the time of presentation of the paper concerned in 1996, had been submitted to publicly available cost-benefit analysis, were public Zones. If Export Processing Zones are indeed created for economic purposes, they are primarily public policy instruments with social and political purposes and are not exclusively limited to purely economic considerations. Indeed, most, if not all, EPZs have been created by political means, through national government legislation, rather than solely economic considerations.

EPZs are designed to provide the 'host' economy with a range of gains and benefits which are difficult to measure. A United Nations publication of 1985 on Export Processing Zones in Developing Countries listed the most common objectives underlying the establishment of Zones as the following:

1. Generating foreign exchange earnings;
2. Creating employment;
3. Attracting foreign capital and advanced technology;
4. Acquiring labour management skills; and
5. Creating linkages between EPZ industries and the domestic economy.

The World Bank, in a 1992 study, stated a more limited range of EPZ objectives, comprising the earning of foreign exchange and the creation of 'employment through exports of manufactured goods'.

In some ways, the EPZ is not a 'normal' component of its national economy. A country establishing a zone hosts a foreign enclave, given that many of the companies establishing operations in an Export Processing Zone are based overseas and are generally multinational corporations. The flows between the EPZ as an enclave and the world are external to the national economy, other than the benefits that they generate for the national economy in terms of employment and export-led revenue and growth, and the latter, that is, export-led revenue and growth, is solely concerned with welfare gains or losses in the flows taking place between the national economy and the zone, with the zone acting as a specific vehicle for export-led revenue and growth. Therefore, a cost-benefit analysis will be limited to these flows and will not consider the national economy as being relevant, as an EPZ is isolated from the constraints of the national economy by way of its international status. In other words, a cost-benefit analysis will not consider the gains made nationally in terms of the national economy as a whole.

The flows which are supposed to impact on the welfare on the 'host' economy's citizens are as follows:

- Profits and losses;
- Foreign exchange earnings;
- Employment;
- Technology transfer;
- Purchase of domestic raw materials and capital goods;
- Use of electricity;
- Domestic borrowing;

- Taxes and development; and
- Recurrent costs.

EPZs generally share several common features:

- They allow duty-free imports of raw materials and intermediate (semi-processed) inputs, components or sub-assemblies, and capital goods for export-based production;
- Government red tape and bureaucracy is streamlined, allowing 'one-stop shopping' for permits, investment applications, Customs clearance simplifications, and so on. In addition, labour laws and profit repatriation regulations are more flexible then for most companies in the domestic market;
- Companies in EPZs are given generous, long-term tax concessions;
- Communications services and infrastructure are more advanced than in other parts of the country. Utility and rental subsidies are common;
- EPZ companies can be domestic, foreign or joint ventures. Foreign Direct Investment plays a prominent role.

Two main features differentiate EPZs. First, EPZs can be publicly or privately owned or managed. Over the past 10–15 years, the number of privately owned or managed Zones has grown substantially because they are believed to achieve superior results. Second, Zones can be 'high-end' or 'low-end', depending upon the quality of the management, facilities and services which they provide to companies using and located in them.

Export Processing Zones (EPZ) are a specific type of FTZ, established generally in developing countries by their governments to promote the export of industrial and commercial exports resulting from production activities using both domestically and internationally procured materials, imported under Customs Duty and VAT Suspension. Once processed, the finished products are re-exported overseas, thus providing much-needed export revenue to the national and regional economies. Most EPZs are located in developing countries, namely Brazil, Colombia, India, Indonesia, El Salvador, China, the Philippines, Malaysia, Bangladesh, Pakistan, Mexico, Costa Rica, Honduras, Guatemala, Kenya, Sri Lanka, Mauritius and Madagascar, and these countries all have major EPZ programs as part of their national economic strategy. In 1997, 93 countries had set up Export Processing Zones employing 22.5 million people, and five years later, in 2003, EPZs in 116 countries employed 43 million people. The main condition of use is that the goods produced in the zone will not be imported or released into the country's domestic Free Circulation.

China, which has several Free Zones in its territory, has specific rules differentiating an EPZ from a FTZ, and, for that matter, a SEZ. For example, 70% of goods manufactured in Chinese EPZs must be exported, but there is no such quota for FTZs. The territory of Hong Kong is designated as FTZ territory as well as a Special Administrative Territory under Chinese law, although Hong Kong itself exports a large amount of products overseas every year. Elsewhere in the Far East, the State of Singapore in South-East Asia is also designated as an FTZ, but also exports goods overseas, as well as to elsewhere in South-East Asia, owing to its central location in the ASEAN bloc and its location at the southern end of the Malay peninsula on the Malacca Strait.

The world's first modern Free-Trade Zone was established at Shannon, on the west coast of Ireland (Shannon Free Zone). This was an attempt by the Irish Government to promote employment within a rural area, make use of a small regional airport and generate revenue for the Irish economy. It was hugely successful, partly owing to its location next to the developing Shannon International Airport, and is still in operation today. The number of worldwide Free-Trade Zones proliferated in the late 20th century. In the United States, Free-Trade Zones were first authorised in 1934, with the US Foreign-Trade Zones Act, and further US legislation developed these Zones from simply being established as general-purpose Customs-controlled storage areas (Foreign-Trade Zones) to large-scale manufacturing areas (Subzones) for the purposes of export of products manufactured within the zone or their release into domestic Free Circulation.

Corporations setting up in a zone may be given tax breaks as an incentive. Usually, these Zones are set up in underdeveloped parts of the host country; the rationale is that the Zones will attract employers and thus reduce poverty and unemployment, and stimulate the area's economy. These Zones are often used by multinational corporations to set up factories to produce goods (such as consumer goods, namely household electrical goods, clothing or shoes). In some cases, the establishment of Free Zones is a national policy designed to develop the national economy as a whole through a combination of export-led growth and the attraction of foreign inward investment in the national economy. This policy is certainly true of the ASEAN, which has adopted this policy as a means of developing the ASEAN bloc on an economic basis. Particular examples of the ASEAN Free Zone initiative include Singapore, Malaysia and the Philippines.

Free-Trade Zones in Latin America date back to the early decades of the 20th century. The first Free-Trade regulations in the region were enacted in Argentina and Uruguay in the 1920s. The LAFTA was created in the 1960 Treaty of Montevideo by Argentina, Brazil, Chile, Mexico, Paraguay, Peru and Uruguay, which brought these countries closer together with a Free Trade Area, that is, the conditional free movement of goods, services and capital within the Free-Trade bloc. However, the rapid development of individual Customs-controlled Free-Trade Zones across the region dates from the late 1960s and the early 1970s. One of the most famous Latin American Free Zones is located in Manaus, Northern Brazil, on the mighty Amazon River. Other FTZs exist in Uruguay and Argentina.

Free-Trade Zones are also known as Special Economic Zones in some countries. SEZs have been established in many countries as testing grounds for the implementation of liberal market economy principles. SEZs are viewed as instruments to enhance the acceptability and the credibility of the transformation policies and to attract domestic and foreign investment.

In 1999, there were 43 million people working in about 3,000 FTZs spanning 116 countries producing clothes, shoes, consumer goods, automotive goods, electronics and toys. The basic objectives of EPZs, which are import and re-export driven, are to enhance foreign exchange earnings, develop export-oriented industries and to generate employment opportunities.

An UNCTAD Report of 2015 concerning the enhancement of EPZs argues that:

- EPZs face a strategic challenge as traditional tax incentives for attracting companies into Zones become incompatible with international trade law and exemptions for developing countries expire.
- EPZs can enhance competitiveness through a 'role reversal': switching from a narrow focus on cost advantages and lower Standards to become champions of

sustainable business. EPZs can find new grounds for competitiveness through meeting the growing expectations on MNEs and their Suppliers to exercise good social and environmental practices. 'Next generation' EPZs can gain a competitive advantage by not only providing conventional commercial benefits (such as modern infrastructure and expedited permitting), but by also providing cost-effective support for good environmental and social practices for firms operating within their boundaries.

- Although some EPZs are making the transition to more of a sustainable development orientation (demonstrating proof of concept), an UNCTAD survey of 100 EPZs' public information undertaken as part of this report suggests that most EPZs are not promoting prominent environmental and social features. Given changes to conventional means of attracting investment into EPZs, this lack of engagement with corporate sustainability could become a missed opportunity for both sustainable development and for EPZ investment promotion.
- EPZ management agencies can develop services to help firms' cost-effective compliance with international Corporate Social Responsibility (CSR) Standards, including provision of training and monitoring, as well as health, safety and waste management services to enable a circular economy.
- EPZ management agencies can develop governments and investment promotion strategies should promote competitiveness through enabling efficient performance on all issues that matter to business success, including economic, social and environmental issues, rather than exempting Zones from their own national laws on labour practices or the environment. They could require Zones to promote economic linkages with their wider economies of host countries and assess progress towards that aim.
- EPZs operating as centres of excellence for sustainable development could act as pilot projects. Lessons learned from these 'Sustainable Economic Zones' could be applied and scaled up by developing country governments at a regional and national level. This can be part of the development of backward and forward linkages to the wider economy so that Zones are catalysts of wider development. In that way, EPZs could play a catalytic role in helping nations achieve, inter alia, SDG 8, on employment and decent work, 9, on sustainable production, and 12, on sustainable industrialisation.
- A 'Framework for Sustainable Economic Zones' is offered to guide consideration of EPZ Standards, infrastructure and administrative assistance to enhance sustainability performance.

This is especially important, as the UNCTAD was the instrumental force behind the creation of the original initiative that introduced the concept of Export Processing Zones in the 1960s in the wake of the initiation of the Mexican Border Industrialization Program (BIP) that established the Mexican Maquiladora program in northern Mexico in 1965. Indeed, the WEPZA was partly the brainchild of the UNCTAD, as well as the UNIDO, and still supervises the operation of the global EPZ initiative and concept. Indeed, the concept of Free Zones has for many years been a pivotal part of the policy of UNCTAD and UNIDO, and is still seen as a major element of global economic and trade development.

Special Economic Zone

An **SEZ** is an area in which the business and trade laws are different from the rest of the country, in that they provide specific economic and fiscal incentives to enterprises operating within these Zones. SEZs are located within a country's national borders, and their aims include increased trade balance, employment, increased investment, job creation and effective administration. To encourage businesses to set up in the zone, financial policies are introduced. These policies typically encompass investing, taxation, trading, quotas, Customs and labour regulations. Additionally, companies may be offered tax holidays, where upon establishing themselves in a zone, they are granted a period of reduced taxation as an economic, commercial and fiscal incentive.

According to UNCTAD, SEZs – geographically delimited areas within which governments facilitate industrial activity through fiscal and regulatory incentives and infrastructure support – are widely used across most developing and many developed economies. Although the performance of some Zones remains below expectations, failing either to attract significant investment or to generate economic impact beyond their confines, new Zones continue to be developed, as governments increasingly compete for internationally mobile industrial activity. Policymakers face not only the traditional challenges of making SEZs succeed, including the need for adequate strategic focus, regulatory and governance models and investment promotion tools, but also new challenges brought about by the sustainable development imperative, the new industrial revolution and changing patterns of international production.

It is more than 50 years since the establishment of the first modern Special Economic Zones. But, as stated by Thomas Farole, Senior Economist at the World Bank, it is only relatively recently, particularly since the 1990s, that their popularity as a policy instrument has increased. The International Labour Organization's 2007 database of Special Economic Zones reported 176 Zones in 47 countries in 1986; by 2006 this had risen to 3,500 Zones in 130 countries. Traditional EPZs were designed to attract investment by enabling countries to better exploit a key source of comparative advantage – low-cost labour – which was otherwise underutilised because of low levels of domestic investment and barriers (regulatory, infrastructure, etc.), preventing Foreign Direct Investment (FDI).

These EPZs have operated under simple principles:

- Allowing investors to import and export free of duties and exchange controls;
- Facilitating licensing and other regulatory processes; and
- Usually freeing companies operating with EPZs from obligations to pay corporate taxes, VAT, or other local taxes.

To maintain control of these facilities, EPZs have normally been fenced-in estates with strict Customs controls at entry, and sales are typically restricted mainly to export markets, hence the definition of EPZs as vehicles for export-led growth.

The model has been extremely successful in many countries. For example, it allowed the Dominican Republic to create more than 100,000 manufacturing jobs and shift dramatically away from reliance on agriculture. Similar stories of industrialisation and job creation can be seen in Mauritius, South Korea, Taiwan, Honduras, El Salvador and Madagascar, and more recently in Bangladesh and Vietnam. However, the success of traditional EPZ programs owes something in part to an unprecedented era of globalisation of trade and investment that has taken place since the 1970s and accelerated during the 1990s and 2000s, enabled by the vertical, horizontal and spatial fragmentation of manufacturing into highly integrated global production networks, and may suggest that a review of EPZ usage is necessary, given the proliferation of Free Trade Agreements and the reduction in global tariffs as driven by the WTO. However, even considering the number of Global Free Trade Agreements and Free Trade Blocs such as the NAFTA, MERCUSUR and ASEAN, the concept of Free Zones or EPZs is still necessary, as FTAs depend on the origin of goods to satisfy the preferential Rules of Origin of such FTAs, and in many cases these Rules of Origin cannot be satisfied and adhered to owing to the nature of manufacturing using large quantities of material imported from overseas. Given the role of EPZs as a means of export-led growth while using imported components for manufacture within the Zones, even the concept of FTAs is still independent from the use of EPZs, given that EPZs are used for export purposes, not necessarily for trade within such Free Trade Blocs. Origin is a vital factor of trade within Free Trade Blocs, and EPZs do not exist for that purpose. Given the fact that products are manufactured in EPZs under Customs control, such products could not be deemed as originating in the country where the EPZ is located, and therefore could not be admitted to the rest of the Free Trade Bloc under preferential duty-free conditions. Indeed, the purpose of such EPZs is to encourage trade outside the bloc, not within it. The advantage of the EPZs for a Free Trade Bloc is that they encourage inward FDI into the bloc as a means of generating and fostering economic and financial investment, thus generating employment and also financial growth based on fiscal incentives. The rule is that if a country is to develop economically, it cannot impose high levels of taxation on its businesses, as this would restrict and even stifle trade and investment initiatives. Lower or reduced levels of taxation encourage national economic development. Given also the demands of international supply chains based on cost structures and constraints, the use of Free-Trade Zones and EPZs is still a major prevalent factor in cost reductions through the elimination of Customs Duties, VAT and other tax reductions as economic and fiscal incentives.

For economic Zones to be a success in the long term, they should contribute to structural transformation of the economy, including diversification and economic upgrading, especially in the case of the world's developing economies. Therefore, there is the requirement for the leveraging of *dynamic economic benefits* from investment and employment. Countries that have been successful in deriving long-term economic benefits from their Special Economic Zone programs have established the conditions for ongoing exchange, and the accompanying hard and soft technology transfer, between the domestic economy and investors based on the Zones. This includes investment by domestic enterprises in the Zones, forward and backward linkages, business support, and the seamless movement of skilled labour and entrepreneurs between the Zones and the domestic economy. This is enhanced by a variety of fiscal incentives designed to encourage such investment.

SEZs are defined by many names and exist in many varieties and sizes. They have one main characteristic in common in that, within a defined perimeter, they provide a regulatory regime for businesses and investors distinct from what normally applies in the broader national or subnational economy where they are established. The most common types of SEZs are variations on Free Zones, which are essentially separate Customs territories. In addition to relief from Customs Duties and tariffs, most Zones also offer fiscal incentives; business-friendly regulations with respect to land access, permits and licenses, or employment rules; and administrative streamlining and facilitation. Infrastructure support is another important feature, especially in developing countries where basic infrastructure for business outside these Zones can be poor. In return for these Customs, fiscal and regulatory concessions; business support measures; and investments in physical infrastructure, governments expect investors operating in SEZs to create jobs, boost exports, diversify the economy and build productive capacity.

The creation of Special Economic Zones by the host country may be motivated by the desire to attract FDI. The benefits a company gains by being in a Special Economic Zone may mean that it can produce and trade goods at a lower price, aimed at being globally competitive.

The definition of an SEZ is determined individually by each country. According to the World Bank in 2008, the modern-day Special Economic Zone typically includes a 'geographically limited area, usually physically secured (fenced in); single management or administration; eligibility for benefits based upon physical location within the zone; separate Customs area (duty-free benefits) and streamlined procedures'. Effectively, this means that an SEZ is a commercial area separated by some means from the rest of the locality owing to the business it conducts which is subject to specific benefits, tax incentives and fiscal privileges. SEZs have contributed significantly to the economic development of many countries, including Ireland (Shannon Free Zone), Uruguay, Argentina, Mexico (Maquiladoras), Mauritius, Hong Kong, China, Singapore and the rest of the ASEAN bloc. Apart from Ireland, Europe never committed itself to the concept of SEZs as an economic generator. The US Free-Trade Zone (Foreign-Trade Zone) system was more specific, having been closely defined as a result of the Foreign-Trade Zones Act of 1934.

SEZs can include:

- Free-Trade Zones (<50 hectares);
- Export Processing Zones (<100 hectares);
- Free Zones (<100 hectares);
- Free Ports (>1,000 hectares);
- Bonded Industrial Parks (varies).

SEZs generally have a designated area defined by the national Revenue Authority and other authorities, but is not necessarily fenced off from the rest of the environment. Freeports tend to be segregated from the rest of the community in the form of fencing and security gates, but this is generally not the case with EPZs and SEZs, as they are designated by lines on a map rather than a physical security segregation. Their main advantage is that they are designed to attract companies by means of tax incentives based on their trading activities, that is, import and export of materials leading to in-zone manufacturing and processing. They are predominantly found in lesser-developed areas of the world, that is, India, South-East Asia and the Far East.

According to the UNCTAD in a report on the effectiveness of Special Economic Zones, SEZs are an important development issue for industrial and investment policymakers, for three primary reasons.

First, the relative ease of implementing business reforms through SEZs

In countries where governance is relatively weak and where the implementation of national reforms is difficult, SEZs are often seen as the only feasible option, or as a first step, towards economic development. Developing countries that have made progress towards more attractive investment climates also continue to rely on SEZs. When such progress fails to deliver better competitiveness rankings or expected foreign investment, SEZs may still be seen as a necessary complement to the investment promotion package and as a signal of the country's progress in building an attractive investment climate.

Second, the perceived low cost of establishing SEZs

A key rationale for SEZs is their low cost in relative terms, compared with that of building equivalent industrial infrastructure in the entire economy. But even in absolute terms, the upfront investment costs can be contained. Capital expenditures for the development of an SEZ, especially basic Zones offering individual plots of land rather than hyper-modern 'plug and play' Zones, as in the case of some of the UAE Zones, are often limited to basic infrastructure connections to the zone perimeter. Additional costs, which are mostly outsourced to a private development company, are then incurred gradually as the zone attracts investors and develops individual areas of land within the zone. In such cases, the government considers basic zone development costs as largely 'no cure, no pay'. The development cost, as well as the cost of common services in the Zones, is subsequently recovered from tenants.

Much of the cost of SEZs is the income foregone from the incentives provided, given the potential loss of fiscal revenue to the governments concerned, which can amount to substantial revenue loss. However, such foregone income is rarely a concern for policymakers when they consider establishing SEZs. Indeed, the loss of fiscal revenue engendered by the sue of the zone is in most cases offset against the increased revenue earned in terms of the influx of foreign investment, which supplies employment to the local community as well as attracting an influx of expatriate staff, who will invest in the local community in terms of renting or purchasing local residential properties and spending money in the local community in terms of amenities and shopping.

Third, increased competitive pressure

SEZs, especially EPZs, traditionally attract internationally mobile efficiency-seeking investments, for which countries compete. Despite the emergence of new forms of Zones linked to natural resources, aimed at domestic markets or targeting innovation capabilities (e.g. science, high-tech or green Zones), most SEZs remain essentially part of countries' competitive investment promotion package, together with other forms of incentives. Global FDI has been weak over the last decade.

It is claimed by the UNCTAD that manufacturing FDI across all developing regions has been structurally lower over the last five years than in the preceding period. In response to the tight market for investment in industrial activity, governments continue to make their investment promotion packages more attractive, often by way of the promotion of service or financial Free Zones, as in the case of the UAE, where the emphasis is that provision of international services rather than the production of physical goods for re-export.

Two major considerations concerning the global success of SEZs can be summarised as follows:

KEY DIMENSIONS DRIVING SEZ SUCCESS

- Strategic focus;
- Regulatory framework and governance;
- Value proposition for investors.

NEW CHALLENGES FACING SEZS

- Sustainable development imperative;
- New industrial revolution and digital economy;
- Changing patterns of international production.

With the long experience and widespread use of SEZs, there is a vast amount of research documenting success stories and failures, describing key characteristics of SEZs and analysing their economic, social, environmental and development impacts. According to the UNCTAD, policy advice tends to centre on three key dimensions, as categorised below:

1. The strategic focus of SEZs;
2. The regulatory framework and governance of SEZs; and
3. The design of the SEZ value proposition, or the package of benefits for investors.

Strategic focus

Economies that have most successfully achieved rapid industrial development through the use of SEZs emphasise that Zones are not only an investment promotion tool, but first and foremost an industrial policy tool. East and South-East Asian economies, by design or by implementation, present many cases of Zones focused on specific industries or on economic activities and value chain components that rely on similar factors of production, skills, technologies and market linkages. The scope for synergies, as well as for sharing resources and costs, in such clusters is an important factor generating the success of these SEZs and their contribution to national economic development.

More recent additions to SEZ strategy as part of national policy, including many of the least developed countries (LDCs), have often followed a multi-activity approach with no active efforts to promote specialisation or clustering, reducing the Zones to mere investment promotion tools – essentially incentives available in limited geographic areas.

Regulatory framework and governance

SEZs, as territories with regimes that are separated from national rules, are by necessity a public initiative. However, the development, ownership and management of individual Zones can be public, private or a public-private partnership (PPP). Private developers are often engaged to minimise initial public outlays and to access international expertise in zone design, construction and marketing. Zone management and oversight can involve various government levels (local, regional, national), investors and businesses operating in the zone, and numerous other stakeholders, such as financiers, industry associations and representatives from local communities or other interest groups. Numerous governance models exist, sometimes within the same jurisdiction, and the choice depends on the objectives and desired strategic focus of individual SEZs. The legal framework for SEZs – mostly national SEZ laws or provisions in Customs or other legal frameworks – often sets the parameters for these Zones' governance and institutional set-up.

Value proposition

SEZ legal frameworks almost always define the package of benefits for investors in Zones, especially exemptions from Customs, tax and other national regulatory regimes. As SEZs are all derived from the concept of Free Zones – free from tariffs, taxes, bureaucracy and red tape – the basic components of incentives packages are very similar across most types of Zones and most geographies. Much research identifies the provision of hard and soft infrastructure around the Zones, the availability of adequate skills and supplier bases, and business facilitation and shared services as critical success factors for zone development and impact. These are also the benefits that can more easily support active clustering and specialisation efforts in the Zones.

In today's global business and investment climate, the strategic focus, the regulatory and governance models and the incentives package offered remain the key ingredients of a successful SEZ policy framework. However, policymakers also face emerging challenges resulting from the sustainable development imperative, the new industrial revolution and changing patterns of international production.

CHALLENGES TO SEZS

The challenges to SEZs can be detailed as follows:

- Global Sustainable Development;
- The New Industrial Revolution;
- Changing Patterns of International Production.

The global sustainable development agenda embodied in the United Nations Sustainable Development Goals (SDGs) is affecting the strategic decisions and operations of businesses around the world. The efficiency and cost savings that might be associated with lower social and environmental Standards are no longer considered a viable competitive advantage, especially in industries that have incurred or are at high risk of reputational damage. As such, offering laxer social and environmental rules or controls is no longer a competitive advantage to attract investment in SEZs. As reported in a recent UNCTAD study on the contribution of SEZs to the SDGs, some Zones are beginning to shift away from lower Standards and are instead incorporating sustainable development into their operating model, with sustainability-related shared services (e.g. common health and safety services, waste management plants, renewable energy installations) among the clustering synergies that SEZs can deliver. This topic is developed in a later section in this text.

The new industrial revolution, namely the adoption across all industries of digital technologies, advanced robotics, 3D printing, big data and the Internet, is transforming manufacturing processes, related services and business models, with wide-ranging implications for international production and global value chains. Some of these changes, mainly the heightened technological scope for reshoring production and the declining importance of labour costs as a locational determinant for investment, have fundamental implications for SEZs and their use in industrial development and investment promotion strategies. The new industrial revolution also comes with opportunities for SEZs (or SEZ development programs) that can offer access to skilled resources and clusters of relevant business and technology service providers.

Changing patterns of international production, as routinely documented in the *World Investment Report* over recent years, are driven in part by structural changes in international business, with a shift towards intangibles and overseas operations that are increasingly asset light. These patterns are therefore less concerned with the production advantages offered by SEZs. They are also driven by economic and policy factors. The growing weight of emerging markets in global trade and investment has implications for SEZ users. The return of protectionist tendencies and slow progress in the international policy regimes for trade and investment are leading industrial investors to constantly assess strategic locations for low-cost production in the light of potential new barriers to trade or shifts in preferential market access, such as FTAs. The regionalisation of trade and investment agreements has further implications for SEZ competitiveness, depending on import sources and export destinations, as well as the status of SEZs in regional agreements.

A paper issued by the World Customs Organisation in September 2019, entitled 'The Extraterritoriality of Free Zones' (WCO Paper No. 47) detailed the need for the enhancement of Customs involvement in Free Zones. It compared the various types of Customs facility, and one specific table details the notable characteristics of Free Zones and related Zones:

Types of characteristics	Examples of characteristics
Characteristics of 'Customs Warehouse' consistent with Specific Annex D Chapter 1 of the Revised Kyoto Convention (RKC) (Customs Warehouses)	Import duties and other indirect taxes on goods brought from abroad/domestic market into the zone are suspended, as long as the goods stay inside the zone. Suspension is typically based on provision of financial security (bond) to Customs.
Characteristics of 'Inward Processing' consistent with Specific Annex F Chapter 1 of the RKC (Inward Processing)	Import duties and other indirect taxes on goods brought from abroad/domestic market are suspended if the goods are intended for manufacturing/processing and actual subsequent exportation of the processed goods (compensating products).
Characteristics unique to 'Free Zone' consistent with Specific Annex D Chapter 2 of RKC (Free Zones)	Goods inside the zone are regarded as being 'outside the Customs territory' only in terms of duty/tax aspects (definition). Duty/tax exemption is applied upon entry into zone (Standard 8). – The entry of goods from domestic market to inside zone is regarded as an 'export' in terms of duty/tax – The fact or intention of actual exportation abroad is not prerequisite for duty/tax exemption Provision of financial security (bond) to Customs is not required when goods are admitted into the zone (Recommended Practice 10) Processing/manufacturing operations are allowed (Standard 12) Typically, exemption of duty/tax for materials and capital goods consumed inside the zone (Standard 13) Unlimited duration for goods to stay inside the zone (Standard 14)

Types of characteristics	Examples of characteristics
Other notable benefits (not directly relevant to Customs procedures/controls)	Exemption of Direct Taxes, such as income tax or real estate tax Unrestricted use of foreign currency Unrestricted transfer of money abroad Unrestricted use of foreign workers

Offshore Supply Bases

Offshore Marine Supply Bases are specialised, dedicated general cargo ports which provide vital support to offshore Oil & Gas exploration and production activities. These facilities are classed as a specific form of Free Zone, specialising in offshore supply operations, including the storage of offshore Oil & Gas drilling and wellhead equipment, drill, conductor and casing pipes, Christmas Tree wellhead pumping mechanisms, offshore maintenance equipment, blow-out preventers and other material associated with offshore Oil & Gas operations management. As well as Customs-controlled storage facilities, other facilities exist which allow companies located on the base to engage in light assembly activities, as well as maintenance and repair of existing Oil & Gas equipment. A typical offshore Supply Base also has an extensive quay, capable of accommodating several AHTS (Anchor Handling Towage and Supply) vessels, PSVs (Platform Supply Vessels) and DSVs (Dive Support Vessels). The quay can also be used for the landing of cargoes destined for the offshore Oil & Gas sector from breakbulk vessels, chartered by the Oil & Gas companies for the movement of maritime cargoes associated with such operations.

Offshore Oil & Gas Supply Bases (OSBs) function as a hub for all material and supply to and from Oil & Gas (O&G) rigs, installations and vessels. O&G companies have operational organisations nearby, or at, the OSBs and it is often a contract claim that main Suppliers establish a department nearby. Some companies even establish a department in front of tendering processes. The level and quantity of services offered by OSBs has increased in both volume and type during many years, and this has attracted many service Suppliers. Offshore Supply Bases are part of a service network for the O&G supply chain, where the outsourcing strategy of the O&G companies determines their role in the network. Also, the phases in developing a field can be divided in exploration, field development, and operation, demanding both different services and logistic focus from the OSBs.

All materials and supplies to offshore operations are sent through an Offshore Supply Base. The ultimate customers in the upstream Oil & Gas supply chain are the Oil & Gas companies such as Royal Dutch Shell, Exxon, Mobil, BP, Philips and so on. Products that need to be shipped out to offshore operations come from the customer's Suppliers, service Suppliers and the Oil & Gas companies themselves. The offshore Supply Bases receive goods from several companies that are to be sent out by different vessels to different installations. The demand for offshore Supply Base services is driven by the offshore Oil & Gas activity and are dependent upon the various phases in Oil & Gas exploration and exploitation. Drilling operations have intense activity over a limited period, and the demand for these services can be uncertain and unpredictable, dependent on what challenges the drilling operations face. However, the supply of material to operational Oil & Gas production installations is more regular and standardised, given the types and quantities of material required during the operational life of a typical offshore oil or gas field. However, due to the high levels of risk associated with offshore operations, offshore Supply Bases must be able to respond to some form of demand on short notice, 24 hours a day, seven days a week, inclusive of national holidays. This demand stems from both exploration and production phases in any offshore operation.

For offshore operations, almost all materials sent out are returned as waste or parts, and tools for repair and maintenance are addressed to different service Suppliers. The Oil & Gas companies operations determine the flow of goods. For offshore Supply Bases, the inbound logistics are delivered from the customers' Suppliers, with which they have no formal business relationship. However, because of import and export Customs formalities, the Supply Bases are also under Customs control, in that they are generally classed as Free Zones, albeit as a specific dedicated function. Where the adjacent ports act as transit points, Supply Bases are classed as Free Zones in that they act as long-term storage and supply points for equipment destined for the offshore sector.

A typical Supply Base is equipped with a quayside, enclosed storage warehouses, open storage areas, handling cranes and vehicles designed to move equipment around the base. The base may also be occupied by several Oil & Gas companies involved in similar offshore projects in the region. Examples of such bases are Great Yarmouth, Teesport and Aberdeen in the UK, Luanda (Angola) and Singapore. These Supply Bases provide cost-effective storage, cargo handling, offshore-certified container handling and provision, quayside management, stevedoring and all supply chain activities associated with the offshore Oil & Gas sector. They are all Customs-controlled, and act as a specialist form of Free Zone. They are all linked with seaports, as they require the fast and efficient movement of materials from the port into the Supply Base, and thence onto the offshore supply vessels by way on an integrated quayside at the base itself.

A recent addition is the Saldanha Supply Base located at the Port of Saldanha, South Africa, to the north of Cape Town. Transnet National Ports Authority (TNPA) and Saldehco, a local South African Company, signed an agreement in 2018 to develop South Africa's first dedicated and customised facility supporting offshore Oil & Gas operations. The Supply Base operates within the SEZ facility at Saldanha, and specialises in offshore Oil & Gas support activities.

TNPA has provided berth infrastructure for the offshore Supply Base (OSSB) at the port's general maintenance quay while Saldehco is responsible for providing warehousing, workshops, offices, canteen, and restroom facilities, as well as equipment such as cranes and other rubber-tyred equipment to operate the facility. The expected activities provided include critical need-based services such as a marine bunkering, lubricants, as well as fresh water for vessels calling at the port and marine traffic passing by the Cape of Good Hope. Additionally, a support facility is intended to allow for fabrication of offshore structures in support of both projects on the Western Cape and up to the West Coast of Africa, as well as capacity to support offshore and onshore pipe-laying projects. The OSSB is designed to serve vessels engaged in supporting offshore exploration and production activities along the West and East coasts of Africa and calling at South African ports for support and logistics services.

Also, the Authority concluded a commercial development lease agreement with the Saldanha Bay Industrial Development Zone (IDZ) for the development of various pockets of land, totalling 35 hectares in the port, as the first tranche of IDZ designated land parcels. The IDZ was granted a permit to operate the SEZ with funding of R303 million ($24.65 million) for the development of the landside area. The core activities within the area include logistics, repair and maintenance, newbuild equipment and fabrication activities for the servicing of upstream and midstream Oil & Gas services. The OSSB is designed to operate within the SEZ and will offer incentives to the industry, both local and international, to establish an Oil & Gas hub to drive the port's and region's overall focus on positioning itself as a global player in the sector.

In Singapore, the 100-hectare (247-acre) Loyang offshore Supply Base in Singapore has been redeveloped into an integrated centre for offshore Oil & Gas exploration and production hub for Asia. The redeveloped base, which accommodates 200 Oil & Gas companies operating in Asia, has been designed to better serve the needs of the Asian offshore industry. It is largely based on the significant growth of Singapore-based Oil & Gas equipment manufacturing companies, with output in 2005 expanding by 68% to $2.6 billion.

Location

Free Zones and Freeports, as well as the more specific Offshore Supply Bases, are generally located outside and adjacent to the defined limits of seaports or airports. However, in some cases, they are part of the port itself, the original Liverpool Freeport being an example. The Liverpool Freeport had to be located within the port confines, as adjacent urban development prevented it from being located outside and adjacent to the port, as the port's confines bordered on other urban development along the whole length of the port. In other cases, however, the Free Zone or Freeport is located adjacent to the seaport/airport, with Customs-approved access from the [air]port facilities directly into the Free zone. This is predominantly the case where there is spare unoccupied land available, which can be easily developed for Free Zone purposes. Offshore Supply Bases, which are used for the Customs-controlled storage of offshore Oil & Gas materials, are also located adjacent to seaports, with the facility to transfer materials directly from the port into the Supply Base, with simplified import clearance formalities. In this respect, transfer from the [air]port to the Free Zone works in exactly the same way, with goods transferred directly from the [air]port into the Free Zone by simplified import clearance into the Free Zone by a Customs-controlled access point.

Free-Trade Zones are generally organised around major seaports, international airports, and national frontiers, namely areas with many geographic advantages for international trade. Examples include Hong Kong, Singapore, Colón (Panama), Copenhagen, Stockholm, Gdańsk (Poland), Los Angeles, and New York City. Alternative facilities such as Bonded Warehouses and associated facilities are used in or close to many large cities, such as London and Amsterdam. The main difference is that Bonded Warehouses are run by individual enterprises in complete isolation from other similar facilities, whereas Free Zones comprise clusters of companies, all involved in Customs-controlled activities, and all located in areas which are more suitable for smooth flows in international trade, inferring proximity to seaports and airports.

Location, however, need not be restricted to seaports or airports. Many Export Processing Zones (EPXs) and SEZs are located close to major cities owing to their proximity to major industrial and employment areas. In China, many of the Zones are located inland, because of their manufacturing nature. In this respect, they may be located throughout the country depending upon need and geographical and demographical convenience.

The primary purpose of a Free-Trade Zone is to remove from a seaport, airport, or border those hindrances to trade caused by high tariffs and complex Customs regulations. Among the advantages of the system are the quicker turnaround of ships and aircraft through the reduction in formalities of Customs examinations, and also the ability to fabricate, refinish, and store goods freely. Streamlined Customs clearance procedures and swift and efficient access from the Free Zones to seaport or airport facilities is also a major factor in determining the location of such Free Zones. Although in many cases Free Zones are located inland, they must still have easy and clear access to frontiers and seaport/airports for the efficient shipment of materials and products into and out of the country in the form of imports and exports.

In many cases, Free Zones are located in national and regional areas in need of economic development. Internationally, Free Zones are located in countries in need of economic development, but in national terms, such economic development is also pertinent to specific regions. One of the driving forces behind the UK's new Freeport policy is that Freeports should be located in areas requiring economic development such as the North and the South-West. Tax incentives included in the UK's Freeport policy mean that investment in these designated areas is actively encouraged, with the promise of reduced or suspended taxes of various kinds, apart from Customs Duty and VAT incentives. The Montréal Mirabel Free-Trade Zone was deliberately located on the site of Montréal Mirabel International Airport to encourage economic growth in the area in the wake of the closure of Mirabel Airport as an international airport.

Other considerations include employment potential, infrastructural considerations, availability of land, and environmental considerations. One of the main deciding factors in Free Zone growth has been the proximity of such Zones to areas in need of employment growth, as well as access to local supporting and supply industries. The US FTZ subzone of BMW at Greenville-Spartanburg, South Carolina, was located there because of the need of BMW for access to industries supplying automotive parts, as well as the urban population of the areas. One of the main conditions for the authorisation of the subzone was that the company should employ much of the local labour force, which it did. The result was that BMW is now one of the major employers in the area. The same is true for the Mercedes-Benz manufacturing plant at Huntsville, Alabama. Given that in the US, FTZ subzones belong to major manufacturing and processing plants such as automotive producers and oil refineries, such subzone activity is a natural catalyst for employment generation as well as the stimulus for greater levels of production and import-export activity.

Employment generation is a major factor in the determination of zone location. Zones are located close to areas of concentrated population. It is unwise to locate a zone far from centres of population, as one of the main purposes of the zone is to generate regional and local employment, where the zone workforce can easily access the zone. It is generally the case that Free Zones are the catalyst for immediate generation of employment, in areas such as logistics and manufacturing. Although such employment may be based on lower wage rates depending upon the nature of the jobs offered by companies operating within the zone, the attraction of such jobs is often the main driver in employment generation, especially in areas where unemployment has been a problem for some years. In developing countries, employment is a key factor in economic development, and the existence of a Free Zone has in general fostered significant economic growth on the basis of the attraction of the workforce to the employment opportunities available within the zone.

Global location

According to UNCTAD, the number of active SEZs worldwide was 5,383 in 2019 present in about 150 countries (out of 193). The analysis of their distribution by country type, but also by major sub-region, is very instructive, as it reveals strong geographical contrasts.

SEZs are predominantly present in developing economies (4,772, or 88.6%). The same is true for Free Zones (1,869, or 81.4%). It is largely as a result of Free Zones and more recently to other types of SEZs that developing economies have been able to attract investors and foreign capital, but also to initiate industrialisation strategies allowing them to gradually participate in international trade. Indeed, Peter Dicken, in his book *Global Shift* (1992), suggested that Export Processing Zones were one of the prime drivers of economic development in the developing world.

Free Zones have emerged in successive waves in these countries. First in South America before and just after the Second World War; then, more gradually, elsewhere in the 1960s and 1970s, in particular to take advantage of the first industrial relocations from Japan, the United States and Western Europe to low-wage Asian countries in sectors such as textiles and clothing and consumer electronics. The development of Free Zones and, more generally SEZs, however, culminated with the globalisation bout of the world economy from the mid-1980s onwards. All emerging countries, without exception, have legislated for the development of Free Zones and SEZs. Moreover, it is the Free Zones that have played an important, even decisive role in the economic emergence of these countries, especially in East Asia, with the notable exception of Brazil, which is still lagging behind, apart from the success of the Manaus Free Economic Zone in the Amazonian are of Brazil. Even other South American countries such as Uruguay and Argentina have invested in Free Zones of some form. Unlike poorer countries, emerging countries offer increasingly sophisticated incentives, such as better training of the workforce, better supervision, efficient infrastructure, diversified and quality services. These benefits offset higher local labour costs. Middle-income countries have also developed SEZ-friendly programs that have generated some significant success. In particular, Kenya, which has 71 Free Zones that vary greatly in size, both public and private, Ghana, Guatemala, Jordan, Nicaragua, Nigeria, Panama, and Tunisia have developed Free Zone strategies that have significantly benefitted the economy. The Nigerian Oil & Gas Free Zone at Onne, in the Niger Delta, has stimulated significant economic development in the region by specifically benefitting the Nigerian Offshore Oil & Gas sector. Likewise, the Panamanian Free Zones adjacent to the Panama Canal, in particular the Colón Free Zone, locate adjacent to the city of Colón, at the entrance to the Panama Canal at the Caribbean end of the Canal, have equally benefitted the Panamanian economy by tapping into the maritime trade using the Panama Canal. The other countries in this group of middle-income countries often have disappointing or modest results, with few ripple effects to local and national economies.

Given the growing interest they have generated in recent decades, several multilateral and bilateral organisations have encouraged SEZ-friendly policies in developing economies.

The WTO has also taken them into account, because they represent one of the few means available to many poor countries to industrialise and participate in international trade.

China accounts for 47.2% of the world's SEZs. The vast majority of Chinese SEZs are intended to produce goods for the Chinese domestic market. Given their size and the number of local and foreign companies they host, the Special Customs Zones make a very large contribution to Chinese exports. According to the website *Asia Briefing*, the country has made the proliferation of SEZs a major focus of its development strategy since 1978. The number of Free Zones in China (called 'Special Customs Zones') stood at only 135 in 2019, 5.9% of the world total of Free Zones. They are divided into six different subtypes: bonded zones (11); Export Processing Zones (27), Bonded Logistics Parks (4), cross-border industrial zones (2), bonded ports (13), comprehensive bonded zones (78). Considerably lagging, Asia is the Latin America-Caribbean region with 486 SEZs, 9% of the world total. Africa has 237 SEZs (4.4%), many of which were developed from 1990 onwards. The transition economies are on the same level as Africa in terms of the number of SEZs, driven in particular by Russia, with its 130 SEZs. Developed economies account for only 7% of global SEZs.

However, the US is characterised by the existence of an effective Free Zone system created in 1934 as a result of the US Foreign-Trade Zones Act, a piece of legislation designed to bolster the US economy in the period following the economic slump and the resulting Smoot-Hawley Tariffs Act of 1930. This distinguishes between general-purpose Zones (which, in fact, correspond to Free Zones), numbering 191, and subzones (free points), numbering 400. By 2015, 2,700 companies were installed within or local to the general-purpose Zones (420,000 jobs). Elsewhere in North America, Canada only has free points, many of these Goods and Services Tax (GST) Warehouses, as does Mexico with its Maquiladoras, although the latter has a small Free Zone. Japan has two small Free Zones on the island of Okinawa.

Western and Eastern Europe have 85 Free Zones, 32 of which are in Western Europe. However, the European Union is far from favourable to Free Zones, which it perceives as distorting competition (as well as what it sees as a major form of tax avoidance). This is the reason why in recent years, particularly from 1995 onwards, the number of Free Zones has decreased in the West, while their number has risen rapidly in the East. Poland (14), Serbia (14), Croatia (13) and the Czech Republic (11) are the countries that have the most Free Zones, largely dating from pre-EU days, and created for the purposes of post-Soviet economic development.

Comparisons

In the introductory section of this text, the various types of Free Zone were detailed according to their function and type. These Zones can therefore be compared according to their respective functions and uses.

Freeports are a special kind of Customs-controlled zone where normal tax and Customs rules do not apply, and are located adjacent to ports or airports. Their significant difference from normal ports and airports is that they can accommodate goods on an unlimited period, whereas in port and airport complexes, goods can only be held in Temporary Storage for a limited period of time, 90 days in the case of the UK. At a Freeport, imports can enter with simplified Customs documentation and without paying import duties, that is, that

Import Duty is suspended on these goods while they are in the zone. Businesses operating inside designated areas in and around the port can manufacture goods using imported materials and add value in the form of productive manufacturing or processing activities, before exporting these goods without facing full tariffs or Customs procedures. However, they need to obtain separate approvals for zone manufacturing, as Freeports are approved for Customs-controlled storage only. This measure is a standard worldwide requirement.

If the goods move out of the Freeport into another part of the country, however, they have to be cleared through the full import process, including the payment of any import duties and taxes. In this respect, Freeports are generally Customs-approved storage areas used by a variety of companies, rather than manufacturing Zones. In the UK, Freeports were not generally used for manufacturing, and were simply extended long-term Customs-controlled storage areas outside the confines of the port areas. They were used partly for transshipments and partly as enhanced Customs warehouses for long-term storage, which is partly why independent Customs Warehousing facilities used by individual companies were viewed as a more favourable solution by the government at the time it allowed UK Freeport licences to expire in 2012. However, given the tight controls imposed by HM Revenue & Customs, as well as rigorous conditions imposed by HMRC for Customs Warehousing operations in the UK, the Freeport solution is becoming increasingly attractive for UK companies following the UK's exit from the EU at the end of 2020, as it offers more flexibility and opportunities to many companies in both the productive and services sectors.

Free Zones, in this case 'Enterprise Zones', are designated areas subject to a broad array of special regulatory requirements, tax breaks and government support. The difference is that a Freeport is designed to specifically encourage businesses that import and re-export goods, rather than more general business support or regeneration objectives. Free Zones in general include manufacturing facilities, either for release into Free Circulation, or for re-export. In the case of a Free Zone being created for predominantly manufacture and re-export purposes, this zone is classed as an EPZ, where imports into Free Circulation are not approved. Export Processing Zones are primarily designed for the purpose of manufacturing for re-export, with materials imported from overseas or supplied from locally to produce finished products which will be exported to overseas markets. However, they are not used as conduits for the supply of such manufactured products to the internal domestic market, owing to the national government's requirements for export-led growth and economic development. In this respect, national EPZ policy centres around the use of EPZs solely for the re-export of manufactured products under Customs-controlled conditions. Furthermore, EPZs also use domestic tax incentives, such as reduced or eliminated Corporate Tax and also reduced or eliminated personal Income Tax. Other incentives, such as reduced or eliminated Property Tax, are also available for such zone activity, in order to encourage and increase Foreign Direct Investment. Expatriates working in such Zones may receive major tax incentives, as the encouragement of specialist foreign labour is also encouraged.

Specifically designated Free Zones such as SEZs are a more flexible solution, as they allow for a combination of Customs-controlled storage and manufacturing for either import into Free Circulation or for re-export, as well as operation of service-based companies in the zone. Indeed, SEZs are becoming increasingly prevalent in major international centres because of their flexibility and diversity of commercial activities. The Free Zones used in other parts of the world have this advantage, and are seen as a major advantage to the economy, encouraging inward investment and substantial economic development, as exemplified by the UAE and Singapore. Both places are important international financial centres as well as being major centres for global trade. SEZs incorporate the incentives of EPZs, but can also be used for the supply of finished products and also services, such as financial services, for international purposes, or for supply into the domestic market. Given that SEZs also include service-based sectors such as IT and the Financial Sector, these services can be combined with manufacturing and processing facilities to make the concept of the SEZ more diverse and flexible.

CHAPTER 6

Customs clearance

Customs clearance into and out of a Free Zone operates in exactly the same way as with a Customs Warehouse. The cargoes are unloaded from the vessel/aircraft, and are pre-cleared through Customs using simplified clearance procedures. They are immediately removed from the [air]port into the Free zone and a designated warehouse, where they are stored under Customs control until required by the customer. When the customer requires an individual consignment, this consignment is cleared through Customs and into Free Circulation, or may be transferred under Customs control into the customer's own Customs-controlled premises, where the consignment is Customs-cleared at that point. Where a customer is located outside the country where the Free Zone is located, the consignment is re-exported, thus resulting in removal of Import Duty and VAT liability.

For consignments to be re-exported, the goods are export cleared out of Customs control in the Free zone and are then moved back into the seaport or airport, where they are loaded aboard vessel/aircraft for shipment overseas.

For all Free Zones, Customs procedures operate around Simplified Procedures. A basic simplified frontier declaration is completed by the Free Zone tenant or their agent, and the goods are cleared from the [air]port into the Free zone. They are then entered into the stock of the Free Zone tenant company, by way of a Supplementary Declaration. When the goods are released into Free Circulation, a further Supplementary Declaration is submitted to Customs for Import Duty and Sales Tax/VAT liability purposes. If the goods are to be re-exported, and export declaration is submitted to the Customs computer, the goods are re-exported accordingly.

This simplified procedure allows the goods to be cleared quickly and efficiently without the need for full Customs clearance for each consignment. Given the number of consignments moving between the port/airport and the Free Zone, the submission of full declarations for each clearance would be completely inefficient and time-consuming, hence the need for simplified electronic clearance procedures.

In the UK, HMRC has already determined the procedures required for the clearance of goods from a Freeport/Free Zone based on previous UK Free Zone operations, originally published in 2016. These are as follows.

The Free Zone tenant must first be authorised for electronic CFSP, which also applies to Customs Warehousing operations. In addition to the standard CFSP criteria and conditions, the trader must additionally:

- Provide any facilities that Customs may require in order to examine goods;
- Inform the Free Zone manager when goods are to be removed from the Free zone;

DOI: 10.4324/9781003232025-7

- Maintain a set of commercial records that allow the goods to be identified from initial receipt, through storage to removal and eventual inclusion on an Import Supplementary Declaration (SDI) – also known as a Bonded Receipt – and Simplified Frontier Declaration (FSD); and
- Comply with the laws on prohibitions, restrictions and rules governing the release of goods to Free Circulation.

The trader's documented procedures must include who, where, when and how the Free Zone procedures will be operated with CFSP EIDR.

As with EIDR removals from Customs Warehousing, traders wishing to use EIDR to remove goods from a Free Zone must comply with additional specific criteria and conditions. The Free Zone approval must also be amended to allow EIDR removals.

A letter must be attached to the CFSP application from the Free Zone manager/operator stating that the Free Zone approval allows goods to be removed using EIDR. This letter must state the means by which the authorised CFSP trader will notify the Free Zone manager/operator of the goods removal. The Free Zone manager must approve these methods before the CFSP EIDR authorisation is granted. As with all other forms of EIDR, the release of the goods is effected by making an entry in the EIDR records followed by a Supplementary Declaration (SD). In the case of Free Zone removals this is an SDI. Specific ex-Free Zone Customs Procedure Codes (CPCs) must be used on the SDI (Supplementary Declaration – Import). These specific CPCs designate the box requirements for the SDI.

The WCO paper on the Extraterritoriality of Free Zones (WCO Paper 47) detailed the standard set of Simplified Customs Procedures and Practices that could be used for each Free Zone on a global basis. These procedures are as follows:

Types of characteristics	*Examples of characteristics of Free Zones (in comparison with goods in Customs warehouses or under the Inward Processing procedure)*
Notable characteristics of FZs under SAD2 of the Revised Kyoto Convention (RKC)	Goods declaration is not required for the cargo's entry from overseas to FZs/exit from FZs to overseas as long as cargo information is available from trade documents (Recommended Practice 9 and 18 of SAD2).
	Security is not required for the cargo's entry to FZs (Recommended Practice 10 of SAD2).
	Bookkeeping (stock-keeping and accounting) for cargo movement is not required inside FZs, while required inside Customs Warehouses (Standard 4 of SAD1 of RKC). *Standard 4 of SAD1 of RKC 'The arrangements for storage of goods in Customs warehouses and for stock-keeping and accounting shall be subject to the approval of the Customs Authority'.
	Unlimited duration for goods to stay inside FZs (Standard 14 of SAD2 of the RKC).
Characteristics unique to each country (simplification of Customs procedure/ practice)	Reduced frequency, or 'bundled' nature, of import declaration for companies operating inside FZs compared with the other companies.

Types of characteristics	*Examples of characteristics of Free Zones (in comparison with goods in Customs warehouses or under the Inward Processing procedure)*
	For entry from overseas to FZs ('e' in Figure 6.3–6.2) and exit from FZs to abroad ('f' in Figure 6.3–6.2), declaration to Customs is not required. On the other hand, when it comes to entry into/exit from Customs warehouses, declaration to Customs is required.
	Simplified supervision of inventory bookkeeping: contract-level bookkeeping (which is usual for goods in Customs Warehouses or under the Inward Processing procedure) is not required (only company-level bookkeeping is required). Once reported as a whole, raw materials consumption in every consumption phase is not required.
	Simplified supervision of inventory bookkeeping: registration of expected per-unit material consumption (which is usually required in for goods in Customs Warehouses or under the Inward Processing procedure) is not required inside FZs.
	Simplified supervision of inventory bookkeeping: bookkeeping is required only for designated sensitive goods, while required for all goods in Customs Warehouses.
	Final products or materials can be selected as taxable standard in case of manufacturing inside FZs and import into the domestic market.
	E-commerce business utilising the characteristic of suspension of import duties and indirect taxes may be conducted only inside FZs.
	Employing a specified expert* (which is mandatory in case of Customs warehouses) is not required. *Accredited expert called 'bonded goods caretaker' unique to the country.

NB. This table should be consulted alongside Specific Annex D (SAD) of the RKC, which can be found in the section on legal status.

The interpretation is that there is no limit on the duration of stay for cargoes inside Free Zones. A cargo can stay inside a Free Zone for an unlimited duration without paying duties and indirect taxes, even if the cargo is transferred from one company to another and the transfer-chain continues repeatedly, as long as the cargo physically stays within the Free Zone.

Release procedures

Any requirements for prior notification (and dwell time if appropriate) must be adhered to before the goods are removed from the Free Zone.

The details of the removal must be entered in the Free Zone stock record. The Free Zone operator/manager should note in the stock account the details of the goods to be removed including the date/time of removals, the Declaration Unique Consignment Reference (DUCR) and details of the CFSP authorisation to which they are being released.

Release procedures when the depositor is a CFSP authorised trader

Where the CFSP authorisation is held by the depositor (owner) of the goods then the depositor must submit a 'request to remove goods' to the Free Zone manager/operator.

(The manager or operator to whom this 'request' is to be submitted should be determined on an individual basis according to the operational practices of the Free Zone in question.) This 'request to remove goods' must include a declaration by the depositor of the goods stating that all Customs formalities will be adhered to and that the goods are being released under the terms of their CFSP authorisation. The request should also include:

- Details of the CFSP authorisation under which they are to be declared;
- Full details of the goods (quantity, weight, description, Commodity Code (as appropriate), value etc.);
- The date and time the removal is to occur;
- Any requirements for a 'prior notification of removal' (including any dwell or standing time) – see CFSP04700 to be made to the Customs Authorities, as noted in the CFSP authorisation;
- Stock rotation number/commercial reference;
- Customs Procedure Code (CPC); and
- DUCR Number.

The Free Zone operator/manager should then cross-reference this request to the Free Zone's stock records. The 'request' and its declaration of intent discharge the Free Zone operator/manager's liability for the Customs debt. If the Free Zone operator/manager is not in possession of the above 'request to remove goods' before allowing the release of the goods then, under the terms of their Free Zone approval they will remain jointly and severally liable with the depositor for any Customs debt arising from the release of the goods.

The CFSP trader must then create the base date and/or tax point and enter the details of the goods in the EIDR records (see CFSP04750 for details) thereby establishing the date for the submission of the SDI (Supplementary Declaration – Import), or Bonded Receipt. If prior notification of removal is required, the trader must first notify Customs of the intention to release the goods.

Release procedures when the Free Zone manager is a CFSP authorised trader

If the CFSP authorisation is held by the Free Zone manager then, upon receipt of a 'request to remove goods' from the owner of the goods, the Free Zone manager should (if prior notification of removal is required) notify Customs of the intention to release the goods, and create the tax point and base date by entering the details of the goods in their EIDR records. These records must also be available to Customs for compliance and accountability purposes, and copies of the release declarations should also be sent to the Free Zone operator, also for compliance and accountability purposes, depending upon whose declarant registration details are used on the declaration.

Release procedures when the Free Zone operator is a CFSP authorised trader

If the CFSP authorisation is held by the Free Zone operator, that is, a company operating within the zone, then upon receipt of a 'request to remove goods' from the depositor, the Free Zone operator must provide a faxed/e-mail written notification, preferably by pdf attachment, to the Free Zone manager of his intent to remove goods using EIDR. This 'request' must include a declaration which states that the goods are being removed under the terms of the operator's CFSP authorisation and that the operator undertakes to fulfil all necessary Customs obligations.

This notification should follow the same format as that specified in the 'request to remove goods' detailed above.

If prior notification of removal is required, the operator should then notify Customs of the intention to release the goods and create the tax point and base date by entering the details of the goods in their EIDR records.

In all cases, the entry in the Free Zone stock records, entry in the EIDR records and any subsequent Import Supplementary Declarations (SDIs) must be able to be cross-referenced to both the 'request to remove goods' and the faxed notification provided to the Free Zone manager.

Consignment stock

One of the key areas in Free Zone storage and clearance centres around the issue of Consignment or Call-Off Stock. This system conventionally applies to the facility of Customs Warehousing, but also applies to the Freeport/Free Zone facility.

If the stock is initially sent to the seller's warehouse which is under their control (including rented storage), then the set-up is treated as Consignment Stock. Typically, there are multiple potential customers for Consignment Stock. This transaction also refers to stock sent to a warehouse in another country which is operated by a logistics company on behalf of the buyer. Even under such circumstances, the stock is still owned by the seller while it is in the receiving warehouse. This is referred to as Call-Off Stock.

Call-Off Stock are goods sent from the seller/exporter's home country to a warehouse or client's storage facility in another country. Title (ownership) of the goods still remains with the seller.

Businesses that source goods from abroad may on import enter the goods into Customs Warehousing (or Freeport facilities) and Import Duty and VAT are suspended. The customer raises a purchase order at a later date and goods are despatched from the warehouse/ Freeport and VAT is deferred or entered on the PVA system (this system is used in the UK and the Republic of Ireland), while the Import Duty is registered to the customer's deferment account. The customer takes ownership of the goods at the time of delivery to either a distribution centre or their premises.

Ordinarily, Import VAT and Customs Duty becomes due when the goods are imported and enter Free Circulation. Where goods are entered into Customs Warehousing, Import VAT becomes due at the point the goods are removed from the warehouse and enter Free Circulation. However, businesses can use a variety of Customs Duty Reliefs, also known as Special Procedures, to suspend, reduce or claim relief on the payment of Customs Duties and VAT under specified conditions.

Special Procedures include:

- **Customs Warehousing** – allows for goods not in Free Circulation to be stored without payment of Customs Duty, and where appropriate Excise Duty or Import VAT, in a Customs Warehouse;

- **Freeports/Free Zones** – as above with Customs Warehousing, but where a series of companies operate form within the Free Zone on a Customs-controlled basis;
- **Inward Processing** – allows for the payment of Customs Duties and Import VAT to be suspended on imported goods while processing is taking place;
- **Outward Processing** – allows for the temporary export of goods for processing or repair, and to re-import the processed products while retaining domestic status or with partial relief from import duties;
- **Temporary Admission** – allows for businesses and individuals who are established outside of the UK to be authorised to import goods with total or partial relief from Customs Duties and other charges because of the specific use to which the goods will be put;
- **Authorised Use** – allows for reduced or nil rates of Customs Duty on certain imported goods, provided they are put to a prescribed end use.

In the above example of Customs Warehousing, when the goods are released from the Customs Warehouse into Free Circulation, the Import VAT becomes due. Where a customer uses their own deferment account and reclaims the Import VAT without having paid for the goods prior to release from the warehouse, this is incorrect. The HMRC policy, as stated in Revenue and Customs Brief 2 (2019), remains correct, in that only the actual owner of the goods can reclaim the Import VAT. On this basis, it is the owner, whose details (EORI) should be shown on the import declaration, who is eligible to reclaim the Import VAT, including the use of PVA.

Where goods are entered into warehouses where VAT and duty is suspended (e.g. Customs Warehouse or Free Zone/Freeport), Import VAT generally becomes due once the goods are removed from the warehouse or Freeport and enter Free Circulation. HMRC have said that it is incorrect for customers to import the goods, use their deferment account and pay the Import VAT if they do not own the goods at the time of their removal from the warehouse, because they only acquire the goods at the point of delivery to their distribution centres/retail premises. To avoid Import VAT becoming a cost for the customer, or the overseas Suppliers having to import the goods and register for and charge UK VAT on the sale to the retailer, HMRC have suggested that retailers should take ownership of the goods prior to their removal from the warehouse or Freeport into Free Circulation. This could impact anyone with call-off/Consignment Stock arrangements for imported goods, and would allow the customer to both act as importer of record and recover the Import VAT. There is no legal issue preventing a sale of the imported goods while within the warehouse regime and this would consequently remove the need for overseas entities to register for UK VAT. In reality, any release of goods from either a Customs Warehouse or a Freeport/Free Zone would enable the warehouse operator to release the goods electronically using the customer's VAT/EORI details, and therefore assign all Import Duty and VAT to the customer's VAT/EORI Number.

Postponed VAT Accounting (PVA)

From 1 January 2021, UK VAT registered businesses are able to use PVA to account for Import VAT on their VAT Return for goods imported for use in their business from anywhere in the world, rather than having to pay Import VAT on the consignment at the point of import either outright or on deferment.

Where a business initially declares goods to Customs Warehousing or into some other Customs Special Procedure including a Freeport, they can use Postponed VAT Accounting when they submit the declaration that releases those goods into Free Circulation.

Businesses do not need to be authorised to use Postponed VAT Accounting, as they simply make the appropriate entry on their Customs Imports Declaration. Ordinarily, Postponed VAT Accounting is not mandatory and businesses can start to use it at any time after 1 January 2021.

However, businesses must use Postponed VAT Accounting if they import non-controlled goods from the EU to Great Britain from 1 January 2021 to 30 June 2021, and either defer their supplementary Customs declaration, or use simplified Customs declaration process where authorised and make an EIDR.

As with existing processes, it is the owner of the goods who is using the goods in the course of their business who can use Postponed VAT Accounting. It means they can declare and recover Import VAT on the same VAT Return, subject to the normal rules on input tax deduction. For businesses which currently import goods into the UK from non-EU countries, this relieves them from having to pay for the Import VAT upfront through their deferment account. Non-owners cannot use Postponed VAT Accounting.

CHAPTER 7

Rules of Origin and Freeports

In simple terms, Rules of Origin are how Customs Authorities classify where an export has come from and originates from in terms of international trade.

There are two main ways:

- **Preferential Rules of Origin**: If the UK and the EU agree under an FTA to remove tariffs for each other's goods, this grants a preference not provided to others. UK goods seeking to enter the EU under this preference will have to prove that they are from the UK under particular rules agreed in an FTA. This prevents a country without a trade deal from accessing the EU market through the UK and vice versa.
- **Non-Preferential Rules of Origin**: Outside a Customs Union, all UK exporters will still have to declare the origin of their goods when trading with other countries, in particular those countries with which the UK has Free Trade Agreements, including the EU. This is used by importing countries to protect their producers and for other monitoring purposes. For instance, if the UK or EU felt that imports are unfairly damaging its own producers, it could apply a temporary tariff to the import. In this case, the EU or the UK would need to differentiate the origin of the import to which it wished to apply duty so that it did not apply tariffs to another country.

The 2013 Trade and Investment Balance of Competence Review states that British companies would be exposed to a combination of administrative and compliance costs linked to Rules of Origin, ranging (based on existing estimates) from 4% to perhaps 15% of the cost of goods sold. The complexity of supply chains can therefore mean that proof of origin can be difficult for traders to supply and hard for authorities to assess. This makes the use of Free Zones for manufacturing for re-export far more attractive to such companies, and this point is elaborated on in the section on the application of Free Zones and Freeports.

The first need is to determine what product is being traded. The WCO has produced a list classifying every product traded under tariff headings. Each product has a unique code which is grouped into broader categories. Once the product is classified, the next step is to establish its 'economic nationality' as opposed to simply the country it came from. This involves determining the product's value and where the contributions were made in *adding value* to the final product, as in the 'sufficient value-added' section below.

If all materials were obtained and processed in one State, it would be 'wholly obtained' in that country. That would apply, for example, to agricultural produce and natural

DOI: 10.4324/9781003232025-8

resources. However, if the materials being used to manufacture the product come from different countries, the resulting product is said to be 'partially originating', and therefore the rules applying to the origin of that product state that:

A majority of the sales value of that product must originate in the country of manufacture, usually 60% of the sales price of the product;

The Commodity Code of the manufactured product must be significantly different from the Commodity Codes of its components or raw materials, that is, it must undergo a significant transformation in terms of the change from on Commodity Code Chapter to another.

A good example of this is a car. A car has multiple components: bumpers, brakes, clutches, computer software, leather seats and rubber tyres, and so on. These can be made in different countries and shipped as needed to be assembled into the final product. With multiple components adding value, it can be very difficult to determine origin for some products. In this case, the final product is determined by the location of the 'last substantial transformation'.

Therefore, for preferential origin, substantial transformation is defined through one or a combination of three main criteria:

- **Change of tariff classification**: When the work undertaken within a country results in a change of classification. For example, the unique code for car parts, 8708, is different to the code for a finished car, 8703. If a country assembles car parts into a finished car, it would qualify as a change of tariff classification.
- **Sufficient value-added**: The originating State must contribute a minimum percentage of the value of a product. Each component will add a certain amount of value, calculated as the percentage of the ex-works price of the final good (i.e. the total price of the inputs to the good exempting transportation and insurance costs). Typically, around 50%+ of value has to be added to claim origin.
- **Specific processing**: Finished products can qualify when particular specific working or processing activities are carried out. For example, a rule may require clothing products to be manufactured from yarn.

The precise rules are very detailed and can change for each product depending on what is agreed in an FTA. Similar principles apply to determining non-preferential origin, but there is a global agreement on what the rules are covering most goods.

Transaction value/Net Cost formulae

For Origin purposes, the Transaction Value Formula that is used for all Global Free Trade Agreements can be expressed as follows, together with the 60/40 or other percentage rules;

$$\frac{\mathbf{TV - VNM}}{\mathbf{TV}} \times \mathbf{100\%}$$

Where:

TV = Transaction Value (i.e. Total EXW Factory Gate Value)
VNM = Value of Non-originating Materials

The other formula is the Net Cost method, where the Net Cost equals the cost of producing the goods, but without the inclusion of profit. This is usually set for most Free Trade Agreements at 50% of the total transaction value of the goods, and is expressed as follows:

$$\frac{\textbf{NC} - \textbf{VNM}}{\textbf{NC}} \times \textbf{100\%}$$

Where:

NC = Net Cost (i.e. Total Cost of Materials + Labour/Processing Costs + Overheads)
VNM = Value of Non-originating Materials

Based on the Net Cost method, the Customs/Revenue Authority generally allows the profit margin to be adjusted to achieve origin status.

Typically, for preferential origin, over 50% of the Ex-Works value (the sales price) of the finished product has to be added to claim origin. Post-Brexit, what was once European value-added will have to be separated into UK and EU value-added. That will make it harder to reach the threshold to export to the EU without tariffs.

One of the ways this problem is avoided by other countries is to allow 'cumulation' of value-added. There are different kinds of cumulation, but the main purpose is to allow the value of components contributed by different countries to be combined to meet the threshold when a product is re-exported. In order to maintain existing supply chains, the UK would want to be able to count EU components toward UK content so that it could reach the threshold to re-export to the EU.

Originating status

Products have originating status if they are either 'wholly obtained' or sufficiently worked or processed. This applies to all preferential origin arrangements.

Wholly obtained

Wholly obtained applies mainly to natural products from the beneficiary country and to goods made entirely from them. This means that a product cannot contain imported non-originating elements.

Sufficiently worked or processed

Non-originating Materials or components must be sufficiently worked in order to obtain origin. Sufficiently worked means sufficiently worked according to the specifications of the list rules.

Comparison of build-down and build-up methods under the FTA Rules of Origin

Main differences between 'Build-down method' and 'Build-up method'

	Build-down method	*Build-up method*
Overview	The use of **foreign input materials** in the manufacturing or processing operations carried out in a contracting party or a specified area is limited to a maximum amount.	The **domestic content**, e.g. the value of originating materials and the manufacturing or processing operations carried out in a contracting party or in a specified area, must be equal to or exceed a given percentage of the value of the final product.
Calculation method	This method requires a comparison between the value of the foreign input or the materials with undetermined origin and the value of the final product.	This method requires a comparison between the value-added in a contracting party or in a specified area, and the value of the final product.
Examples of Calculation Method	Indirect method Transaction value method Net Cost method Focused value method Maximum Allowance for Non-originating Material	Direct method Minimum Requirement of Domestic Content

Calculation method of build down

RVC = (FOB Value – Value of Non-originating Materials)/FOB Value × 100%

Calculation method of build up

RVC = (Value of locally-produced materials + direct labour and overheads + profit)/ FOB Value × 100%.
Where RVC = Regional Value Content
Features of the Ad Valorem Rule/Value-Added Criterion are as follows:

- The exact methods for calculating the input materials and the final product are stipulated in the applicable agreement.
- A direct comparison between the percentages used in the different methodologies cannot be made because of the different calculation bases.
- The higher the allowed percentage for use of Non-originating Material, the more liberal the origin rule.
- The higher the minimum requirement for the domestic content, the more stringent the origin rule.

The ad valorem calculation may also vary according to the price basis used for the final product, that is, the price of the final product at the moment when it leaves the factory (ex-works price), or the price of the final product at the time of exportation or importation (FOB or CIF price).

1. Suitable for goods which have been further refined or processed without a change of tariff classification;

2. Value-added criterion is relatively easy to understand and to apply in practice; value-added rules allow simple and flexible adjustments for different stages of development of developing countries;
3. Economic operators are familiar with the cost components of their inputs as the values are known for commercial and Customs purposes;
4. The administration of value-added rules is complex for small and medium-sized companies and may demand additional bookkeeping and sophisticated accounting systems;
5. Requires disclosure of sensitive commercial information by Suppliers;
6. Relatively high administrative burden due to the necessity to calculate the various cost components;
7. Susceptible to the impact of fluctuating exchange rates. A weakening of the exchange rate raises the value of the foreign inputs in relation to the total cost/ex-works price of a given product. An increase of the exchange rate of a foreign currency (imported goods are often invoiced in foreign currencies) will cause an increase of the value of all imported components priced in a foreign currency. This will render a given ad valorem rule more restrictive;
8. Susceptible to commodity value fluctuations.

(*Source*: WCO ORIGIN COMPENDIUM)

Cumulation

Cumulation is the term used to describe a system that allows originating products of country A to be further processed or added to products originating in country B, just as if they had originated in country B. The resulting product would have the origin of country B. It can only be applied between countries operating with identical origin rules.

An important point to remember is that in the case of cumulation the working or processing carried out in each partner country on originating products does not have to be 'sufficient working or processing' as set out in the list rules.

There are four types of cumulation: bilateral, diagonal, regional and full.

Bilateral cumulation

Bilateral cumulation operates between two countries where a Free Trade Agreement or autonomous arrangement contains a provision allowing them to cumulate origin. This is the basic type of cumulation and is common to all origin arrangements. Only originating products or materials can benefit from it.

Diagonal cumulation

Diagonal cumulation operates between more than two countries provided they have Free Trade Agreements containing identical origin rules and provision for cumulation between them. As with bilateral cumulation, only originating products or materials can benefit from diagonal cumulation.

Although more than two countries can be involved in the manufacture of a product, it will have the origin of the country where the last working or processing operation took place, provided that it was more than a minimal operation. Diagonal cumulation operates between the community and the countries of the so-called 'pan-Euro-Mediterranean cumulation zone'.

Regional cumulation

Regional cumulation is a form of diagonal cumulation, which only exists under the Generalised System of Preferences (GSP) and operates between members of a regional group of beneficiary countries (e.g. ASEAN).

Full cumulation

Full cumulation allows the parties to an agreement to carry out working or processing on non-originating products in the area formed by them. Full cumulation means that all operations carried out in the participating countries are taken into account. While other forms of cumulation require that the goods be originating before being exported from one party to another for further working or processing, this is not the case with full cumulation. Full cumulation simply demands that all the working or processing in the list rules must be carried out on Non-originating Materials in order for the final product to obtain origin.

Full cumulation is in operation between the community and, for example, the countries of the European Economic Area, Maghreb, Other Countries and Territories or Africa Caribbean and Pacific.

Minimal operations

Minimal operations are operations that when carried out either individually or in combination are regarded as being of such minor importance that they never confer originating status. All **preferential** origin rules contain an article, which defines the working or processing which is to be regarded as insufficient to confer origin. (e.g. Article 7 of Protocol No. 4 of the Europe (Association) Agreement with Bulgaria).

Working or processing carried out on a product that satisfies the list rule shall not result in the product obtaining origin if that working or processing is mentioned as a minimal operation set out in the relevant article.

However, when allocating origin **within a cumulation system**, any working or processing carried out must exceed the above-mentioned minimal operations but does not necessarily need to satisfy the relevant list rule of the arrangement.

If no operations are carried out on EU goods entering the UK and then re-exported to the UK, these goods lose their preferential status and will be subject to import duties on re-entry into the EU. For preferential status to apply, the goods must be imported into a UK Customs Warehouse, meaning that they do not enter UK Free Circulation and therefore can retain their original EU origin status, thus meaning that they can be re-imported into the EU on a duty-free basis.

General tolerance rule

The general tolerance rule permits manufacturers to use Non-originating Materials up to a specific percentage value of the ex-works price. However, should the specific working or processing rule already allow the use of Non-originating Materials the tolerance cannot be used to exceed the percentage amount specified in the list rule. The maximum will always be that allowed by the specific rule. The percentage of the tolerance allowed varies from one preferential regime to another.

The general tolerance rule does not apply to textile goods of Chapters 50 to 63 (inclusive). Specific tolerance rules for textiles are included in the introductory notes to the list rules.

'No drawback' rule

The term drawback means refunding duties paid on imported goods and the 'no drawback' provision where provided for prohibits this. This rule ensures that duties applicable to third country materials are paid. The objective of this rule is to prevent unfair competition in national markets.

However, some agreements allow for **partial drawback** for a limited period. The reason for this derogation is because the Customs Duties applicable to Non-originating Materials in some countries are considerable higher than those applicable in the community and by allowing a refund to a certain level the imbalance, which could be seen as favouring community producers, is reduced.

Principle of territoriality

The principle of territoriality means that the working or processing must be carried out in the territories of the parties.

Due to modern manufacturing processes, it is not always possible to fulfil this requirement. It may be necessary to do some processing in a country not party to the preferential arrangement. Some arrangements allow such external working or processing provided it conforms to certain specified conditions.

Failure to comply with the specified conditions will result in the returning product being treated as non-originating.

In most cases the derogation from the principle of territoriality does not apply to textile products of Chapters 50 to 63 (inclusive) and nor can a product benefit from both this derogation and the general tolerance rule at the same time.

When determining the origin of the final product, working or processing performed outside the territory of the contracting parties is not to be taken into account. However, when calculating the value-added, the total added value of the working or processing done outside the territory of the contracting parties must be taken together with the value of the Non-originating Materials incorporated in the territory of the other contracting party.

The combined values (the value-added outside the territory and the value of the Non-originating Materials) should not exceed the percentages stated in the relevant list rule.

Direct transport rule

Preferential arrangements contain rules concerning the transportation of preferential goods from one party's territory to another. The purpose of direct transport is to ensure that the goods arriving in the country of import are the same as those which left the country of export. However, if for any reason the goods pass through or stop-over in the territory of a third country, provided that they stay under Customs supervision, including a Freeport, the conditions of direct transport are considered to have been fulfilled.

Proof of compliance with the Direct Transport Rule may be given by a single transport document covering the passage of the goods through the country of transit or, for example, a 'non-manipulation certificate' issued by the authorities of that country.

Proof of origin

When goods are claimed to have a particular preferential origin, the Customs Authorities of the importing country must be satisfied that the claim is correct and thus a proof of that origin is required. The different preferential arrangements require specific proofs of origin relevant to specific arrangements. For example, the preferential arrangements the community has with certain countries require a movement certificate EUR.1 or EUR-MED whereas under GSP a Certificate of Origin Form A is required. Traders are advised to check which particular proof of origin is required to substantiate their claims to preferential origin. Declaration on certain commercial documents (an invoice, a delivery note or any other commercial document which describes the products concerned in sufficient detail to enable them to be identified – the so-called 'invoice declaration') can replace the specific proof of origin. This is subject to prior authorisation by the Customs Authorities granted to Approved Exporters. Additionally, most arrangements allow the use of 'invoice declarations' made out by the exporter for any consignment under a certain value.

The Freeport/Free Zone application

Freeports are Customs-controlled Zones where storage and production activities take place under Customs control. This means that all goods entering the zone and leaving it are under Customs control, and therefore do not enter domestic Free Circulation, that is, they are duty and tax suspended. This means that under the conventional Rules of Origin, they cannot be classified as originating in the country where they are stored or manufactured. These rules apply as much to EPZs and SEZs as they do to Freeports, and to this extent these rules therefore apply to the UK's Freeport regime. In this respect, this rule operates in the same way as an IP regime, as under such a regime goods produced under Customs control cannot be eligible for origin of the country of production, as they do not enter that country's Free Circulation regime, that is, duty and tax paid, to be processed for re-export. Since an IP regime predominantly exists for production for re-export under Customs control, there is no way that any goods produced under such a regime will qualify for origin status, and will therefore be subject to Import Duty and tax in the country of ultimate import. Indeed the IP regime used for this purpose also applies to manufacture under Freeport conditions as well, given that this facility will be allowed for UK Freeport operations and activities.

The advantage of such a regime is that where materials enter a country to be processed for re-export, a Customs-controlled production facility means that the Import Duty and tax on such imported materials is suspended pending re-export of the product manufactured under this regime. That means that such duty is not added on to the sales price to the customer, and therefore reduces the effective value of that product when it is imported into the country of ultimate destination. This therefore reduces the Import Duty and tax liable on that product at the point and time of import.

Given the application of the Rules of Origin, there is still no guarantee that the product could be eligible for preferential status on import into the country of destination, as in many cases the value of the imported material constituting that product exceeds the maximum value of Non-originating Material (MAXNOM) allowed for that product. Given that in such cases preferential duty-free status could not be accorded on that product, there is no point in importing the materials into Free Circulation in the country of production, and therefore a Freeport/Free Zone is an ideal solution, as at very least it means that the product can be manufactured under Customs-controlled conditions, that is, duty and tax suspended. This is exactly the *modus operandi* of EPZs and SEZs, as the point of the exercise is to manufacture goods under Customs control, that is, duty and tax suspended, for re-export to any part of the world, regardless of the existence of any Free Trade Agreements. In most cases where EPZs and SEZs exist, there are very few Free Trade Agreements with other countries. In the case of the UK, origin is a very sensitive issue given the levels of import of materials from elsewhere for incorporation in products manufactured either for distribution in the UK or for re-export, and therefore the question of the origin of the finished products is far less clear-cut given the application of the MAXNOM rule.

There are arguments prevailing within the UK Government that more could have been done to explain this scenario to UK companies. However, the FTAs concluded with other countries by the UK would (or should) have explained that goods produced in Freeports cannot be eligible for duty-free preferential status, given that production is not carried out in domestic Free Circulation. However, all Free Trade Agreements apply this rule anyway, and therefore such arguments being put forward do not hold any validity, as there is a need to apply the standard Rules of Origin to any FTA, given that such rules apply on a global basis, and are not limited to any specific FTA. As previously stated, what has not been made clear is that many goods (re-)exported from the UK do not originate in the UK anyway, so therefore duty-free preferential status cannot apply on these goods on import into the country of destination, thus obviating the advantages of a Free Trade Agreement with that country.

CHAPTER 8

Business clustering and economic development

Business clustering

The purpose of Free Zones, be they Freeports, Free-Trade Zones or EPZs, is to encourage the grouping or clustering of associated businesses within the zone for the purposes of the storage and distribution of goods, as well as processing and manufacturing activities. Although individual Customs Warehousing facilities throughout the country are useful and of fiscal and economic benefit, as in the case of sites owned and managed by 3PL Logistics Providers and even private commercial traders, there are issues concerning the security of the movement of goods between the ports and these locations, especially concerning Customs requirements for goods moving in transit under Customs control, as well as the additional logistics costs associated with the movement of goods by trailer or container between the ports and these locations. Freeports and Free Zones largely eliminate these issues, as Free Zones and Freeports are located adjacent to seaports or airports. In the case of the US, subzones are located inland, where the operating company is located, although they are connected to specific Foreign-Trade Zones. However, on a national level, the other purpose is to stimulate national economic development by the use of Foreign Direct Investment and the use of local labour to stimulate the local, regional and national economy through export-led growth, and also the supply of the local economy with goods manufactured under tax-reduced incentives. This not only enables such companies to locate within and alongside port and airport complexes in terms of the rapid and efficient movement of import and export goods, but also encourages companies to cluster together in terms of regional economic development. Even within the EU, which does not actively encourage Free zone development, several Free Zones exist in Central and Eastern Europe, as well as the Free zone at Barcelona and the Free zone status of the Portuguese island of Madeira. These Zones exist primarily for the economic development of these regions and have done much to stimulate and develop the local economies where the Zones are located. In many cases, the location of businesses in Free Zone clusters close to or adjacent to seaport or airport facilities has facilitated more convenient and cost-effective operations, with immediate access from the Free Zone to the port or airport facilities for the ease of shipping goods into and out of the zone. Furthermore, where associated businesses are clustered near to each other, such as manufacturers, Suppliers and logistics providers, supply and movement costs are reduced to a minimum.

It has been shown in various countries, including the US and China, that Free Zones as a means of economic, commercial and logistics concentration lead to rapid economic development. The Foreign-Trade Zones Act of the US led to a pronounced recovery in

DOI: 10.4324/9781003232025-9

the US economy in the wake of the economic slump of the 1930s, and contributed greatly to economic development in the smaller, less-developed States of the US such as South Carolina and Alabama, especially where specific companies, especially in the automotive sector, developed production plants using the subzone concept. Elsewhere, the Export Processing Zones of China have done much to develop the export economy of the country, and in the UAE, the mighty Jebel Ali Free Zone, located just outside Dubai, has done much to reduce the country's reliance on the oil industry as its major source of income.

Furthermore, Free Zones adjacent to ports and airports enable their operators and tenants to reduce logistics costs, as the need to transport goods long distance from the ports and airports to inland destinations miles away from such facilities. This also enhances security issues in terms of transport movements, since security risks can be significantly reduced if goods are simply transported out of the port or airport into an adjacent Free Zone. This is especially true for goods imported in large quantities for industries such as FMCG logistics operations, the automotive sector and even the offshore Oil & Gas sector, which relies heavily on Free Zones in the form of Customs-controlled Offshore Supply Bases as bases for the storage and handling of offshore materials destined for offshore Oil & Gas platforms. Such facilities are seen as standard practice in such industrial sectors, as they concentrate associated activities in one location, rather than spreading it out over wide areas and thus creating issues such as logistics and security.

Economic development

This study has addressed the various types of Free Zone that exist in different parts of the world. In the developing world, Free Zones, in the form of EPZs or SEZs, have been established as a means of fostering economic development and growth through the attraction of Foreign Direct Investment, largely through the use of fiscal incentives. However, the same is not necessarily true of many of the Zones located in western countries, especially the fully developed countries. In these cases, the Free Zone concept has more largely been used to enable companies to use Customs facilities to avoid duty and indirect tax burdens, such as Sales Tax and VAT. Indeed, much of the Free Zone concept in the US and the Americas in general has been to enable companies to import and manufacture goods for the domestic sector, rather than for export, although one of the primary objectives of the Manaus Free Zone has always been to stimulate Customs-controlled production for the export of goods to the international sector, as well as supplying the domestic and South American markets with products manufactured in the zone. The case of the UK Freeports is as an enclave for the Customs-controlled storage and possibly manufacture of goods destined for the domestic market, rather more along the lines of the US Foreign-Trade Zone concept. However, such Zones are beneficial to local and regional communities in terms of the generation of employment, but are not necessarily seen as a vehicle for national economic development, in that they serve a local or regional community, rather than a national one.

Elsewhere in the world, the emphasis has been the use of the Free Zone for the re-export of products based on Customs-controlled manufacture. EPZs are also Customs-controlled Zones, but exist primarily for the purposes of the manufacture of goods for re-export and not for the entry of these goods into domestic Free Circulation. However, the additional advantages in terms of EPZs is that the governments establishing these types of Zones also incorporate the economic advantages of the reduction or elimination of Corporation Tax and personal income taxes, in order to attract Foreign Direct Investment, as well as personnel from overseas. This investment incentive is designed to enable economic development of the country using a combination of fiscal incentives to companies to contribute to this economic growth.

An SEZ is similar to an Export Processing Zone, and is a geographically delineated area subject to differentiated regulation and administration from the host country in which it is located, in the form of duty and tax incentive advantages, for the purpose of attracting Foreign Direct Investment in economic activity that could not otherwise be achieved owing to normal domestic fiscal regulation. SEZs have evolved from a relatively simple proposition to an increasingly diverse range of propositions, designed to achieve more specific development objectives. SEZs play varied roles in facilitating national, regional and local economic development and global economic connections, with some Zones remarkably successful in doing so. As a national development strategy, SEZs have become a global phenomenon. From an estimated 500 in 1995, SEZs have now grown to around 4,300 in over 130 countries and employ more than 68 million workers, according to figures released in 2015.

SEZs play varied roles in facilitating national, regional and local economic development, and global economic connections, with some remarkably successful in doing so. However, many others fail to achieve a fraction of their intended objectives.

Special Manufacturing Zones, that is, those SEZs dedicated to manufacturing activities, originally sought to develop manufacturing activity in a country through leveraging an abundance of low-cost land and labour (and potential raw material availability) to overcome the absence of a domestic market through export. Historically, significant financial incentives were also required to attract investment. As global manufacturing has evolved, so too have SMZs – reflecting both the increasing competition and sophistication of manufacturing, and the realigned outcomes of economic development that accompanies it.

Special Service Zones typically started with a simple focus on trade and trade facilitation, with a number of successful examples emerging, especially in Dubai, UAE. While manufacturing Zones will always have a place in the global economic framework, the scope and sophistication of services offered by the Service and Financial Zones has dramatically increased in absolute value, the scope of services covered and share of the global economy, underlining their relevance as an SEZ archetype.

While important from an evolutionary perspective, two increasingly powerful trends require a re-framing of SEZs to reflect the ever more global and dynamic environment in which they exist:

- The shift of the global manufacturing landscape from (now) higher-cost domains (North America, Western Europe, East Asia) to cheaper locations elsewhere, such as Africa – coupled with increasingly global supply chain dynamics and more fragmented distribution of advanced and innovative manufacturing; and
- The rise and fall of cities and regions achieving highly variable levels of success based on new national policies, locally niched competitive strengths, and global connectivity.

These trends, coupled with a substantial volume of competing SEZs across the globe, have created a more diverse and fragmented field of 'winners' and 'losers' across the SEZ archetypes and their offshoots. Some Zones, especially those in India and elsewhere, have seen lower degrees of success, while other Zones, especially in the UAE, South-East Asia and China, have witnessed massive success, especially in the levels to which they have attracted foreign investment.

From this, the question can be asked as to what the requirements are for an SEZ to succeed in such shifting national and global economic conditions.

In a global arena crowded with both nationally/regionally promoted and private sector-led SEZs competing for every amount of new business available, it is necessary to examine how a new SEZ can possibly succeed. The answer is the old economic principle of Comparative Advantage, first conceptualised by the English economist David Ricardo in the early 19th century.

Comparative advantages typically fall into three main groups:

Abundance of cheap factors of production

This is the essential element of Opportunity Cost, and the value of such a proposition is largely limited to Special Manufacturing Zones, in host countries at their earliest stage of development. Ironically, the greater the success of the zone, the faster such comparative advantages dissolve as the host country enjoys economic growth, resulting in increasing factor costs and, perhaps, a progressive reduction in fiscal advantages with the progress of time. As has been witnessed in East Asia, in a global supply chain environment, many cases of low-cost, low-skilled manufacturing in commodities such as garments and footwear has already moved from China, as it progresses its industrial upgrading journey, to South-East Asian countries such as Cambodia and Vietnam.

Incentives

Evidence provided by various streams of data from Free Zone operations shows that the historical 'blunt' tool of straightforward fiscal incentives as a sole means of the attraction of Foreign Direct Investment rarely achieves any sustainable value. They may have a place in attracting the pioneer investors during Stage 1 type of SEZ formation, but otherwise risk simply attracting investors that leave the day after the incentives expire, or artificially sustaining unnecessary subsidies and uneconomical activities at the cost of the host economy. An example is the Montréal Mirabel Free-Trade Zone in Canada. Once the tax incentives offered by the zone expired in 2013, ten years after their implementation, especially as Customs and GST incentives were not part of the general Free Zone advantages, many companies realised that they could relocate outside the zone and still apply for Customs and GST incentives, which in reality became part of the Canadian government's incentives for overall foreign investment, and opened up the whole of Canada to a variety of incentives.

It has already been established that over-generous financial incentives rarely succeed. All they do is to attract companies of any size or viability to invest in the specific zone, without proving that they can bring large economic benefits to the region or can indeed maintain viability in such surroundings. It is necessary to ensure that incentives generate an economic return on investment rather than artificially sustain uneconomical business activity.

Some of the most successful incentives today focus increasingly on encouraging target investors to consume local content and employ local human capital, with the aim of deriving an economic 'return on investment' in the form of increased national economic activity and knowledge transfer and labour force upskilling.

Institutional factors

Providing an efficient and robust institutional environment remains one of the most important success factors in any SEZ. The highest quality physical infrastructure, access to labour and cheap input factors will simply not be enough for many investors considering a new location due to their 'risk-adjusted' return calculations. In the 'global arms race', to be at the peak of 'Ease of Doing Business', many host nations simply do not have the requisite institutional apparatus to support this (the correlation between a base economy's ease of doing business ranking and its sustainable economic growth performance is no coincidence).

SEZs represent a valuable 'low-risk' environment to provide an institutional proposition that could not otherwise be offered by the base economy for a host of reasons, whether bureaucratic inertia, political or social constraints. In some cases, the success of SEZ regulation then provides the host nation the impetus and confidence to enhance their national regulation and extend other institutional reforms, resulting in even greater economic benefit.

Reflecting on the functional and temporal evolution of SEZs highlights just how difficult it can be to create a sustainable comparative advantage.

There are at present many barriers to entering the established and competitive realm of Special Manufacturing Zones in today's mature globalised production model, including:

- The relevance of cheap labour and basic factors of production remain predominant in many areas of manufacturing, without which a country has limited chance of (economic) success, however there is an ever-reducing number of such countries; and
- Even with comparative factors of production advantages, the ability to 'reconfigure' or restructure global supply chains requires a very compelling policy, namely the use of incentives that almost certainly could or might deliver negative economic return on investment but would still be dictated by competition.

Despite these points, there are still specific pockets of viable opportunity under the right circumstances, including geographies where there is not yet a sufficiently broad and dense manufacturing base, for example the Middle East.

Low-cost factors have become less of a differentiating factor (typically in the later stages of development), and the emphasis is more on access to talent, valuable domestic or regional market for consumption, and opportunity spread across all industrial sectors. Low wages and social issues are still issues of concern, and these have been addressed in several books and papers relating to Special Economic Zones.

The intelligent design of mutually beneficial incentives, both financial and non-financial, can create a differentiated proposition, and the institutional environment for a specific industry or activity could become a specific differentiator, as in highly regulated, complex or frontier sector activity, such as the institutional and industrial experimentation in China's Shenzhen Special Economic Zone in the 1980s, which was subsequently replicated in the Waigaoqiao and Jinqiao Special Economic Zones at Shanghai.

Factors such as nationalisation objectives and a well-educated national labour force pose important challenges to success in this domain for the Gulf Co-operation Council (GCC) countries of the Middle East, significantly reducing their chances of success given their greater levels of economic development. The exception to this is Dubai, which has established a wide range of Free Zones in both the manufacturing and service sectors. Where such countries and ventures have gained a significant level of success, they remain heavily reliant on the lower-cost expatriate labour force, ultimately reducing the net economic impact of the zone in terms of benefits to the local or national community. However, the development of such Zones has resulted in an influx of people from overseas in both professional and tourism capacities, resulting in a major generation of income and economic wellbeing for the whole community.

While many of the considerations for Special Manufacturing Zones are relevant for all zone archetypes, there are also some important differences concerning incentives, location and other requirements and enablers. Where late entry may limit a new SMZ to a small number of manufacturing industries, this is much less the case with respect to Special Service Zones (SSZs), with more flexible fiscal incentives and location choices.

A pertinent lesson may be learned from the uneven experience of Kazakhstan with its SEZs as an oil-rich and dominant economy in transition to more diverse sectors and activities. Of its ten SEZs, Seaport Aktau and Astana account for over 83% of total goods and services produced. While Seaport Aktau is a Special Service Zone, the Astana zone is located at Astana, the capital of Kazakhstan, and can be compared with the Chinese city-like SEZs.

Trade and logistics also dominate the design and functionality of the China-Kazakhstan Horgos International Border Cooperation Centre, located on the border between Kazakhstan and China. International Trade and Logistics are two of the most important services supporting manufacturing in countries that feature energy industries and main ports. Consequently, emphasis is placed more on simplified Customs clearance, efficient warehousing and expedient transport connections than generous upfront fiscal incentives such as tax holidays on corporate tax and other Direct Taxes. With simple and fast electronic Customs clearance, the China-Kazakhstan border trade zone functions efficiently to allow through large numbers of Chinese and Kazakh freight trucks on a daily basis.

In the UAE, Jebel Ali Free Zone (JAFZA) is one such example that has increasingly sought to expand its role from pure trade and shipping to a complete logistics and supply chain venture, capturing an increasing share of the value chain of trade and logistics in the process, thus making it a true crossroads in international trade. The test is whether the existence of an SEZ brings economic benefit to the area where it is located as a result of all the incentives conferred on it. If the zone succeeds, the area around it will succeed as well, and will prosper as a result. If, however, the zone brings little benefit to the area in which it is located, and, for that matter, the area concerned does not prosper as a result of the zone being located there, then it is pointless maintaining the zone, and it should be either closed down or simply converted into an industrial zone within the national Customs jurisdiction as part of national territory. Indeed, some Zones had a limited life by nature of government policy concerning tax reductions or breaks. The Montréal Mirabel Free-Trade Zone was designed with a limited lifespan of ten years, and once its tax incentives expired, it simply became an industrial zone located next to what had been Mirabel airport. A study of the zone is contained in Part Two of this text.

CHAPTER 9

Tax incentives, duty deferral savings

Tax incentives: direct vs indirect

Much of the definition of any Free Zone revolves around the kind of tax incentives available in the zone. Some Zones, such as the Dubai Financial Free Zone and the Madeira Free Zone, as well as several Special Economic Zones, operate purely around the use of Direct Tax incentives such as Corporation Tax and VAT, whereas Freeports and Export Processing Zones incorporate other essential incentives, namely Import Duty Reliefs, Customs Warehousing and Inward Processing Relief. The original Montréal Mirabel Free-Trade Zone primarily used Direct Tax incentives, that is, breaks from Corporation Tax, as a means of the encouragement of inward investment, and companies wishing to make use of Indirect tax reliefs, that is, Import Duty and GST, had to apply separately to Canada Customs for these reliefs, as well as establishing Export Distribution Centres (EDCs) within the zone as separate facilities. Foreign-Trade Zones and Freeports, on the other hand, use the Indirect Tax reliefs as the primary form of tax incentives to encourage the growth of international trade facilities.

Both forms of tax incentive, that is, Direct and Indirect, are substantial benefits to any Free Zone user. However, these depend upon the activities carried out by the zone user. Companies involved in international services are more likely to use Zones where Direct tax incentives are available, whereas manufacturing companies will use Zones where Indirect tax incentives are available. The encouragement of foreign investment into such Zones requires the application of both Direct and Indirect Tax incentives to justify the use of such Zones, hence the use of Export Processing Zones as such a means of fiscal incentives.

The ideal solution is a hybrid, where both Direct and Indirect Tax incentives are offered by the zone, as in the case of EPZs and SEZs. However, one of the main rules for EPZs is that they are used to encourage export-led activities by encouraging investment (especially foreign investment) from companies wishing to set up operations in the zone for the purposes of the import of raw materials and components into the zone for production for the duty-free re-export of finished products. Additional tax incentives include holidays from Corporation Tax and PAYE Income Tax, as well as exemption from property tax and other fiscal burdens. However, such Zones do not encourage the manufacture of goods under the Customs-controlled environment for import of these

DOI: 10.4324/9781003232025-10

goods from the EPZ into national Free Circulation. They are, effectively, for re-export purposes only.

This would suggest that one can have some of the tax incentives in a Free Zone, but not all of them. The US Foreign-Trade Zones allow for the re-export of goods from a Customs-controlled environment or the release of these goods as well as the manufacture of finished goods from a Customs-controlled environment into US Free Circulation, but they do not allow for Direct Tax incentives. They exist to encourage international trade by Customs-controlled incentives. The same is true of Freeports, although the UK Government is considering allowing the use of direct, as well as indirect, tax incentives to promote the use of the proposed UK Freeports.

The outline of the tax incentive approach is as follows:

- Freeports – Import Duty and VAT incentives;
- FTZs – Import Duty and Sales Tax incentives;
- EPZs – Import Duty and Sales Tax/VAT incentives plus Direct Tax incentives (Export Oriented);
- SEZs – Direct and Indirect Tax incentives.

The ideal Free Zone facilities should include a combination of both Direct and Indirect Tax incentives, plus the ability to manufacture goods in the zone for re-export or for release into national Free Circulation based on the Tariff Inversion principle as described earlier in the text. This flexibility gives far more incentives for companies to use the Free Zone for either production, storage or general operation purposes, such as international trading of services, thus allowing a wide variety of companies to use the zone while enjoying a wide variety of fiscal incentives.

However, it must also be stated that, even within the above set of criteria and categories, there is no absolute demarcation between many of the Free Zone concepts. Each country where such Zones are located is host to different types of Free Zone depending upon national Free Zone policy as determined by national government. In the developing world, Free Zones have a much more varied function given that they are designed as vehicles for a combination of tax incentives in general as well as the encouragement of foreign inward investment. Foreign investment generated income for the country from external sources, and the concept of the EPZ encourages export-led economic growth. Therefore, government policies which engender such activity promote economic growth in their countries and thus seek to encourage greater levels of economic development in line with the policies of the UNCTAD. Indeed, the WEPZA, an organisation which was established by the UNIDO as an umbrella organisation coordinating and promoting the worldwide network of Export Processing Zones, existed as a means of promoting the development of EPZs on a global scale and encouraging their implementation and success. Although the organisation's secretariat has relocated from its previous base in Arizona, US, to the UK, it is still possible to access many of its publications in its form of the erstwhile Flagstaff Institute, and to determine the extent to which it promoted the whole concept of both Export Processing Zones and Free Zones in general. (The website is www.wepza.org.)

The supply chain

Freeports and Free Zones are intended to stimulate economic activity in their designated areas. Supporters argue that benefits can arise due to the government stimulus or tax incentives and breaks available. There can also be some benefits due to the 'agglomeration effect', which is where increased economic benefits are seen as a result of concentrating the economic activity of a particular sector, or related sectors, in one place.

Economic studies have found the main advantage of Freeports is that they encourage imports by lowering duty and paperwork costs, as well as a decrease in bureaucracy and red tape. Manufacturing businesses that are inside the Freeport can benefit from cheaper imported inputs/components in comparison to those outside the area and are subject to conventional Customs Imports controls and import duties.

In terms of the international supply chain, Free Zones eliminate much of the costs associated with the international flow of goods, especially materials and finished products. When one considers the implications of the international supply chain, from secondary Suppliers through primary Suppliers to the processor, and onwards to primary and secondary customers, it is easy to see where the increase in associated costs arises. Take the following sequence of the International Supply Chain concerning the relationship between Suppliers, Processors/Manufacturers and Customers, and these implications become evident:

SECONDARY SUPPLIERS

↓

PRIMARY SUPPLIERS

↓

PROCESSORS/MANUFACTURERS

↓

PRIMARY CUSTOMERS

↓

SECONDARY CUSTOMERS

A typical Supply Chain Diagram is as follows:

THE INTEGRATED SUPPLY-CHAIN NETWORK MODEL: A CUSTOMS PERSPECTIVE

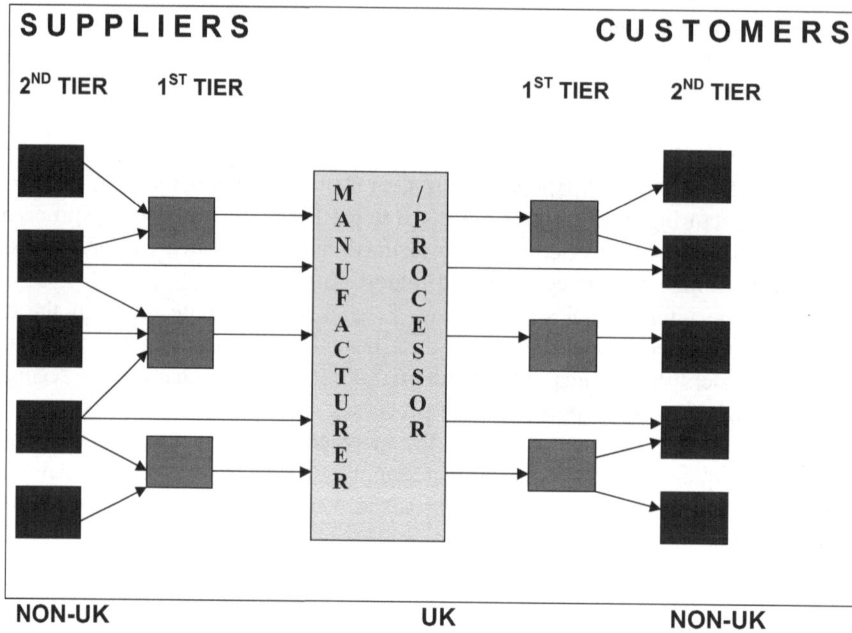

1. The Suppliers at **2nd Tier level** outside the UK supply the Suppliers at **1st Tier level** with raw materials.
2. The **1st Tier Suppliers** in turn supply the Manufacturer/Processor with semi-processed Components for incorporation in the finished product.
3. The Processor supplies the finished product to the **1st tier Customer**, which in turn may act as a Distributor (or as an onward Processor) and supply the finished product to the End-Customer, or the End-User, located at **2nd Tier level**.

Given the above scenario, as long as the Manufacturer knows that some or all of the raw materials (and hence the **2nd Tier Suppliers**) originate outside the UK, and that some or all of their 2nd Tier Customers are also located outside the EU, then they may use a Duty Relief Facility mechanism, in particular **Inward Processing Relief (IP)**, to ensure that they can minimise Import Duty liability on the products they manufacture. The only time where Import Duty becomes liable is where the finished product is destined for the UK market under Free Circulation conditions. In using an IP facility, the Manufacturer may also ensure that their **1st Tier Suppliers and Customers** are authorised to use the same IP authorisation or their own IP authorisation in order to complete the minimisation of Import Duty and Tax liabilities.

International movements of materials between secondary Suppliers and primary Suppliers accrue logistics and fiscal costs along the way; these costs are further compounded with each subsequent stage in the international supply chain. Import duties are always calculated on the combination of the purchase cost of the materials plus international transport costs on a CIF basis. It would normally be assumed that at each stage in the process, logistics costs, duties and taxes would be incurred at each import stage in the supply chain and would thus be absorbed into the overall supply chain costs. However, it must also be taken into account that at each of the stages in the supply chain, materials are imported, processed and subsequently re-exported. Customs provisions allow for Import Duty relief on materials that are imported, processed and then re-exported, and these can apply to both individual companies and Free Zone operations. In this case, the Free Zone concept removes Customs Duties and Taxes on goods that undergo this set of import and re-export activities. EPZs are specifically created for these kind of activities to take place, as the EPZ facility allows for the duty-suspended import of materials which are to be processed into finished or semi-finished products and then re-exported. Instead of these processes taking place in individual companies at a distance from each other, the EPZ allows companies collectively involved in these activities to cluster together in a designated Customs-approved EPZ. In this way, much, if not all, of the costs associated with import duties and taxes is automatically removed from the supply chain process. The net result is that the overall ultimate cost to the final customer or end-user is significantly removed because of the elimination in import duties along the way during the supply chain process. Logistics costs remain, but these would exist anyway as part of the supply chain process.

Duty deferral/suspension

The size of potential savings that businesses could accrue from duty deferral or suspension will depend on the following:

1. The value of goods imported;
2. The size of the tariff;
3. The interest rates on loans (i.e. cost of money); and
4. The average time that intermediate inputs are stored in a Free Zone before they are released for circulation.

For example, assume the following:

- Value of imports = £10,000
- Tariff (Import Duty rate) = 3%
- Interest rate = 5%
- Time in inventory in Free Zones = 3 months

The savings on duty deferral will then be equal to £3.75, a marginal amount.

The formula used to arrive at the £3.75 is as follows:

Tariff liability = value of imports x Import Duty rate
Savings on duty deferral = tariff liability x interest rate x (days in inventory/365)

Assuming that the average tariff rate on manufactured products stands at 3%, the prevailing interest rates on loans stand at 5% (p.a.) and that it takes three months for the inputs to be processed in a Free Zone and then released for circulation, the savings in duty deferral account for 0.0375% of the value of goods imported. However, this still presents cashflow savings, especially where the imported value is greater, essentially implying economies of scale. The other reason for this is that the importer of materials in bulk may not use these materials in a short space of time. It would be imprudent to pay Import Duty on the full imported amount when the sales of these materials may not materialise for some time; it is better to pay Import Duty on only the materials released into Free Circulation at the time of sale and supply of each individual consignment from the bulk load to the customer.

Of course, the higher the value of goods imported, the higher the value of savings that businesses can make from duty deferral. However, even if the goods imported were worth much more, for example £1,000,000, this still leaves £375 made in savings. The overall benefit is that the higher the Import Duty rates are, the greater the savings that can be achieved. Many products still have Import Duty rates of 5–6%, which increases the level of savings offered by a Freeport.

An example is automotive gearboxes (**HS code 870840**).

In 2017, the UK imported some US$3.037 billion worth of these (i.e. total UK imports). These originally faced an MFN (Most Favoured Nation) tariff of 3.81%, later reduced to 3% (with a further reduction to 2% in the UK Global Tariff following the UK's withdrawal from the EU Single Market at the end of 2020). Assume that only 10% of these gearboxes can be imported and processed in Free Zones (this is because of space constraints). And as above, let us assume an interest rate of 5%, and an average processing time in a Free Zone of three months. The total value of savings that will be made on deferring duty payments on gearboxes imported to Free Zones will be equal to US$140,000, which at the USD/GBP exchange rate of $1.29 = £1 makes it equal to a total of £110,000.

However, it should be pointed out that an automotive manufacturer such as Nissan or Toyota will require the import of a large number of gearboxes at any time to satisfy their production requirements, it makes better sense to import these consignments in bulk per 40-foot container into a Freeport, then only release smaller consignments into Free Circulation from the Freeport for delivery to the automotive production plant as required according to production schedules, and leave the rest of the load in the Freeport until required. Import Duty and VAT would therefore only be paid on the release of each smaller consignment from the Freeport as required by the automotive producer. The rest of the load remains in the Freeport on a duty-suspended basis.

The other element is re-export. Where goods are exported, they are zero-rated for VAT purposes. Where goods are re-exported from duty relief mechanisms such as IP, Customs Warehousing or Freeports/Free Zones, they are completely suspended from both Import Duty and VAT. If these goods were re-exported from Free Circulation, they would have been duty paid and thus import paid on them at import could not be reclaimed. If they are held in a Free zone/ Freeport, this Import Duty and VAT is suspended at the time of import, and thus remains suspended until the goods have been re-exported, along with the correct information entered upon the Customs Export Declaration at the time of re-export. This also means that there are less costs passed on to the ultimate importer, as Import Duty costs incurred when the goods arrive in the country of transit will not be levied, as the goods in question will not enter Free Circulation while in transit. This also benefits the overall supply chain, as much of the costs incurred in the international supply chain occur when goods are imported into Free Circulation at any point along the supply chain up until the point of ultimate consumption or end use of the finished product at its ultimate destination. Since these costs relate to import duties, where such duties can be removed as a result of using Free Zones or Freeports is of evident benefit in terms of onward costs being passed on through each stage in the chain. Indeed, the argument states that Import Duty should only be paid at the point that the finished product arrives in the ultimate country of destination, that is, where it is to be consumed or used by the consumer or end-user. Elsewhere, such duty should be suspended on the grounds that the materials involved in the supply chain are to be imported and processed into another product which will subsequently be re-exported to its next stage in the processing chain. This process thus continues until the ultimate finished product reaches its final country of destination, where Import Duty and tax (often VAT) will be paid by the ultimate importer. This implies that all goods in transit should be subject to some form of Import Duty relief at each stage in the process.

There is also a question of whether it will cost businesses more to store goods in a Free Zone, consequently reducing any savings made on duty deferral. On the one hand, storage costs will be incurred by businesses regardless of whether goods are stored in a Free Zone or elsewhere. On the other hand, it is possible to argue that storage costs will be higher in a Free Zone, because of the added security, and potential for businesses to make these additional savings in duty deferral and Tariff Inversion. This issue can be set aside but is something to bear in mind. However, against this, the whole aim is to overcome costly demurrage costs of goods being kept in Temporary Storage, and this is why Free Zone costs will be kept much more competitive in line with conventional Customs Warehousing costs, especially where 3PL logistics providers are concerned.

In addition to these potential savings that businesses can accrue from a Free Zone location, there is also the question of the costs that will be incurred by the taxpayers as a result of operating Free Zones. While this is a valid question to ask, it is intentionally left unanswered as there are no hard facts and numbers to provide strong answers. In reality, it is more than likely that the establishment and operational costs will be borne by the authorities implementing each of the Freeports, as each of the Zones is intended to be an individual autonomous venture.

Tariff Inversion applications

The US Foreign-Trade Zones are driven very much by the desire to avoid higher tariffs on inputs – than final outputs – and the US motor vehicle sector is one of the sectors where tariffs on inputs are higher. For example, because of inverted tariffs, a Volkswagen plant in Tennessee was estimated to save $1.9 million – or $13 per car – on producing 150,000 cars annually in Foreign-Trade Zones.

This issue is less significant for EU tariffs or likely UK tariffs. For example, in the motor vehicle sector (ISIC4 2910) EU tariffs are not inverted: importers of automotive parts face lower tariffs (4.5%) than importers of final cars (10%). The EU is, in fact, more often accused of tariff escalation rather than inversion.

A more tangible application of this to the EU is the example of computers (HS Code Tariff Chapter 8471). The UK Import Duty rate on computers is 0%, whereas the plastic moulds for casings are classed as Articles of Plastic, attracting an Import Duty rate of 6%. It makes better sense to import the components for the computers into a Free Zone, manufacture the products under Customs-controlled conditions (Inward Processing Relief), then release the finished product into Free Circulation at the duty rate of 0% but at the value of the imported components, using the principle of Tariff Inversion. Assuming that the finished products are re-exported to the EU, they still have an Import Duty rate of 0% under the EU tariff, notwithstanding their ineligibility for UK Origin status. This is surely a case of the whole not being equal to the sum of its parts.

CHAPTER 10

Financial and service Free Zones

Free Economic Zones (FEZ), Free Economic Territories (FETs) or Free Zones (FZ) are all defined as a class of SEZ, designated by the trade and commerce administrations of various countries, and are in many cases more flexible versions of the conventional Free Zone in terms of activities carried out in the zone. The term is generally used to designate areas in which companies are taxed very lightly or not at all to encourage economic activity, and the taxation rules for these Zones are determined by each country. The WTO Agreement on Subsidies and Countervailing Measures (SCM) has content on the conditions and benefits of Free Zones, and these Zones also include service-based Zones dealing in international financial and IT activities as well as physical merchandise. Indeed, such Zones are experiencing significant growth alongside existing physical product-based SEZs as a means of the attraction of inward overseas investment.

Although Free Zones are generally associated with the Customs-controlled storage and manufacture of materials and goods, other initiatives exist concerning Free Zones for the service-based sector, including finance, IT and other services. The financial and IT sectors in particular are favoured by many governments worldwide, as they promote inward investment by international companies, including banks, insurance companies, and in the case of the IT sector, software developers and Suppliers.

Dubai, in the UAE, is no exception, and indeed is a pioneer in this type of Free Zone. The area of Media City in the western part of the metropolis is an example of how the Free Zone concept can be used to attract inward investment based on fiscal incentives, including tax breaks. Dubai is a crossroads of international trade, and this has led to inward investment from all around the globe concerning a wide variety of international companies engaged in a variety of activities, including the trade in both goods and services. Most of the Free Zones in Dubai, of which there are more than 30 at present (2020), broadly offer trading, services and industrial licences to investors looking to establish their businesses in the zone. The section on Dubai in Part Two provides greater detail about several of the Dubai Free Zones.

Financial Free Zones

Free Zones are specific geographic areas within the UAE. Each Free Zone complies with special laws aimed at encouraging new business and attracting foreign investment.

DOI: 10.4324/9781003232025-11

Currently, there are about 30 Free Zones distributed among the different Emirates, all dealing with different types of commerce, from goods and materials to services of various kinds.

Financial Free Zones (FFZs) are Free Zones engaged in financial activities.

In the UAE, there are currently two FFZs:

- The Global Marketplace Abu Dhabi (under construction);
- The Dubai International Financial Centre (DIFC).

Activities within Financial Free Zones

Financial activities within FFZs include:

- Banking and finance;
- Insurance and reinsurance;
- Financial markets.

Support activities within FFZs include:

- Fiscal and monetary intermediation services;
- Providing services and consultations;
- Providing services to individuals or companies;
- Providing goods for companies, institutions and individuals within the financial Free Zones.

Established companies operating within an FFZ must comply with all UAE laws that apply outside the FFZ, except for civil and commercial laws, which are subject to the laws of the FFZ authority in question.

Branches of companies registered in an FFZ that also operate in the UAE outside the FFZ are subject to all UAE laws that apply outside the Free Zone, including civil and commercial laws.

Restrictions on organisations and individuals working in Free Zones

There are certain restrictions that FFZ authorities, companies and individuals working within them must follow.

In relation to banking activities, licensing is limited to companies and institutions that have:

- A strong financial status;
- An integrated organisational and management structure;
- Management with experience and knowledge of banking activities.

Companies inside a FFZ cannot deal in UAE currency and cannot take deposits from UAE markets.

Financial intermediaries authorised to trade in UAE financial markets are only allowed to operate in a FFZ market after obtaining approval from the Securities and Commodities Authority (SCA).

Companies listed on UAE trade markets are only allowed to be listed in any FFZ market after obtaining permission from the SCA.

Companies operating within a FFZ should not break any international treaty signed by the UAE.

Companies operating within a FFZ can:

- Operate outside the geographical boundaries of an FFZ, after obtaining a licence from the FFZ authority, for a period of up to four years from the date the FFZ was established;
- Work outside the UAE after obtaining a licence from the FFZ authority.

The main benefits of such Zones are that they are free from corporation and income taxes. However, the applicant companies must be able to justify to the authorities why they wish to take advantage of the fiscal incentives offered within the zone, and what benefits they will bring to the State, for example employment, contribution to the local and national economy, and overall national economic development. The service sector is a major source of economic development to many countries, and in many cases, Special Economic Zones encompass a hybrid set of activities relating to not only the trade in tangible goods, but also the trade in services. Logistics as a service facilitates the international movement of goods, but in most cases, logistics as a service is already a major element of international Free Zone activities.

Dubai Internet City

Dubai Internet City (DIC) is a specific service-based IT Free-Trade Zone, and provides a knowledge economy ecosystem designed to support the business development of information and communications technology (ICT) companies. It is the Middle East's biggest ICT infrastructure, built inside the Technology and Media Free-Trade Zone already established in the Emirate of Dubai, and located to the west of the main city. It is effectively a Special Economic Zone, although it does not trade in goods and is therefore not subject to Customs controls, but rather tax incentives.

Dubai Internet City, a member of Dubai Holding subsidiary TECOM Investments, was founded in October 1999, and it commenced activities in October 2000. Dubai Internet City is the Middle East and North Africa's largest information and communications technology hub. DIC has been created and designed to support ICT companies, standing out as the biggest ICT infrastructure built inside a Free Zone.

DIC, a forerunner in carrying forward Dubai's vision of transitioning into a knowledge-based economy, has successfully developed an ecosystem for technology organisations. It is home to the most prestigious global ICT giants, including Microsoft, Oracle, HP, IBM, Dell, Siemens, Canon, Logica, Sony Ericsson, Schlumberger and Cisco, as well as many small and medium enterprises and entrepreneurial ventures. Companies from various sectors, namely software development, business services, e-commerce, consultancy and sales and marketing are benefitting from various cost-effective solutions through Firststeps@dic, a facility that enables companies to conduct feasibility studies, evaluate future potential and search the market for new business or collaborative ventures, as well as working alongside existing and future enterprises operating within DIC without needing to make a large initial investment. However, even if large investments were necessary, these would soon be offset by the potential for business growth engendered by the significant fiscal incentives offered by the State to this facility.

Dubai Internet City business benefits include:

- No personal, income and corporate taxes (50-year exemption);
- 100% foreign ownership;
- Full repatriation of profits;
- Metro Ethernet environment;
- Dynamic international community;
- Networking opportunities;
- Market development opportunities;
- World-class communications infrastructure on new innovative technologies;
- Digital voice and high-speed data services offered at competitive rates;
- Commercial offices, Business Centres (Executive Desk and Executive Office) and Conference Facilities.

Legal entities inside Dubai Internet City

- Free Zone Limited Liability Company (FZ-LLC);
- Branch of a Foreign Company, where the applicant is a foreign registered corporate person;
- Branch of a UAE Company, where the applicant is a UAE registered corporate person.

Business infrastructure in Dubai Internet City

- Commercial offices;
- Business Centres with Executive Desk and Executive Office;
- Conference Facilities;
- Amenities – Star Hotels, Fitness Facilities, Dining and Retail, Banking & ATM, Medical, Security and Public Safety.

VAT on transactions within designated Zones

The UAE introduced VAT at 5% on all domestic business transactions as well as imported goods on 1 January 2018. However, the UAE also made the provision that for all designated and non-designated Free Zones in the UAE, VAT would not be applicable in certain circumstances. The rules concerning these specific VAT conditions are:

a) Goods transferred between designated Zones are not subject to VAT. However, goods supplied by an entity in the designated zone to entities outside the designated zone are subject to 5% VAT.
b) Services provided by an entity to other entities inside the designated zone or outside the designated zone are subject to 5% VAT.
c) Professional fees for services are subject to VAT @ 5%.

To this extent, the Dubai Financial and Internet City Free-Trade Zones are not Customs-controlled Zones, but are SEZs defined by location and area and subject to government tax incentives in order to foster international business growth, hence their tax-free status.

These incentives are specifically allowed and encouraged in order to boost the influx of Foreign Direct Investment and hence commercial growth in the specific fields of Finance and Information Technology, which are seen as global economic growth trends and catalysts, and which have become an integral part of the UAE economy in terms of the attraction of overseas investment.

Dubai Technology and Media Free Zone

The Dubai Technology and Media Free Zone **(DTMFZ)** was developed by TECOM Investments and is made up of nine business parks operating as separate entities. The Dubai Technology and Media Free Zone Authority (DTMFZA) has divided the Free Zone into four clusters:

- The Media cluster;
- The Education cluster;
- The Information and communication (ICT) cluster;
- The Sciences cluster.

The Dubai Technology and Media Free Zone Authority is also the only regulator in the Free Zone. In 2003, the DTMFZA enabled the Technology and Media Free Zone Companies Regulations which applies to other Free Zones among which the Dubai Internet City, Knowledge Village, the Dubai Outsource Zone and Dubai Studio City.

According to the DTMFZA, each type of company will be issued a business license depending on the cluster it belongs to. License categories have been classified under different segments and each segment encompasses an established number of activities. The types of licences issued by the Dubai Technology and Media Free Zone Authority are:

- Free zone limited liability companies licenses under the publishing segment;
- Licences under the broadcasting TV and radio segments;
- Licences under the food segment;
- Licences under the storage activity segment;
- Licences under the manufacturing and productivity segment;
- Licences under the higher education provider segment.

Each type of company registered in the Dubai Technology and Media Free Zone is subject to certain requirements, such as a minimum number of shareholders and minimum capital requirements.

One of the greatest advantages for setting up a company in the Technology and Media Free Zone in Dubai is the variety of licences available for company incorporation. In a Dubai Free Zone, investors may set up companies with 100% foreign ownership. No personal or corporate taxes will be applied to Dubai Free Zone companies for 50 years. Other tax advantages are full repatriation of capital and profits and no Customs Duties for goods and services.

CHAPTER 11

WEPZA and WFZO

WEPZA

Given its role in the development and overall oversight over the operation and function of the global EPZ network, it is only fair and justifiable to make reference to the existence and function of the WEPZA. The WEPZA was the creation of the UNIDO throughout the 1970s to enable and help developing countries enhance export production through the concept of Export Processing Zones. Based on the success of forerunner EPZs like the Shannon Free Zone in Ireland and Masan in South Korea, as well as the Mexican Maquiladora sector established as a result of the Mexican BIP of 1965, UNIDO concluded that EPZs could simultaneously serve as pilots for initiating trade-liberalisation reforms nationwide and as mechanisms for diversifying and increasing exports. It therefore engaged numerous experts from successful EPZ projects and began offering technical assistance to countries considering EPZ projects.

By 1974, representatives of UNIDO formed a working group to consider the creation of a more formal association of EPZ experts. Through this association, UNIDO could devise international Standards for EPZs and offer consultation on feasibility studies, site development, operation and other aspects of EPZ development. Finally, on 4 February 1978, representatives of UNIDO and of EPZ regulatory authorities in 29 countries gathered in Manila, Philippines, to officially form WEPZA, or the 'World Export Processing Zones Association' as it was then known. It was headed up by Richard Bolin, who had previously been involved with the Mexican Border Industrialisation Program of 1965, and Robert Haywood, who also directed the Flagstaff Institute, the publication arm of WEPZA, at its home at Flagstaff, Arizona. Together, these two leaders not only promoted the work of WEPZA and its influencing role over the direction and function of the global network of Export Processing Zones, but also produced a series of informative articles and papers on various characteristics, aspects and facets of EPZ operations and functions. Even after the passing of Richard Bolin and under the organisation's present leadership, the work of WEPZA is still an influential factor in how EPZs operate throughout the world.

From 1978 to 1985, WEPZA consisted of representatives of governments with EPZs and operated under the auspices of UNIDO. For UNIDO, WEPZA provided crucial training programs for zone officials. Other partner organisations also supplied UNIDO with studies to help improve EPZ performance: the Asian Productivity Organization, which measured the productivity and efficiency of Zones, and the International Labour Organisation (ILO), which measured the social, economic and employment-generation effects of Zones.

DOI: 10.4324/9781003232025-12

In 1985, WEPZA reorganised as an independent entity. Instead of consisting exclusively of governmental members, WEPZA became a unique hybrid, with both governmental and non-governmental members, including private EPZ developers and operators and consultants. The Flagstaff Institute, a non-profit research organisation, took over management of WEPZA as its secretariat.

In the succeeding years, WEPZA membership grew to include 60 EPZs and 66 countries and provided training seminars, conferences, and workshops dedicated to improving the performance of EPZs as a vehicle for development. It published a journal, then called the *Journal of the Flagstaff Institute*, which provided a full breadth of empirical scholarship and academic articles on EPZs for the public, the academic world, professionals and industry.

As stated by WEPZA, the Free Zone concept continues to evolve and expand to include new terminology and functions. There are now 'Special Economic Zones', 'Free Zones', 'Free-Trade Zones', 'Foreign-Trade Zones', 'Industrial Development Zones', and so on, with each zone classified according to the national requirements of the governments establishing their own type of zone, as well as by UNCTAD. Because of this, WEPZA is no longer simply an acronym but exists to promote all special-status spatial-development Zones. WEPZA has also renamed its journal as the *Flagstaff Journal of Special Economic Zones*.

Today, WEPZA is, as stated on its website, an association of zone operators and developers, consultants and academics offering practical assistance to Zones through collaboration and knowledge sharing. Its efforts continue to enhance the development impact of Zones all over the world. WEPZA is presently based in Deal, Kent, in the south-east of the UK, and currently advises EPZs and national governments on the merits and advantages of Free Zones in general, as well as providing direction in such activities. More details on the organisation, its activities and its management can be found at www.wepza.org. Alongside the websites of other organisations associated with Free Zone activity, WEPZA is one of the prime drivers of Free Zone operations, especially those of Export Processing Zones.

It should also be pointed out that WEPZA is not the only organisation representing Free Zones. There are several other organisations providing similar services and acting as catalysts for Free Zone operations and networking, including, *inter alia*, the WFZO. WEPZA may be one of the best-known of these organisations, but it is by no means unique. The WFZO is equally a major influence on Free Zone development, collaboration and coordination, and, like the WEPZA, covers the operations of the global network of Free Zones.

WFZO

The World Free Zones Organization (World FZO) is a global not-for-profit organisation that claims to provide one authoritative, collective voice representing the interests of Free Zones around the world.

The World FZO was launched in Dubai, UAE, in May 2014, by its 14 founding members and under the auspices of His Highness Sheikh Mohammed bin Rashid Al Maktoum, Vice President and Prime Minister of the UAE, and Ruler of Dubai, the home of one of the largest international Free Zones in the world, namely the Jebel Ali Free Zone. Registered in Geneva and headquartered in Dubai, the World FZO also claims to be the only truly international, multilateral organisation for Zones in the world today.

As stated by the WFZO, the Free Zone concept, in its many forms, has gained popularity over the past few decades, particularly in the emerging economies of Asia, the Middle East and Africa. From the first Free Zone at Shannon Airport in 1959, the model has proliferated to the point where there are an estimated 2,260 Free Zones around the world, which support approximately 70 million jobs.

In addition, to ensure they receive the international recognition and support they deserve, the role of these Zones as exemplary models of modern infrastructure, as creators of employment opportunities and as integrators of services, logistics and transport networks, should be highlighted and emphasised.

The WFZO states that Free Zones have played a critical role in the economies of many countries and to ensure they have the greatest possible impact, they need a global, unifying association to bring them together. One that can represent their interests, share their achievements and support their continuous positive development. It is to address this need that the World FZO has been created.

The Board of Directors and Executive Management of the World FZO has established a number of key objectives which form the mandate for the association and underpin all the World FZO's activities:

1. Bring together Free Zones; regional, national, subnational and local Free Zone associations; consultants and advisers to Free Zones; Free Zone users; interested governmental organisations; and international trade-related organisations, for knowledge exchange, education and training, networking and business development;
2. Provide a forum for Free Zones around the world to learn, grow and prosper through unrivalled access to exclusive in-depth research and insights;
3. Create 'best-in-class' Standards for Free Zones that enhance the economic ecosystem both globally and in local markets, as well as guidelines for the establishment and administration of Free Zones;
4. Gather, create, expand and disseminate the knowledge of, and about, Free Zones internationally;
5. Improve the perception of Free Zones globally and position them as areas that make valuable contributions to the local economy and promote sustainable business;
6. Provide specialised operational, administrative, educational and networking services to Members, Partners and Observers through trainings as well as physical and electronic resources;
7. Support and advise new Free Zones internationally as they develop;
8. Become the global leader on Free Zones and issues relating to them.

On 13 and 14 January 2014, a steering committee of 26 leaders and academics met to finalise the details on the creation of a unifying non-governmental entity to bring together Zones from across the globe to share their achievements, exchange best practices and knowledge, support their continuous positive development and to ensure the sustainability and continued success of the Free Zone model. This initiative led to the official launch of the World Free Zones Organization on 19 May 2014, in Dubai, UAE.

The CEO of WFZO is Dr Samir Hamrouni, and the following are members of the steering committee and the first Board of Directors (as at 2021):

Dr. Mohammed Alzarooni
Director General of Dubai Airport Free Zone (DAFZA)
Martin Ibarra
Honorary President and founder of the Free Zones Association of the Americas (AZFA)
PC Nambiar
Director of SEZ Biotech Services PVT Ltd, Pune, India
Rose Hynes
Chairman of Shannon Group plc
Julie Brown
President & CEO of Georgia Foreign-Trade Zone
Kenneth Carlstedt
Global Trade Compliance Manager for Momentive
Isidoro Hodara
Isidoro Hodara, Director Zonamérica, Vicepresident Uruguay
Chris Ndibe
CEO of Carclon Group
Jose Luis Rodriguez
Director Comercial y Director de la Zona Franca Aduanera del Consorcio La Zona Franca De Barcelona (Commercial Director and Director of the Customs Free Zone of the Consortium of the Free Zone of Barcelona)
Mehdi Tazi
Board Member at TMSA, Tanger-Med Special Agency and Managing Director of Tanger Free Zone
François Bost
Professor of Economic Geography at the University of Reims Champagne-Ardenne (URCA) in France. He is a member of the laboratory HABITER (EA 2076) and has written the UNCTAD Report on Free Zones.
Nasser Al Madani
Assistant Director General at Dubai Airport Free Zone (DAFZA)

WFZO National Contact Points exist in several countries, namely:

Afghanistan
Argentina
Armenia
Bosnia/Herzegovina
Bulgaria
China
Colombia
Costa Rica
Croatia
Dominican Republic

Gabon
Georgia
Ghana
Haïti
India
Ivory Coast
Jamaica
Jordan
Kazakhstan
Latvia
Lithuania
Mali
Mauretania
Mexico
Mozambique
Morocco
Nigeria
North Macedonia
Senegal
Serbia
Spain
Sri Lanka
Togo
Tunisia
Uganda
Uruguay
USA

Other countries which operate Free Zones are not represented on this list, such as Brazil, Canada, Mauritius, Russia and Turkey.

The representatives of these countries are mainly national representatives of their respective national or individual Free Zone Authorities, as well as promotional agencies, and serve as contact points for those companies wishing to ascertain more information about the various national Free Zone regimes and how these Zones may be of use to the companies concerned.

The WFZO and WEPZA are not necessarily rivals, as WFZO is a more modern organisation dealing with global Free Zones, and operates on a more practical basis. WEPZA, however, has done more to highlight and promote the use of Export Processing Zones, and, through its Flagstaff publishing arm, has produced more academic and professional articles about the subject over several years, thus demonstrating a greater degree of maturity and historical basis than its counterparts.

CHAPTER 12

Free Zone security and risk

Because of the nature of the Free Zone as a Customs-controlled enclave, there is always the need for tight security. Although tax-Free Zones function as parts of other urban and commercial communities, the companies operating within these Zones are subject to constant monitoring by the revenue authorities, and must submit copious reports and statements about their operating and commercial activities in order to satisfy the authorities of their level of compliance. In 2020, the UAE Central Bank signed an agreement with the Dubai Multi-Commodities Centre requiring that Free Zone to share information on any financial transaction suspected of having links to money laundering for the possible purpose of terrorist financing. The agreement requires that a compliance officer will operate within the Free Zone and monitor financial transactions.

Security in general is required as part of any Customs approval. All national Customs and Revenue Authorities impose strict conditions as part of Free Zone applications, and both the Free Zone Authority and its tenants must be able to show as part of their application process that they are able to impose strict security conditions as required by national Free Zone law.

Customs-controlled Free Zones and Freeports are no exception. Any typical Free Zone must operate a set of controllable security systems, including its access control systems, perimeter intruder detection, automated vehicle identification and visitor management systems. It is not possible for unauthorised people to access the zone, as it is a controlled area, and all visitors must report to the reception in the Free Zone office or a manned gatehouse. Indeed, in most cases, all visitors must register with the zone operator in advance of arrival, so that their personal details can be checked and verified. This prevents any form of criminal or suspicious activities, especially concerning contraband or smuggling. Furthermore, the Free Zone or Freeport must be surrounded by secure fencing as a designated zone segregated form the surrounding areas, with a single gatehouse leading to the external environment, and a further gatehouse leading to the port environment as deemed appropriate. However, in some cases, Free Zones are deemed to be an extension of the port and may have nominal controls between the port and the Free Zone depending upon the level of security deemed necessary in the specific location. In terms of documentation, goods will not be allowed to leave a zone unless the driver of the vehicle carrying the consignments concerned has the correct clearance paperwork with him at the time of exit, or at the very least the reference numbers relating to the Customs clearance. It is normal practice that an appropriately endorsed document called a Goods Release Note or Out-of-Charge Note (C130 in the case of the UK) is issued to the driver for presentation to the gatehouse at the point of exit from the port/Free Zone.

DOI: 10.4324/9781003232025-13

If such a document is not available, the goods cannot be released from the zone until the appropriate document has been correctly issued and submitted.

Crime

It has been intimated in some quarters that Free-Trade Zones are attractions for criminal activity. This view, although based on certain figures and reported activities, is not a foregone conclusion. Journals such as the *New York Times* have reported that some of the Middle East Free Zones have been the target for criminals, and indeed the EU published a report that suggested that works of art and antiques that had been stolen from elsewhere were seized at a Geneva Freeport. The *NY Times* reported that counterfeiting and money laundering can flourish in these Zones, typically manufacturing and warehousing sites near ports and airports, where governments relax tax and regulatory requirements to attract foreign investment and ease the rapid movement of goods.

A report by Richard Heath and James Tumbridge of Venner & Shipley, issued in February 2020 and which severely criticised the [ab]use of Free Zones, stated that throughout the world there has been abuse of Free Zones by organised crime syndicates, often known to Interpol, that facilitate the manufacture, distribution and sale of counterfeit goods but this is not to suggest that all FTZs accommodate or facilitate such illegal activity. The 2010 OECD report on Money Laundering Vulnerabilities of Free-Trade Zones, for example, delineates these abuses to include 'participation in an organised criminal group and racketeering, illicit trafficking in narcotics, fraud, counterfeiting and piracy of products, and smuggling'.

The report states that most FTZs operate as an important and legitimate tool within a country's economy, facilitating international trade and development. However, the same features of FTZs that provide legitimate business opportunities can be exploited and misused by organised crime groups to produce, distribute and sell counterfeit goods. When this criminal activity is allowed to occur in full sight without enforcement, or worse is simply ignored, the underlying objectives of the Free Zones to promote trade and economic growth are eventually destroyed. The report states that there is therefore an urgent need to address this type of abuse before it takes hold, preferably in advance of the system being launched in a country largely new to FTZs, such as the UK.

According to the definitive OECD report on the Economic Impact of Counterfeiting and Piracy (2008, updated 2016), the total global economic value of counterfeit and pirated products was US$509 billion in 2016, which is equivalent to 2.5% of imported goods worldwide and within the EU the number is even higher, at 5%. The OECD notes that FTZs have emerged as a facilitator of IPR (Intellectual Property Rights) abuses and concludes that 'the lack of controls has made the Free-Trade areas attractive locations for parties engaging in trade of counterfeit/pirated products'. The report goes on to explain how parties import counterfeit goods into FTZs to 'sanitise' shipments, disguise origin, add counterfeit trademarks, manufacture and repackage finished counterfeit goods for export, and use FTZs as 'gateways' for smuggling and trans-shipping fake products. The OECD notes that these parties conduct these illicit activities with little or no risk of IPR-related enforcement. In their 2018 report to the EU's Intellectual Property Office, they noted that where economic activity is driven by reduced taxes and Customs controls, light regulation and limited oversight, it can unintentionally foster growth in counterfeit goods trafficking. Another OECD report on the Governance Frameworks to Counter Illicit Trade pointed to poor oversight of Free-Trade Zones, insufficient screening of small parcels and inconsistent penalties on shippers of fake goods as three key areas where lax policy is facilitating trafficking of fake goods. As well as infringing trademarks and copyright, counterfeit and pirated goods entail health and safety risks, product malfunctions and loss of income for companies and governments.

The point about limited oversight is one of the inherent weaknesses with some Customs and Revenue Authorities. Although typical Free Zone law states what Free Zone Authorities and operators are supposed to do as allowed by national Free Zone legislation, such legislation does not necessarily detail what security measures are supposed to be implemented and enforced by Free Zone Authorities, hence the variation in levels of security between Free Zones on both a regional and national basis. Authorities such as HMRC place very strict rules and regulations on Freeport management, as this essential set of rules and regulations has been in place ever since the UK's 1984 Finance Act, and has never been replaced, although it has been amended and updated in line with the UK Government's latest Freeport initiative of 2020. However, although compromise to the national revenue through duty and tax suspension has been largely taken care of in most cases, the issue of monitoring what happens inside the zone is a significantly vague area, given the range of allowable activities that take place within the Zones.

The report continues by stating that, unfortunately, organised crime groups and counterfeiters have also taken an interest in FTZs, and they are exploiting the very system that governments have put in place to help FTZs contribute to economic development. There are now more than 3,500 Free-Trade Zones around the world, often located at key ports, in 130 countries in every continent. This is up from just 79 in only 25 countries in 1975. They have certainly facilitated trade and by so doing have helped emerging economies to attract foreign investment and generate jobs and growth; they have also benefitted wealthier economies such as the USA, Singapore and Hong Kong. The Standards, oversight and regulations governing FTZs have not kept pace with these developments and, as a result, organised criminal syndicates are increasingly exploiting FTZs. Halting this trend from the outset therefore is paramount, but, according to Venner & Shipley, it must start with three fundamental understandings:

1. FTZs are part of the National Territory and Jurisdiction in which they are located;
2. FTZs are physical locations for goods of a particular status for Customs' purposes;
3. Simplified regulation does not mean impunity.

Point 1 is somewhat erroneous. FTZs are outside national Customs jurisdiction, given that goods held in an FTZ are suspended from Import Duty and VAT. This means that such goods are under Customs control, and therefore effectively in international status, as they have not yet been brought into Free Circulation. In this respect, FTZs are therefore not part of national territory and jurisdiction, especially from a duty, tax and fiscal perspective.

Owing to a concerted campaign of awareness raising and capacity building by IP (Intellectual Property) Rights holders (brand owners) through Public-Private Partnerships with International Governmental and Non-Governmental Organisations and Institutions over the past 20 years or more, government policymakers are now increasingly recognising the economic drain caused by counterfeiting and piracy. They understand the vulnerabilities of FTZs which are exacerbating the problem, and they know that they face the daunting task of balancing trade controls with trade facilitation. Since FTZs are geared towards free movement of goods, potential measures to tighten governance could hinder trade. Nevertheless, effective IPR enforcement in FTZs does not mean that policymakers must sacrifice their goal of using FTZs to facilitate legitimate international trade and development.

Rather, voluntary establishment of Standards and improved practices, along with the implementation of specific FTZ legislative and regulatory measures, can help address the global threat of counterfeiting and piracy in FTZs, without impeding their effectiveness. The risk accepted, FTZs have become significant contributors to both national economic growth in the countries in which they are located as well as becoming critical to the integrated global economy – and their impact continues to grow.

A report issued by CICAD, the Inter-American Drug Abuse Control Commission, part of the organisation of American States (OAS), detailed a series of best practices covering Port and Free Zone security, in the face of security challenges being faced by both ports and Free Zones in the Americas. It stated as follows:

> Such facilities, coupled with the variety and volume of goods that are traded in these areas are attractive to criminal groups engaged in drug trafficking and related crimes, which makes it mandatory to adopt mechanisms to control the activities that are developed. These areas are attractive to organised crime because there are a lot of movement of goods whose control is difficult and, therefore, are vulnerable to, *inter alia*, the following threats: terrorism, drug trafficking, money laundering, Intellectual Property, Unfair Competition, Theft of Trade, trafficking, Sabotage.

Under this perspective, there is a need to harmonise the rules for use of areas, to combat the above threats and promote the principle of social responsibility between the State and individuals, to prevent areas (i.e. Free Zones) from being used for activities related to drug trafficking, promoting information exchange among member countries.

Therefore, it is necessary to create a model of best practices to try to harmonise the rules at international level in order to safeguard all countries of the potential threats for the Free-Trade Zones in Ports and Tax-Free Ports.

1. **To have a system to verify the identity of all persons who must enter the port facilities and limit access to people outside the area.**

Implementation of the use of an access control system to the areas can be achieved through the following mechanisms:

- Visible passes.
- Control of the areas in which there are people outside the Free Zone.
- Number of employees in uniforms.

2. **Manage a proper control of vehicles.**

To effectuate the control of entry and exit of vehicles to the areas, the following controls must be generated:

- Numbers of people in vehicles.
- Have visible registration in the transportation.
- A limited number of members within the vehicle entering.

3. **Inspections of persons, personal effects, vehicles entering and leaving the commercial area.**

The preventive activity and investigation of crimes, under the use of records, avoids the destruction of evidence, which may itself determine the flagrancy of the offence, thus:

- In the entrances and exits to detect weapons, drugs or illegal items, and search for technology to take photographs or capture images.

4. **Identify the doors not used regularly and close them permanently.**

This action will limit the number of access points to the zone, with the effect of increasing the existing controls.

5. **Keep strict records of employees and others who work in the open area.**

It is essential to promote the implementation of physical security activities in the common areas and companies, through:

- 24-hour security;
- Spinning doors at entrances and exits of the area;
- Electronic passes reader;
- Use of metal detectors;
- Check of briefcases and suitcases.

6. **Maintaining a unit to detect narcotics.**

Having a specialised unit or an interdisciplinary group in the detection and monitoring of both narcotics and precursor chemicals in the Free-Trade Zones in Ports and Freeports and Free Zones will lead to direct efforts to counteract maritime narcotrafficking on strategic points of the terminal, to monitor the perimeters of the springs and the access channel for ships, as well as coverage of the area.

7. **Establish a system of closed circuit video and secure technology.**

Electronic surveillance in areas of common use, the development of effective media, the fingerprint control of the entry and exit of employees and the computerisation of business records are highly productive tools in the fight against drug trafficking, especially if promoted by the following means:

- Closed circuit video system;
- Perimeter alarm system;
- Intrusion detection system;
- Use of radios for internal communication connected to a control centre;
- Control of entrance and exit of employees system;
- Carrier identification system.

8. To have a system of advanced information for movement of goods.

With this type of action you can have information about the cargo 24 hours prior to the arrival at the port and at the same time control its departure with the same amount of time, thus enabling the profiling and assessment risk, but principally will rise the verification of full compliance of the requirements that the cargo in Free-Trade Zones demand.

- This measure ensures the execution of all tasks related to the protection of the port facility.
- Allows to control the restricted areas so only authorised personal can have access.
- Facilitate the supervision of cargo handling.
- Ensure the immediate availability of the means of communications about protection.

9. Establish a special and segregated area for inspection of suspicious cargo.

In this special area where all the goods entering and leaving the area are examined, based on a risk profile, a methodology should be developed for security assessments, and there should be plans and procedures to react against drug trafficking activities.

10. Collection and use of scanners for non-intrusive or invasive inspections.

This technology will allow the detection of explosives and narcotics, in the cargo that enters, departs or passes through the port, as well as prevent and combat the use of installations and port facilities for illegal purposes, thereby affecting the enhancement of security and protection against maritime narcotrafficking.

11. Institute a program to perform routine inspections of warehouses and stores in the Tax-Free Zones with canine units to verify the cargo or existing merchandise.

The implementation of mechanisms for regular monitoring and control of warehouses and stores of the companies established in the areas aims to prevent activities related to drug trafficking and related crimes. This can be made effective through the use of:

- Dogs to detect narcotics (passive and active);
- Patrol dogs and handlers;
- Qualified guides for the detection of illegal substances;
- Service available on a 24-hour basis.

12. In the case of Free-Trade Zones in ports, the documentation of cargo that was declared should be analysed along with the certification of the existing cargo at the warehouse.

It is necessary to promote the analysis and monitoring of the commercial labour that reflects in each company within the Free-Trade Zone in Port. The analysis suggested in this case is designed to prevent activities related to drug trafficking, in particular:

- Search for indicators or warning signs.
- Indicators with unanswered logic will generate a higher level of risk.
- The frequency of analysing the documents by 90% reduces the search for suspicious cargo to 10%.
- According to the results, profiles can be established.

For more certainty of the analysis is essential to encourage the computerisation of the records of the commercial enterprises established in the Zones.

13. Constitute a risk analysis group to establish criminal profiles according to the type of merchandise.

This group will generate matrices, profiles and risk assessments of routes, from the ports of origin, transit and destination of the cargo of the economic agents involved and the nature of it, in order to limit the actions of drug traffickers.

14. Implement a continuous training of staff in procedures and techniques to search for narcotics and other dangerous substances.

It is required to encourage the inter-agency training of public and private in subjects related with the traffic of illegal substances. This has the objective to assist with the help in the fight against drug trafficking, especially in the following aspects:

- Knowledge of current trends and threats related to protection.
- Recognition and detection of weapons and narcotics.
- Recognition of characteristics and behavioural patterns of persons who are likely to threaten security.
- Techniques for managing and controlling crowds.
- Communications related with protection.
- Operation of equipment and protection systems.
- Testing, calibration and maintenance of protection systems.
- Techniques for inspection, monitoring and observation.
- Methods of physical searches of persons, personal effects and baggage loading.

The above practices may appear to be radical, but they are seen as a general guideline for all global Free Zone operations, and are incorporated in some form or other in all national legislation concerning the security of Free Zone operations, especially where the Free Zones concerned are defined by security fencing and gatehouses. In the case of more flexible Zones, such as Special Economic Zones and Financial Free Zones, such security is delegated to companies located within the zone to manage their own security affairs, as specific security measure such as fencing and CCTV cameras are not in evidence.

Another report, commissioned by the Royal United Services Institute (RUSI) and published in 2020, highlighted other concerns. The report identified factors that render Free-Trade Zones vulnerable to illicit trade and financial crime and proposes measures to detect and prevent it. To explore common challenges and responses that transcend countries' individual circumstances, it examines four country case studies: Morocco, Panama, Singapore and the UAE.

Based on 74 interviews, two research workshops and an analysis of publicly available literature, the report identified key challenges faced by the case study countries, which were also likely to apply to other countries hosting FTZs.

- **The lack of consistent international Standards and incentives for the policing of goods passing through FTZs in transit.** Ensuring that FTZs are not abused for criminal gain tends to be a secondary national objective, especially if the goods transiting or being processed in an FTZ never enter the host jurisdiction. Although this gives rise to illicit trade risks that adversely impact foreign trading partners, the experience of case study countries suggests that they face much more international pressure in relation to tax competition matters, whereas illicit trade prevention has not been nearly as prominent an issue.
- **Inadequate understanding of FTZ-related criminal risks in general and financial crime risks specifically, including at the stage of planning and approving the establishment of an FTZ.** At a universal level, all logistics hubs – including sea and rail terminals and airports – are vulnerable by virtue of facilitating high volumes of trade at the fastest pace possible. What makes FTZs different, however, is that they operate under liberalised conditions, including simplified Customs procedures. These risks are not always taken into account at the stage of planning and approving an FTZ. Even once an FTZ is in operation, disagreements may persist in relation to key facts pertinent to its criminal profile, such as the volume of cash transactions in the zone. This patchy understanding of risk impedes risk-based law enforcement efforts, anti-money laundering/counterterrorist-financing (AML/CTF) supervision and efforts to prevent sanctions and export control evasion.
- **Uncertainty in the division of responsibility for the monitoring, governance and regulation of FTZs, including limited information sharing and failure to involve Customs agencies in FTZ-level risks assessment.** Despite the variety of approaches to FTZ governance, there is in general some degree of reliance by governments on FTZ administrators to operate the zone, who in turn expect FTZ users to abide by the rules. With the multiplicity of other authorities governing the zone in some capacity, from Customs agencies to the police, this arrangement requires clarity about responsibilities and effective coordination, including information sharing. Intuitive though they are, these principles are more honoured in the breach than in the observance. For instance, simply because an FTZ administrator is supposed to carry out due diligence on prospective users does not mean that this takes place to a high standard and the administrator has the right staffing, training and IT resources.
- **The absence of credible monitoring of FTZ administrators and users, as well as the resulting gap in enforcement.** With little to no information publicly available on the monitoring of FTZ administrators' security-related performance, it does not appear likely to entail any more robust approach than having an informal conversation with the administrator if the zone's activities reflect poorly on the country's reputation. Similarly, FTZ users frequently operate in the absence of meaningful oversight. In some cases, there is little to oversee to begin with, as FTZ users face no significant obligations to ascertain that they are not facilitating illicit trade when acting on behalf of third parties.

- **The lack of proportionate sanctions and AML/CTF supervision of FTZ-based businesses that would take account of the risk profile and volume of FTZ activities.** Although no less exacting AML/CTF rules tend to apply within FTZs than in the rest of the territory, the volume and diverse nature of activities in FTZs present challenges that compound the usual difficulties of AML/CTF supervision.
- **Limited cooperation with the private sector**. Despite the contribution that logistics companies and intellectual property rights holders can make to FTZ integrity by volunteering information to FTZ administrators and/or State authorities, gaps remain in both incentivising them to do so and providing avenues for regular submission of information. In contrast, the financial sector is both obligated to report suspicious activity and has a formal process for doing so, but regulators do not often tell financial institutions how to recognise suspicious activity relating to FTZs.

The report stated that these challenges are formidable but not insurmountable. Over the past year, progress has been made, including by the OECD with its Code of Conduct for Clean Free-Trade Zones and the World Free Zones Organization – an industry group representing over 600 FTZs around the world – with its Safe Zone certification program. Advances have also been made at the national level.

To support the implementation of the new international Standards, as well as to address other issues identified in the course of the research, the report made a range of recommendations in the areas of policing FTZs, namely;

- Understanding FTZ-related criminal risks;
- Dividing responsibilities in FTZ governance and ensuring coordination;
- Implementing AML/CTF and sanctions measures; and
- Cooperating with the private sector.

According to data from European Union Customs, the Emirates were the second source of counterfeit goods, after only China, in 2008 and 2009. The Zones' susceptibility to illegal activities was also cited earlier this year by the Financial Action Task Force, an international watchdog organisation based in Paris that coordinates and monitors government efforts to block money laundering and terrorist financing. Free-Trade Zones do improve economic opportunity, but the characteristics that make these enclaves attractive to business also create chances for illicit programs that can finance terrorism, the task force warned.

According to the Financial Action Task Force, the screening of cargo is often carried out by random selection more than on risk assessment or indicators. It also stated that no clear procedure, authority or documentation was identified to organise and execute the examinations. In Jebel Ali, however, security is at its tightest, owing to the sheer volume of cargoes entering and leaving the zone at any time. It should be noted that Dubai Customs regularly track and seize items ranging from toothpaste to medicine suspected of being counterfeit goods.

The EU itself decided to conduct investigations on 82 free ports and Free Zones in the EU, mostly in Central and Eastern Europe, after apparently identifying that their special tariff and duty status had aided the financing of terrorism, money laundering and organised crime. Evidence supporting this view is questionable, and it may be that such a stance on the part of the EU may be at best questionable itself, given that there is little proof that such illicit activities have indeed been taking place. A set of new rules was introduced by the European Commission just weeks before the launch of the UK Government consultation on the creation of up to ten free ports in the post-Brexit UK, and this set of rules restricts EU Free Zone operations and functions to a large degree, even to the point that some Free Zones, including the famous Shannon Free Zones, no longer have Free Zone status but have been relegated to simple industrial zone status within the national fiscal regimes where they are located. Indeed, the EU is not favourable to Free Zone regimes in general, and it is perceived that the EU administration wishes to remove Free Zone status from many such Zones if at all possible, especially in Western Europe. In Central and Eastern Europe, Free Zones still have a part to play in regional economic development, and it is to be hoped that such Free Zones will continue to exist for a long time forward.

Authorities across the EU have been obliged to take extra measures to identify and report suspicious activities at the ports and Zones as a result of what has been claimed to be the high incidence of corruption, tax evasion and criminal activity, although this was never proven. The EU Commission claimed that Freeports, popular for the storage of art, precious stones, antiques, gold and wine as alternative assets to cash, posed an emerging threat in multiple ways. It was alleged that the ports allowed counterfeiters to land consignments, tamper with loads or associated paperwork and re-export the products without Customs intervention, disguising the true origin and nature of the goods, and the identity of the original supplier. The Commission said they were also used for narcotics trafficking, the illegal ivory trade, people smuggling, VAT fraud, corruption and money laundering. However, this was never proven, although it has been seized upon by a sceptical press. Indeed, the newspaper *The Daily Telegraph* reported on 12 October 2020 that Carolyn Fairbairn, the Director General of the Confederation of British Industry (CBI), stated that Freeports were the target for criminal activities. There is little proof of this, and such comments do no justice whatsoever to the reality of Free Zones as centres of investment and legitimate trading under Customs and Tax controls. However, the EU is not generally in favour of Free Zones in its territory for tax reasons, and wishes, where at all possible, to discourage the use of Free Zones as part of EU commercial activity.

HM Revenue & Customs have a policy of no toleration of criminal activities inside any UK ports or airports, and take radical measures to stamp any illicit activities out as soon as possible, indeed to the point that UK Border Force, which controls the UK ports and airports, ensures absolute control over all activities conducted in these establishments. Any Revenue Authority that has controls over Free Zones has the obligation and duty to ensure that all Free Zone activities are stringently monitored and scrutinised at all times.

It is, however, accepted that certain Free Zones choose to overlook certain dubious activities as part of their drive to allow tax incentives and other investment tools in the Free Zone environment, but it cannot be said or proven that Free Zones are a natural haven for contraband or fraudulent activities. There are, however, exceptions. As an example of the illicit activities taking place at such sites, the Commission noted that in December 2016, Swiss authorities seized cultural relics looted from Syria, Libya and Yemen that were being stored in Geneva's free ports. This was more of an individual set of criminal activities and was not widespread. The fact that the Geneva Freeport regime was being used for such activities is thankfully the exception rather than the norm, and appears to be an isolated case.

Free Zone risk

There are of course many compelling practical opportunities and economic benefits that the establishment of Free Zones brings to any given country, but there are also many risks and vulnerabilities which can have the reverse effect, depending upon the levels of security imposed upon the Free Zones in question. However, with sufficient care and attention to regulatory detail and control, such risks can be eliminated or at least mitigated to a large extent, provided that policymakers and regulators act proactively, before any criminal system becomes established and entrenched in illicit or illegal activities and practices that are hard, if not impossible, to reverse. For the establishment of any Free Zone, the following risk matrix should be applied when determining the perceived and inherent levels of risk applying to the establishment of any Free Zone.

The **Composite Risk Matrix (CRI)** works on the basis of two factors: **Likelihood** and **Impact**. Each factor is graduated in the form of five levels, ranging from:

Likelihood: 1 = Very Unlikely; to 5 = Highly Likely;
Impact: 1 = Minimal; to 5 = Critical.

Multiplying these factors together, we derive a scale of 1(1×1) – 25 (5×5).

These scales then equate as follows to form the **Composite Risk Index (CRI)**:

1–8 (Low);
9–16 (Medium);
17–25 (High).

They are then arranged in the 5×5 Risk Matrix as shown below.

The 5×5 method can be used where data is available or a good degree of judgement can be applied to estimates of the frequency and consequences of each hazardous event in the form of a simplified matrix. This risk ranking approach allows for a normal level of accuracy and consistency in the risk estimates that can be obtained.

Note: The size of the matrix and the factor difference in frequency and consequence rankings can be altered to give the best ranges to suit a particular organisation's operation.

This solution works for any factor difference (two, five, ten, 100, etc.) providing both the frequency and consequence ranking estimates are separated by the same factor.

I M P A C T

Likelihood ↓	*Minimal (1)*	*Low (2)*	*Moderate (3)*	*High (4)*	*Critical (5)*
Very likely (5)	5	10	15	20	25
Regular (4)	4	8	12	16	20
Frequent (3)	3	6	9	12	15
Infrequent (2)	2	4	6	8	10
Very unlikely (1)	1	2	3	4	5

Levels:
1-8; Low (ALARP – As Low As Reasonably Possible)
9-16; Medium
17-25; High

These CRI numerical levels and codes are used in the Risk Register, to show the levels of risk for each column, namely **L** (Low), **M** (Medium), and **H** (High). The acronym ALARP means **A**s **L**ow **A**s **R**easonably **P**ossible.

In the case of Free Zone operations, the risk relates to the security of the relevant Free Zone and its activities, especially concerning potential or perceived levels of criminal activity occurring within the zone, as well as perceived compromise and prejudice to the national revenue. Any form of Customs-controlled operation, be it Temporary Storage, Customs Warehousing or Free Zones, has a perceived level of risk, because the good stored in any of these facilities is subject to Import Duty and VAT Suspension, and therefore potential national revenue in the form of Import Duty and VAT is at risk. Any national Customs or Revenue Authority imposes strict regimes on such operations and takes such steps as to ensure that Import Duty and VAT will not be compromised or lost for whatever reason. This is also why the Revenue Authority carries out a suitable revenue protection risk analysis on any such project at the time of application and ensures that any risk to the national revenue is kept to a minimum. Every Freeport of Free Zone applicant must, in line with internal Revenue Authority policy and guidelines, be able to show as part of its Free Zone proposals that it will implement a regime of safety and security that can be vetted, scrutinised and approved by the Revenue Authority prior to any application being accepted and approved. The Revenue Authority's risk analysis must therefore show that the risk levels pertinent to the Free Zone application must be at worst Medium, and at best Low, corresponding to CRI levels of 1–8 (**Low**) to 9–15 (**Medium**). Where risk levels are at a medium level, the application may not be rejected, but the Free Zone applicant will be required to review their proposals and take the appropriate steps to reduce risk levels of security by ensuring that tight and strict internal and external security levels, including monitoring of Free Zone activities, as well as the control of goods entering and leaving the zone, are maintained or will be guaranteed to be maintained at all times.

With regard to Free Zone operations, the primary risk areas are:

- Security;
- Loss;
- Damage;
- Pilferage;
- Fraud;
- Accountability;
- Customs compliance;
- Tax compliance;
- Illicit trade;
- Viability.

Security has already been covered in this chapter. Loss, damage to goods and pilferage are all issues that relate to the Customs-controlled storage of goods. One of the main conditions of any Free Zone operation is that in the event of unaccountable loss or damage, the Free Zone tenant will be liable to the Revenue Authority for the Customs Duty and VAT on the goods in question. These are also conditions of Customs Warehousing operations, and are part of any Customs authorisation for such facilities.

Fraud is based on false accounting, false declarations to Customs and Revenue Authorities and overall tax evasion. Although the OECD and WCO have undertaken extensive studies into the potential and incidence of illicit operations, much of any Free Zone operation depends upon the honesty and integrity of both the Free Zone Authority and its tenants. However, given that all Free Zone Authorities and their tenants are approved by the Customs and Revenue Authorities for Free Zone authorisation and operations, it is their responsibility to prove to the Revenue and Customs Authorities that they can be trusted to operate a Free Zone within the scope of the Free Zone regulations of the country concerned. Failure to do so would result in the revocation of the Free Zone licence by the government authorities of that country.

Accountability, although linked to fraud, is in itself a major element of Free Zone activity. All Free Zone tenants are accountable to the Free Zone authority and the government authorities. Both the Free Zone authority and its tenants must keep copious accounts and records of all goods passing through and stored within the zone at any time. This is one of the prime requirements of the Customs and Revenue Authorities, and indeed this is also a prime requirement for any trader applying to the Customs Authority for Import Duty and VAT Reliefs such as Inward Processing, Processing for Free Circulation (Tariff Inversion/Reversed Cascading) and Customs Warehousing. Every trader applying for such authorisations must be able to show to the Customs Authority that it has copious electronic import and export transaction spreadsheet records, completed, kept and maintained on a monthly basis. In the UK, this takes the form of EIDR, a facility which will be part of the Free Zone Simplified Procedures.

Customs and Tax Compliance are also major issues in Free Zone authorisations and operations. Part of the conditions of Free Zone operation is that the Free Zone authority and its tenants must be able to show that they can comply with Customs and Tax requirements at all times, generally by established Import and Export Procedures and Documentation. The Customs and Tax Authorities maintain the right to investigate and examine the documentation and records of all Free Zone authorities and tenants at any time, and determine whether full compliance is being maintained. The AEO facility partly ensures compliance, as Customs and Tax Compliance, including proven compliance history, is a major area which determines whether the company applying for the facility is suitable for being authorised for the AEO facility.

Illicit trade is an area of concern, particularly to Customs Authorities. Smuggling and contraband are always a problem for any Customs Authority, not only in terms of Customs controls but also because of VAT fraud. Although there is a significant degree of success on the part of the Customs Authorities worldwide in combatting illicit trade, there are still many countries where illicit trade remains a significant problem. Although it has been inferred that Free Zones have been the target for illicit trading activities, the discovery of such activities is still rare, and has been focused on specific cases.

Free zone viability depends upon the ability of the Free Zone authority to attract enough business to make the Free Zone project work. Industries will locate in a Free Zone if they see an economic and fiscal reason to do so. In many cases, Free Zone success depends upon the number of economic, financial and fiscal advantages that it has to offer. Zones with more limited financial and fiscal advantages will never succeed in the same way that Free Zones offering a wide range of financial and fiscal advantages will. The original Freeport concept initiated in the UK in 1984 was very much more limited than Free Zones such as Shannon, in Western Ireland, and, as a result, the UK Freeports of the era never enjoyed outstanding success, other than perhaps the Freeport adjacent to the Port of Liverpool, which was a very successful venture throughout its duration until 2012, when its Freeport status was removed as part of overall UK Government policy in line with EU policy.

Government Free Zone initiatives establish the national Free Zone policy, but do not exist to actually develop or run any of the country's Free Zones. This is the function and responsibility of the individual Free Zone authority itself, using methods such as promotion through websites and other means. In many ways, the long-term success of many Free Zones has been generated by reputation and efficiency, especially in the case of the Jebel Ali Free Zone at Dubai, UAE. Ever since it was first inaugurated in the mid-1980s, it has served as a crossroads for global trade, as well as being a very efficient Customs-controlled centre of storage and manufacturing operations.

A means of measuring such viability can be found in the Viable Systems Model (VSM), developed by the English cybernetician and erstwhile Professor of Business at Manchester University, Stafford Beer. He developed the model in the 1970s to analyse the viability of major businesses following a management position he originally held within the company British Steel, and it became a major tool in determining the extent to which such businesses are viable in their present State, and therefore any rectification, amendments or adjustments required to make the enterprise more viable. To this extent, it is an equally useful tool in determining the extent to which a Free Zone may be viable based on its function, its aspirations and its overall coordination and efficiency. Indeed, it should be noted that if certain other Free Zones had adopted this model, more of these Zones would have been far more viable than they actually were. This is borne out by the UNCTAD Report on Special Economic Zones of 2019.

This Quick Guide to how the VSM as a cybernetic function looks at organisations and how it ensures the various parts are balanced, and introduces the following brief points:

- Autonomous or Individual Operational units.
- Metasystem – concerned with ensuring the Operational units work together, integrate or cohere into a single integrated organisation.
- Synergy – the added efficiency which comes from working together in a cooperative fashion.
- Daily Performance Indicators – which measure the goings on within each Operational unit.
- Algedonics – signals which are generated to say 'Look out . . . something unusual has occurred', leading to the rectification of the problem.

It also uses the five systems to describe the various functions within the organisation.

System 1	The entire collection of interacting Operational units.
System 2	The system responsible for stability/resolving conflict between and within Operational units.
System 3	The systems responsible for optimisation/generating overall synergy between Operational units.
System 3*	Monitoring and Checking; Auditing.
System 4	Future plans and strategies. Adaptation to a changing environment. Externalities.
System 5	Overall Policy.

In terms of Free Zone viability, each system applies to both the Free Zone Authority and its tenants. As any FZ Authority has a collection of departments, sections and functions, each section or department must be able to not only run its own affairs but also be able to communicate with other departments, as well as its tenants. This means that there has also to be an efficient set of control mechanisms to ensure the smooth, efficient and compliant operation of the whole enterprise, especially in line with government requirements, both in terms of Free Zone law and operational regulations laid down by the Customs and Revenue Authorities. Where System 1 may refer to the FZ Authority as a whole, the activities of each operational unit of the Free Zone Administration are dealt with by Systems 2 and 3, which also refer to the FZ Authority's relationships with the Free Zone tenants. System 4 relates to the relationship between the FZ Authority and government agencies, that is, the Customs and Tax Authorities. System 5 refers to the overall policy of the Free Zone Authority and its mission statement, assuming that it has one. However, this overall policy can also be shaped by the Free Zone policy of the national government itself. In brief, the systematic approach of the VSM can be translated into the following:

System 1	The entire collection of interacting Operational units within the Free Zone and its Tenants.
System 2	The system responsible for stability/resolving conflict between and within Operational units of the Free Zone Authority and its Tenants.
System 3	The system responsible for optimisation/generating overall synergy between Operational units of the Free Zone Authority and its Tenants.
System 3*	Monitoring and Checking; Auditing (Customs and Tax Compliance).
System 4	Future plans and strategies. Adaptation to a changing environment. Externalities. International Trade policy, global Free Zone policy and national government Tax and Fiscal Controls.
System 5	Overall Free Zone Policy.

As part of their overall approach concerning risk analysis and management, the national Customs and Revenue Authorities generally require all Free Zone applicants and potential tenants to undertake a risk analysis as part of their eligibility to become approved for Free Zone operations. This risk analysis takes the form of the following typical spreadsheet:

Subject	*Ownership*	*Low risk*	*Medium risk*	*High risk*	*Mitigating action*
Import Documentation	Logistics		**X**		Improve Documentation
Export Documentation	Logistics		**X**		
Import Procedures	Logistics			**X**	Implement Procedures
Export Procedures	Logistics			**X**	Implement Procedures
Import Transaction Records	Finance		**X**		Maintain Records
Export Transaction Records	Finance		**X**		Maintain Records
Audit Trail	Logistics		**X**		Maintain Audit Trail

This risk analysis allows for Raw Risk to be established at the time of the audit based on all the main areas being analysed, followed by a set of mitigating actions which are designed to rectify the main prevalent issues. This will result in Residual Risk, not shown on the table, which determines the risk levels for each subject area following the implementation of such mitigating actions. Risk reduction results in greater levels of compliance, meaning that the company will be considered more suitable and eligible for Free Zone operations by the Customs and Tax Authorities.

As a summary, Free Zone risk is crucial at all times, and must be monitored and analysed on very frequent intervals to ensure that it is kept low and does not rise at any time. Free Zone regulatory control and governance is vital to the process, and must be implemented in any Free Zone project from the outset. Such governance and control must include a combination of vigilance and due diligence, and specific documented procedures, in the form of Security Standard Operating Procedures (SOPs), created and implemented by the Free Zone authority, are vital and essential to this process. Failure to do so can result in revocation of the project and facility licence by the national Revenue Authority, although such radical action is rare. In general, where it is proven that illicit activity has taken place inside a Free Zone, the Revenue Authority gives the Free Zone authority the opportunity to review its activities and take steps such as to reduce the chance of such illicit activity continuing.

CHAPTER 13

The political perspective

Behind every Free Zone/Freeport venture, as well as fiscal and economic incentives, there are also political considerations. Free Zones are considered a means of Import Duty and tax relief, which, to a degree, conflicts with the tax policies of any government. Indeed, the political spectrum shows us how Free Zones may be favoured or disliked. In general, socialist regimes dislike Free Zones as they see them as a means of avoiding duties and taxes which are vital to the government's sources of revenue. However, right-wing regimes see Free Zones as a means of economic development through the implementation of fiscal incentives, and thus economic development of the nation. Indeed, in developing countries, the implementation of Free Zones and the existence of these Zones shows the extent to which the Free Zone concept, whether pure Free Zone, Export Processing Zone, or Special Economic Zone, has benefitted many nations. Turkey, the UAE, Mauritius, China, Mexico, Brazil, Ireland and Morocco are classic cases where this premise holds true, and these cases are exemplified and analysed in the Part Two of this study. Free Zones can therefore be seen as a political tool in a government's national economic and fiscal policy.

In the vast majority of cases, such Free Zone initiatives are private ventures, established by way of specific dedicated Free Zone authorities, such as JAFZA (Jebel Ali Free Zone Authority). However, as well as government policy favouring such ventures, national legislation has been needed to establish the facility in each country where Free Zones operate. The US Foreign-Trade Zones were established by the FTZ Act of 1934. The Manaus Free Zone in its present form was established by Decree-Law in 1967, and the original UK Freeports were established by legislation in the form of the UK's Finance Act of 1984, although the original UK Freeport concept dates back to 1981, where the idea was first mooted. The UK Government has announced that the Freeport concept is to return to the UK, and is passing legislation in 2020 to allow this.

However, politics is at best a strange animal, and there are always those who criticise Free Zones and Freeports within the parliamentary environment. The Socialists in the UK have long argued that Freeports are a means of duty exemption, which is completely false, as there is no such thing as duty exemption. VAT may be exempted in certain circumstances, but duty, whether it be Customs or Excise Duty, cannot. That is set in statute law. Duties can be subject to conditional reliefs or suspensions, but only that. The levying of duties and taxes is enshrined in every national legislation, as it is this fiscal tool which sustains government policy in terms of spending on all necessary requirements, be they

DOI: 10.4324/9781003232025-14

defence, health, education, welfare, national infrastructure and so on. No government even entertains the policy of duty exemption, as such a measure would be extremely foolish at best, and downright illegal at worst. Duty exemption is a national form of tax evasion, which is illegal.

National government, therefore, must approve and sanction any Free Zone concept by national legislation, in order to facilitate the creation of designated Free Zones according to need and expediency. At the time of the passing of the Finance Act in 1984, certain questions were raised as to the viability of certain Zones, including the Free Zone at Ballasalla on the Isle of Man, and it was proven over time that only some of the original Freeports that were established in the UK were truly viable, including the Freeport at Prestwick, adjacent to Prestwick International Airport, on the Clyde Coast in South-West Scotland. The author had the opportunity to address several meetings concerning the future of the zone in the face of competition from the Bonded storage area at the Airport's cargo centre, and indeed there were valid arguments concerning the viability of the zone at the time, especially as very few companies had located in the Freeport. The author presented a paper at Glasgow University shortly afterwards, comparing the Glasgow Prestwick Freeport with the Montréal Mirabel Free-Trade Zone, the first of its kind in Canada, and made several points concerning the fact that, while both Free Zones were located to international airports, the Mirabel Free Zone was significantly more successful than its Scottish counterpart, largely through a greater range of fiscal incentives.

State aid

Although government support for Free Zones in the form of State aid is somewhat questionable, it depends upon the extent to which government is prepared to financially support such ventures. In general, although government may sanction the existence and operation of Free Zones, it does not run them. The nearest for State intervention of some kind is in China, where although each of the Chinese SEZs and EPZs is run by a separate authority, these authorities are still answerable to the Chinese State system owing to the political nature of the Chinese economic system. In some cases, State aid has been necessary to support certain Free Zones, such as the Subic Bay Free Zone in the Philippines, which is part of the Subic Bay Metropolitan Authority. In short, national government supports and sanctions the concept and operation of Free Zones, but devolves and delegates their operation to separate autonomous authorities. Such will be the case in the UK, where the various projected Freeports will be run by separate authorities, possibly part of the adjacent port authorities, with, at very least, moral support from the local regional authorities, although some regional authorities may express some degree of interest in contributing to the operation of some of these Freeports.

State aid concerning Free Zones has been an issue of controversy within the European Union, which places strict limitations on State aid in some sectors, including Free Zones, leading many to believe that the EU does not favour the use of Free Zones. A case in point as that of the Madeira Free Zone, on the Portuguese island of Madeira, where a Free Zone was established to bolster the island's fragile economy. According to the Europa.eu website, in 2018, the European Commission opened an in-depth investigation to examine whether Portugal has applied the Madeira Free Zone regional aid scheme in conformity with the 2007 and 2013 Commission decisions approving it. In particular, the Commission has concerns that tax exemptions granted by Portugal to companies established in the Madeira Free Zone are not in line with the Commission decisions and EU State aid rules.

Commissioner Margrethe Vestager, in charge of competition policy, said:

> Our regional aid rules are particularly flexible when it comes to supporting the EU's outermost regions, including Madeira. Under these rules, fiscal aid can only be granted if it contributes to the creation of real economic activity and jobs in the assisted region. We will now investigate whether the Zona Franca Madeira fiscal aid scheme approved by the Commission in the past has been applied correctly by Portugal.

The Madeira Free Zone

The Madeira Free Zone (*Zona Franca da Madeira*, 'ZFM') was created by Portugal on the island of Madeira in 1987 to support economic development in its outermost region Madeira. The ZFM's objective is, and always has been, to attract investment to and create jobs in Madeira, although in its true sense it is not so much a Free Zone but more a Tax-Incentive Zone, in that it does not confer duty-suspended status on products imported into and manufactured in the Zone.

In this context, Portugal put in place a regional aid scheme providing support to companies establishing themselves in the ZFM through:

- Corporate income tax reductions on profits resulting from activities performed in Madeira; and
- Other tax reductions, such as an exemption from municipal and local taxes, as well as exemption from transfer tax payable on real estate for setting up a business in the ZFM.

The Commission approved successive versions of the ZFM regional aid scheme under EU State aid rules on several occasions between 1987 and 2014.

EU State aid rules provide ample scope for Member States to support the economic development of outermost regions, such as Madeira, and to address the structural challenges of companies active in such regions.

At the same time, in order for such measures to be fit for purpose, State aid must be granted exclusively to companies generating economic activity and real jobs in the outermost regions. That is why, under the approved ZFM regional aid scheme, the amount of aid granted to companies through corporate income tax reductions or other tax reductions is linked to the number of jobs that they create in Madeira.

The Commission's investigation

As part of its standard monitoring of the implementation of State aid decisions, the Commission carried out a preliminary assessment of how Portugal applied the ZFM aid scheme until its expiry at the end of 2014, taking into account the framework of the 2007 and 2013 Commission decisions approving the scheme.

The Commission had concerns that the Portuguese authorities may have failed to respect some of the basic conditions under the 2007 and 2013 decisions. In particular, the Commission had doubts that Portugal complied with the requirements that:

- The company profits benefitting from the income tax reductions originated exclusively from activities carried out in Madeira; and
- The beneficiary companies actually created and maintained jobs in Madeira.

The Commission is at present investigating further to find out whether its initial concerns are confirmed. The opening of an in-depth investigation gives Portugal and interested third parties an opportunity to submit comments. It does not prejudge the outcome of the investigation.

Background

Each year, the Commission selects a number of State aid measures in order to monitor whether Member States implement them in compliance with EU State aid rules. In this context, the Commission asked Portugal for information on the implementation of the ZFM scheme in 2012 and 2013.

The scheme in question expired at the end of 2014. Portugal has informed the Commission that, since 2015, it has implemented a similar aid scheme on the basis of the 2014 General Block Exemption Regulation (GBER). Under this regulation, Member States can implement regional operating aid schemes for companies established in outermost regions, without notification and approval by the Commission, as long as certain conditions are respected.

Article 349 of the Treaty on the Functioning of the European Union acknowledges the special characteristics of the outermost regions and affords them a special status. All outermost regions, including Madeira, have been granted special regional aid status to help address their specific handicaps, namely remoteness, insularity, small size, difficult topography and climate, and economic dependence on a few products.

In recognition of the serious nature of the structural disadvantages that the companies located in these regions face, the Commission established specific State aid rules for the outermost regions, within both the Regional Aid Guidelines and the GBER. These regions are all automatically considered assisted areas where the economic situation is extremely unfavourable in relation to the rest of the European Union as a whole. Due to this status, all companies with economic activity in these areas may benefit from additional bonuses of up to 20% on top of the normal regional investment aid ceilings. Additionally, Member States can provide operating aid to companies located in these regions to compensate them for the additional costs they are facing in these remote regions.

The non-confidential version of the decision will be made available under the case number SA.21259 in the State Aid Register on the Commission's competition website once any confidentiality issues have been resolved. New publications of State aid decisions on the Internet and in the EU official journal are listed in the *State Aid Weekly e-News*.

Some of this investigation originated in the revelation that two companies operating on Madeira were owned by the dictator of Equatorial Guinea, coupled with the fact that Madeira has one of the lowest minimum wage rates in Europe, at €700/month. Whether this can be seen as an instrument in attracting companies to the island may be seen as either cause or effect. However, the Madeira Free Zone is now known as the International Business Centre of Madeira, rather than a Free-Trade Zone, mainly because of its generous Corporation Tax rates at 5%, and this is where there is a clear dividing line between Freeports and many Free Zones, especially EPZs and SEZs. These latter two concepts attract many companies because of tax breaks other than simply Import Duty and VAT Suspension. Such tax breaks include reduction or freedom from Corporation Tax and personal income tax, to name but two incentives, and these incentives are seen as being elements of State aid. Each country reserves the right to operate its own national State aid policies, especially where it seeks to develop its economy through fiscal incentives, which in turn are designed to encourage inward foreign investment. However, in many cases, such fiscal incentives operate for a fixed number of years, usually ten years, and are then subject to either revocation or extension. In many cases, such fiscal incentives are subsequently extended in order to enhance the long-term potential of the Free Zones in question. Whether the new set of UK Freeports are to be given State aid in the form of Direct Tax breaks in the form of reductions in Corporation Tax as well as indirect tax incentives is as yet a matter of conjecture.

One deliberate policy of governments in favour of Free Zones is to locate them in areas of economic need, and in this respect, they adhere to international rules concerning the application of State aid, in that the Free Zones concerned exist to generate employment and commercial and economic development. In developing countries Free Zones have generally been located in specific economically disadvantaged or strategically important regions to generate investment and employment, especially in areas which have been abandoned by other organisations. The Free Zone at Subic Bay, Philippines, was implemented to for two specific reasons: it was located close to commercial maritime activities, and it was designed to provide badly needed employment following the closure of the US Naval Base there. In the US, FTZs have been encouraged in the States less economically advantaged, especially in the south-eastern States of South Carolina and Alabama. The Moroccan Free Zones were partly established to provide vital employment to the area around Tangier, the home of the Tanger-Med Free Zone. Similar strategies surrounded the development of several of the Turkish Free Zones. In each case, such policies have met with significant success, although the performance of some Zones has significantly exceeded that of others. In the UK, this will be no exception. It is envisaged that the majority of the first ten Freeports projected for the UK will be in the North and the provinces, namely Wales, Scotland and Northern Ireland. Despite local political misgivings, there is reason to believe that such ventures will foster economic growth where the Zones will be located, certainly in the North of England, and will provide badly needed employment to these regions. However, that said, given that the major seaports of the UK are located in the south of the country, there is equally the argument that Freeports located adjacent to the major ports of Tilbury, London Gateway, Felixstowe and Southampton would also provide significant fiscal and logistical advantages, as they also would at ports such as Teesport, Liverpool and Bristol. Indeed, lessons learned from the past concerning Freeports such as Prestwick, adjacent to Glasgow Prestwick Airport, which proved to be much less successful than its counterparts further south, would suggest that the idea of locating a Freeport in Scotland would reap few economic and trade benefits.

In conclusion, government strategy and policy may be admirable, but it must linked to economic and fiscal benefit, leading to economic growth with a net gain for taxpayers and businesses alike, especially in justifying an increase in employment and overall economic wellbeing. The Freeport concept can provide this, but it must be supported from all parts of the national political spectrum, as well as by local authorities and business itself. Freeports are designed to be of fiscal and economic benefit to the nation as a whole, not specific little enclaves dotted around the country. However, the risk is that they will simply benefit the local region, rather than the country as a whole.

CHAPTER 14

Sustainability and the future

Apart from the issues already analysed in this text, another issue is that of sustainability and the overall capacity of Free Zones to adapt to future trends, including the environment. In the past, controversies have surrounded the use of some Free Zones, particularly the Mexican Maquiladoras, which had a reputation for lax environmental rules and the propensity for pollution problems and their effects on the northern Mexican environment. The United Nations sought to address these issues, and in 2015 issued a set of SDGs alongside its objectives for global economic development.

Several of the SDGs provide a significant opportunity for the World Free Zones Organization (World FZO) and its constituents to make a notable contribution in lifting the living Standards of people, in protecting and optimally utilising the planet's finite natural resources, and more generally spreading prosperity and peace for all.

The World FZO launched the 'Free Zone of the Future' Program (FZF Program), a global initiative for local prosperity that seeks to empower Free Zones and assist them to build and contribute to a sustainable and prosperous future, and an initiative that supports the growth of local economies and communities while simultaneously benefitting from global market dynamics.

Central to the World FZO's present and planned future activities, specifically advancing the 'Free Zone of the future' concept, are three SDGs, namely:

- Decent work and economic growth (number 8);
- Industry, innovation and infrastructure (number 9); and
- Partnerships for the goals (number 17).

Other goals are, of course, important additional elements of this list, and are equally important SDGs.

Conceptually, the World FZO's FZF Program seeks to promote economic growth, boost industrial and commercial activities, create livelihood opportunities, foster innovation, make optimal use of natural resources and achieve all these and more by networking and striking appropriate partnerships.

The FZF Program consists of three pillars, including best-in-class practices, Innovation and sustainability, and each contains three elements. **Best-in-class practices** include knowledge-based, certified and tech-ready Zones; **Innovation** includes entrepreneurial, small and medium-sized enterprises (SME) developer and innovative Zones; and **sustainability** includes environmentally friendly, good-place-to-work and socially responsible Zones. There are strong links between the nine elements of the FZF Program and their contribution to the SDGs.

DOI: 10.4324/9781003232025-15

SDG relevance

As economic entities, Free Zones across the world have played a key role in promoting investment and Free-Trade as well as generating employment and income. To this extent, the conviction that they can make a positive and notable contribution to the advancement of SDGs is gaining ground. It is against this background that the World FZO, one of the facilitating organisations of Free Zones around the world along with other organisations such as the WEPZA, decided to seek the views of experts from across geographies about the relevance of SDGs and the role that Free Zones can play in advancing them.

Through interviews based on questionnaires and telephone conversations, the World FZO's knowledge management unit approached several domain experts to elicit their views, perceptions and suggestions. Not unexpectedly, there was unanimity among them about the relevance of SDGs to Free Zones and the positive role that Free Zones can play to advance relevant SDGs. The following is a summarised version of the excerpts of the interviews.

The role of Free Zones with respect to SDGs

While there is little doubt that Free Zones contribute to advancing SDGs, different types of Free Zones contribute differently to them. The nature of economic activity and even location or geography may influence this. In reality, the core activity of the Free Zone may be a key determinant of the nature of contribution. For instance, the work style or functional aspects of Free Zones that are manufacturing-oriented, where physical materials are used in manufacturing processes and can produce wastage, would be different from those that are, for example, service-oriented, such as financial Free Zones, where there are no physical productive activities, and therefore their contribution to sustainable development would also be different. It is important to bear this in mind.

In a country such as India, where Free Zones are called Special Economic Zones, there has been notable flow of investment, creation of jobs, promotion of industrial production and exports, all of which go to foster economic growth. In this case, it may be said that the contribution of Free Zones to SDGs is less direct, but no less relevant. In other words, Free Zones can and do contribute to moving towards some of the SDGs.

Contribution of Free Zones to achieving SDGs

Across geographies, expert respondents highlighted the fact that Free Zones have invariably encouraged investment, built infrastructure, generated economic activity, created employment and promoted exports in addition to skills development and the fostering of gender equality. Each of these activities has contributed to moving towards many of the goals. Indeed, the positive contribution of Free Zones towards SDGs is seen as more relevant in emerging or low-income economies.

ILO's Decent Work Agenda and Free Zones

According to the ILO, 'decent work' involves the following opportunities for work:

- Productive and deliver a fair income;
- Security in the workplace and social protection for families;

- Better prospects for personal development and social integration;
- Freedom for people to express their concerns, organise and participate in the decisions that affect their lives; and
- Equal opportunity and treatment for all people.

The ILO is developing an agenda for the community of work, represented by its tripartite constituents, to mobilise their considerable resources to create those opportunities and to help reduce and eradicate poverty. The Decent Work Agenda is the balanced and integrated programmatic approach to pursue the objectives of full and productive employment and decent work for all at global, regional, national, sectoral and local levels. It has four pillars: Standards and rights at work; employment creation and enterprise development; social protection; and social dialogue.

The SDGs also proclaim decent work for sustainable economic growth. However, not all Free Zones contribute uniformly to a Decent Work Agenda or, for that matter, sustainable development. Bringing in uniformity and standardisation in work practices is a challenge, as the local labour laws, minimum wages legislation, employment conditions and working environment vary widely in different Zones across the globe.

Evidence of contribution by Free Zones

Experts have listed a wide variety of evidence across geographies to demonstrate the contribution made by Free Zones to the global economy. It encompassed on-the-ground environmental activities such as the creation of green Zones, the generation of solar energy, improved sanitation and cleanliness, strict law and order and improving the overall workplace experience. More solid evidence from India highlighted that in the past decade incremental investment in Free Zones was $55 billion, the increase in employment amounted to $1.4 billion and exports nearly doubled to about $70 billion.

It may be relevant to record that what has been proffered as evidence by the experts may be only a small part of arguably large contributions made by Free Zones around the world in recent years. Some of the suggested ways in which Free Zones can contribute in the future include: to focus on sustainability; create a 'healthy' workplace; promote transparency; and focus on the health and energy sectors.

Conversion of Oil & Gas offshore Supply Bases to Marine Renewables

The organisation DAI published an article on the Internet in 2020 concerning the transition of Offshore Supply Bases to use for the Marine Renewables sector, namely the construction and operation of offshore wind farms. The article stated that the past few decades have seen an intense effort to encourage investment in forward-looking renewable energy technologies, principally in onshore solar and wind generation. Over this time, a global supply chain that involves both large businesses and SMEs has emerged to service these onshore projects. More recently, new technology is expanding the ability to harness *offshore*, marine-based renewables, specifically, offshore wind and tidal. In January 2020, the Hornsea one wind farm, 170 kilometres off the UK's North Sea coast, became the world's largest offshore wind generator, with a capacity of 1,218 megawatts. In 2018,

DAI's research for Marine Renewables Canada found that countries such as the United Kingdom, South Korea, France, Indonesia and the North-Eastern United States are home to marine renewable investments exceeding $500 billion.

Indeed, in many locations the groundwork has already been laid for this transition to Marine Renewables. Many coastal cities and portside towns where new projects are blooming already boast sizeable Oil & Gas supply chains that employ tens of thousands of people. With appropriate support, this growing stream of renewables investment could and should become a source of market growth opportunities for those companies and communities largely dependent today on Oil & Gas, a dependency that increasingly looks like a vulnerability in the light of the COVID-19 crisis and the global oil production wars, where oil is apparently plentiful yet the market appears to be diminishing in the face of environmental pressure.

Fostering local content and SME participation in this emerging energy space should be a priority for governments pursuing energy sustainability and new pathways to economic growth. If they are to seize this opportunity to refit and convert an existing Supply Base, governments should take a systematic approach in collaboration with developers and operators.

The relative immaturity of the Marine Renewables subsector means that there is as yet no generally accepted and streamlined way to measure the readiness and even ability of companies located in the existing Supply Base, especially given their possible lack of experience in the offshore Marine Renewables sector. Furthermore, the sheer diversity of new technologies, especially in tidal energy, makes it difficult to determine the services, goods and skills that might constitute industry Standards. This landscape will consolidate and develop as technologies are proven and more projects come online, but it is likely that there will not be global technical Standards in place in the immediate future.

Nonetheless, significant progress in setting new competitiveness criteria for those seeking to work in Marine Renewables has been made in both Atlantic Canada and Mexico, where the business communities have partnered with government to identify a preliminary list of supply chain categories that can then be assessed. In both jurisdictions, this work has been based on the supply chain categories and criteria used to qualify Suppliers and workers in the Oil & Gas industry. It is evident that some of the facilities found in offshore Supply Bases, such as construction techniques and the storage of materials for wind turbines, can be easily adapted for the Marine Renewables sector. Similarly, the supply vessels used to transport materials to the offshore Oil & Gas installations can be easily adapted to carry components and materials for the offshore wind turbines to the offshore wind farm sites.

In terms of Customs controls, much depends upon the location of the wind farms. Those farms located outside the 12-mile limit fall under the same category as do offshore Oil & Gas installations, that is, outside national territorial jurisdiction. However, those wind farms located within the 12-mile limit are within national territorial jurisdiction, and therefore are not considered eligible to qualify for Customs Duty relief. These considerations must be taken into account when storing materials destined for such offshore projects within the confines of the Supply Base, as they must be accounted for separately from the equipment destined for the extra-territorial offshore Marine Renewables projects. In most cases, the materials destined for each of these types of projects are generally the same, therefore strict accountability applies to the Customs status of such materials, and the information relating to these materials must be carefully recorded and accounted for in terms of Customs status.

The next step in preparing the Supply Base is building a foundation of data on the current capabilities of the local enterprises and workforce. This mapping exercise will be more difficult than it would be for the Oil & Gas sector, where there have been decades of experience and established industry Standards, and it will require an extremely localised evaluation of skills to establish how well they are equipped to deal with the needs of new marine projects. However, related analytical work already conducted in Atlantic Canada found that almost three-quarters of the traditional supply chain categories associated with servicing offshore Oil & Gas installations are applicable to Marine Renewables. Examples include work on the transmission infrastructure required to transfer energy back into the onshore grid, which in some ways bears a similarity to the installation of subsea pipelines. Further examples include the storage and supply of wind turbine structures and other support materials that are transported to the offshore wind turbine locations from the Supply Base.

An important component of such a mapping exercise is estimating the market size and opportunities available for local enterprises, both locally and globally. Doing so will help to match supply with demand and pinpoint the growth opportunities for local Suppliers of materials used in the sector.

Equally important will be for government to establish policies that encourage businesses to make the transition. Policy incentives can take several forms, such as:

- Grants to help qualifying SMEs invest in new technology, training and systems;
- Fiscal incentives such as tax reductions for investments in upgrades related to Marine Renewables;
- Customs incentives where projects are located outside national maritime territorial limits;
- Facilitation of partnerships such as joint ventures;
- Brokering and arrangement of outward trade missions and supplier forums; and
- Network building events such as conferences and workshops.

Industry advocacy may be required to strengthen the business case for relaxing some policies that restrict the percentage of energy derived from renewables. By demonstrating how marine renewable projects can benefit the local Supply Base through job creation and SME inclusion, the value proposition for these forward-leaning energy investments can be expanded to include benefits beyond those related to climate change.

In brief, the marine renewable sector can help the development of Offshore Supply Bases and Free Zones in general. Given the need for the construction and development of offshore wind farms, there is also the need for the development of the offshore Supply Base and associated Free Zone or Freeport to accommodate companies engaged in associated activities, such as supply, manufacture and logistics. It is largely impossible to manufacture and assemble much of the offshore wind farm infrastructure inland, as the sheer size of the turbine blades and support pillars can only be fully constructed in an area close to the port of despatch and loading. There is also the need to transport such large structures initially by breakbulk vessel in the form of project cargoes to the port immediately accessible to the offshore wind farm, and then transfer these structures offshore to the wind farm itself for final assembly into the wind turbine installations. This whole type of venture requires meticulous management and execution, and the Freeport/ Free Zone plays a major part in the venture.

CHAPTER 15

Challenges and secrets to success

Challenges

As the UK was proposing the creation of ten Freeports after the UK's exit from the EU in early 2020, the EU was clamping down on 82 Free Zones after 'finding', or at least claiming, that their special status had aided the financing of terrorism, money laundering and organised crime. More details can be found in a previous chapter on Free Zone Security.

Although the OECD has long supported the use and promotion of Free Zones, in early 2020 the European Union introduced new stricter rules to identify and report suspicious activities at free ports and Zones in response to what was claimed to be the 'high incidence of corruption, tax evasion, and criminal activity', with a further review to take place in the following year, the European Parliament suggested that increasing demand for free ports could be partly a response to global crackdowns on tax evasion. The European Commission in a report said that free ports were popular for the storage of art, precious stones, antiques, gold and wine as alternative assets to cash, and posed an emerging threat in multiple ways: allowing counterfeiters to land consignments and tamper with loads and paperwork, then re-export the products without Customs formalities, disguising the actual origin and nature of the goods and their supplier. The Commission said that they were also used for narcotics trafficking, the illegal ivory trade, people smuggling, VAT fraud, corruption and money laundering, a claim which was never substantiated or proven, and which in many ways was seen as highly controversial and contentious, given that it was deemed an excuse for the EU to remove Free Zone status from many of the EU Free Zones. According to the EU Commission, 'Legal businesses owned by criminals remain key to money-laundering activities . . . Free ports are perceived as facilities that protect their clients' identity and financial dealings, much as private banks used to.' As an example, the Commission cited the Swiss authorities' 2016 seizure of cultural relics looted from the Middle East being stored in Geneva's free ports. The free port system has been accused of facilitating international art crime, allowing stolen artworks to remain undetected in storage for decades. However, behind the scenes, it has been suspected that the true motive of the EU for wanting to abolish Free Zones is that it saw Free Zones as a means to legally avoid paying duties and taxes on any form of import and processing activities, especially where the beneficial use of tariffs and the practice of re-exporting finished products was concerned. The EU has long taken the view that imported goods from overseas yield large amounts of revenue in the form of Import Duty and VAT, and indeed have thrown up many obstacles to the use of Import Duty and VAT Reliefs, especially following the introduction of the Union Customs Code in May 2016. In 2012, the

DOI: 10.4324/9781003232025-16

decision was taken by the EU to limit the scope of all Freeports and Free Zones in EU territory, a decision seen as many as being counter-productive and against international economic interests, as well as stifling economic development in parts of Europe where the concept would have succeeded the most, especially the countries bordering the Mediterranean Sea and also the countries of Central Europe.

Social and employment challenges

Free Zones have been perhaps seen as exploiting labour forces, with some enterprises using the Free Zone concept to deliberately employing cheap labour. It is true that Free Zones are designed to use local labour, especially where wage levels may be comparatively lower than elsewhere in the national economy, but they do not imply that there is a deliberate policy on the part of Free Zone operators to employ unskilled or cheap labour. In some cases, there is, however, the suggestion that Free Zones do provide the catalyst for labour exploitation. Papers produced by various authors suggest that the Indian SEZs have a policy of employing cheap unskilled labour, especially female labour, in companies occupying the Zones.

The employment effect of many Indian SEZs operates through three channels. First, SEZs generate direct employment for skilled and unskilled labour; Second, they also generate indirect employment; and third, they generate employment for female workers. It is believed that employment creation generates incomes, creates non-pecuniary benefits, improves the quality of life in terms of labour and enhances their productivity. These, in turn, lead to poverty reduction effects.

In so far as SEZs comprise labour-intensive activities, enterprises in SEZs constitute, a priori, a significant source of new employment. Due to the availability of labour at low wages, developing countries generally attract investment into simple labour-intensive processing industries. This increases the demand for unskilled labour within the zone. The shift towards higher value-added activities as SEZs grow might also increase demand for skilled labour. SEZs also generate employment for unskilled labour by creating demand for physical infrastructure within the zone. This stimulates the local construction industry, giving employment to unskilled or semi-skilled labour.

The indirect effect is manifested as ancillary employment opportunities generated in sectors of the economy affected by or benefitting from the operations of the SEZ. These include transport, communication, automobile, civil aviation, shipping, tourism, hospitality, packaging, banking and insurance. Employment opportunities are thus generated for both unskilled and skilled labour.

In addition to the above, there are three other channels through which SEZs generate a favourable impact on employment generation.

First, SEZs provide foreign exchange earnings that slacken the foreign exchange constraints of the rest of the economy regarding the import needs of the rest of the economy and accelerate investment activities. SEZs thus generate development funds, which facilitate the generation of economic activities and employment.

Second, they also generate economic activity outside the zone due to the transformation of investment funds into fixed assets and purchase of inputs and services from the rest of the economy. Also, economic activity is generated by the supply of external services and materials to the SEZ, thus generating the local supply-based economy.

Third, once additional incomes are generated, there is an increase in demand for various goods and services such as housing, education, health and transport. This in turn has multiplier effects on income and employment.

Technology

SEZs attract export-oriented FDI and promote other forms of collaboration between local companies and multinational corporations (MNCs). For instance, SEZs facilitate the inclusion of domestic SMEs into global value chains by offering them an enabling investment climate. Global Standards, low-cost competition and advances in technology raise challenges for the SEZ units competing in global value chains. This stimulates learning and innovation which are crucial aspects of human development.

Two distinct types of value chains have been identified, namely those that are producer-driven and others that are buyer-driven. The former type characterises those value chains in which multinational enterprises (MNEs) outsource the production of components and play the central role in controlling the system. They provide technology to the networked producers. This arrangement is common in capital- and technology-intensive industries such as the automotive sector, computers and electronics. In contrast, the latter type refers to primarily low-tech labour-intensive industries in which large retailers, branded marketers and trading companies play the pivotal role in setting up decentralised production networks in a variety of exporting companies, typically located in the 'Third World' or Developing World. In this case, MNEs are marketers of products only; networked producers need to arrange for the supply and provision of raw materials and technology themselves. Participation in these chains allows producers to upgrade themselves technologically on a continuous basis. For instance, many local companies become responsible for original equipment manufacturing (OEM) wherein they source raw materials locally and manufacture products to the specifications of foreign buyers. However, having established a range of technological skills through learning, these companies transfer into 'original brand name manufacturing' (OBM) enterprises.

Learning and knowledge created in SEZs is eventually transmitted to domestic companies supplying to the SEZ-based companies through backward linkages when the companies within the SEZ buy inputs from the host country. Direct transaction of technology and indirect spill-overs through various channels such as copying, reverse engineering, and the movement of workers and managers between foreign and domestic companies also facilitate transmission of knowledge to the rest of the economy, thus benefitting everybody. Furthermore, trade bodies, manufacturers' associations and export marketing bodies which provide a useful platform to interact and to foster closer rapport among members act as valuable forums and conduits for information sharing. Thus, SEZs are not enclaves or foreign territories that function in isolation. They are very much part of the local economic community, albeit with a degree of specific economic incentives which are set apart from the economic community as a whole, but which contribute to the local, regional and national economy in a very significant way.

One could be led to believe that SEZs and other Free Zones are simply a catalyst for the use of unskilled labour. This is definitely not the case. Free Zones as a whole accommodate hi-tech companies with a need for specialist labour and skills as much as they do conventional manufacturing companies. Multinational corporations seek to invest in such

Zones for a variety of reasons, of which just one is the availability of labour, whether skilled or unskilled. Much has been written about labour exploitation, but in reality the ability of Free Zones to generate business and wealth is itself a catalyst for the attraction of local labour in pursuit of a better lifestyle and guaranteed employment.

Relevance

How relevant are Free Zones? This question may seem somewhat generic, but it does hold a significant degree of meaning. The concept of Free Zones has developed over many decades, especially concerning the type of Free Zone in question and equally the function of the specific Free Zones. In some cases, such as in the case of the US FTZs and Shannon Free Zone in Western Ireland, Free Zones were born of necessity, to stimulate the national or regional economies. The 1934 Foreign-Trade Zones Act of the US was designed to lift the US out of severe economic stagnation following the Great Depression by encouraging the use of Customs Duty incentives to stimulate growth in international trade with the US, whereas the Shannon Free Zone was developed in 1959 to bring essential life to an otherwise-declining Shannon International Airport in the form of the generation of international trade and foreign investment.

The developing nations saw Free Zones, especially EPZs and SEZs, as an essential means of generating export-led growth, and the examples of the UAE, South-East Asia and China have certainly proven that, given the evidence of significant economic growth in all these areas. Indeed, such development has been sustained over several decades, and shows no sign of decrease, even considering present global challenges. Such use of Free Zones has generated significant case studies concerning the success of such ventures, and many countries use the example of the Dubai-based Jebel Ali Free Zone as an ideal case study, given its resounding success as a hub for global trade.

However, this does not mean that every nation should invest in a Free Zone policy. The EU actively seeks to restrict Free Zone activity for a variety of reasons, and indeed the Western nations have not pursued the policy with absolute zeal, especially given their economic status and their desire to maintain strict fiscal policies. The developing world, however, has sought to use the concept as a major form of economic development, and has, to a major extent, succeeded. The raison d'être depends upon the country concerned and its desire to develop its national economy by way of the stimulation of international trade through a reduction in trade barriers, either tariff or non-tariff related. Free Zones are very much relevant in today's economic world, but should be given careful consideration in relation to the country's economic aspirations. Free Zones should not be seen as a drain on a country's economic resources through subsidy or unfair economic advantage, but instead should be seen as a viable means of economic growth and development which is designed to benefit all concerned, both nationally and internationally.

Secrets to success

The CEO of the WFZO, Dr. Samir Hamrouni, suggests a series of key points that can influence a successful strategy concerning the encouragement and development of Free Zones. He states that host governments have undertaken to provide various kinds of fiscal and financial incentives through Free-Trade Zones. The fiscal incentives include reduced tax burdens and tax holidays, streamlined or fast-tracked business administration, or exemption from duties on imports and exports. The financial incentives consist of grants and preferential/subsidised loans, as well as preferential access to markets, infrastructure and capital.

An increasing number of countries are striving to create a favourable and enabling climate to attract FDI, and there are reasonable arguments both for, and against investment incentives with regards to efficacy and return on investment for host governments (national or local). What cannot be argued, however, is the increasingly fierce competition by authorities to attract FDI, usually in the form of incentive bidding wars between competing jurisdictions.

Although there is nothing wrong with competition, and indeed competition is encouraged in a free market economy, government authorities and Free-Trade Zones should avoid competing solely on incentives. This would amount to nothing more than a price war, setting competing jurisdictions against each other to see who can provide the most lucrative arrangements to potential investors. Besides which, incentives may be good in the short term, but in the long term they cost, as incentives granted by government must be paid for in another way, and that usually means that in the long term the taxpayer foots the bill through being subject to higher taxes imposed elsewhere.

Therefore, the question is how to move beyond incentives. Free-Trade Zones in their generic function must change the way that competition is to be encouraged, and must compete on their own terms by offering potential investors what they really require in order to stimulate business growth. However, this does not mean that one Free Zone may flourish at another's expense. Different Free Zones often specialise in different industrial or commercial sectors, such as industrial goods, consumer goods, maritime-related activities or even aviation-related activities. It is often the case that even Export Processing Zones or Special Economic Zones specialise in the attraction of specific companies for a variety of reasons, and this often reflects in the markets covered and supplied by these Zones. Furthermore, the geographic location of a Free Zone often influences the markets which it serves. The US Foreign-Trade Zones have always been designed to benefit the US economy, whereas the UAE Free Zones, especially in Dubai, are considered to be the crossroads of global trade. The Export Processing Zones and Special Economic Zones of China are designed to stimulate the Chinese economy through the export of large quantities of finished products, much of which is destined for the global consumer markets.

Identify a niche

It is important to ask this question: What is different, or potentially different, about a specific zone or regime? One of the advantages of specialisation amongst Free Zones is that they can target a specific market and provide unique benefits to satisfy the needs of their investors and tenants. It is no surprise that the most successful Free Zones are the ones which have been able to carve out a niche for themselves, especially concerning the commercial and industrial sectors which they serve, or, for that matter, the specific global markets which they serve.

Compete on value

Whether it is streamlined administration, next generation infrastructure, or best-in-class services, Free Zones of the future must be able to adapt to the rapidly evolving global economic landscape and be agile enough to capitalise on emerging trends early so as to create perceived value differentiation.

Target the right investors

Not all investments are created equal. Free Zones must work to attract the right kind of FDI, and focus on those activities that create the strongest potential for return on investment, including linkages between foreign-owned and domestic companies, education, training, technology and R&D.

Build loyalty

When one sees government authorities and Free Zones that compete on price alone to attract investors, it usually means that they are paying too much attention to what the competition is doing and not enough on the investors they want to serve. In other words, they are too busy trying to compete with everybody else rather than concentrating on the activities to which they are best suited. After all, one cannot be a specialist in everything. Instead, the focus should be shifted to developing forward-looking relationships and strategies that grow over time and create real long-term value and prosperity. Short-term fixes never work; long-term strategies demand meticulous planning and undertaking. No Free Zone has ever sprung up overnight and become an instant success. Successful Free Zones such as Jebel Ali in Dubai have taken years to become what they are today.

For an example of these four key elements working together, a good example of this practice is the Dubai Silicon Oasis (DSO), a zone that has managed to transcend the typical Free Zone model to become a thriving, fully integrated ecosystem catering to the needs of the technology sector. Through state-of-the-art facilities, infrastructure and best-in-class amenities and service, DSO has managed to attract top tier tenants and investors in their niche, while providing exceptional value to high-tech enterprises. Details of the DSO can be found in Part Two of this text.

By translating this success in to targeted investments in R&D and incubation centres such as the Dubai Technology Entrepreneur Campus (DTEC), DSO has managed to foster a perpetual engine for growth and loyalty whereby start-ups from DTEC produce outputs which then go back as inputs to the larger organisations and multinationals within DSO, creating a mutually beneficial scenario for all parties involved in the venture.

Sustainability

The other key area is sustainability, referred to in a previous section. The protection of the environment and the ability to operate an accountable, sustainable Free Zone regime is one of the key considerations of any national Free Zone policy, and is an issue which has become increasingly important over the past several decades. Society is increasingly holding businesses accountable, forcing companies to change the way they think about products, technologies, processes and business models, and Free Zones must also come to grips with this new reality. In the past, the Mexican maquilas were the focus of major controversy, as US companies used them to manufacture goods for re-export to the US without any form of environmental controls or anti-pollution legislation. In time, the maquilas were cleaned up as environmental legislation was passed by the Mexican government, but elsewhere in the world, environmental issues concerning Free Zone activity remain in various places.

Beyond the moral imperatives for adopting sustainable development practices, it can be seen that investing in sustainability is proven to have significant outcomes, including, but not limited to gaining competitive advantage, increasing market share and boosting shareholder value. The same also applies to Free-Trade Zones. While no single company, government or institution alone can solve these inter-connected global challenges alone, it can be argued that Free Zones, which by their very nature are uniquely positioned at the core of the key issues and stakeholders, can and should play a critical role in addressing the key issues of sustainable development.

For Free Zones to succeed, it is necessary to approach sustainability from multiple fronts. First, it is necessary to look inwards to establish a framework for how Free Zones can be designed, developed and operated sustainably. Second, it is also necessary to look outwards to provide investors and tenants with an already-optimised environment in which sustainability is already integrated within facilities, amenities, logistics and zone management.

For investors, Free Zones can act as a tool which can help to compensate or overcome their shortcomings in sustainable development. In this way, Free Zones can find new opportunities for competitiveness through meeting the growing expectations on multinational companies and their Suppliers to exercise good social and environmental practices.

In brief, Free Zones that are able to tackle issues of sustainable development are those most likely to succeed in the future. These Zones are flexible enough to adapt to changing global policy, yet maintain all the advantages and incentives that are vital to the stimulation of both economic development and international trade.

CHAPTER 16

The UK perspective

The UK Freeports are covered in both this section and a section at the end of Part Two of this text. This first section deals with the overall theory and concept of the UK Freeports, while the section in Part Two deals with the UK Freeport structure as part of the global study covered in Part Two.

The Institute for government has published an article on Freeports and Free Zones on its website, outlining the main issues concerning the establishment of Freeports in the UK, with ten Freeports envisaged in the UK. This is in support of the UK Government's Consultation on Freeports, published in February 2020, and the government's response to the outcomes of the Consultation, published in October 2020, which paved the way for the government's decision in early 2021 to grant licences to eight UK Freeport applicants, all located in England. These locations are:

- Teesport;
- Humber;
- Harwich/Felixstowe;
- Tilbury/London Gateway;
- Solent;
- Plymouth;
- East Midlands Airport;
- Liverpool.

All but one of the new UK Freeports are to be located next to existing port facilities; the only exception in the Freeport to be located adjacent to East Midlands Airport, mainly because of the extensive international airfreight activities located at the airport. The Freeports of Liverpool, Tilbury/London Gateway and Solent are effectively revivals of the original Freeport facilities located at these ports, other than the Thames, where the Tilbury Freeport is to be extended to include the new port of London Gateway, constructed on the former Thames Haven oil refinery and tanker terminal site, situated in deeper water downstream from the Port of Tilbury.

Freeports are a designated extension of the port where normal tax and Customs rules do not apply, in the sense that Freeports are controlled by Customs. These are generally designed to be located at international airports as well as maritime ports. At a Freeport, imports can enter with simplified Customs documentation and without paying tariffs, as they are deemed to be under Customs Duty and tax suspension at the time of entry. Depending upon the Customs approval granted, such as IP Relief, businesses operating inside designated areas in and around the port can manufacture goods using the imported

DOI: 10.4324/9781003232025-17

material and thus add value to the products concerned, before being exported again without ever facing full tariffs or procedures. However, under present Customs legislation and regulations, separate approvals would be required for Customs-controlled manufacturing activities over and above Freeport authorisation.

From the UK perspective, Freeports were originally defined in the 1984 Finance Act as Customs-controlled Zones, adjacent to or close to UK Seaports and Airports, where goods could be stored under Import Duty and VAT Suspension until released for movement to inland destinations, or re-exported. Some Zones, such as Liverpool Freeport, were more successful than others, and indeed the Liverpool Freeport was to become the most successful of all the UK Freeports at its zenith. Indeed, so successful did it become, that it was handling cargoes of all kinds from the other side of the UK.

No provision was made for Customs-controlled manufacture, as the Freeport concept was based on the principles of Customs Warehousing, where goods could simply be stored and repackaged under Customs control. Customs-controlled manufacturing facilities could only be carried out by individual companies located within the zone, as long as they were approved by HM Customs & Excise (later HM Revenue & Customs) for Inward Processing Relief (IP), which was not deemed to be part of Free Zone approval. As a result, all Freeports were simply used for the storage of materials in bulk, with only light activities such as storage, repackaging, sorting and testing, carried out within the Freeport confines. Assuming similar Customs Freeport approvals, the same activities will be stipulated under the new arrangements unless specific provision is included for Customs-controlled manufacturing purposes.

If the goods move out of the Freeport into another part of the country, however, they have to go through the rest of the import process, including the payment of any import duties and VAT. However, if the recipient trader is also Customs-approved for Customs Warehousing or Inward Processing Relief, the goods released from the Free Zone can be transported under Customs-controlled Import Duty and VAT Suspension to the recipient trader's premises.

It should be noted that Freeports do not include suspension from Excise Duty as part of their overall remit. Excise traders will still have to apply for and be approved by HMRC for Excise Duty suspension authorisations separate from Customs-controlled Freeport activities. Freeports are approved for Customs-related activities, with VAT liability included in this remit. Excise activities, such as trade facility or tax warehouses, are not included in this remit.

Furthermore, Freeports are not classed as Temporary Storage facilities, that is, Transit Sheds. Temporary Storage facilities allow a maximum of 90 days' storage before they must be declared to HM Customs for import or export purposes. Such facilities must remain separate to Freeport facilities, as Freeports are effectively Zones used as integrated long-term Customs Warehousing facilities for several companies on the same site. Freeports allow an unlimited timescale for goods to be stored in Customs-controlled Import Duty and VAT Suspension, in a manner similar to Customs Warehousing facilities. Indeed, to become a Freeport user, individual Freeport tenants must apply to HMRC for approval to be located within a Freeport for Customs-controlled purposes. This means that not only must a Freeport operator (i.e. the owner and operator of the Freeport site) be approved for such purposes by HMRC, but so too must the Freeport tenants, that is, the individual companies operating within the Freeport.

Freeports are similar to Free Zones, or 'enterprise Zones', which are designated areas subject to a broad array of special regulatory requirements, tax breaks and government support. The difference is that a Freeport is designed to specifically encourage businesses that import, distribute and re-export goods, rather than more general business support or regeneration objectives. A full Free Zone also allows the provision for manufacturing and processing activities as well as those allowed for in a Freeport. In general, however, Freeports have historically remained limited to activities associated with import, stockholding and re-export activities, in other words, facilities associated with logistics activities rather than processing and manufacture. Indeed, one of the specialist functions in Freeports is Customs-controlled breakbulk and storage activities. In contrast, the UK Government has stated that it will allow manufacturing activities to take place within the Freeport environment, given the Customs authorisations available for this, thus making the new UK Freeport concept more flexible and viable.

Given the proximity of the majority of the new UK Freeports to ports accessing the EU, another advantage of the UK Freeport concept is that goods can be brought into the Freeports under T2 Community Transit status, stored in the zone for a defined period, and then re-exported back to EU customers under Community Transit status using what is known as the Direct Transport Rule, that is, that the goods pass through the UK in Customs-controlled Transit without touching UK Free Circulation. This means that movements from and to the EU can be made on a Simplified basis without the need for full Customs Declarations in either the EU or the UK, thus simplifying the whole logistics process. The facility would also allow for the use of the UK landbridge as a Customs-controlled Transit movement, thus facilitating the movement of goods across the UK from Ireland to the rest of the EU and vice versa. This would enable the goods to be temporarily stored in a UK Freeport such as Liverpool or the Humber or even Teesport under Customs control while en route between Ireland and the continent, enabling the Freeport to act as a Customs-controlled logistics hub.

Freeports and Free Zones are intended to stimulate economic activity in their designated areas. Supporters argue that benefits can arise due to the government stimulus or tax breaks available. There can also be some benefits due to the 'agglomeration effect', which is where increased economic benefits are seen as a result of concentrating the economic activity of a particular sector, or related sectors, in one place.

Economic studies have found that the main advantage of Freeports is that they encourage imports by lowering Import Duty and paperwork costs. Manufacturing businesses that are located inside the Freeport can benefit from cheaper imported inputs/components in comparison to those outside the facility, although rigorous Customs compliance requirements still apply concerning the use of Import Duty and VAT relief facilities.

Securing the boundary around the entire Freeport/Free Zone and how to control and monitor rights of access to and from it also needs to be considered from the outset, as this will have an impact on choosing their exact location, and therefore Town and Country Planning considerations will become paramount in those towns or cities with successful bids, especially where the proposed zone encroaches upon other urban development. If they are well-placed, they can be a great benefit to the final assembly or local distribution businesses that may be located, or indeed relocated, near them thereby generating local employment opportunities.

On the other hand, the UK Trade Policy Observatory (UKTPO) cautions that the evidence of wider economic benefits of Freeports and other Zones are mixed, as they depend heavily on the design of the Zones, access to transport infrastructure, skilled labour and the use of capital within the zone in question, as well as the nature of companies operating within the zone. There is also a risk that Freeports and Free Zones do not create new economic activity, but rather divert existing business into the area with the allure of tax breaks – at a cost to the taxpayer in the form of lost revenue. (Author's note: such tax breaks normally apply to new FDI, not local enterprises, as they are already registered in UK domestic territory.) The argument of lost revenue is equally doubtful, as revenue lost in terms of fiscal incentives is significantly compensated for in terms of economic benefits to the community, where business growth leads to greater levels of employment and business and economic regeneration in the region, thus resulting in an injection of wealth into the local and regional economy.

Ultimately, the UKTPO concludes that whilst some form of Free Zones could help with shaping export-oriented and place-based regional development programs, policy makers should:

1. Devise measures that counteract the possible diversion of economic activity from elsewhere; and
2. Offer a wider set of incentives than just Free Zones, while keeping within the WTO [World Trade Organisation] and any 'level playing field' obligations that arise from our trade agreements.

The UKTPO observations partly arise from the fact that, while elsewhere in the world the Free Zone concept has largely been very successful, in the UK it was never taken seriously, especially given the amount of trade conducted within the EU Single Market. This partly due to the limitations imposed by HM Customs & Excise (later HM Revenue & Customs) on the functions of the UK Freeports as largely Zones for the storage of goods under Customs control, without the facility of Customs-controlled manufacturing, namely IP Relief, which would have to be applied for by individual Free Zone tenants, and was, at the time, limited to re-export activities. Whereas the Free Zone at Shannon, on the west coast of Ireland, was very successful, partly because of its strategic location in trade flows between Ireland and the US, as well as relations with other countries such as Russia, and partly because of the flexible Customs regime conferred upon it by Irish Customs in terms of Customs-controlled manufacturing as well as storage, the UK Freeports were more constricted because of the tight regimes imposed on them by HM Customs & Excise as a result of the 1984 Finance Act, and were consequently less popular in terms of business and fiscal advantages. Indeed, at the time, the Freeport concept in the UK was never fully embraced, nor was it properly understood or even managed.

In October 2020, the government announced a review of its plans for a series of Freeports to be based in the UK. This included:

- Next steps set out on 7 October for the creation of Freeports, driving investment and creating jobs after the end of the transition period;
- Freeport bidding process in England to open before the end of the year;
- The first Freeports on track to be open by the end of 2021.

Responding to the consultation on the proposals the government confirmed that sea, air and rail ports in England will be invited to bid for Freeport status before the end of the year, with the government aiming for the first of the new sites to be open for business in 2021.

It also confirmed that the Freeports will benefit from:

- Streamlined planning processes to aid brownfield redevelopment;
- A package of tax reliefs to help drive jobs, growth and innovation;
- Simplified Customs procedures and duty suspensions on goods.

Seizing on the opportunities presented by leaving the EU, Freeports will be created across the nation to help drive Britain's post-Brexit growth. Designed to attract major domestic and international investment, the hubs of enterprise will allow places to carry out business inside a country's land border but where different Customs rules apply. The Chancellor of the Exchequer, Rishi Sunak, stated that the UK's new Freeports will create national hubs for trade, innovation and commerce, regenerating communities across the UK and supporting jobs. They will attract investment from around the world as the UK embraces new opportunities following its departure from the EU and will be a key driver for economic recovery as the UK builds back a better economy post coronavirus. He added that the government is working constructively and collaboratively with the devolved administrations to seek to establish at least one Freeport in each nation of the UK.

In brief, the UK Government outlined in its Freeport consultation several facilities that will be made available as part of the UK Freeport regime. These are:

Duty Suspension – no Import Duty, Import VAT or Excise Duty to be paid on goods brought into a Freeport from overseas (Duty and VAT Suspension) until they leave the Freeport and enter the UK's domestic market (however, separate excise approvals would be required for such activities);

Duty/Tariff Inversion – if the duty on a finished product is lower than that on the component parts, a company could benefit by importing components duty-free, manufacture the final product in the Freeport and then pay the duty at the rate of the finished product when it enters the UK's domestic market;

Duty-Free Re-exports – a company could import components duty-free, manufacture the final product in the Freeport and then pay no tariffs on the components when the final product is re-exported;

Simplified Customs Procedures – the government intends to introduce streamlined procedures to enable businesses to access Freeports.

These measures engender exactly the operations that could be carried out in the UK Freeports, and should, as a matter of course, be adopted in the UK's Free Zone initiative. However, further advantages such as Corporation Tax and Property Tax incentives, enhanced regulatory freedoms and reduced overall bureaucracy, should also be granted, equally as a matter of course, to companies wishing to locate in the envisaged Free Zones/Freeports as additional incentives in order to foster economic and commercial growth through the Free Zone initiative, namely the opportunities afforded by SEZs in their international perspective. The main issues are that each Freeport, or Free Zone, will differ from others depending upon the region where it is located, and even the specific activities likely to take place within the Free Zone in particular. Although most, if not all, proposed Freeports are likely to be located next to major seaports in the UK, their activities will also be influenced by the ports where they are located. The ports of the east coast handle different traffic from the ports located in the south-west of the UK, and indeed the specific activities envisaged by each of the Freeports will vary according to their location. One of the main driving factors behind the Freeports to be located on the River Thames is the large automotive plant at Dagenham, while much of the driving force behind the Teesport Freeport is likely to be the automotive plant belonging to Nissan up in Washington, Tyne & Wear.

Further information on the Freeport initiative (as supplied by UK Government in 2020)

- At the centre of the new Freeports policy is a new Customs model, based on international best practice. The flexible model will improve upon both the UK's existing Customs arrangements and the Freeports that previously existed in the UK;
- The government will also introduce a package of tax reliefs on investment by businesses within Freeport tax sites, new measures to speed up planning processes to accelerate development in and around Freeports and new initiatives to encourage innovators to generate new ideas to create additional economic growth and jobs;
- A company can import goods into a Freeport without paying tariffs, process them into a final product and then either pay a tariff, that is, Import Duty, on goods sold into the domestic market, or export the final goods without paying UK tariffs;
- The government wishes to deliver Freeports as soon as possible and will make further announcements in due course (estimated implementation late 2021);
- It is intended that all the nations of the UK should be able to share in the benefits of Freeports. As such, the government is working collaboratively with the devolved administrations to ensure Freeports are a UK-wide offer that will enable the creation of Freeports in England, Wales, Scotland and Northern Ireland;
- Freeports will be selected through a fair, transparent and competitive process, and will be expected to collaborate closely with key partners across the public and private sectors. The bidding process for locations to become a Freeport in England opened by the end of 2020, and bids were submitted to the UK Government at the beginning of 2021.

The government approach towards the UK Freeport initiative is designed to be as flexible as possible, enabling investors in the Freeport initiative to use the Freeport facilities as widely as possible depending upon their proposed commercial activities. Although the project is at an early stage in its development, there is in reality a huge potential for development of the UK Freeport initiative, with significant economic, commercial, social and fiscal benefits for all concerned.

CHAPTER 17

Conclusions

Since their first establishment more than 50 years ago in the West of Ireland at Shannon (1959), Free Zones have played an important role in the economic development of both national and international economies. From Ireland throughout the world, the overall concept of Free Zones has attracted national business start-ups, development and multinational conglomerates. They are particularly beneficial to economic and commercial development and have been especially prevalent and influential to economic policy in lesser-developed or economically developing countries. Although the primary purpose of Free Zones is to reduce or eliminate import duties and taxes by way of duty and tax suspension concerning operations in the Zones themselves, the other purpose of the Zones is to provide a vehicle for economic development and Foreign Direct Investment, especially where re-export activities are involved.

Studies carried out by various economic organisations, including the World Bank, UNCTAD and UNIDO, have shown that UAE-based Free Zones, especially those in Dubai, have had a significant economic impact on both regional and global trade. The combined trade value of UAE Free Zones account for more than 80% of the country's non-oil exports. A good example is Dubai's JAFZA, whose 2014 levels of exports reached a staggering US$90 billion, providing more than 200,000 jobs to the region.

It is clear that Free Zones generate positive macro and microeconomic impact. The following is a summary of some of the benefits:

- Macroeconomic: attraction of Foreign Direct Investment, increase in exports, diversification and development of the economy, and the creation of employment as well as a larger market-base through the inflow of an expatriate workforce, leading to an overall increase in national revenue and greater national economic prosperity;
- Microeconomic: reduction or suspension of import duties and taxes, improved competition, transfer of knowledge as well as greater export orientation and sophistication of local companies;
- Strategically: greater economic stability and higher levels of local economic power and influence, as well as greater influence on regional trade.

Overall, Free Zones of any kind have brought significant benefits to the economies of the countries where they are located. Some examples have been more successful than others. Some of the African Free Zones have not met with resounding success, nor have they been managed well. The Onne Free Zone, also known as the Onne Export Free Zone, based in the Niger Delta in Nigeria, has been plagued with accusations of corruption

DOI: 10.4324/9781003232025-18

and mismanagement, as well as disputes between the main logistics company, Integrated Logistics Services (INTELS) and the Free Zone Authority. Various online reports about the Subic Bay Free Zone in the Philippines have suggested that the zone has met with limited success, and has not enjoyed the economic and fiscal benefits once envisaged when it was originally established, to the point that several companies located in the zone have had to close down. Conversely, the economic fortunes of the United Arab Emirates have resulted in the creation of at least 30 Free Zones of different kinds in Dubai alone, all vigorously contributing to the UAE economy. The US FTZs have also contributed greatly to the US national economy, and indeed also contribute to the economies of other countries in both North and South America, as well as the Caribbean basin. Much of the success of Free Zones lies in their operational efficiency, their fiscal benefits to the economy and their overall promotion. Certain criticisms have been levelled at various global Free Zones, including the exploitation of workforces, the illegal us of child labour, low wages, as well as the illegal use of Free Zones for smuggling and contraband. Indeed, EU legislation was tightened up to eliminate the illegal use of Free Zones within the European Union. However, these criticisms have been somewhat exaggerated in their content, and in general the overall effect of Free Zones has been to significantly benefit the national economy, especially in the case of the developing countries. Even in fully developed countries such as Canada and the US, the Free Zone concept has provided significant economic benefits to a variety of commercial sectors. On the negative side, some Free Zones have been implicated in illicit activities such as money laundering, smuggling and organised crime, although many of the accusations levelled at particular Zones have yet to be proven.

Every Free Zone initiative carries a level of risk. However, regulatory control and governance over each Free Zone will reduce this level of risk, making the Free Zone more efficient and competitive as a result. Risk control and analysis is crucial in Free Zone management, and must be exercised at all times if the Free Zone is to be viable and reliable in terms of national economic development. However, risk is variable, and can only be ascertained by way of perception, calculation and analysis. Risk also depends upon the steps that have been taken to implement strict controls over Free Zone operations, and the extent to which those controls are all-embracing.

Planning is also vital to the process. Many Free Zones have come into existence largely as a result of government Free Zone legislation, not because of a prior need. Free zone legislation may occur because of a need for it and the prior need for some form of major economic development. The developing world saw Free Zones as a means of swift economic development, coupled with the incentives for the attraction of Foreign Direct Investment. This challenge resulted in Free Zone legislation being enacted in many developing countries across the globe, where the need for Free Zone regimes had already been defined. However, in other cases, Free Zones have developed on the back of existing Free Zone regimes. In some cases, these ventures have been very successful, such as in Dubai, while in other cases, they were seen simply as a means of attempting to bring economic life to deprived areas or areas where previous ventures or establishments such as military bases had already left. Such was the case with the Subic Bay Free Zone in the Philippines, which was developed in the wake of the departure of US Forces from the Subic Bay Naval Base in 1991, and the nearby Clark Air Force Base, which was vacated at about the same time. The principle of the Free Zone at Subic Bay was admirable; it was designed to create employment which had been lost after the departure of the US

Forces. However, its planning failed to establish the actual need for a Free Zone in the area and indeed how it would attract Foreign Direct Investment, and the result has been that the Free Zone has seen mixed fortunes, to the extent that it never enjoyed the same fortunes as its counterparts elsewhere in South-East Asia. It has largely become an area for shipbuilding and maintenance, rather than pure industrial development.

In mid-2019, there were about 135,000 workers employed in the Subic Bay Freeport, 68.37% of which were engaged in the service industry and 17.03% in the manufacturing industry. Subic was also a hub in shipbuilding, with the now-defunct Hanjin Philippines yard previously being the single biggest employer in the area prior to its bankruptcy in January 2019. As of mid-2019, there were 5,901 workers, or 4.36% of the whole zone, employed in the shipbuilding and maritime industry from 96 companies, compared to 26,559 workers from 110 companies in 2018, perhaps showing the relative decline in the facility. It could be argued that the Subic Bay facility was never properly planned or managed, but the global economic climate could be a contributor to this decline coupled with a failure on the part of the project to recognise its full potential. The Free Zone was heralded as an ideal replacement for the military facilities originally in the location, but it never lived up to the aspirations that the authorities originally held. Today, it is more of a Freeport rather than a fully-fledged Free Zone, as it concentrates on maritime-related activities, many of which are services-oriented. Although the whole fenced-off area of 14,000 hectares (35,000 acres) is referred to as the Subic Bay Freeport Zone, where much of the development of the Special Economic Zone has taken place, out of this area only some 2,800 hectares (6,900 acres) is suitable for commercial development, with the remaining portions consisting of high slopes, forests, or protected areas.

Where Part One has dealt with the theory and practice of the various types of Free Zone, Part Two deals with specific examples of Free Zones and Free Zone activity around the world, and comparisons can therefore be made of how Free Zones operate in each location analysed. These Zones differ in function according to their location, but in each case, they demonstrate how Free Zone development has shaped the regional and national economies, and how the Free Zone concept has proved overall to be a significant enhancement to national economic development for both developing and fully developed countries. These case studies show how the concept of Freeports in the UK, especially in the North of England, could be a significant benefit to the regional economy, as well as encouraging overall economic growth in the UK, at a time when it is most needed. There is no one specific case study which provide all the answers, and on this basis alone it is essential to analyse each Free Zone example as pertinent to the needs of the national economy which it serves. However, given that most of the Free Zone examples quoted have common elements such as duty and tax incentives, the model that each zone represents is entirely unique according to the varying levels and types of tax incentives conferred upon it by the national government. Free Zones selected from different parts of the world illustrate the extent to which national Free Zone policy has determined the type of zone used in each country quoted, and how it has benefitted that country's economy. As shown, there is no common denominator to all the Zones analysed, and this demonstrates the diversity and variety of each Free Zone project. The only common denominator for all examples is that they are all classed as some form of Free Zone. In this respect, they are all grouped in a generic description, yet all are distinguishable and thus identifiable in their own way.

PART TWO

SPECIFIC GLOBAL FREE ZONE EXAMPLES

SECTION 1

North America

The US FTZ program

A US Foreign-Trade Zone (FTZ) is a secure, geographical area authorised by the US Federal Government, where commercial merchandise, both domestic and foreign, receives the same treatment by US Customs as if it were outside the commercial remit of the United States and also outside the Customs jurisdiction of the US. Many companies use FTZs to defer the payment of duties and taxes, and in the case of re-export of cargo, to avoid the applicable duties and taxes altogether, as the merchandise was considered to have never entered the national US consumption area, known as Free Circulation.

FTZs can be operated by both public and private entities, either in general-purpose Zones or specific subzones.

Merchandise of every description may be held in FTZs without being subject to US Customs Duties or other value-added taxes. Importers, manufacturers and distributors can achieve significant cost-savings benefits because, normally, when foreign cargo lands on US territory, it is subject to clearance through US Customs, and requires the immediate payment of US Customs Duties. However, if it is moved into a distant Foreign-Trade Zone, that is, an inland zone away from or even adjacent to the port or airport itself, it is held in the zone on a duty and tax-suspended basis, which amounts to a form of duty and tax relief while the goods are located within the zone. This tariff and tax relief is designed to lower the costs of US-based businesses engaged in international trade, and thereby create and retain the employment and capital investment opportunities which result from these operations.

FTZs operate under the oversight and supervision of US Customs & Border Protection (USCBP), as part of the US Homeland Security Council. They are also subscribers to the NAFTZ (National Association of Foreign-Trade Zones), based in Washington DC. Even though FTZs are considered to be outside the national Customs territory of the United States, they are located on US soil, including Alaska, Hawaii and Puerto Rico, which itself has three FTZs located on its territory. For that reason, goods and activities in FTZs are subject to federal, State and local laws and regulations. Articles prohibited by law are not allowed admission, nor are articles that violate copyright, trademark or patent laws. Animal quarantine restrictions apply as well. As long as the merchandise remains in an FTZ, it is not subject to US Customs laws governing the entry of goods into Customs territory or payment of Import Duty on the goods concerned.

In the United States, a Foreign-Trade Zone **(FTZ)** is a geographical area, in (or adjacent to) a US Port of Entry, where commercial merchandise, both domestic and foreign receives the same Customs treatment it would if it were outside the commerce of the United States. The purpose of such Zones is to help American businesses to be competitive in the global economy by reducing tariff burdens on the importation of foreign inputs and

DOI: 10.4324/9781003232025-20

on exported finished products. Another definition of an FTZ states that it is an isolated, enclosed and policed area operated as a public utility, furnished with facilities for loading, unloading, handling, storing, manipulating, manufacturing and exhibiting goods and for reshipping them by land, water or air. Merchandise of every description may be held in the zone without being subject to US tariffs (Customs Duties) and other ad valorem taxes. This tariff and tax relief is designed to lower the costs of US-based operations engaged in international trade activities and thereby create and retain the employment and capital investment opportunities that result from those operations.

These special geographic areas that constitute Foreign-Trade Zones are established 'in or adjacent to' US Ports of Entry and are under the supervision of the US Customs and Border Protection department under the US Homeland Security Council. The relevant State government must also have passed a law enabling the establishment of such Zones.

Since 1986, US Customs' oversight of FTZ operations has been conducted on an audit-inspection basis known as Compliance Reviews, whereby compliance is assured through audits and spot checks under a surety bond, rather than through on-site supervision by Customs personnel.

There are at present some 300 Foreign-Trade Zone projects and nearly 400 subzones in the United States.

There are two types of FTZs: General-Purpose Zones, also known as ***magnet sites***, and Special-purpose subzones, which are owned and operated by individual specific companies for more specific use, such as manufacturing or processing activities. General-purpose Zones operate as public utilities, providing a variety of services to many users. Special-purpose subzones are single-use facilities which cannot be accommodated within the general-purpose Zones. Magnet sites are usually located at ports or industrial parks, and are open to multiple zone users. Subzones or ***Usage-Driven sites*** are approved for a specific company or use.

The benefits to zone users are:

- **Duty Suspension**. No duties on or quota charges on goods in the zone or on re-exports;
- **Duty Deferral**. Customs Duties and federal excise tax deferred on imports;
- **Inverted Tariff**. In situations where zone production results in a finished product that has a lower duty rate than the rates on foreign inputs (inverted tariff), the finished products may be entered at the duty rate that applies to its condition as it leaves the zone (requires prior authorisation);
- **Logistical Benefits**. Companies using FTZ procedures may have access to streamlined Customs procedures (e.g. 'weekly entry' or 'direct delivery');
- **Other Benefits**. Foreign goods and domestic goods held for export are exempt from State/local inventory taxes. FTZ status may also make a site eligible for State/local benefits which are unrelated to the FTZ Act.

The public and regional/national economic benefits are:

- Help facilitate and expedite international trade;
- Provide special Customs procedures as a public service to help US companies to conduct international trade-related operations in competition with foreign plants;

- Encourage and facilitate exports and imports;
- Help attract offshore activity and encourage retention of domestic activity;
- Assist State/local economic development efforts;
- Help create employment opportunities.

Activities permitted in FTZs are:

- Merchandise in a zone may be assembled, exhibited, cleaned, manipulated, manufactured, mixed, processed, relabelled, repackaged, repaired, salvaged, sampled, stored, tested, displayed and destroyed;
- Production activity must be specifically authorised by the FTZ Board. (Production activity is defined as activity involving the substantial transformation of a foreign article or activity involving a change in the condition of the article which results in a change in the Customs classification of the article or in its eligibility for entry for consumption, i.e. manufacturing and processing activities.);
- Retail trade is prohibited in Zones.

Foreign-Trade Zone sites must be within or adjacent to a US Customs and Border Protection (CBP) port of entry.

The adjacency requirement can be satisfied if one of the following factors is met:

1. The zone or subzone site is within the limits of a CBP port of entry.
2. The zone or subzone site is within 60 statute miles of the outer limits of a CBP port of entry.
3. The zone or subzone site is within 90 minutes' driving time from the outer limits of a CBP port of entry as verified by the CBP Service Port Director.
4. For subzones only: subzone sites that are outside the 60 miles/90 minutes driving time from the outer limits of the CBP port of entry may alternatively qualify to be considered adjacent if they work with the CBP Port Director to ensure that proper oversight measures are in place.

The largest industry currently using zone procedures in the US is the petroleum refining industry. Significant zone manufacturing also occurs in the automotive, electronics and pharmaceutical product areas.

There is also the facility of ASF (Alternative Site framework). The ASF is an optional framework for organising and designating sites that allows Zones to use quicker and less complex procedures to obtain FTZ designation for eligible facilities. In January 2009, the Foreign-Trade Zones Board adopted a FTZ Board staff proposal to make the ASF as a means of designating and managing general-purpose FTZ sites through reorganisation. The ASF provides Foreign-Trade Zone Grantees with greater flexibility to meet specific requests for zone status by utilising the minor boundary modification process. The theory of the ASF is that by more closely linking the amount of FTZ designated space to the amount of space activated with Customs and Border Protection, Zone users would have better and quicker access to benefits. When a FTZ Grantee evaluates whether or not to expand its FTZ project in order to improve the ease in which the Zone may be utilised by existing companies, as well as how it attracts new prospective companies, the ASF should be considered. The ASF may be an appropriate option for certain Foreign-Trade Zone projects, but the decision of whether to adopt the new framework and what the configuration of the sites should be will require careful analysis and planning. Regardless of the choice to expand the FTZ project, the sites should be selected and the application should be drafted in such a manner as to receive swift approval, while maximising benefit to those that locate in the Zone. Successful zone projects are generally the result of a plan developed and implemented by individuals that understand all aspects of the FTZ program.

To reorganise under the ASF, each zone grantee, that is, the organisation owning and operating the zone, will propose a 'service area', namely a local region where the zone is designated to operate, for example Spartanburg County, South Carolina. Once approved by the FTZ Board, a subzone or usage-driven site can be designated anywhere in the service area within 30 days using a simple application form. The ASF allows subzone designation to be brought to any company that needs it, eliminating the need for zone grantees to predict where the zone will be needed and pre-designate sites. It is this facility that has allowed automotive companies such as BMW and Mercedes to establish subzones in the overall area covered by an FTZ operation.

Other countries around the world have Free-Trade Zones that are often confused with the US Foreign-Trade Zones program. While there are similarities, the FTZ program is very different from other countries' Free-Trade Zones. In a number of 'Free-Trade Zones' in other countries – particularly those in developing countries – the sole benefit is the avoidance of internal Customs Duties on products that are re-exported from the Free-Trade Zone. Often, the goods are not even allowed to be sold in the country where the Free-Trade Zone exists. One often hears these Zones referred to as 'Export Processing Zones'. The US Foreign-Trade Zones program not only allows the sale and importation of merchandise to the US Commerce, but in many cases enables companies to reduce or eliminate duties on products manufactured for domestic consumption. This relief from inverted tariff benefit is one of the key distinctions between the US Foreign-Trade Zones program and other countries Free-Trade Zone programs. Generally Free-Trade Zones offer significantly less opportunity for benefits and tariff savings. As previously mentioned, in many cases the company must actually export all the merchandise they bring into a Free-Trade Zone (if it is an Export Processing Zone). In other cases, importation is allowed, but not manufacturing of merchandise. Under the US FTZ program, companies can obtain FTZ benefits such as, duty exemption on re-exports, duty elimination on waste, scrap, and yield loss, duty exemption on damaged, or nonconforming items, reduction in Merchandise Processing Fees (MPF) and brokerage fees through weekly entry, cash flow savings, and relief from ad valorem tax, and the previously described relief from inverted tariffs. They can also establish manufacturing activities subject to US government approval in the form of a subzone, as long as such activities benefit the local economy.

In the US, the Foreign-Trade Zone Board is led by the Secretary of Commerce and the Secretary of the Treasury. The FTZ Board, and indeed, the FTZ program, was created with the Foreign-Trade Zones Act of 1934 to combat the prevalent economic slump that resulted from the 1929 Wall Street Crash, and to mitigate some of the destructive economic adversities caused by the implementation of the Smoot-Hawley tariffs, which had been imposed in 1930 as a means of attempting to protect the US economy from cheap foreign imports. The FTZ initiative was designed to stimulate international trade, as well as to stimulate economic investment in FTZ activities and create large numbers of jobs for the struggling US economy. In all these aspects, the result was a progressive success, and indeed, the program contributed to the US's major recovery from the slump.

In 1950, the original act was amended to open up FTZs to manufacturing, but it had little impact until 1980. In that year, Congress again amended the act so that products manufactured in the Zones would not be assessed on US value-added content, that is, that all US value-added activities, that is, the use of local labour and US-sourced materials, would not be included in the liability of the finished product for US Import Duty. This ensured that the only tariffs that a producer inside the zone selling to US customers would pay, would be on the value of the raw materials imported into the zone from outside the US. This integrated model, which replaced the previous 'island' model, spurred growth in the US Foreign-Trade Zones program and resulted in a massive development of the Zones from the 1980s onwards.

Some of the benefits of operating a FTZ include:

- Improved inventory management;
- Automated record-keeping and document storage;
- Increased visibility of the supply chain;
- Improved cash flow;
- Improved company compliance;
- Lessened US regulatory agency requirements for re-export.

Inverted tariff benefits exist when the duty rate for the overall finished good is lower than the duty rate of the component parts. For example, US automobiles have an ad valorem import tariff rate of 2.5%, while their component parts may have import tariff rates of up to 6.5%. This means that it is far more advantageous to import the parts into a US subzone manufacturing plant under Import Duty suspension, manufacture the car in the subzone using additional US-procured components, and declare the finished product into Free Circulation with the Customs declaration based on the value of the imported components but at the lower import tariff rate of the finished automobile. Therefore, by manufacturing finished goods within an FTZ, US importers can take advantage of the inverted tariff duty rate, all while keeping manufacturing operations within the US. Inverted tariff works when an importer with manufacturing authority within an FTZ is allowed to admit their components into the zone duty-free, manufacture the finished good and pay CBP duties on the foreign content in the finished good at the lower duty rate of the finished goods at the time of entry. The importer avoids paying the higher duty rate on the component parts and defers the lower duty payment on the value of the foreign content until the time of consumption in the commerce of the US. Inverted tariff is seen predominantly in the manufacturing industry, benefitting automotive, petroleum, pharmaceutical, aerospace, electronics, textile companies and many more.

The Foreign-Trade Zone Board (FTZB), based in Washington DC, approved the reorganisation of Foreign-Trade Zone (FTZ) #32 (Miami) under the ASF, allowing the FTZ operator to expand its site area without the need for re-application for FTZ approval. The application submitted by its grantee, The Greater Miami Foreign-Trade Zone, was approved and officially ordered by the FTZB on 8 January 2013. From California, to Oklahoma to North Carolina to New York State, FTZs all across the nation have recently been making use of the flexible opportunities offered by the ASF program. The ASF program is designed to serve zone projects that want the flexibility to both attract users/operators to certain fixed sites but also want the ability to serve companies at other locations where the demand for FTZ services arises in the future. FTZ #32 was founded in

1979 and processes over $1 billion in goods with products from more than 65 countries and exported to more than 75 countries worldwide, with speed and efficiency. According to the official order from the FTZB, FTZ #32 existing site 1, Miami Free Zone will be classified as a magnet site, that is, an industrial park or multi-tenant site designated as a Foreign-Trade Zone. Today, there are over 260 FTZs operating in the US, all dealing with a wide variety of products and materials, importing from and exporting to various parts of the world, as well as supplying the US national economy.

US FTZ Corporations have a remarkable record of success with preparing, submitting, and obtaining approval of Foreign-Trade Zone Board subzone and manufacturing applications. In many cases, the FTZ Corporation has received Foreign-Trade Zone Board approval for subzone and manufacturing applications and been successful in industries where other consulting or law firms have failed. The FTZ Corporation's extraordinary success is even more noteworthy considering the FTZ Corporation has prepared and submitted over 100 Foreign-Trade Zone Board applications or requests.

Too often, consulting or law firms place insufficient focus on trade policy issues and the proper presentation of data due to a lack of understanding of the Foreign-Trade Zone Board review process. This type of oversight can result not only in costly delays of the application's approval, but even more expensive Foreign-Trade Zone Board restrictions that greatly reduce, or even eliminate FTZ savings.

The Foreign-Trade Zone Corporation has established its remarkable record of success by utilising its in-depth knowledge of trade policy as well as its understanding of the criteria and methodology by which the FTZ Board evaluates applications in the careful preparation of our client's Foreign-Trade Zone Board applications. This attentive, informed approach combined with both the FTZ Corporation's vigilant monitoring of the application through the review process, and its skill in organising political support, when necessary, will help ensure a company's application receives a positive outcome.

Most recently, the FTZ Corporation has again broken new ground by preparing and securing the first FTZ manufacturing or subzone application ever that allowed the reduction of textile duty rates utilising Foreign-Trade Zone manufacturing procedures. Prior to the recent furniture manufacturing successes, the FTZ Corporation had the same success in the Forklift Industry (previous service providers' applications were denied), the first space launch vehicle application success, and other successes too numerous to mention. Other subzones include the BMW manufacturing plant at Greenville-Spartanburg, South Carolina (Subzone 38A), and the Mercedes plant at Huntsville, Alabama. On the Gulf coast, oil refineries between Mobile, Alabama and South-West Texas are all classified as subzones, bringing in crude oil and re-exporting it as refined oil products overseas. These subzones were all approved by the US Federal Government partly because of their duty and tax suspension facilities, but also because they attracted a large number of jobs owing to the resulting economic and financial incentives that they offered.

A general-purpose zone is a warehouse, industrial park, or seaport or airport that has been designated as an FTZ. Multiple companies can use general-purpose Zones simultaneously for the purpose of storing merchandise, equipment, parts, and other goods. The biggest benefit for the companies leasing space within a general-purpose zone is that the costs associated with the space are shared, thus, reducing each companies' liability.

General-purpose Zones are well suited to those that import or export finished products, parts, or components. They are also a good choice for those companies that need an FTZ for a shorter length of time. These companies are able to use an FTZ on an as-needed basis, which avoids the costs associated with investing in building, operating, and maintaining a stand-alone warehouse structure. In addition, general-purpose warehouses offer companies services such as packaging, inventory control, and other logistics services.

FTZ subzones

Although most FTZs are general-purpose Zones, many manufacturing FTZs are classed as subzones, that is, Foreign-Trade Zones dedicated specifically to a single company.

A subzone is an FTZ site that is dedicated to a single company for a specific activity or purpose, and which is associated with a local general-purpose FTZ. This scenario is only the case when operations cannot be accommodated within an existing general-purpose zone. Typical users of a Special-purpose zone are manufacturing plants and distribution facilities that are not geographically close to other industrial and commercial spaces.

All financial responsibilities to build, maintain, secure and operate the zone lie with the company since they are the sole tenant. Subzones generally work better for large companies, as they are considered to be cost-prohibitive for smaller manufacturing businesses. In reality, smaller business can locate in a general-purpose FTZ as long as the space exists for their operations and that they are able to satisfy the requirements laid down by the national federal authorities. Car manufacturers such as BMW and Mercedes are a good example of the type of company that uses the subzone type of facility.

Companies wishing to operate a subzone are required to submit a detailed application that can take between 9 and 12 months to process by the authorities. If there are concerns from the public, this process can take much longer. In order to gain approval, the company must demonstrate that such a site would be of significant public and economic benefit. Therefore, companies cannot simply state that operating in a subzone will save them money, or improve their production and expect to be approved. This is why companies such as BMW were able to satisfy the authorities that a dedicated subzone for their proposed US manufacturing operations would be beneficial not only for them but also for the South Carolina economy, where they proposed to establish a manufacturing plant.

These subzones include automotive plants and oil refineries, as well as other companies involved in manufacturing based on the import of raw materials and the re-export of finished products. A particular case is that of the BMW plant at Greenville-Spartanburg, South Carolina, that was established in 1992 and commenced operations in 1994. The German car manufacturer BMW wanted to use the US FTZ regime to take advantage of lower tariffs by establishing its own FTZ, and it chose the State of South Carolina because of its development potential, as well as the business incentives offered by the US government for doing so. One of the main arguments was that it would guarantee the employment of around 500 people in the plant, as well as 10,000 further jobs in the surrounding supply sector. It also had access to the major seaport at Charleston, also in South Carolina, for the purpose of the import of materials and the re-export of finished vehicles.

The other main advantage of FTZ status was that BMW could import the components from Europe into the FTZ, manufacture these components into the finished cars under Customs control, and then either import the cars into US Free Circulation by paying US Import Duty on the cars themselves or re-exporting the cars worldwide, therefore avoiding any US Import Duty or tax. The added advantage was that the imported components were liable for higher Import Duty rates than were the finished vehicles which only had a US Import Duty of 2.5%, thus resulting in a phenomenon called **Tariff Inversion** or **Reversed Cascading**. The resulting solution was that cars imported into US Free Circulation were liable for US Import Duty based on the *ad valorem* duty rate of the finished car, but at the value of the imported components. This facility also allows for the import of components under this principle, combine these with locally sourced materials, and then declare the finished product into Free Circulation at the value of the imported materials but at the Import Duty rate of the finished product, excluding the value of the locally sourced materials. In the UK, this facility is also known as Tariff Inversion, and is used within the Inward Processing facility as PFC. The Mercedes manufacturing facility at the FTZ subzone in Huntsville, Alabama, uses the same kind of facility.

The first cars to roll off the Greenville-Spartanburg assembly line using this facility were the famous BMW Z3 convertible, and since then many other types of BMW have been produced at the plant. In 2011, BMW's South Carolina facility produced over 276,000 vehicles for over 130 markets around the world, representing a 73% increase from the previous year: 70% of the vehicles produced were exported, making BMW the United States' largest automotive exporter to non-NAFTA countries.

BMW Manufacturing Company, LLC is part of BMW Group's global manufacturing network and is the exclusive manufacturing plant for all X5 and X3 Sports Activity Vehicles and X6 Sports Activity Coupes. The company generated output volumes of 350,000 vehicles per year by 2014. In addition, BMW introduced plans to manufacture a new sport activity vehicle, the X4, at this location soon after. Since 1994, the plant has undergone four major expansions and produced six different BMW models. As a result, employment has grown from 500 in 1994 to more than 7,000 today. In 2012, the facility celebrated the production of its two-millionth vehicle since the company began US production in 1994. This concept has therefore become one of the main features of many US subzones, and an increasing number of companies are submitting applications to the US FTZ Board to create their own subzones to use Customs-controlled facilities for manufacturing purposes, for either release of finished products into US Free Circulation, or for the re-export of these products overseas.

Canada

The Montréal Mirabel Free-Trade Zone

The international airport at Mirabel, several kilometres to the North-east of the city of Montréal, was created to cater primarily for the Montréal Olympic Games in 1976, but the overall plan was to create a massive international airport to rival any other North American Airport. The plan was to create several main terminals with satellite offshoots, and was masterminded by the Canadian Prime Minister of the time, Pierre Trudeau. However, most of the airport was never developed. It had one major terminal with its satellites, and two long runways, designed for the intercontinental jetliners. The airport was considered too far out of the city centre to be economical and viable, and the decision was taken in the late 1980s under the administration of Prime Minister Brian Mulroney to transfer all major airline activities to the International Airport of Dorval, located to the south-west of the city of Montréal on Montréal Island, which was, in any case, much closer to the city itself.

To foster optimum utilisation of the remaining airport facilities at Montréal Mirabel Airport, which was therefore being downgraded in the face of the transfer of all major international flights to Montréal Dorval Airport, and to attract strategic companies which could contribute to the development of Mirabel as a hub of international trade, a package of tax benefits was introduced in the 1999–2000 federal budget of 9 March 1999, establishing a Free-Trade Zone at Mirabel, adjacent to the airport complex. The tax benefits relating to the Montréal Foreign-Trade Zone at Mirabel (ZCIMM) comprised a holiday from income tax, the tax on capital and employer contributions to the Canadian Health Services Fund (HSF), and various refundable tax credits, as well as relief from Customs Duties and GST/TVQ (Goods and Services Tax/Taxe de Vente Québecoise), with all tax holidays ending by the close of December 2013. In addition, certain foreign specialists employed by an eligible corporation could be granted a tax exemption.

The main purpose of the Mirabel Free-Trade Zone was primarily to induce economic investment in the region by fiscal means, while supplying a means of swift and efficient inward and outward movement of air cargo to and from the region. In order to ensure investment potential by attracting companies into the Free Zone, the fiscal incentives introduced were as follows:

Tax holidays (until December 2013)

- Corporate income tax;
- Personal income tax for foreign specialist employees of investing companies;
- Tax on capital;
- Employer contribution to health services fund.

Refundable tax credits (until December 2004)

- Salaries of eligible employees (excluding light manufacturing companies); 30%

Other incentives were:

- Priority assistance for companies wishing to apply for individual Customs approvals, for example, to operate Customs Warehousing or other Import Duty relief facilities;
- Export Distribution Centre (EDC) status;
- Recruiting, training and assistance in human resources management (until December 2013).

Although it was never intended that the general-purpose of the zone would be as a Customs-controlled entity, as in the case of the zone's US neighbours within the regime of the US Foreign-Trade Zone (FTZ) network, Customs facilities were to be made available for individual companies operating from within the zone, thus making the zone a hybrid Free Zone for both Direct and Indirect Tax incentive purposes, which was a similar function to the Free Zones of Dubai and other EPZs. It should be noted that while the generic zone facilities of tax incentives were available for the zone in general, Customs-controlled facilities were available purely on a company-by-company basis depending upon the individual needs of the company concerned.

Customs approvals from Revenue Canada were seen as being indirectly part of the package of benefits, as it was intended that the zone should be promoted for the use of companies engaged in international trade activities, that is, import and export to and from the region. For this reason, partial refunds of Customs brokerage fees were made part of the overall scheme of benefits to zone users, thus stimulating Customs-related activity within the zone. It was envisaged that the zone would attract companies involved in importing and exporting and which would thus enhance Québec's international trade profile. Furthermore, the incentive of EDC status would also enable companies involved in import/export activities to gain the benefit of being rendered exempt from GST (General Sales Tax) liability by means of using the EDC status for the purpose of export activities. However, this exemption was in fact conditional, as it depended upon the compliance of companies using the facility with GST/Provincial Sales Tax (PST) requirements laid down by Revenue Canada and was therefore completely separate from Customs authorisations granted by the authorities. It was stated by the Mirabel Zone Authority that in order for companies to make full use of the Free-Trade Zone facilities available, they had to also apply for the operation of a number of Customs programs available through the Canada Customs and Revenue Agency (CCRA). These programs include:

- Import Duty Processing Relief;
- Customs Warehousing;
- Export Distribution Centres (EDCs) (initiated 1 January 2001).

It should also be noted that such programs were not governed by the provincial government structure (other than Provincial Sales Taxes), but by the Federal Government based in Ottawa, as the Customs system is of a national nature and not a provincial one.

Companies wishing to take advantage of the financial and tax incentives offered by the Free-Trade Zone had to apply in writing to the zone authority and had to be able to satisfy special economic criteria before they could be admitted for operating from within the zone. Each specific project was evaluated by the zone authority and had to be accompanied by a certificate of eligibility issued by the [Canadian] Ministry of Finance.

Activities considered eligible for zone operations included:

- Aerospace;
- Aircraft, navigational equipment and ground services equipment, maintenance and repair services;
- Advanced aviation training;
- International logistics (supply, distribution and value-added services) – transportation services are excluded;
- Light manufacturing.

The criteria for operational eligibility within the zone were as follows:

- Projects should involve new activities in order to avoid the displacement of existing activities from elsewhere in Québec;

- Projects should not compete with enterprises already engaged in similar operations elsewhere in Québec;
- Each enterprise had to maintain separate accounting procedures for its operations in the Foreign-Trade Zone;
- Each project had to generate a total operating payroll of over C$400,000;
- At least 90% of the operations carried out in the Foreign-Trade Zone had to be related to eligible activities.

The implication of the above criteria was that no company operating from within the Foreign-Trade Zone could use its fiscally advantageous position unfairly to compete against other companies operating within the confines of the provincial Québecois economic structure, that is, not subject to the zone's fiscal advantages.

Among the conditions to satisfy to be eligible for the ZCIMM tax measure, a corporation needed to, during one year, have an establishment in Québec Province and carry on an eligible business outside the ZCIMM. In addition, the corporation could not be:

- A Corporation that was tax-exempt for the year in question;
- A Crown Corporation or a wholly-owned subsidiary of such a corporation;
- A Corporation governed, during the year, by an act incorporating a labour fund.

Special rules applied for corporations that temporarily carried on an eligible business outside the ZCIMM.

In general, for the purposes of the ZCIMM tax measure, an 'eligible business' had to be carrying out activities in at least one of the following sectors:

- International Logistics;
- Aircraft Maintenance and Repair;
- Aircraft Construction (e.g. Bombardier);
- Supplemental Training in the field of Aviation;
- Light Processing and Manufacture.

Investissement Québec could also issue an Eligibility Certificate to any other businesses carried on by a Corporation in the ZCIMM whose activities were of particular interest to the Québec economy. The assistance measures available to companies investing in the zone included:

- Facilitating the enterprises' establishment on the site;
- Reduction of operating costs in the Foreign-Trade Zone;
- Assistance in operating in a Customs Free Zone;
- Training and recruiting the workers required;
- Attracting foreign specialists.

The organisation operating the zone was the Société de Développement de la Zone de Commerce International de Montréal à Mirabel (ZCIMM). This organisation was responsible for:

- Acting a as a multiservice outlet for enterprises;
- Promoting the Foreign-Trade Zone;
- Submitting recommendations to the Ministry of Finance concerning the eligibility of projects for assistance measures.

Operating assistance included:

- Income Tax exemption;
- Exemption from tax on capital;
- Exemption from Health Services Fund contributions;
- Refundable Tax Credit on salaries of eligible employees, except the employees of a manufacturing concern. Credit started at 40%, and reduced by 10% each successive year.

Assistance to operate in a Customs Free Zone included:

- Access to specialists from the Development Corporation to help enterprises manage Customs Duty and Sales Tax exemption or deferral programs;
- Loan guarantees and Interest Holiday programs to overcome certain shortcomings that did not allow some enterprises to operate fully in a Customs Free Zone pursuant to existing programs in Canada and thus streamline the working capital of enterprises;
- A refundable tax credit on fees paid to Customs brokers of up to C$30,000 per enterprise per year for the first two years, diminishing to C$24,000 over the following three years, and C$16,000 thereafter.

However, in order to use Customs-controlled facilities within the zone, that is, Customs Warehousing, Processing Relief and GST Relief, companies had to apply separately on an individual corporate basis for the use of these facilities to Customs Canada. They also had to gain approval from Revenue Canada for the creation and use of EDC status, in order to gain relief from Canadian GST (Goods and Services Tax) and PST. This meant that the primary purpose of the zone was to offer Direct Tax incentives, that is, Corporation Tax reliefs and so on, rather than indirect tax incentives, that is, Customs and GST/PST, as a primary fiscal incentive, and thus encourage foreign investment where possible.

In 2013, the Mirabel Zone ended as a Customs Free Zone. Canadian legislation allowed for individual companies to establish their own GST Warehouses that could also be approved as Canadian Customs warehouses, thus obviating the need for specific designated Free Zones in Canada. Today, the zone still exists as a technology zone, and includes the major manufacturing plant of the aircraft manufacturer Bombardier, whose aircraft are flown off the adjacent runway, once part of Mirabel International Airport.

In terms of international logistics criteria, the province of Québec could be neither the destination nor the origin for more than 20% of the value of goods, by category of goods handled, unless it was merchandise which was not distributed by companies already operating in the province of Québec. This implied that the goods handled must have come from either elsewhere in Canada or from another country, for example the United States or the European Union, or had to be handled by a non-Québecois logistics provider.

The added value in the assembly and component purchase phase undertaken in the Foreign-Trade Zone could not exceed 50% of the overall value of the finished products shipped. This implied that the origin of the manufactured finished product leaving the zone had to be Québecois (and hence Canadian). This also implied that such products could enter either of the other NAFTA member countries free of Import Duty pertinent to that country, as allowed by the NAFTA Rules of Origin.

Projects had to demonstrate that one or more of the following factors were vital to the enterprise's establishment within the zone:

- Proximity to an international airport;
- Easy access to the four main modes of transportation;
- A large surface area at the time of start-up.

The above conditions could easily be fulfilled in the case of Mirabel, as the Foreign-Trade Zone was located adjacent to the airport complex itself, and in particular the air cargo facility which allowed for speedy and efficient onward shipment of goods leaving the zone for foreign destinations.

Such air cargo movements could benefit from the use of the air cargo centre at Mirabel Airport. The cargo area covered 18 hectares and had a storage area of 64,000 m^2 (695,000 square feet). Pallets and cargoes could be stored in centres allowing for the storage of a variety of goods, including perishable goods such as foodstuffs. There was also a permanent presence by Customs Canada, allowing for the full control of import and export activities.

The other advantage of the Mirabel Zone was its proximity to the regional surface infrastructure, including the road and rail networks across Canada and North America, and also the international maritime service offered by the Port of Montréal, which is one of North America's busiest container ports. In short, Mirabel's geographic location provided rapid access to a market of 100 million consumers within a 1,000-kilometre radius, namely the whole of the NAFTA region. Its proximity to the Eastern Atlantic seaboard allowed for additional easy access to the markets of Europe, and the nature of the aviation industry allowed for equal access to the trans-Pacific markets, thus allowing for a flexibility of activities relating to the fast-moving industrial sectors so reliant upon air cargo movement.

The range of companies investing in the Foreign-Trade Zone varied from cargo logistics companies, through aviation and aerospace companies, to manufacturing companies. Examples of well-known names that invested in the zone were:

- **Bombardier Aerospace** (manufacturing the CRJ-700 and CRJ-900 regional aircraft);
- **Messier-Dowty** (manufacture of landing gear for the Airbus 319 and 320 aircraft);
- **Technicolor** (reproduction of film copying);
- **Turbomeca Canada** (aero-engine repair and overhaul facility).

At the time (as at 2004), 15 companies, including the above plus Bell Helicopters (Canada), had invested in the zone, most operating aviation-related activities of either a repair/overhaul nature or a manufacturing nature. One of the highest investments by a single company in the zone at the time was that of Bombardier Aerospace, with a total investment of some C$170 million, second only to Mediterranean Aviation, engaged in the maintenance, repair and overhaul of aircraft engines, which invested some C$214 million in its own operations within the zone.

It must be pointed out at this stage that for Customs purposes, aviation-related activities do not generally attract high rates of Customs Imports duties, and thus are less subject to Import Duty liability than other sectors. However, given that GST still applies, the nature of their business implies that the products they are involved with (aviation-related engineering activities) are still used under international conditions, and are thus not subject to the same national fiscal constraints as are other industrial sectors.

Although the main fiscal incentives offered by the zone related to direct taxation in the form of corporate income tax holidays, it was still a major condition of zone operations that any company investing in the zone applied for Customs-controlled facilities as well, in order to take full advantage of international trade incentives on offer. Customs programs could only be applied for through Customs Canada, as Customs programs operate on a standard basis throughout Canada as a federal nation.

The Canadian Customs regime operates in a similar manner to that of the UK, with a set of Customs Duty relief facilities designed to stimulate international trade activities where both import and export functions are maintained. There are specific forms of duty relief programs, and these are centred around:

- Processing Reliefs;
- Customs Warehousing.

These facilities still apply today in terms of Canadian Customs facilities.

Processing reliefs concern activities where an importing company can gain Import Duty relief if the products which it imports are to be used in processing activities which will result in the re-export of the finished product, either to another NAFTA country (i.e. the United States or Mexico) or further afield, such as Latin America, the Pacific Rim or Europe. Given that the NAFTA is not a single integrated market, as in the case of the European Union, a different import tariff regime exists in each of the other NAFTA member countries. In this way, there is no integrated system of Free Circulation throughout the NAFTA, and any product originating in one NAFTA country must be declared to the appropriate national Customs Authority of the other member countries if it is to enter into either of the other NAFTA countries. As such, it is treated as an export from the originating country. In the case of the Mirabel Zone, this is no exception. If the product were to be released into Canadian Free Circulation from a Customs-controlled activity within the Mirabel Zone, it would have to be declared to Canadian Customs and Import Duty and GST/PST (Taxe de Vente Québecoise in the case of Québec) would be liable on the consignment. However, if the consignment leaves the zone and is destined for another country, even elsewhere within the NAFTA regime, the consignment is treated by Canadian Customs as an export and is therefore not subject to Canadian import duties and taxes.

In the case of Customs Warehousing, products are imported into the facility to be simply stored under Customs control and then re-exported to another country, or to be released as smaller individual consignments for the purpose of delivery to individual customers on the payment of Import Duty and GST/PST at the point of release from the warehouse. Import Duty and GST/PST is liable on each individual consignment when it is released from the warehouse, not on the imported consignment as a whole at the time of importation.

In the case of processing reliefs, a consignment of raw materials or components is imported by a company for the purposes of processing or manufacturing into a finished product. The components or raw materials incorporated in the finished product thus undergo a substantial **Transformation**, that is, they change their tariff Commodity Code as a result of the process performed on them. Therefore, the tariff Commodity Code applicable to the imported consignment changes to the tariff Commodity Code of the finished product. This Commodity Code is then use to classify the finished product at the time of re-export. As long as the finished product is re-exported in its entirety or in a vast majority of the total production, then such a processing relief may apply.

There are two forms of relief, namely **Duty Suspension** and **Duty Drawback**. As with the EU regime known as Inward Processing Relief (IPR), if the entire product resulting from the imported consignment is re-exported, then duty suspension applies, that is, that the importing company pays no Import Duty at the point of import. However, if the company decides to release some of the finished product into Canadian Free Circulation, then the company must pay Import Duty at the time of import of the consignment, and then seek a refund of Import Duty pertaining to the value of the consignment being re-exported. This refund is payable once the specific part of the consignment for export has been re-exported, and the proof of re-export in the form of the Customs Export Declaration has been lodged with and accepted by Canadian Customs. The refund of Import Duty thus depends upon the value of the consignment which has been re-exported.

It was thus possible for a company operating within the Mirabel Zone to apply for any of the Import Duty and tax reliefs mentioned, as long as the applicant company was involved in eligible activities pertaining to such duty and tax reliefs. The stipulation by the Mirabel Zone Authority, that zone-based activities should include aviation-related activities, accounted for such Customs requirements, as aviation activities automatically include international movements of materials. The nature and location of the zone and the fact that zone activities revolved around air cargo movements also influenced the nature of general processing activities permissible within the zone, as it was doubtful whether heavy engineering would be suitable for air cargo movements to and from the zone. Besides which, light processing activities allowed for the fast turnaround of products within a manufacturing environment, implying the speedy and efficient movement of both imports and exports with relation to zone-based activity.

The present Canadian FTZs

More recently, the policy of FTZs in Canada was reviewed and revived. The Canadian government more closely defined and extended the FTZ concept in 2013, allowing for further development of the Canadian FTZ concept. In 2019, Montréal acquired Foreign-Trade Zone (FTZ) status, covering the entire Montréal metropolitan area, allowing companies to import goods for manufacturing or assembly on a duty-suspended basis for up to four years, provided the final product leaving the zone is for export and is exported within four years of its imported elements having been imported into the zone in the first place. This FTZ status acts more as an EPZ facility rather than a pure Free Zone or the US version of the Foreign-Trade Zone. Montréal is the 13th zone in Canada, with Québec City and Halifax, Nova Scotia, already having FTZ status. Québec City obtained FTZ status in September 2017. By 2018, there were 9 FTZs in Canada, mostly attached to Canadian ports, including Windsor, Edmonton, Calgary, Winnipeg, Québec and Halifax.

Over the past few years, the Canadian government has endeavoured to position Canada as a desirable destination for foreign investment. To this end, import tariffs have been eliminated on essentially all manufacturing inputs, including machinery, equipment, and other inputs used in the industrial manufacturing sector. According to the Canadian government, this initiative has made Canada the first country in the G-20 group to offer a tariff-Free Zone for industrial manufacturers. Furthermore, since this a nationwide initiative, the Federal Government has promoted this tariff elimination as essentially making Canada one large FTZ for companies importing manufacturing inputs, that is, components.

Unlike other countries, such as the United States, which focus on location-specific FTZs, Canada's unique FTZ program allows for geographically flexible duty and tax relief, including excise taxes and anti-dumping duties. Since FTZs are not restricted to any particular part of the country, businesses are free to choose any location for an FTZ that best fits their needs. Indeed, programs such as the Duty Deferral Program, the Export Distribution Centre Program and Exporters of Processing Services Program essentially make it possible to create an FTZ anywhere in Canada.

On this basis, Canada's unique FTZ program would appear to benefit both foreign business and investors since it allows them to enjoy the benefits of a traditional FTZ anywhere in Canada. That said, the lack of designated FTZ locations does, however, have the potential to be confusing to foreign entities that are accustomed to the traditional idea of FTZs being located in specific designated geographic areas.

To help market and familiarise foreign entities with Canada's unique FTZ program, specialised Foreign-Trade Zone Points have been created throughout Canada. These Foreign-Trade Zone Points are designated geographical areas where public and private organisations have set up a FTZ Task Force that is coordinated by the regional development agency to ease access to government policies and programs, and thereby promote local and international trade.

According to the Canadian Finance Department, a Foreign-Trade Zone Point is generally a well-defined location in a given country where the purchase or import of raw materials, inputs or finished goods is officially eligible for exemption from Customs Duties and Taxes, that is, GST/PST. Such materials and goods may generally be stored, processed or assembled in the FTZ for re-export (in which case they are generally not subject to taxes and Customs Duties), or for sale on the domestic market (in which case taxes and duties are deferred until the finished goods enter the domestic market). Indeed, the main difference between the Canadian FTZs and the US FTZs is that the Canadian FTZs are more export oriented to encourage export-led growth, while the US FTZs encourage the import of goods and raw materials for distribution within the US, although many US general-purpose FTZs and subzones are used for export purposes.

FTZ requirements

Export Requirement – All imported goods must be exported from Canada within four years from the day it crosses the border into Canada, except for imported spirits used to manufacture distilled spirits which must be exported within five years.

Non-Qualifying Goods Reporting – When the goods no longer qualify for duty relief under this program (i.e. goods were sold in Canada or no longer will be exported) they must be reported and duties paid within 90 days. Failure to do so will result in the assessment of a penalty and applicable fines and duty with interest payable.

NAFTA Restriction – When foreign goods are imported into Canada then exported to a NAFTA country (USA or MEX) the entire amount of Import Duty may not be eliminated under the FTZ program. The Canadian duty amount must be compared to the NAFTA country duty and the 'lesser of the two duties' can be claimed for savings.

Approved FTZ locations must have adequate control records in place to track the imported goods while they remain in Canada. The records, including tracking of all receipts, activities and movement of the goods included under the program, must be sufficient to enable the Canadian Border Services Agency (CBSA) to conduct an audit. The ongoing maintenance and tracking of shipments are critical for continued participation in the program.

Applicant companies will be scheduled for an initial visit from the CBSA to confirm adequate control records exist as indicated in the company's application. The company will also be subject to periodic audits or validations that will be conducted at their premises to monitor compliance and activity summaries.

The benefits of the Canadian Foreign-Trade Zone programs include:

- Reduction of administration burden;
- No geographical restrictions – programs available regardless of location;
- Improved cash flow;
- Reduction of operating costs;
- Increased international competitiveness.

It should also be noted that there are distinct differences between Foreign-Trade Zones and Free Trade Agreements between various countries, for example the USMCA FTA, the successor to the NAFTA.

- Free Trade Agreements do not exempt companies from taxes (e.g. GST Goods and Services Tax, VAT);
- Free Trade Agreements impose strict rules that must be respected;
- Foreign-Trade Zones can be a complementary alternative to Free Trade Agreements.

In many ways, the present Canadian FTZs are a development of the original Montréal Mirabel FTZ, but with a more defined status, namely that of an EPZ. The aim of the Canadian FTZ initiative is to promote international trade with Canada, investment in the Zones by international companies and the generation of an export-driven economy.

SECTION 2

Latin America

The Mexican Maquiladoras

A **Maquiladora** (assembly plant) is a manufacturing operation or factory established in Mexico, usually near the border with the US, that imports raw materials and equipment for assembly, processing or manufacturing. Its products are then exported under a special program that grants them tax breaks, including Import Duties and Sales Taxes, and other economic, financial and fiscal benefits. Most Maquiladoras in Mexico produce a vast range of electronic equipment, clothing, plastics, furniture, appliances and auto parts, with clothing being the top product.

A Maquiladora in Mexico is therefore an assembly, manufacturing or processing factory that operates under preferential tariff programs established and administered by the United States and Mexico. Materials, assembly components, and production equipment used in Maquiladoras are allowed to enter Mexico duty-free. Products made can be exported into the US at lower tariffs than those from other countries. Recently, the term 'Maquiladora' has been used for similar operations in Latin America and Asia as well, though its roots are deeply embedded in its Mexican origins. As such, a Maquiladora in Mexico, and especially the border areas of Tijuana, close to San Diego, and Ciudad Juarez, over the border from El Paso, has economic and fiscal advantages for both Mexico and the US.

The Maquiladora program, which allowed Maquiladoras to be 100% foreign owned, was initiated in Mexico in 1964, and followed the National BIP, which was implemented three years earlier in 1961. The Industrialization Program was created to increase foreign investment and stimulate Mexico's internal market. Resulting from this, the Maquiladora program was developed to foster border region employment rates as well as the further attraction of foreign investment, and a 1989 decree further relaxed Mexico's foreign investment laws, allowing Maquiladoras to sell up to 50% of their products to Mexican domestic markets.

During the latter half of the 1960s, Maquiladora industries rapidly expanded in Mexico, geographically and economically, especially along the border with the US, and by 1985 had become Mexico's second largest source of income from exports, behind oil. Since 1973, Maquiladoras have also accounted for nearly half of Mexico's export assembly. Between 1995 and 2000, exports of assembled products in Mexico tripled, and the rate of the industry's growth amounted to about one new factory per day. By the late 20th century, the industry accounted for 25% of Mexico's Gross Domestic Product (GDP), and 17% of total Mexican employment.

DOI: 10.4324/9781003232025-21

Despite its impressive, successful history, the Maquiladora industry in Mexico never fully realised its maximum potential until the NAFTA was approved in 1994. Interestingly, NAFTA was not entirely a benefit to the industry, as it eliminated certain Customs benefits enjoyed by the Maquiladora program and determined strict 'Rules of Origin' for products to qualify for preferential tariffs. However, it did allow products manufactured in Maquiladoras to be sold in Mexico without the prior limits in place and eliminated certain quotas that further impeded full penetration of US and Mexican markets.

Constantly changing Mexican laws continue to make establishment and management of a Maquiladora in Mexico intimidating and confusing to even the most intrepid and savvy businessmen. Yet thousands of manufacturing companies, including a substantial number of small to medium-sized American companies, have been able to negotiate the process and establish a Maquiladora. Reduced labour costs of 50% or more, a highly skilled and conscientious workforce, six-day working week and logistical advantages over other offshore locations persuaded these businesses to explore manufacturing options and opportunities in Mexico.

There is no question that the task of establishing a Maquiladora in Mexico is a considerable challenge for an American company. Fortune 500 companies often embark on the process themselves, but still require a large and diverse pool of consultants. Some companies choose to use a contract manufacturer if they can find a reliable company. Others decide on what is known as a corporate shelter service. Although the quickest and simplest way to establish a Mexican Maquiladora, the way in which this system works is often misunderstood.

Corporate shelters allow manufacturing companies to establish a Maquiladora in Mexico without actually owning a Mexican business. Indeed, many of the maquila companies are owned by non-Mexican companies, especially from the US or the Far East. The process is simple when an American or foreign-owned company contracts with a corporate shelter service company. Using production volumes and specifications required to assemble or manufacture the client's product, the corporate shelter company looks for appropriately sized and designed buildings. Once the client chooses a building, the shelter company leases it for them, and takes care of all of the property (real estate) transactions, permits and legal work necessary to acquire and operate in the facility. The shelter service also secures the Maquiladora register, import permits and local and federal licenses and permits, as well as opening bank accounts and establishing an accounting and tax payment program. Prospective employees are interviewed and hired as the client firm moves or purchases equipment and machinery required for assembly or manufacturing its product. The client also designates a production supervisor to oversee manufacturing.

Once operational, the shelter company ensures that the Maquiladora complies with all Mexican laws addressing taxes, Customs, labour, zoning, facility management and environmental protection. The shelter firm also handles research and management necessary for fiscal compliance with transfer pricing, permanent establishment, safe storage, asset taxes and payroll, withholding tax and employee benefits packages. Ongoing recruitment, termination, incentive and disciplinary programs and compliance with labour laws and the labour board are performed as part of the shelter package as well.

The shelter company can also complete all border crossing documentation, US and Mexico broker coordination and transportation arrangements. The client now has a

Maquiladora in Mexico, and has avoided the myriad of challenges related to cultural differences, employee management and compensation policies, accounting and payment of taxes and compliance with local and federal laws and regulations. The client firm focuses on production quality while the shelter service performs all administrative functions required to keep the operation running efficiently.

Panama Free Zones

The **Colón Free Trade Zone** is a Free Zone in Panama dedicated to re-exporting a wide variety of merchandise to Latin America and the Caribbean. It is located on the Caribbean coast, near the Atlantic entrance to the Panama Canal, in the province of Colón, within the city of Colón but outside its municipal jurisdiction, and operates as an autonomous entity of Panama.

In 1917, three years after the opening of the Panama Canal, the possibility of building a Free Zone in the area in Colón was discussed. The Colón Chamber of Commerce raised the project of a Free Zone in 1929, and the project was initiated in 1948, following the Second World War.

During the war, many Panamanian landowners rented land for the construction of defence installations and centres to provide services for the movement of US troops. With the end of the arrival of the troops, difficulties began. In order to alleviate these difficulties, Enrique A. Jiménez, Panama's President in 1945, led the initiative to make the Free Zone project a reality, using for this purpose the geographical position of the ports and the interoceanic Panama Canal, a crucial link between the Atlantic and Pacific Oceans. Jiménez recommended the reconsideration of the project prepared by George E. Roberts, Vice President of the First National City Bank of New York, which contemplated the creation of the Colón Free Zone and which had been presented to the government in 1929.

In 1946, the Panamanian government hired the American Thomas E. Lyons, an official of the United States Department of Commerce and recognised authority in the design of Free Zones, to carry out a feasibility study in the area suggested by the project. Based on its recommendations, the government gave its approval two years later, in June 1948, to creating an autonomous entity of 36 hectares where the trade of products was exempt from tariffs and had little paperwork. The Colón Free Zone will have its own legal status only dependent on the Presidency of the Republic and the Comptroller General of Panama. Lyons conceived the Free Zone as a strategic centre of trade that would connect the industries of the United States and Europe with the clients of Latin America, concentrating in the same geographic point mainly warehouses but also supplier industries, which in turn would bring collateral benefits to Panama in the area of construction, land prices, transfer of managerial knowledge, stimulation of business tourism, industrialisation of Panama, increased revenues from the Panama Canal and increased air traffic.

Lyons' projections were duly achieved and hundreds of companies moved to the Zona Libre de Colón (CFZ). Starting in 1970, when Panama became an international banking centre, more companies established themselves in the Free Zone, and in 1988 its area expanded to almost 300 hectares, becoming the largest Free Zone in the Western Hemisphere and the second largest in the world, following Hong Kong. In the 1980s, the Free Zone began to have competition from other Free Zones in Miami and the Caribbean, and it was also affected by the debt crisis in other Latin American countries which reduced their imports.

In the 1990s, the Colón Free Zone regained its strength by becoming the Latin American headquarters for companies from Japan and recently industrialised countries in Asia, and a centre for re-exports to the United States.

Of all imports to the Free Zone during 2004, 87% came mainly from Hong Kong, Taiwan, the United States, Japan, Korea, France, Mexico, Italy, Switzerland, the United Kingdom, Malaysia and Germany. In the same year, Colombia was the largest buyer of merchandise, with almost 16% of all its exports. Other important buyers were Venezuela, the domestic market of Panama, Guatemala, Ecuador, Costa Rica, the Dominican Republic, the United States, Chile, Honduras, Brazil, Nicaragua and El Salvador. These countries acquired around 83% of all exports from the Colón Free Zone.

In the 21st century, an idea promoted by some businessmen was to expand some of the benefits of the Colón Free Zone to the city of Colón to improve the socio-economic conditions of the latter. This project is called Colón Puerto Libre (Colón Free Port).

The Colón Free Trade Zone is the largest Free Zone in the Americas, and the second largest such zone in the world. Since the start of its operations in 1948, it now occupies about 2.4 km^2 (600 acres). It is divided in two large areas: one located in Colón city, segregated from the city by a wall, and the other a relatively new venture, in the harbour area, which is designated for warehouses, covering 0.53 km^2 (130 acres) and 370 m (400 yards) from Colón's commercial sector.

Exports from the Free-Trade Zone into neighbouring countries are still subject to local rules, regulations, and payment requirements of the importing country. Venezuela, one of the larger buyers from the zone, has had difficulty meeting its obligations to exporters from the zone resulting in unpaid debts. Colombia implemented a series of tariffs which had the effect of reducing imports, primarily from Asia.

The Zone was created by Decree-Law No. 18 of 17 June 1948, as an autonomous entity to develop the country's competitive advantages. More recently, the legislation for the Zone was modernised by Decree-Law No. 8 of 4 April 2016, to allow for new businesses, such as electronic commerce, construction and operation of ports and other commercial activities.

Profits from foreign operations are totally exempt from income tax. Dividends that come from external operations or those carried out abroad are subject to Dividend Tax of 5%, as established by law 8 of 2010:

- Legal persons or companies established in the Colón Free Zone or in any other zone or existing free area or that is created in the future are obliged to retain the Dividend Tax or participation fee of 5% of the profits that it distributes to its shareholders or partners when they come from:

1. Panamanian source or internal or local operations;
2. Foreign source or foreign or export operations;
3. Income exempt from Income Tax, provided for in paragraphs f, l and n of article 708 of the Code.

Companies located in the Colón Free Zone are subject to a payment of 1% per year on the value of their net worth at the end of their fiscal period, as an Operation Notice Tax.

The Colón Free Trade Zone (CFZ) is considered as Panama's duty-free paradise. With over 3,000 companies either represented or operating on its complex of more than 1065 acres, and a massive turnover of US$19 billion per year of imports and exports move in and out. Everything from the latest electronics from Japan, silks from Italy, designer perfumes from France, clothing, jewellery, computers, appliances and just about anything else imaginable from around the world, all at very competitive prices, it can be found at the CFZ straight from the factory.

Latin American and Caribbean buyers prefer to buy at the CFZ instead of travelling to Asia. In the CFZ, buyers can have containers filled with a variety of items. In some Asian countries, they would likely have to buy container loads of goods comprising just one product. For this and many other reasons, the CFZ is considered as an ideal shopping centre for buyers and wholesalers across the Americas.

For consumer retail companies, using the CFZ as a method for export in Latin America will experience the following benefits:

- Time Savings. Instead of travelling to every Latin American country where there might be export prospects, talking with merchants, agents, representatives and distributors, you would only need to go to one location – Panama, which is very accessible given its prominence as a regional air hub.
- Sales Growth. Because the CFZ is the world's second largest Free-Trade Zone, with exports of US$11.5 billion and growing, retailers from many countries in Latin America simply schedule regular shopping trips to CFZ merchants. When they order, they order in wholesale quantities – the target retailer buying in the CFZ is frequently a department store owner with 10–15 stores in his country of origin.
- Reduction in Complexity. Products can be purchased in US dollars from a CFZ merchant. The entry is duty-free. And as the buyer only purchases from one company, therefore there is only have one relationship to manage. Finally, the CFZ is co-located with some of the world's largest transshipment ports, meaning that it is easy for merchants to pick and pack customised shipments to any one of a number of otherwise small Latin American ports of entry.
- Reduction in Financial Risk. The producer sells to established CFZ merchants. They in turn make their money by showcasing the producer's products. They know their customers and can offer financial terms based on creditworthiness. These terms in turn allow the producer to sell more products instead of having to bear the risk of offering terms or losing the sale. In addition, there are no duties payable – those end up being the responsibility of the final buyer once the goods enter that country.

Companies operating from the CFZ enjoy many trade advantages along with special tax incentives such as tax credits, depending on the number of Panamanian employees, and special income tax rates on foreign trade operations. Companies in the Free Zone do not pay corporate income tax. Dividends paid on profits from foreign trade operations and from direct sales are subject to 5% to 10% of Dividend Tax respectively. Merchandise arriving at, stored in or leaving the CFZ destined for a foreign country is exempt from taxes, charges or any type of tariff. Also, CFZ companies are not subject to any type of federal or municipal tax.

Advantages

The existence of modern shipping ports with modern facilities, large facilities for containers, direct access by the Pan American highway, air and rail access transporting containers from the Pacific Ocean to the Atlantic Ocean daily, enables the Colón Free Zone to claim to be the best place to invest for its many advantages over other Free Zone areas in the world. Its advantages include:

PERMITTED ACTIVITIES

- Exportation;
- Re-exportation;
- Importation;
- Manufacture;
- Sale, commercialisation and distribution;
- Refining and processing of goods;
- Operations, transactions, negotiations or incidental activities appropriate to the establishment and operation of international Free-Trade Zones.

TAX INCENTIVES

- 0% taxes on income from overseas operations;
- 0% taxes on the products imported for re-exportation;
- Tax exemptions on services involving overseas activities;
- Significantly competitive costs.

IMMIGRATION INCENTIVES

- Streamlined migration procedures are granted for foreign executives and investors.

WAYS OF ESTABLISHING OPERATIONS

- Operation Permit;
- Representation Agreement;
- Lease of Premises;
- Lease of Land Lots;
- Public Storage.

The Colón Free Zone is located a few kilometres from the Panama Canal in the Caribbean sector, in the Colón Province and it is considered the first Free Zone in the Western hemisphere and the second largest worldwide.

Other Panamanian Free-Trade Zones

Free-Trade Zones are part of a special, comprehensive and simplified regime for the establishment and operation of companies that contribute to national development and the generation of employment and foreign exchange, incorporated into the global economy of goods and services, promoting investment and promote economic, scientific, technological, cultural, educational and social development.

The Panamanian government has granted a total of 16 licences to operate Free-Trade Zones, between the cities of Panama and Colón. There are currently 12 Free Zones in operation in Panama, of which the main Zones are the Colón Free Zone and the Pacifico Free Zone.

The Panama Pacifico Area is one of the most important projects of the Panamanian government that develops an international trade hub and attracts large multinational companies, logistics services, commerce and industry. The main objective of this Special Economic Area is the attraction of new direct foreign investment and the creation of jobs in Panama. The Pacifico Free Zone offers a variety of benefits including exemption from all indirect taxes, an increase in the maximum number of foreign employees to 15% of the workforce, and the availability of five-year investor visas, as opposed to the two-year investor visas available elsewhere.

With this ambitious project which includes economic and legal benefits, the Republic of Panama promotes the development of different industries such as logistics, sea and air transportation, high-technology, call centres, shared services, among others.

Tax incentives exemption from indirect taxes for all companies, full tax exemptions on income, dividends and transfer/withholding for 12 'Specific Business Activities', legal stability for ten years; one-stop-shop with access to 15 government entities; on-site Customs operations; special labour incentives; expanded immigration benefits and on-site workforce training centre are some of the benefits of operating a business in the Panama Pacifico Special Economic Area.

Logistic parks

Panama is considered the best logistic centre in the Americas for its privileged geographical position and has adopted laws and regulations that encourage activities and proper integration of infrastructure and world-class logistics services, among which are included the Panama Canal, multiple ports in the Pacific and the Caribbean, Interoceanic Highway and Railroad, air Hub of the Americas, Free-Trade Zones and Special Economic Zones, among others.

Panama Logistics Park is a Real Estate Industrial Project and Logistics, developed with world-class Standards, strategically located in the east of Panama City a short distance from Tocumen Airport and fast connectivity with the rest of the infrastructure offered by the country.

Export Zones

Panama's strategic location makes it the best destination in America to export and import products. It is situated between North and South America, bordered by the Caribbean Sea and the Pacific Ocean. A majority of Panama's trade transactions are carried out in the Colón Free Trade Zone, which is one of the biggest Free-Trade Zones in the world.

During 2018, the value of exports, excluding those of the Colón Free Zone, totalled US$672.3 million, 1.9% more than the previous year, according to the Comptroller General of the Republic. The United States was the largest export market. Other top export destinations of Panama are Netherlands, China (Continental), China – Taiwan and Costa Rica.

Manaus Free Trade Zone (Zona Franca de Manaus)

The **Free Economic Zone of Manaus (Portuguese**: *Zona Franca de Manaus* – **ZFM)** is a free economic zone in the city of Manaus, the capital of the State of Amazonas, Northern Brazil. The initial concept, a Free-Trade port in Manaus, was formed by Congressman Francisco Pereira da Silva and was subsequently formalised by Law No. 3.173 on 6 June 1957. The project was approved by the National Congress on 23 October 1957 under Law No. 1.310 and regulated by Decree No. 47.757 on 2 February 1960. It was then amended by the engineer and entrepreneur Maurício Jopper, who by agreement with the original founder, reinforced and justified the creation of a free economic zone instead of a Free-Trade port.

Located near the *encontro das aguas*, where two mighty arms of the Amazon River, the Rio Negro and Rio Solimões, meet, Manaus had its heyday during the rubber boom of the late 19th and early 20th century, when rubber was the most important commodity export in Brazil after coffee. Some of the city's most impressive monuments, such as the pink-and-white opera house, date from this period, when immensely rich rubber barons imported acts from overseas. After smuggling out seeds, the British eventually started producing rubber in Asia, sending Manaus into decline, until it was revived by the governments of the 1960s. They were afraid that if Brazil did not populate the Amazon region, someone else might. In order to encourage settlement, the Federal Government awarded the city a system of Import Duty and fiscal incentives, offering generous relief from a taxation system widely seen as one of the world's most burdensome. As a result, manufacturers flocked to the city. During its historical evolution, the Manaus Free Trade Zone has enabled three economic hubs to be developed: industrial, commercial and agricultural. The first of these, represented by the Manaus Industrial Sector (PIM), is considered to be the foundation stone that sustains the model.

The Manaus Free Trade Zone (MFTZ), which is regulated by Decree-Law No. 288/1967, was conceived as a free import and export trade area with special tax incentives. It was set up with the object of creating an industrial, commercial and agricultural centre in the hinterland of the Amazon region, which would be equipped with economic conditions that would enable the region to be occupied and developed. For the first ten years the ZFM (Manaus Free Trade Zone) was located in a warehouse rented from Manaus Harbour, in the Port of Manaus, and relied on federal funds. It was perhaps due to this lack of its own resources that there was little credibility or viability in the project at the time.

However, nearly ten years later, on 28 February 1967, President Humberto Castello Branco (the first President of Brazil in the new military regime) signed Decree-Law No. 288, whose draft accompanied the Exposition of Motives. Decree-Law No. 288 amended the provisions of Law No. 3.173/57 and redefined the Manaus Free Trade Zone in more concrete and definable terms. The new Decree-Law stipulated that the Manaus Free Trade Zone would have an area of 10,000 km^2 (3,900 miles squared) with an industrial centre as well as an agricultural centre and that these would be given the economic means to allow for regional development in order to lift the Amazon out of the economic isolation that it had fallen into at that time. Decree No. 61.244 of 28 August 1967 created the Manaus Free Trade Zone Superintendency, SUFRAMA (Superintência da Zona Franca de Manaus), which administers and operates the Free Zone. It is an independent Federal Agency under the Brazilian Ministry of Development, Industry and Foreign Trade (MDIC).

Tax incentives and the subsequent complementary legislation created comparative advantages in the region with respect to other parts of the country and as a result the Manaus Free Trade Zone attracted new investment to the area. These incentives constituted tax exemptions administered federally by SUFRAMA and SUDAM.

Created as a Free-Trade Zone for the development of Western Amazonia, the Manaus Free Trade Zone has rapidly become a focus for intensive commercial and industrial activity. Within the zone, there is a concentration of principal industries such as electro-electronic goods, watches, bicycles, computers, toys, jet skis, spectacles and motorbikes, which are supplied to the Brazilian internal market. International companies operating from the zone include Nokia, Siemens, Panasonic, LG Electronics, Flextronics, Samsung, Honda, Harley-Davidson, Pepsi, Coca-Cola and Philips, along with several Brazil-based companies. The main industrial sectors represented are:

- Bicycles and motorbikes: 29.38%;
- Electrical and Electronics: 25.64%;
- Computer goods: 15.21%;
- Chemicals: 8.67%;
- Metallurgy: 6.88%;
- Thermoplastics: 5.67%;
- Mechanical: 2.42%;
- Disposables: 2.44%;
- Watchmakers: 0.96%.

This dynamic commerce, offering imported hi-tech products at affordable prices, has attracted tourists from every part of Brazil and even beyond, extending to elsewhere in Latin America. With the recent establishment of Customs Warehousing, Manaus has become the major Customs-controlled business enclave in Latin America and is the gateway for the export of products to the markets of the Caribbean and the United States.

The reputation of the Manaus Free Zone for the manufacture of electronic products embraced the whole of Brazil some time ago, and continues unabated to the present. Colour TVs and photographic equipment, for example, are still a major part of the economy in terms of visitor purchases. However, because of Customs controls, there is a limit in terms of the purchase of products in the zone and what is imported into the country itself. This has not stopped many thousands of Brazilians making the tourist trip to Manaus and purchasing goods from the Free Zone to take home with them. Indeed, for many years there has been a daily major flight between Rio de Janeiro and Manaus, mainly for tourism purposes.

In its first years following its reformation, the Manaus Free Zone functioned like a large shopping centre for all Brazilians. The military regime in power at the time did not permit imports or even the exit of Brazilians overseas. The Free Zone functioned like an escape valve for those with extensive purchasing power, who were able to find in Manaus new items imported from all over the world. To account for this increase in purchases, the city expanded its services. According to data from the Commercial Council of Amazonas, in 1967 alone a total of 1,339 new companies were registered in the region because of the zone's activities.

The scope of the Manaus Free Zone has been constantly redefined over the last 30 years, the period initially forecast for its duration. The Free Zone model was then assured by law up to 2013, and was then extended by the President of the time, Dilma Rousseff.

Products of well-known brands with the guarantee of origin and quality are produced and supplied to both national and international markets, including audio, video, computer/IT, clothing and perfumes. Tourists have the right to carry in their personal baggage the equivalent of US$2,000 worth of zone-produced goods and double this amount for couples. Up to US$500, there are no quantitative limits per product, and each passenger has the right of a further US$50 of household goods. Baggage declarations must be submitted along with goods receipts, when checking in for flights at Manaus International airport.

Today, around 50 years after it was founded, the Manaus Free Trade Zone represents a virtuous Brazilian government development model that has managed to make a socio-economic base in the Amazon region feasible, promote the better productive and social integration of the region with the rest of Brazil, and guarantee national sovereignty over its borders.

Manaus has a population of 2 million and the Free Zone employs 120,000 people directly and 500,000 indirectly. It produces most of Brazil's motorcycles and bicycles, and a large quantity of its electronic products. The tax breaks make manufacturing 35% cheaper here than in the rest of the country, according to Ernst & Young, the professional services and management consultancy company. These benefits include a reduction of up to an 88% on Import Duty, depending on the product; an exemption from the Federal Government's Excise Duty, which can reach 35%; and reductions of 55–100% in Sales Tax, again according to the product. Aside from these tax incentives, there is an extra incentive in terms of land. The government runs schemes to provide land to manufacturers at virtually no cost. Manaus also benefitted from a further decision by Dilma Rousseff, the country's president at the time, when she agreed to extend its tax privileges for another 50 years. However, even with these guarantees, Manaus needs to remain vigilant. With such poor transport links and situated so far from its markets, it would quickly fade back into the jungle without its tax advantages. Indeed, Amazonas stands to lose the most from the so-called 'tax wars' between Brazilian States, where each State tries to undercut the other by offering incentives to manufacturers to settle in their jurisdictions. By law, States are not permitted to offer tax breaks without the approval of their peers, but in the past this requirement has been ignored. However, for now, the outlook is very promising for Manaus, which is continuing to attract new factories and investors. One of the most recent newcomers is a sister company of Flextronics, the electronics group, which is planning to make the Xbox games console for 30% less than it would cost to import it. The State of Amazonas boasts that it is the only region that has this model of development, which explains its huge success.

The Uruguay Free-Trade Zones

Uruguay is one of the smallest countries in South America, but it is also one of the richest. It is the centre of the MERCUSUR, the South American Free Trade Bloc, as well as being the crossroads of South American Trade. Much of South American banking is concentrated on Montevideo, the capital of Uruguay, and the country also has a series of active and strategic Free Zones. These are especially useful given Uruguay's strategic position as an international trade hub, located between Brazil and Argentina, and therefore in a position to import materials from around the world on a duty-suspended basis and re-export them to the rest of the region.

The Free-Trade Zone Regime in Uruguay provides companies with tax and Customs benefits. Likewise, it is an effective tool for businesses to efficiently manage their business ventures and activities, especially concerning import and export activities, allowing them to avoid long delays, unnecessary bureaucratic administrative processes and, of course, providing attractive fiscal benefits. Uruguay is one of the most attractive Latin American jurisdictions for the establishment of companies, with its business system often being compared with that of Switzerland. Uruguay allows 100% foreign ownership of local companies, and companies can be formed with only one shareholder.

The promotion and development of the Uruguayan Free Zone regime has been declared of national interest, with the objective of promoting investments, diversifying the productive model, creating job opportunities, increasing the number of qualified national jobs, increasing the national added value, promoting innovative and technological activities and promoting the decentralisation of economic activities and regional development. In general terms, it aims to increase the country's participation in the international trade of goods and services and international investment flows.

The Uruguayan Free Zone regulations seek to make the regime more dynamic and specialised, encouraging activities of special interest for the country and promoting new investments. Additionally, the Free Zone regime is aligned with the process that Uruguay has been developing to align tax incentives with international Standards regarding guidelines and requirements in terms of international taxation. The government's implementation of legislation relating to tax regimes and Free-Trade Zones has turned Uruguay into a commercial paradise for companies looking to establish their operations abroad. Moreover, Uruguay is a very stable country from the political, economic and social point of view.

The Uruguayan Free-Trade Zones are areas in Uruguayan territory which can be both public or privately owned. These are highly secured locations with the following features:

- State monopolies do not apply;
- The business activities of companies operating in these Free Zones have Tax and Customs exemptions/suspensions;
- There is total freedom for the entry and exit of goods, fixed or capital assets, with exemptions/suspensions in taxes and duties, including VAT.

Companies can develop any business, industrial and service activity in these Zones. Some examples are given below:

- Marketing, deposit, storage, conditioning, selection, fractioning, assembly, disassembly, handling or mixture or goods or raw materials with other materials of foreign or national origin;
- Installation and operation of manufacturing equipment;

- Financial, IT, repair and maintenance services, professional services and others required for the operation of the activities.

To date, Uruguay has 11 Free Zones, all with a variety of specialisations, and most of these areas are located near the metropolitan area. The metropolitan area is defined by Law 19.566 as the geographical area which lies within a 40 kilometre radius of the Centre of Montevideo.

The 11 Free-Trade Zones are:

- Zona Franca Punta Pereira;
- WTC Free Zone;
- Zona Franca Colonia Suiza;
- Aguada Park;
- Zona Franca Nueva Palmira;
- Parque de las Ciencias;
- Zona Franca Florida;
- Zona Franca Libertad;
- UPM Fray Bentos;
- Zona Franca Colonia;
- Zonamérica.

In Uruguay, both private owners and the State operate the Free-Trade Zones. The government duly authorises companies to manage some of the Free Zones and the government itself manages others. Additionally, the government is responsible for the supervision and monitoring of the whole system through the General Agency of Commerce – Free Zones Areas (Dirección General de Comercio – Área Zonas Francas).

Free Zone operations will give companies various attractive tax advantages which are granted by law. In order to be granted the status of a Free-Trade Zone user, the company will need to be registered at the Dirección de Zonas Francas. It should be noted that there are two types of Free-Trade Zone users:

1. **The Direct User**: This user gets the right to operate in the Free-Trade Zone and the process occurs through signing a contract with the entity that manages the Free-Trade Zone.
2. **The Indirect User**: This user acquires the right to operate in a Free-Trade Zone and has to sign a contract with the owner and then has the right to use or exploit the zone for commercial purposes.

According to national legislation, only legal persons (i.e. companies and corporations) can operate in Free-Trade Zones. Most often, Uruguayan corporations are chosen as the vehicle to manage operations in these Zones. However, a branch office of a foreign company can also be used to carry out commercial activities.

Companies operating in Free-Trade Zones should choose the most appropriate zone to develop their business. The choice of the Free-Trade Zone will depend on the company's planned business activity. Such activities include the delivery of services, storage and inventory, import and export of components and finished products, and the manufacture of products.

The Uruguayan State must have previously authorised Uruguayan Free-Trade Zones in order for them to legally operate. Moreover, the State must deliver the necessary infrastructure for them to function, that is, warehouses, offices and a minimum level of urban development. Additionally, Free-Trade Zones must include basic services such as electricity, waste disposal, communication, security, and surveillance and so on.

Companies involved in construction can operate free of taxes and with limited paperwork, if they meet the requirements below:

- The construction of buildings with the aim of developing industrial or service activities.
- The construction of yard space.
- The creation of office space.
- The development of green areas designed to improve the environment.

Free-Trade Zone users are free from all existing and future national Uruguayan taxes. Additionally, fiscal benefits are incorporated within the following taxes for companies operating in Uruguayan Free-Trade Zones:

- Corporate Income Tax (IRAE);
- Net worth taxes (IP);
- Value Added Tax (VAT);
- Internal Specific Tax (IMESI);
- Tax on Public Limited Companies (ICOSA).

Free-Trade Zones in Uruguay play an important role in attracting investment and capital to the nation. Above all, the Free-Trade Zones highlight the governments drive to develop industrial, business and service activities in Uruguay. As the government shows its support for foreign business and foreign capital, the investment opportunities in the region grow. It comes as no surprise that businesses see Uruguay as one of the most appealing destinations in Latin America to expand their business to.

The following text, although similar to the details above, fully explains the regulatory framework of the Uruguayan Free Zone regime.

Regulatory framework of Uruguayan Free Zones National interest

The promotion and development of the Uruguayan Free Zone regime has been declared of national interest, with the objective of promoting investments, diversifying the productive model, creating job opportunities, increasing the number of qualified national jobs, increasing the national added value, promoting innovative and technological activities and promoting the decentralisation of economic activities and regional development. In general terms, it aims to increase the country's participation in the international trade of goods and services and international investment flows.

The regulations seek to make the regime more dynamic and specialised, encouraging activities of special interest for the country and promoting new investments.

Additionally, the Free Zone regime is aligned with the process that Uruguay has been developing to align tax incentives with international Standards regarding guidelines and requirements in terms of international taxation.

Structure of the Free Zones

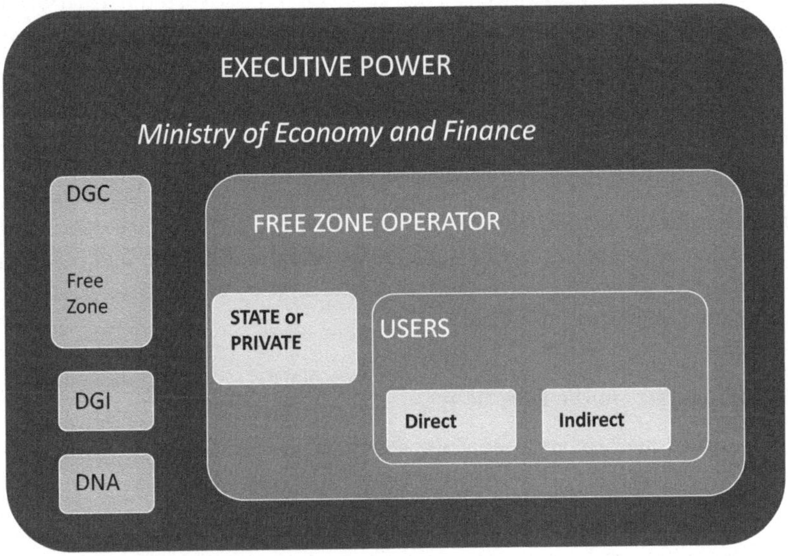

Source: Uruguay FZ Authority.

Operator/developer

It can be the State itself or a private person. In this case, the operator or developer can be a natural or legal person and must provide the appropriate infrastructure for the installation and operations of a Free Zone, in exchange for a price. Authorisations are therefore to be paid, and such payment can be cancelled as a lump sum, or paid as regular operation fees to the State; being the latter the most frequent regime.

Users

They are natural or legal persons that acquire the right to develop their activities within the Free Zone, but they are not allowed to conduct any other type of activity outside the Free Zone.

There are two categories of users: Direct and Indirect

Direct Users are those who contract directly with the operator, while Indirect Users contract with the Direct User, and are entitled to use the facilities of the latter.

Management, supervision and control

Management and supervision are in charge of the Ministry of Economy and Finance through the General Commerce Directorate – Free Zones Department. This directorate is the main interlocutor concerning any regulations, permits and controls regarding all the country's Free Zones.

Since the Uruguayan New Customs Code (CAROU), Law 19.276 dated 19/SEP/2014, was passed, Free Zones moved from being an exclave to be part of the Customs territory, and, therefore, under the control of the National Customs Directorate (DNA).

International business platforms

The Free Zones primary objective is to develop **commercial and industrial activities and services**, with the benefits and in the terms foreseen in the legislation in force.

The introduction to Free Zones of guns, gunpowder, ammunition and other materials used for warlike purposes, as well as those declared contrary to the interests of the country by the Executive Power, is prohibited.

Activities of the users in the Free Zone

These are some of the primary Free Zone activities:

- Commercialisation of goods, warehousing, storage, conditioning, selection, classification, division, assembly, disassembly, handling or mixing of goods or raw materials of foreign or national origin.
- Installation and operation of manufacturing establishments.
- Service provision in the following way:
  - From the Free Zone to other users in other Free Zones.
  - From the Free Zone to companies located in the national territory (not a Free Zone): all types of services can be provided, on the condition that the company located in the non-Free Zone is a taxpayer of the Income Tax on Economic Activities (IRAE), which must be communicated to the Free Zone user and performed in the terms established by the Tax Administration Department (DGI).
  - From the Free Zone to third countries.
- Other ways which, according to the Executive Power, are beneficial for the national economy or for economic and social integration.

Activities of zone users outside the Free Zone

General rule

As a general rule, the users of a Free Zone will not be able to perform industrial and commercial activities or activities related to services outside the Free Zones. Some exceptions may be applied. These are outlined below.

Exceptional activities

Exceptionally, the users will be able to perform the following activities in non-Free Zones:

- Collection of delinquent portfolios, provided that it is made through third parties. 'Delinquent' refers to credits whose payment has been delayed for more than

180 days. The Free Zone Area will control that third parties that provide the service are not linked to the user and that they develop this activity regularly.
- Merchandise display in Montevideo, only for users that are installed in Free Zones located outside the metropolitan area, in an area provided by the developer, with prior authorisation by the Free Zones Department.

Ancillary activities

It will be possible to develop certain ancillary activities in the national territory (non-Free Zone), in a single fixed place, with prior authorisation of the Free Zones Department.

Complementary activities

The users of the Free Zone located outside the metropolitan area will be able to develop the following activities, in a single place provided by the developer:

- Public relations;
- Management of ancillary documents;
- Invoicing;
- Collection of goods and services of non-delinquent portfolios.

Full exemptions

The users are exempted from any national tax, standing or to be created in the future, including any taxes whose implementation requires special exemptions, with respect to the activities developed in the Free Zone, provided that they are carried out within the law. These include:

- Tax on the Control of Public Limited Companies (ICOSA);
- Internal Specific Tax (IMESI);
- Wealth Tax (IP);
- Income Tax on Economic Activities (IRAE);
- Value Added Tax (IVA).

As previously stated, the Executive Power may enable the provision of other services from the Free Zones to the rest of the national territory. These activities will be regulated by the general tax regime, which may be established according to tax withholding regimes which are final, in accordance with what the Executive Power establishes.

Staff

In order to maintain the quality of users of a Free Zone and the benefits and rights that this law gives them, the users of Free Zones will hire for the activities they need to carry out within the Free Zone a minimum of 75% of staff who are Uruguayan citizens, natural or legal. On a transitional basis, this percentage can be reduced, with the authorisation of the Free Zones Department. To this end, the reasons for the request must be expressed. The aforementioned office will submit a report to the Ministry of Economy and Finance, in charge of taking a decision. The following will be assessed by them: specific reasons of the activity of the company, situations of beginning or extension of activities, reasons of general interest and consideration of objectives set forth in this decree. Furthermore, the implementation of training plans so that users reach the minimum percentage required by the regulations may be necessary.

The same procedure must be done in the Free Zones Department by those users who develop activities related to services and intend to have a maximum percentage of foreign staff equivalent to 50% for the entire term of the user agreement.

Terms of agreements

The law establishes maximum terms for Free Zone user agreements:

- Direct users: maximum of 15 years to carry out industrial activities and ten years for commercial activities or services.
- Indirect users: maximum of five years to carry out any type of activity.

Additionally, in the cases mentioned below longer terms for the agreements can be authorised:

The users of Free Zones located outside the metropolitan area must meet one of the following conditions during the first three years:

- More than 50 employees.
- Investment greater than 20,000,000 Indexed Units (UI), which is equivalent to approximately US$2,500,000 (as at September 2018).
- The users of Free Zones located within the metropolitan area must meet one of the following conditions during the first two years:
  - More than 100 employees.
  - Investment greater than 40,000,000 Indexed Units (UI), which is equivalent to approximately US$5,000,000 (as at September 2018).

Revocation

The Free Zones Department may revoke the authorisation of the user agreement, when it is understood that it does not comply with the established requirements and the commitments assumed in the investment project. Among others, it will be understood that there is no default when:

- Jobs are not created in the area in an adequate proportion in relation to the activities developed;
- The activities are not carried out within the Free Zone;
- There is no fiscal address in the area.

Developments since 2019

Since its inception, the Uruguayan Free-Trade Zone regime was intended to be a driving force for development of the national economy through which new investments and employment generation are to be encouraged. The success of Law 15.921 allowed the development of private FTZs in a framework of security and legal stability guaranteed by the State, but with its minimal intervention. Important infrastructure, Tax and Customs exemptions and adequate and qualified human resources became very attractive for multinational companies that came to our country. The growth of FTZs specialising in rendering services has been exponential in recent years, achieving the success of the model and its undeniable contribution to the country. As stated previously, Uruguay currently has 11 operating FTZs in which almost 15,000 people are employed.

The recently approved rule changes keep in essence the objectives of the regime (investment increase, employment generation and exports growth), making some matters far more flexible, but increasing the Administration's controls over companies. The additional controls and certain recently approved limitations and restrictions have allowed the Uruguayan FTZ regime to comply with the OECD transparency Standards established in the BEPS (Base Erosion and Profit Shifting) project instigated by the OECD, concerning the combatting of tax avoidance.

Provision of services to non-FTZ areas

The main provision of the new regulatory framework refers to the possibility that FTZ companies may provide services to companies established in local Uruguayan areas (it was allowed to provide services exclusively for abroad or within the FTZ). The main condition required is that the entity receiving the service must be a regular taxpayer of the Corporate Income Tax (IRAE). We do not know, to date, the interpretation that will be made of this provision, because the concept of IRAE taxpayer can lead to different meanings. What is indisputable is that this modification makes the regime more flexible, and will allow several FTZ users to expand their target market.

It should be noted that entities providing services to local Uruguayan areas must first be authorised for such purposes by the 'Área de Zonas Francas' (FTZs Free Zone Area Administration Office) at the time of submission of its business plan that determines this activity.

Entities that receive services from the FTZ will not be able to deduct the abovementioned expense in their local Corporate Income Tax Return (IRAE affidavit).

New permitted activities

FTZ user companies will be able to carry out additional exceptional activities (collection of debts by third parties) and auxiliary activities (not classed as substantial, but still authorised by the Executive) outside the designated territory of the Free Zones. Those companies established in FTZs outside the Metropolitan Area may also exceptionally exhibit merchandise and carry out certain complementary activities in Montevideo (Uruguay's capital city). The new Law also enables the possibility of establishing thematic FTZs for audio-visual services and activities related to entertainment, similar to Free Zone activities carried out in Dubai, UAE.

Restrictions and emphasis on controls

In order to modernise the regime with transparency measures and controls (and comply with international Standards), certain restrictions and controls were established for FTZ users. First of all, contract terms have become limited:

- Direct FTZ user contracts may have a maximum term of 15 years for industrial activities, and ten years for commercial and service activities.
- Indirect FTZ user contracts (those agreed with Direct users) may not exceed five years in all cases.

Longer deadlines may be authorised when the company commits to a significant volume of personnel and investment. Clauses for automatic renewal of contracts are prohibited, but every contract can be extended for further periods after a formal request and submission of a new business plan.

New regulations also grant greater powers to the FTZ's Administration Office which can revoke the authorisation to operate when gathering evidence of the user not fulfilling the objectives set out in the investment project and business plan. To this end, controls were established for verifying that the commitments assumed have been reasonably met. The main focus will be on demonstrating that the activity was effectively carried out within the FTZ, that the company generated employment in sufficient quantity and quality to develop its activity, and effectively established its fiscal domicile in the FTZ.

Final considerations

Changes to a successful active regime generate expectation and uncertainty for agents affected by these changes. The increase of the involvement of the Administration in its control role has become necessary to comply with international demands. It is understood that the recently approved regulations preserve and enhance the substance of the FTZ regime. In the long term, the criteria adopted by the FTZ's Administration Office in the application of new regulations should lead to growth and improvement of this sector of the economy that has contributed so much to the development of Uruguay and its economic importance within not only the MERCOSUR, but also South America as a whole.

SECTION 3

MENA

In the MENA region, there are around 73 Free Zones, and 17 MENA countries have some type of Free Zone in place or in development. MENA Free Zones have tended to focus on trading (importing goods and re-exporting to other destinations), but lately there has been a trend away from traditional Free Zones towards the more channelled variety of Special Economic Zones and industrial Zones, in part to boost value-added and revenue, but also to promote economic diversification and generate more employment.

A classic example is the Free Zone at Jebel Ali, a deep-water port in Dubai established in 1985 and widely considered to be among the most successful. It started as a trans-shipment port where large vessels unloaded goods that smaller ships would move on to other ports around the Gulf. Activities and goods involved were exempt from Import Duty. Jebel Ali triggered a wave of new Free Zone type initiatives, and the UAE now accounts for over a third of all MENA Free Zones, with Zones all the way from Dubai to Ras-al-Khaimah.

This has led UAE governments, especially Dubai, to establish industrial Zones to target particular sectors. There are now 24 such Zones, with Dubai Media City being one of the best known. Six of Egypt's nine Free Zones were established before 1994. The three established since then include the famous Media Production City, and one large Special Economic Zone called Northwest Gulf of Suez. Since 2007, Egypt has been concentrating on more focused industrial Zones, known there as investment Zones. These depend less on tax incentives and more on facilitating administrative procedures, quality infrastructure and private sector management to attract investment.

As of June 2008, Free Zones in Egypt employed nearly 136,000 people. In 2007/2008 they accounted for 20.3% of Egypt's total exports, and FDI in Free Zones represented 9.5% of Egypt's total FDI in 2007/2008. Jordan has seven Free Zones, with the Aqaba Special Economic Zone the most successful. It has attracted more than 300 companies and an estimated $400 million of investment. Three new Zones have been established since 2001.

As a general rule, Free Zones in the MENA region provide regulatory incentives. In many Zones, the authorities act as a one-stop shop, cutting related red tape and simplifying administrative procedures. A further regulatory incentive is an exemption from limits on foreign ownership. In many Gulf countries, such as Kuwait, Bahrain and the UAE, land ownership regulations are relaxed either through renewable long-term leases or outright waivers. Similarly, labour market regulation can be eased, particularly regarding the employment of expatriates, as in the case of Jordan and Kuwait, or waiving regulations

DOI: 10.4324/9781003232025-22

on limited duration contracts, such as in Tunisia. In some cases, foreign exchange regulations can also be foregone, as in Morocco, Syria, and Tunisia.

Free Zones often offer programs of fiscal incentives that go beyond those offered to investors in the wider economy. Algeria, Egypt, Kuwait and the UAE, for example, offer complete exemption from private and corporate income taxes. Lebanon, Morocco and Yemen offer corporate tax holidays of variable duration. With regard to the private income taxes of foreign employees, Yemen offers full exemption, Jordan a 12-year holiday and Tunisia a flat income tax rate of 20%.

Subsidies are not prevalent, if, that is, they exist at all. Indeed, the Free Zone concept does not allow for the implementation of subsidies, be they commercial or government. Tax and Duty incentives remove the fiscal burdens normally suffered by most businesses, and that means that untaxed profits can be invested in corporate growth, as well as bringing obvious economic benefits to the regional and national community as a whole. Financial incentives take the form of low land rental and utilities rates, as in Egypt, Lebanon, Tunisia, Kuwait and UAE, State aid for acquiring land, as in Morocco, or subsidies for training expenses, as in Jordan's Aqaba zone.

The question must, of course, be asked as to whether Free Zones actually work. In the case of the MENA area, they do, and the proof exists in the form of data-based evidence shown in this text. Some investments may have taken place anyway, although the existence of Zones does encourage governments to develop their investment policies, satisfy investors and promote opportunities for new businesses. They also create jobs: the World Bank estimates that Free Zones account for just over 1.5% of national employment throughout MENA as a whole.

The Zones in the MENA region that have performed best over a long period tend to be in countries where the enabling environment is in any case relatively favourable, in terms of macroeconomic and exchange rate policies, private property and investment laws, labour market regulations, productivity of human capital and rule of law. Incentives and economic Zones supplement, but cannot replace, a good enabling environment. Zones should not be seen as a substitute for a country's larger trade and investment reform efforts.

Another question is whether the fiscal incentives that most MENA countries offer are effective. On the one hand, such incentives are rule-based and relatively transparent. On the other hand, they result in foregone public revenue, although the loss or reduction in fiscal revenue through duties and taxes is offset by higher employment rates and increased foreign and regional investment in Free Zone operations. Thorough cost-benefit analyses should be done prior to establishing the Zones and sunset clauses should be used.

Morocco's Free-Trade Zones

As laid down by Law 19–94 (Dahir No. 1–95–1 dated 26 January 1995), Morocco's Export Processing Zones are areas of the Customs territory where industrial and commercial export activities are exempt from Customs regulations, import duties and taxes, foreign trade and exchange controls. Each zone is created and defined by a decree which stipulates the nature and activities of the companies that can operate in the zone. Goods entering and leaving the Free Zones are tax-exempt. After a company's fifth year of operation, a business tax of 8.75% is charged, versus the usual tax of 30%. Companies with export Free Zone status have no minimum export requirement and no limit on the share of goods that they may sell in Moroccan national territory.

As of 2015, there were 13 Free Zones in Morocco, including the Nouaceur Free Zone in Casablanca; the Free Zone at Tanger-Med Ksar el Majaz Mellousa 1 and 2; Oujda Free Zone; the Export Processing Zone in Kenitra; the Export Processing Zone of Tangier; Tangier Automotive City; Technopolis; Technopole d'Oujda; Tetouan Shore; Casanear Shore; Fès Shore; Oujda Shore; and the Free Storage Zone of hydrocarbons at Kebdana and Nador.

Morocco has made great strides in improving the release and clearance procedures for these Free Zones. Known operators are now able to conduct 30 operations remotely, such as the release and clearance of goods, digital signature of Customs Declarations, and e-payment. Moreover, an agreement between Customs and the Directorate General of Taxation permits approved economic operators to exchange tax data, reducing tax-related procedures.

Prior to 2017, the principal Free Zones in Morocco were:

- Export Processing Zone of Tangier;
- Free Zones at Tanger-Med Ksar el Majaz Mellousa 1 and 2;
- Free Zone in Dakhla and Laayoune (Western Sahara);
- Free Storage Zone of hydrocarbons: Kebdana and Nador;
- Export Processing Zone in Kenitra.

These have been expanded to include the present regime of Free Zones in the area close to Tangier, which is detailed later in this section.

Tangier Free Zone – Tanger-Med

Located on the African side of the Straits of Gibraltar, just 14 kilometres from Europe, the Moroccan port of Tangier, a city of great cultural significance and intrigue that has long attracted writers, musicians and tourists from around the world, is now using Free Zones to build a new reputation as a business hub, not just for North Africa but for the whole of the Mediterranean basin and beyond.

The Tangier Free Zone (TFZ) reflects the emerging trend of moving away from classical Export Processing Zone development towards Zones with a multi-sectoral development approach. It was inaugurated in 1999 and became operational in 2000. Located inland near the airport, it covers some 345 hectares and houses some 400 companies. In the ten years since its inception, the industrial users of the Free Zone have invested some €500 million in their facilities. Some 40,000 jobs have been created, and workers have added significantly to Morocco's exports. In 2008, the Free Zone accounted for a tenth of Morocco's industrial exports, totalling €1.2 billion.

Free Zones are also considered a lever for boosting technological skills, particularly in the auto-components industry. Major clients such as Yazaki, Sumitomo and Delphi now supply the automobile industry, and new demand is likely, thanks to investments by Renault. Tangier's Free Zone is one of several successful such areas in MENA, though the landscape is also dotted with slower performing ones.

The creation of the TEFZ (Tangier Exportation Free Zone) has increased the economic output of the city significantly. The TEFZ is a protected Free-Trade environment where companies from around the world can operate tax-free. It covers an area of 345 hectares and incorporates a vast container port at the junction of the biggest maritime routes in the world with the capacity to handle both cargo and passenger ships. The Free Zone has allowed Tangier to develop into an industrial pillar of the country.

The Tanger-Med Project will contain the largest port in Africa and on the Mediterranean Sea. The project is a strategic priority of the Moroccan government for the economic and social development of the North Morocco region. It is part of the economic policy orienting Morocco towards exports, based on eight clearly identified export sectors, with particular emphasis on the Free Trade Agreement with the European Union to be implemented by 2012.

Completion of the Tanger-Med project will have important economic effects in terms of jobs, creation of added value and foreign investment. Its particular position on the Straits of Gibraltar, at the crossing of two major maritime routes, and 15 kilometres from the European Union will enable it to serve a market of hundreds of millions of consumers through the industrial and commercial Free Zones which will be run by well-known private operators. It will also win part of the strong growth market of container transshipment and become the leading hub for cereal transshipment, a facility which is non-existent in the north-west African region at present.

The project is being implemented, coordinated and managed by TMSA, a private company with public prerogatives, operating under an agreement with the State and interacting with the different ministries involved.

The port complex will have important economic effects in terms of jobs, creation of added value and foreign investment. In addition to the economic effects of the operation of the port, there will be important effects resulting from its construction, particularly through foreign investments, and others from the operation of the Free Zones.

A draft loan contract of $180 million to fund the expansion works of Tanger-Med port was signed in October 2008 for building a second deep-water port, dubbed 'Tanger-Med II', to meet the growing demand for containers treatment at the international level in sea transport. The port, to be operational by the second half of 2012, will include two container terminals with a total length of 2,800 m and a nominal capacity of 5 million containers. The city's new port is set to become one of the largest in the world, transforming the region into a competitive hub, and rivalling that of Algeciras, across the Strait of Gibraltar in Spain.

The overall aim has always been that Tanger-Med will increase Morocco's competitiveness by attracting foreign investments and boosting the country's industries (textile and manufacturing). The port's container activities will be complemented by a series of Free Zones, which will develop the country's import and export capacity. The philosophy is to take advantage of Tanger's geographical location, but the objective is to boost the development of a real industrial platform for Europe, North America and West Africa, according to the Tanger Mediterranée Special Agency (TMSA), the governing body overseeing the development of Tanger-Med.

Under original plans, the port was to have a capacity of 3.5 million Twenty-Foot Equivalent Units (TEU) by 2010, with an extension could add 5 million TEU. With a total capacity approaching 9 million, Tanger-Med would be among the 15 largest ports in the world. The port and the Free Zones were projected to employ 150,000 people in the long run.

The TFZ is a pioneer of what is set to become a crucial part of Tanger-Med's success. Started in 1999, the TFZ was designed to attract foreign investors to Morocco through a comprehensive package of incentives: no import tax, no benefit tax for the first five years (8.75% thereafter), no custom duty, business conducted in home currency (no exchange rate) and State subsidies for industrial estates in priority industries such as automotive, aeronautics and electronics.

TFZ also pioneered a management concept known as 'facilitator' that TMSA now uses: it is a private company with State prerogatives. In other words, companies wishing to establish operations in the TFZ are able to avoid all the usual bureaucratic and red tape obstacles. In a country such as Morocco, ranked 115 out of 175 on the World Bank's index on ease of doing business, this is a major selling point. It was explained that investors usually allow a year to initiate the process of operation in the TFZ. The facilitator can deliver building permits, giving the Free Zone operator the parameters. If the architect works fast, it can be done in a week. The plans are obtained, and the following day the permits are signed.

There are presently 352 companies in the TFZ, with a strong emphasis on automotive and aeronautics. Some EU companies now come to the zone so that they can sell their products to the US without being affected by the WTO restrictions between the EU and US, given that the products concerned are manufactured outside the EU. TMSA is now a shareholder of the TFZ and is likely to capitalise on this to develop two more industrial Free Zones in the port's hinterland. Tanger-Med will also benefit from a logistics Free Zone, Medhub, located behind the container terminals, which is designed to focus on light, value-added activities and process container goods in transit. Third party logistics companies that specialise in distribution, such as TNT or UPS, can use the zone as a distribution platform.

The concept was tried and tested in Dubai with immense success and it was a logical step for the parent company Jebel Ali Free Zone (JAFZA) to run Medhub. The Jebel Ali Free Zone was built around the port, just outside Dubai, and indeed the city has steadily expanded to reach almost to the eastern reaches of the Free Zone. The Jebel Ali Free Zone Authority brings 20 years' experience to Medhub, so Morocco is buying itself time and experience, as well as significant economic and fiscal advantages.

As with TFZ, Medhub clients benefit from a worry-free environment, proximity to large markets, low-cost logistics and cheap labour. However, the organisation States that it is the possibility of working 'just-in-time' with Europe that constitutes the biggest draw. A good example is a retail business such as a consumer goods supermarket chain. It consolidates orders at Shanghai out of products originating from China and neighbouring Asian countries. The order preparation is labour-intensive. If products were ordered directly from China, it would be cheap, but it would take over a month to deliver. If production were carried out in Morocco, the order could be sent directly to the supermarkets at a competitive labour cost. In reality, the Moroccan Free Zone is capable of delivering anywhere in Europe within 12 to 48 hours, owing to frequent marine links to the rest of the Mediterranean and trailer links to elsewhere in mainland Europe.

The message that cost-effective manufacturing solutions can be found in Tangier has clearly been understood, as the US automobile manufacturer Delphi Group created 3,441 jobs in 2008 through an agreement signed with the National Agency for the Promotion of Employment and Skills (ANAPEC). The French automotive manufacturer Renault has adopted the same policy creating its own Free Zone automotive manufacturing plant as part of the Tangier Free Zone network.

Jobs have been recruited in the Delphi Automotive Systems Morocco Unit in Tangier, which already employs 2,289 workers, and the new Delphi Packard Systems Morocco Unit in the Tangier Free Zone which employs 1,152 workers. Delphi has indeed become the largest car component manufacturer in Tangier. The Michigan-based group which has been present in Morocco since 1999, employs 170,000 workers in 36 countries and chose Morocco because of its attractive incentives for investment and its key geographical location.

In addition, Renault Nissan reached a manufacturing agreement in the Tangier Free Zone to build a €600 million plant to make 200,000 cars by 2010. Further investment by the Group of another €200–400 million has been envisaged depending upon the type and number of vehicles produced. Ancillary component-producing companies for the plants have also located in the zone.

This automobile manufacturing plant is designed to be the biggest in the Mediterranean and provides 6,000 direct and up to 30,0000 indirect jobs. When the zone was first planned, the Chief Executive of Renault Nissan, Carlos Ghosn, commented that the plant would supply low-cost cars to the international market, noting that it was now impossible to achieve this level of production in Western European plants because of cost factors. This is a highly significant success for Morocco, and today the Renault plant is the largest car plant on the African continent.

Today (2021), the whole Tanger-Med Free Zone complex has six distinct areas, namely:

- Tanger Free Zone (400 hectares) – Automotive, Aeronautics, Textile;
- Tanger Automotive City (600 ha) – Automotive;
- Renault Tanger-Med (300 ha) – Largest Car Plant in Africa;
- Logistics Free Zone (150 ha) – Logistics;
- Tetouan Shore (20 ha) – Services, Offshoring;
- Tetouan Park (150 ha) – Light Industrial Units, Light Processing.

The whole of the Tanger-Med complex is the primary Free Zone complex in Africa and the Mediterranean area. The Tanger Free Zone alone, which is a general-purpose Free Zone, accommodates 600 companies serving a wide range of industrial and commercial sectors, employing over 30,000 people. The Tanger Automotive Zone, established in 2012, accommodates 55 companies, and is 2 kilometres from the Renault Tanger-Med Zone, thus facilitating the easy and efficient transport of components from the zone to the Renault plant. The Tetouan Park, located to the east, was established in 2015, has a surface area of 156 hectares, and accommodates 110 companies.

Sectors

Automotive

The automotive sector is the number one exporter in the Kingdom; it is one of the key areas of the Moroccan economy. Thanks to the implantation of Renault Tanger-Med, the largest automobile production factory in Africa is based in Morocco.

In addition to the vehicle manufacturer, various equipment such as seats, wiring, air conditioning, stamping, lighting, plastic injection, and airbags and so on, are manufactured in Tanger-Med industrial zone.

Aeronautic

Due to its proximity to Europe and its very attractive policy regarding industrial development, Morocco has naturally attracted players in the aviation industry.

The companies located in the Zones, many of which are subsidiaries of foreign companies, manufacture the following:

- Composite parts;
- Air Exchangers;
- Pressure parts;
- Surface coating;
- High-performance interconnection solutions.

Textiles

The textile sector, which is almost exclusively present in the northern Moroccan region, is one of the primary industries in Morocco. This historic industry represents a significant market share in the total industrial production in Morocco. Companies are involved in numerous areas, namely clothing, leather goods and digital printing on clothing.

The food-processing industry

The food industry plays a major role in the industrial development in Morocco, specifically in the Tanger-Tetouan region, with companies involved in the following activities:

- Packaging of food products;
- Processing of seafood products;
- Development of frozen home-made pastries;
- Drinks bottling.

Electronics

The electronics industry plays an important role in the Tanger-Med industrial Zones with job-creating companies operating in many target markets:

- Fibre-optic cables;
- Connectors;
- Optical cords;
- Hydraulic and pneumatic components;
- Electronic cards and subsets.

Turkish Free Zones

Beginning by 1987, Turkey established a number of **Free Zones**. Free Zones are defined in Turkish law as fenced-in areas in which special regulatory treatment exists for the operating users in order to promote exports of goods and services. Free Zones offer more convenient and flexible business climate in order to increase trade volume and export for some industrial and commercial activities as compared to the other parts of the country. The basic objectives of the Foundation and Operation of Free Zones are promoting export-oriented investment and production, accelerating Foreign Direct Investment and technology access, directing enterprises towards export and developing international trade.

Below is the list of Free Zones in Turkey, as provided by the Turkish Ministry of the Economy.

Free Zones in Turkey

SN	*Name*	*Province*	*Foundation date*
1	Mersin Free Zone	Mersin	1987
2	Antalya Free Zone	Antalya	1987
3	Aegean Free Zone [1]	İzmir	1990
4	İstanbul Atatürk Airport Free Zone	İstanbul	1990
5	Trabzon Free Zone	Trabzon	1992
6	İstanbul Leather Industry Free Zone [2]	İstanbul	1995
7	East Anatolia Free Zone	Erzurum	1995
8	Mardin Free Zone	Mardin	1995
9	İstanbul Stock Exchange Free Zone (İMKB)	İstanbul	1997
10	İzmir Menemen Leather Free Zone	İzmir (Menemen)	1998
11	Rize Free Zone	Rize	1998
12	Samsun Free Zone	Samsun	1998
13	İstanbul Tracia Free Zone	İstanbul	1998
14	Kayseri Free Zone	Kayseri	1998
15	Adana Yumurtalık Free Zone	Adana (Yumurtalık)	1998
16	European Free Zone	Tekirdağ (Çorlu)	1999
17	Gaziantep Free Zone	Gaziantep	1999
18	Bursa Free Zone	Bursa	2001
19	Kocaeli Free Zone	Kocaeli	2001
20	Denizli Free Zone	Denizli	2002
21	Tubitak Free Zone	Kocaeli (Gebze)	2002

The European Free-Trade Zone (EFZ) (www.asb.com.tr), İstanbul-Leather and Industrial Free Zone (www.desbas.com.tr) and Aegean Free Zone (www.esbas.com.tr) are among the largest Free Zones in Turkey. Free Zones offer ready offices, warehouses, open stock areas, production facilities for rent or sale and lands with ready infrastructure. All kinds of infrastructure services (electricity, water, gas, waste water, purification, communication) are provided in these technocities. In addition to these facilitations, Free Zones such as the EFZ also offer construction services, catering, IT Services, Maintenance Services, Insurance, Loading/Unloading, Warehousing, Consulting Services, 24-hour Private Security and Conference Halls.

Incentives and advantages of the Turkish Free-Trade Zones:

- Companies are 100% exempt from Corporate Tax (20%) and Income Tax (15–35%).
- Free Zones are considered to be outside the Customs border, meaning that no Customs Duty, VAT or KKDF (6% over the credit payments) is applied on the goods that enter the zone.
- Companies that sell at least 85% of their products abroad are 100% exempt from income tax on employee salaries.
- Due to the Customs Union Agreement between Turkey & EU, goods of Turkish origin can enter Free Circulation in the EU Market (No Tax between TR & EU).
- Companies can freely transfer their profits and earnings to Turkey or any other country.
- As Free Zones are outside domestic Customs jurisdiction, companies can purchase goods from Turkey for export prices, excluding VAT.
- Infrastructure services are provided exempt from VAT (Electricity, Water, Gas, telecommunication).
- Companies are free to bring second-hand (used) machinery to the Free Zones and there is no age limitation for the importation of second-hand (used) machinery.
- As the transactions within the zone are performed with convertible foreign currencies, the domestic inflation rate will not influence purchasing and selling activities, inventory control and accounting procedures in general.
- Faulty or substandard goods can easily be returned to their origin by just issuing an invoice.
- Companies can keep their stock in the Zones on a duty-free basis for an unlimited period of time.

The European Free Zone

BCCT member European Free Zone Founder and Operator Co. (EFZ)/Avrupa Serbest Bölgesi (ASB) is a Free-Trade Zone that includes a multi-sectoral industrial site and finds appropriate solutions for the requirements of all its investors. Established in 1999, it is located in the Çorlu district of Tekirdağ on an area covering 2 million m^2 of land.

More than **150 companies** from all over the world – such as 3M, Foxconn, Polyplex Resins, Indorama, Bekaert Textile, Flamaerotec and MTU Motor – have invested into the European Free Zone, where 4,000 people are currently employed.

In 2015, the trade volume generated in EFZ was US$2.5 billion, making it 4th among the existing 19 Free Zones in Turkey.

Jordanian Free Zones

Jordan's Free Zones were established to promote export-oriented industries and transit trade. Commodities and goods of various origins are deposited in the Free Zone areas for the purpose of storage and manufacturing, without having to pay the usual excise fees and other taxes, as they are treated like goods outside Jordan. There are currently six operating Free-Trade Zones in Jordan, at Aqaba, the country's largest operating Free Zone, with the greatest number of fiscal benefits, Zarqa, Al Karama, Al Karak, Sahab, and Queen Alia International Airport, and they are operated by the Jordanian Free Zones Corporation, an autonomous government agency.

Jordanian Free Zone advantages include:

- 100% foreign ownership of zone tenant companies;
- Subsidised real estate;
- Customs Duty suspension on materials imported into the Zones for company operations, including storage and production.

In addition, the Aqaba Free Zone offers a reduced Corporation Tax of 5%, exemption from property tax, and a 70% quota on foreign employees.

In order to conduct operations in a Jordanian Free-Trade Zone, a company must obtain approval from the Aqaba Special Economic Zone Authority if incorporating in Aqaba, or the Jordanian Free Zone Corporation, if incorporating in the other Free Zones.

The **Aqaba Special Economic Zone Authority** (ASEZA) is the financially and administratively autonomous authority responsible for the management, regulation and the development of the Aqaba Special Economic Zone (ASEZ). **ASEZA** was inaugurated in 2001 as an initiative by the Jordanian government to ensure that Aqaba's commercial and cultural prominence developed to become a regional hub for trade, tourism and culture. Six ministerial-level commissioners, each responsible for a major area of regulatory or operational activity, govern the ASEZ. ASEZA is a service-oriented organisation offering one-stop assistance covering all investment needs.

In 2002, ASEZA adopted a comprehensive Master Plan that encompasses development activities in the Zone for the promotion of portal, urban, tourist, commercial, academic and other investment sectors. Developed planning already covers five special areas:

Aqaba town

- Modern architecture is to complement the old city traditional elements, thus creating a unique cultural environment, and which is more, new opportunities for investors especially in the tourist, commercial, and residential areas of development.

Port areas

- The Aqaba Port areas include the Main Port, the Container Port and the Southern Industrial Port. According to the Master Plan, a common location – the Main Port – is established to merge the three existing port area activities into one expanded entertainment, residential, hotel and cruises service centre.

Coral Coastal Zone

- The Coral Coastal Zone is undergoing a wide residential, hotel and entertainment facilities construction process for the development of an advanced community resort, with respect to relative beach and coral reef protection requirements.

Southern industrial zone

- The Zone extends along the Southern Industrial Zone Port and consists of reorganised and expanded current sites. New transportation systems, including a rail terminal, serve the developed area.

Airport industrial zone

- Ideal for industrial facilities, permitted land uses in the Zone include logistics and distribution, high-tech industries, warehousing, light manufacturing, showrooms, office complexes and airport-related business activities.

The Master Plan aims at preserving natural resources within the construction frame. It comprises several Zones and reserves for the protection of Aqaba's cultural, archaeological, historical and natural heritage and diversity. Areas include: Five environmental Zones, coral reserves, archaeological reserves, natural area reserves and a Beach Protection Zone.

ASEZA incentives include:

- 5% income tax on net profit;
- No Customs Duties;
- No Sales Tax on final consumption of vast majority of goods and services;
- No restrictions on foreign equity or foreign currency exchange;
- No income tax for registered enterprises operating in logistics centres (transit, export, re-export);
- 40% Discount on Handling of Transit Shipments;
- 50% Discount on Containers Exported from ASEZ;
- 50% Discount on Suez Canal Fees for Goods Shipped to ASEZ;
- Automated Customs Procedures (ASYCUDA);
- Access to 1.5 billion customers in 161 countries through trade agreements.

The Aqaba Free Zone covers one million square metres, although an additional 2.5 million square metres has been allocated for the purpose of establishing industrial projects, similar to the Jebel Ali Free Zone in Dubai. The Zarqa Free Zone lies 35 kilometres northeast of Amman, along a route which connects Jordan with neighbouring countries. It covers 5.5 million square metres and houses about 65 licensed industrial companies and more than 175 warehouses. There are currently about 700 commercial trading and industrial projects based in Jordan's two Free Zone areas. They include storage, repackaging, mixing and manufacturing operations. Land and buildings in the Free Zone areas are available for rent at concessionary prices.

The Free Zone project at Sahab covers a total area of 63,000 square metres at the Sahab Industrial Estate, and has been designated for serving its industrial investors in addition to aiding in the establishment of export-oriented industries. Meanwhile, the Free Zone project at Queen Alia International Airport covers an area of 120,000 square metres, and has been allocated for the purpose of serving transit trade and establishing light high-tech, pollution-free industries. In addition, plans are under consideration for promoting private Free Zones in Jordan, as well as for setting up a trilateral Free Zone including Jordan, the Palestinian National Authority territories and Israel.

Jordanian Development Zones

The Jordanian authorities also operate six Development Zones, which are industrial estates located within Jordan's main cities, namely:

- King Hussein bin Talal Mafraq Development Zone;
- Ma'an Development Zone;
- Irbid Development Zone;
- Dead Sea Development Zone;
- Jabal Ajloun Development Zone;
- Amman Business Park Development Zone.

All six Development Zones offer identical benefits for operations conducted in the Free Zone, including:

- 100% foreign ownership of companies operating within the zone;
- Reduced corporate tax rate of 5%;
- Exemption from VAT;
- Suspension from all Customs Imports Duties for all materials imported into the zone required for company operations, including storage and manufacture;
- No quota on foreign employees;
- No social security contributions and payroll tax on the salaries of foreign employees.

In order to conduct operations in a Development Zone, the company must obtain approval from the Development and Free Zones Commission (DFZC), and it normally takes between four and eight weeks (one to two months) to set the company up inside the zone. The Free-Trade Zones are largely used by manufacturing companies, while the Development Zones are largely use by IT companies.

Foreign and local companies established in Free Zones enjoy the following incentives and exemptions:

- The profits of projects operating in the Free Zones are exempt from income and social affairs taxes for a period of 12 years.
- Salaries and bonuses of non-Jordanian employees working in the Free Zones are exempt from income and social affairs taxes.
- All commodities imported or exported through the Free Zones and bound for external markets are exempt from Customs, imports and all other taxes and fees.
- Buildings, including production and storage facilities, erected in the Free Zones are exempt from licence fees, and land is exempt from property taxes.
- The transfer of capital invested in the Free Zones and the profits accrued from them is permitted to anywhere outside Jordan, without any constraints or restrictions.

- The products of Free Zone industries are exempt from Customs fees in the case of offering them for consumption in the local market, limited by the cost of the local material and the expenses which go into their manufacture.

Additionally, the government of Jordan has embarked on a comprehensive plan to transform the entire Aqaba region, Jordan's only seaport area, into a 'world-class' free port area. Moreover, there are plans to transform some of the southern part of Aqaba into an integrated Free Zone measuring four kilometres in width and 10–20 kilometres in length. The location of this zone will be on the southern shore, and will include industrial and commercial sections for storage similar to that of the Jebel Ali Free Zone in Dubai.

United Arab Emirates

Most of the United Arab Emirates' 36 Free-Trade Zones are located in Dubai, but other Emirates are also creating them as a means of investment, including Masdar, a green-energy zone located in Abu Dhabi. The oldest Free-Trade Zone in the Emirates, the Jebel Ali Free Trade Zone, is one of the largest Free Zones in the world, and handles 11 million containers each month.

Free Zones in Dubai are managed and operated by the relevant authority. For instance, the Jebel Ali Free Zone Authority in Dubai is responsible for managing, operating and supervising the Jebel Ali Free Zone (JAFZ), one of the largest seaport Free Zones in Dubai. It has a subsidised rate of 32% on the country's FDI. As for other Free Zones in Dubai, the Dubai Multi-Commodities Centre (DMCC) has 7,330 active registered companies (as per 2013), offers a retention rate of 94%, and estimates an application of over 200 companies every year. The DIFC is another jurisdiction demonstrating the growth of expansion. It contributes 12% to the GDP of Dubai and has an estimated a growth rate of 27% (as per 2015). The authorities speculate that the region will triple in size by 2024. Others include the Dubai Airport Free Zone (DAFZA); the Dubai Internet City; and the Dubai Media City.

In the UAE, a designated zone is a specified fenced geographical area having security measures and Customs controls in place to monitor entry and exit of individuals and the movement of goods to and from the area. The following Free Zones are declared as designated Zones.

- Free Trade Zone of Khalifa Port;
- Abu Dhabi Airport Free Zone;
- Khalifa Industrial Zone;
- Jebel Ali Free Zone (North-South);
- Dubai Cars and Automotive Zone (DUCAMZ);
- Dubai Textile City;
- Free Zone Area in Al Quoz;
- Free Zone Area in Al Qusais;
- Dubai Aviation City;
- Dubai Airport Free Zone;
- Hamriyah Free Zone;
- Sharjah Airport International Free Zone;
- Ajman Free Zone;

- Umm Al Quwain Free Trade Zone in Ahmed Bin Rashid Port;
- Umm Al Quwain Free Trade Zone on Sheikh Mohammed Bin Zayed Road;
- RAK (Ras Al-Khaimah) Free Trade Zone;
- RAK Maritime City Free Zone;
- RAK Airport Free Zone;
- Fujairah Free Zone;
- FOIZ (Fujairah Oil Industry Zone).

Any Free Zone which is not declared as designated zone is a non-designated zone. In other words, a non-designated zone is any geographical area within UAE which does not have any security measures and Customs controls in place to monitor entry and exit of goods and individuals. The primary examples of this are DMCC, Dubai Media City, DIFC and Dubai Internet City.

The Jebel Ali Free Zone (JAFZ)

Due to growing business opportunities in the UAE, the UAE government has introduced 'Free Zones' to make it easier for foreigners to invest and operate in the UAE. In these Free Zones, investors benefit from maintaining full business ownership and receiving tax exemptions.

Some of the benefits of setting up business in UAE Free Zones are:

- Tax exemption;
- 100% ownership of business (Outside a Free Zone, you are required to use the services of a local sponsor);
- Bank accounts can be opened in a business's name;
- Reasonable renewal fees;
- 100% import and export tax exemptions;
- 100% repatriation of profits and capital;
- No personal income tax.

Currently, there are 45 FTZs active in the UAE, including the Jebel Ali Free Zone and the Dubai Airport Free Zone.

In 1985, an independent authority named JAFZA was established to manage and promote the Free Zone, which had just opened adjacent to the port of Jebel Ali. Key benefits from Jebel Ali Port and Free Zone combination to foreign investors include: Developed infrastructure claimed to be 'plug and play' ready within the Free Zone, immediate and easy access to seaport with good infrastructure and efficiency, independent Free Zone authority and 'one-stop-shop' bureaucracy, Customs-free trading zone and no foreign ownership restrictions.

The successful combination of port and SEZ at Jebel Ali propelled growth of its cargo volumes and placed it in the league of world's Top 10 container ports despite being purely reliant on transshipment and re-export cargo. Jebel Ali Port plays a vital role in the UAE's (especially Dubai) economy by serving the world markets with over 180 shipping lines and more than 90 weekly services connecting the port to over 140 ports worldwide. It is primarily a container port and its container terminals are equipped with a total of 23 berths and 78 cranes to cater to the world's largest container vessels (including those being built). In 2013, Jebel Ali Port achieved a throughput 13.6 million TEUs and was ranked ninth-largest container port worldwide.

The success or growth of SEZs in a given location is driven by the potential of industrialisation and the level of investment in industrial infrastructure done by the local (State) government in providing necessities like electricity, water, transport connectivity, defined land banks, land acquisition guidelines and uniform taxation structure, amongst others.

Unevenly distributed SEZs in the GCC is also an issue leading to lower realisation of benefits in locations of crowded establishments and missing potential gains in other locations. Further, almost all of these port-SEZ combinations are heavily reliant on re-exports for their volumes and the available volume within the region is being fragmented between these multiple ports.

Even in case of port-based SEZs, despite the significant additional advantages they offer over land-locked SEZs, experts say that they cannot be recommended for every port. While availability of suitable infrastructure is one of the most important factors while deciding on a Special Economic Zone, there are other factors like proximity of potential cargo-feeding industrial clusters, environmental impact, State-level regulations, displacement of labour (primarily fishermen), weather conditions, and, last, scope for long-term growth and expansion that need to be taken into account before deciding on a port-based SEZ.

The combined development of ports and Special Economic Zones offer high potential to accelerate the economic prosperity of the countries in the GCC. It can also possibly cover up the less-than-expected benefits from conventional SEZs to a certain extent. Several operational and planned SEZs at ports in countries like the UAE, Oman, Qatar and Kuwait are likely to add significant success to those ports and trade revenues for the countries. However, it should be noted that not every port can be developed into an integrated one and SEZ entity and several factors have to be considered to approve the development of such facilities.

Investors need to have proven expertise in development of such Zones and have a clear business plan for justified/optimal use of the allocated port and land banks. Simultaneously, governments must eliminate the limitations in the existing SEZ policies and define a specific policy for port-based SEZs. Best practices and key factors that contributed to the success of this model in nations like China and the UAE have to be adopted in other the GCC countries, too, by improvising them to suit the specific country needs context. Such constructive efforts from both the government and investors would definitely lead to high potential gains for the economy from these Zones.

JAFZA is Economic Zones World's flagship operation, and is one of the world's largest and fastest growing Free Zones. Established in 1985, JAFZA today is spread over an area of 48 km^2 and is home to over 6,400 companies, including over 120 of the Fortune Global 500 enterprises, from across the world. It is a leading driver of the burgeoning UAE economy. With its impeccable track record, JAFZA stands for innovation, customer centricity, transparent operations and entrepreneurial dynamism.

As the leading business hub of the Middle East, the zone focuses on long-term customer relationships and fosters alliances with global investors by providing them with world-class infrastructure supported with value-added services and incentives. JAFZA also offers the benefit of huge business opportunities from a potential market of over two billion people in the greater Middle East region. Its products include office units, warehouses, light industrial units and land on long-term lease. These land sites are suitable for a variety of purpose-built facilities. Other value-added products include business centres, hotels for visitors and customised Build-to-Suit options.

As one of the fastest growing Free Zones in the world, over the last four years, the zone has:

- Grown its customer base by over 60%;
- Increased its revenue at an average of 34% year-on-year;
- Contributed to Dubai's GDP at 25% on a year-to-year basis;
- Sustained more than 160,000 jobs in the UAE through its companies;
- Accounted for more than 50% of Dubai's total exports. It also accounts for 25% of all container throughputs through the Jebel Ali Port and 12% of all air freight at Dubai International Airport;
- Accounted for 20% of all FDI inflow into the UAE.

Today, the Jebel Ali Free Zone is one of the largest and most successful Free Zones in the world, accommodating several thousand companies and allowing for a wide variety of operations, from manufacturing and processing to storage and distribution.

Dubai Silicon Oasis (DSO)

Dubai Silicon Oasis was established by the Government of Dubai in 2004 and is a unique Free Zone reputed for world-class innovation, design and development in the field of photovoltaic, nanotechnology, electronics optoelectronic technology and supporting industries providing equipment and materials for the production of information and communications technologies using semiconductors. It is the only technology park in the UAE to provide integrated living and working community.

DSO was established as a global and collaborative initiative to facilitate and promote modern technology-based industries in the Middle East, and provide the world's best business climate to the entire electronics value chain in the form of highly educated personnel and access to shared capital.

Spread across 7.2 km^2, DSO is superbly governed by Dubai Silicon Oasis Authority (DSOA) and enjoys advanced public, industrial, living & residential, commercial, and education facilities. Dubai Silicon Oasis aims at attracting companies engaged in Semiconductor Manufacturing, Electronic Manufacturing Systems, Microelectronics, Fabless IC Design, Test & Assembly and optoelectronics related enterprises.

Strategically located in Dubai at the trade crossroads of Europe & Asia, DSO is easily accessible from Dubai's International Airport, Jebel Ali Port & Port Rashid and central business district, making it a popular investment destination. Dubai Silicon Oasis has lived up to its economic diversification strategy and has successfully transformed UAE into a knowledge-based economy by positively impacting almost all economic sectors including trade and services, finance, employment, and banking and so on.

Business establishment in Dubai Silicon Oasis

Companies operating within the Dubai Silicon Oasis Free Zone avail a wide range of Free Zone incentives and additional benefits; like 100% ownership, advanced IT network, and business-friendly environment specifically designed for the technology industry. Therefore, company formation in Dubai Silicon Oasis is an ideal objective for anyone associated with the technology domain, and as a result, popular global companies have their presence in DSO, including AMD, Fujitsu, Henkel, Nortel Networks, Philips, Schneider Electric, Synopsys, Wavetec and Western Digital, among others.

Business establishment in Dubai Silicon Oasis has also received a substantial boost due to its dynamic commercial and social environment, and presence of advanced industrial Zones, office towers, villas & apartments, R&D units, educational institutions and healthcare units. The DSO facilities include:

- 'Plug and Play' offices and R&D centres;
- Advanced logistics facilities including light industrial units, operational warehouse units, high-bay warehouses, and industrial spaces;
- Shovel ready industrial land plots of varying sizes;
- Excellent conference facilities including meeting rooms and lecture facility for executive presentations;
- Shops, amenities, and restaurants.

Business creation in DSO

Company incorporation in Dubai Silicon Oasis is a lucrative proposition due to excellent business infrastructure, liberal government policies and the following reasons:

- 100% foreign ownership;
- 100% personal and corporate tax exemptions;
- 100% repatriation of capital and profits;
- Competitive pricing;
- No Customs Duty;
- No quotas or trade barriers;
- State-of-the-art IT infrastructure – fibre rings, Wi-Fi coverage, on-site data centre, high-speed Internet access and a full suite of services with 3rd Tier data centre;
- Plug and play offices;
- Subsidised top-end Electronic Design Automation (EDA) tools;
- Faster processing of employee visas;
- Bureaucracy-free Customs clearance;
- Business support and conference facilities;
- Stringent IP laws and support;
- Thriving urban community with core technology zone, surrounded by a master-planned residential environment, consisting of villas, technologically advanced commercial and residential high-rise buildings;
- Fast-track process for business set-up;
- Dedicated business support services including integrated online E-business system offering tenants fast and efficient services at the touch of a button;
- Access to a talented pool of technical and engineering professionals;
- Stable and clear regulation laws;
- Access to a 5-billion consumer market with tourists from the Middle East, North Africa and the Indian Subcontinent.

Types of legal entities in Dubai Silicon Oasis

DSO offers a lucrative value chain to investors in the form of multiple incentives and allows an individual or a corporate entity to register a business in any of the following legal forms:

- Free Zone Establishment (FZE) – FZE is an entity with a single shareholder (an individual or a corporate), which can be set up with a minimum capital investment of AED 100,000;
- Free Zone Company (FZC/FZCO) – FZC is an entity with two to five shareholders (individual or corporates) and needs a minimum capital investment of AED 100,000 for company formation;
- Branch of a Foreign Company – Any UAE or foreign-based company can register its branch in the DSO without any capital investment on the condition that it conducts same business activity as the parent company;
- Branch of a Local Company.

Business licensing segments in DSO

Dubai Silicon Oasis is the hub for companies belonging to the semiconductor sector, both regionally and internationally. Additionally, the Dubai Silicon Oasis Free Zone focuses on the companies belonging to any of the following hi-tech sectors:

- Aerospace;
- Alternative Energy;
- Automobile;
- Biotechnology;
- Consultancy & Business Development;
- Data Centre;
- EDA Tools;
- Electrical Appliances & Equipment;
- Engineering Related to Technology;
- Finance Institutions;
- General Activities;
- IC Design;
- Information Technology and Localization of Technologies;
- Internet;
- IP Protection;
- IT Security;
- Law Firms;
- Logistics;
- Microelectronics;
- Mobile Technologies;
- Oil & Gas;
- Pharmaceutical;
- Semiconductor;

- Software Development & Solutions or Software-as-a-Service (SAAS);
- Talent Development and Recruitment;
- Telecommunications Equipment.

Types of licences issued for company formation in DSO

Based on the type of business activity to be performed, three types of business licences are issued in Dubai Silicon Oasis by the DSOA:

- **Service Licence** – Allows the registered entities (like accounting firms, business consultants, and lawyers) to carry out services specified by the DSOA;
- **Industrial Licence** – Allows the registered entity to import raw material, manufacture, process, assemble, package and export the finished product;
- **Trade Licence** – Allows the registered entity to import, export and distribute the items specified in the licence.

Special licences

- **Business Operation Permit**: This is a special permit given to companies by the Dubai Economic Department (DED) operating under the areas owned by private;
- **Entrepreneurial Business Licence (EBL)**: EBL is a low-cost license that offers a lesser business stake, and is designed to offer a wide range of support resources and services to budding entrepreneurs who are members of DSO's incubator program.

Business establishment process in Dubai Silicon Oasis

There is a lot to do for business incorporation in DSO, like choosing appropriate legal business structures, deciding the business activity, getting required staff, creating a detailed business plan and so on. Company formation in Dubai Silicon Oasis is easy for companies that understand the DSO's pre-defined rules and regulations, and plan their business decisions accordingly; however, you need to be sure that all the procedures are followed in accordance to the UAE laws, as a slight error can elongate the business set up process unnecessarily.

Therefore, getting professional help from reliable business partners like Commitbiz is preferred, as they are well-versed with the required legal formalities pertaining to employment, getting office or residential space on lease, capital requirements, business registration and licensing, dispute resolution, getting visa and so on, thus making the entire company formation process easy and streamlined.

Financial Free Zones

UAE Free Zones are a major attraction to foreign investors and businesses wishing to conduct business in the UAE and encompass a wide variety of commercial activities.

Until the introduction of the UAE's Foreign Direct Investment Law in late 2018, it was a federal requirement for at least 51% of the shares of a company to be held by a UAE national, excluding the companies already established in the Jebel Ali and Airport Free Zones. However, investors in the existing Free Zones still required a local UAE 'sponsor', that is, a local legal representative, to legitimise their businesses in the Zones. As a result, a variety of Free Zones were established in order to attract foreign businesses to the region wishing to have full control of their business.

In the UAE, Free Zones are geographically demarcated areas within the UAE (even if most of them are not fenced or gated), permitting 100% foreign ownership and are, in most cases, dedicated to a specific industry. They were designed to support strategic transformation in key industries (e.g. finance, IT, logistics and manufacturing) and many are built with public finance and boast State-of-the-art facilities.

For instance, the Dubai Media City, which is a Free Zone in the Emirate of Dubai and at the western end of the metropolis, close to the port of Jebel Ali, has infrastructure and licences adapted to the needs of the media industry. Similarly, the DIFC attracts companies in the financial services sector, drawing in insurance, financial services and investment firms and banks wanting to grow their international client-base.

Accordingly, each Free Zone has its own specific requirements regarding minimum capital requirements, office or warehouse space and permitted activities; with each possessing the relevant licences and adequate legislation to enable their dedicated industry to flourish.

With more than 50 different Free Zones across the UAE and with many more under development, Free Zones have helped make the UAE an attractive option for foreign businesses looking to relocate or expand their global footprint. The common benefits of doing business in a UAE Free Zone include:

- 100% foreign ownership of the enterprise;
- Access to world-class logistic facilities;
- Availability of a large pool of multicultural, skilled professionals;
- Benefits from economies of concentration (given the Zones dedicated to industries);
- Ease of recruiting international employees, with all Free Zones providing one-stop-shop services for work visas;
- Tax holidays – usually guaranteed for 15 or 50 years;
- 100% import and export tax exemption;
- 100% repatriation of capital and profits;
- Corporate tax exemptions for up to 50 years;
- Eligibility to apply for the UAE Tax Residency Certificate.

Dubai International Financial Centre (DIFC)

The Dubai International Financial Centre is recognised as the leading financial centre in the Middle East, Africa and South Asia region. The DIFC Free Zone is distinct from other Free Zones in the UAE as it has its own court with independent regulations abiding by an English Common Law framework.

The main features of the DIFC, in addition to the ones stated above, are:

- Access to laws and courts (including arbitration system) based on English Common Law;
- Access to DIFC Will and Probate Registry;
- Access to a recognised and international stock exchange with primary and secondary listings of debt and equity instruments;
- Choice of a large number of regulated, non-regulated and financial activities licences;
- A platform to access regional wealth and investment opportunities.

With over 65 significant funds domiciled in the DIFC and well over 2,000 companies resident within its regulatory parameters, the DIFC provides a flexible and hospitable business ecosystem for financial firms wishing to expand their global footprint.

Dubai Multi-Commodities Centre (DMCC)

In 2013, the DMCC became the UAE's largest Free Zone, overtaking Jebel Ali. DMCC now has more than 7,330 active registrations, with an average of 200 companies joining each month and a 94% retention rate. The centre trades in international commodities, and uses Dubai as its major centre for international trading activities.

As a global commodities broker, the centre innovates and complements key trading hubs across the globe to further support Dubai's ambitious economic development program. It serves markets along the new Silk Route and has become a strong facilitator of trade for producing countries in African and consuming nations in Asia, ASEAN, Europe, South America and the US. To this extent, its tax incentives enable it to trade internationally on a much more cost-effective basis.

Eilat – Israel's only Free-Trade Zone

Eilat, the port and town at the southern extremity of Israel which is also a centre for Israel's tourism industry, has since 1985 also been enjoying a status as Israel's only Free-Trade area, that is, free from duties and consumption taxes. This status was granted despite a very modest level of international trade, given that the port handles only 1% of cargo arriving in Israel. The main reason for the Free-Trade status was as a response to pleas by the city's leaders for incentives to maintain Eilat's economic viability. The plea was made at a time when the city's population had decreased from 25,000 in 1982 to 19,000 in 1985. The opening of the Suez Canal to Israeli ships following the Egypt-Israeli peace treaty seemed to make Eilat's port even less vital than previously, except for its continuing role as an oil port, previously a storage point for Iranian oil, but latterly oil from Egypt's Gulf of Suez. This was in direct contrast to Eilat's Jordanian neighbour, Aqaba, which was beginning to enjoy a greater degree of economic success and which later was to implement and establish its own Free Zone to boost its economy.

High prices charged by local hotels and restaurants, blamed on transportation costs from the centre of the country (Eilat is completely isolated form the main economic centre of Israel by the Negev desert) were also threatening Eilat's tourism status. Several foreign tourism package companies had said that they would transfer business to the Canary Islands and other holiday locations where sun, sea, sand and bottles of beer were cheaper. In the case of the Canary Islands, this was definitely the case, as the islands are an offshore territory under Spanish rule and are therefore considered to be advantageous for tax purposes, as tax levels in the Canaries are lower than in mainland Spain.

Because of the political importance to Israel of maintaining a strong presence in its strategically vulnerable southern Negev Desert, the Israeli government decided to assist Eilat by granting it a limited Free-Trade status that would make it cheaper to live there and therefore make it more economically attractive and therefore more economically attractive for tourists to visit the region. Under the terms of the Eilat Free Trade Area Law which took effect from 1 November 1985, goods sold in Eilat for local consumption are exempt from the 15% VAT applicable to the rest of the country. However, specifically excluded from the exemption are cars, televisions, videos and certain electrical appliances. Goods imported into Eilat by an approved dealer for sale to foreign tourists are exempt from all import duties and other taxes, similar to the fiscal conditions applying to the Manaus Free Zone in northern Brazil. In addition to these fiscal incentives in Eilat, for local residents the most important provision is a 10% income tax credit.

The law, passed by the Israeli Knesset (the Israeli Parliament), is given a large share of the credit for the turnaround that Eilat has experienced since the implementation of its Free-Trade and overall fiscal status. In two years since the implementation of the Free-Trade law, the population of Eilat rose to 21,000, and is now held from increasing further only because of a housing bottleneck, in that the rate at which new houses are being built is exceeded by the number of people wishing to move to Eilat because of its economic advantages. A combination of reduced taxes and pressure by the town's municipal authorities persuaded local hoteliers and restaurant owners to decrease prices to the point where they became competitive with process overseas, thus encouraging domestic, as well as international, tourism to the location.

An upsurge in tourism has renewed interest by local and foreign investors in the construction of more hotels, with increasing numbers of hotel rooms available for tourists. This is coupled with an increase in the number of flights, both charter and scheduled, heading for the location from both Tel Aviv and elsewhere. The industrial base of Tel Aviv was also proposed for expansion given Israel's Free Trade Agreements with the United States, Canada and the European Union, now part of the Pan-Euro-Med Free Trade Agreement. In 1987, preliminary studies were launched into the feasibility of importing semi-finished goods from the Far East and parts of Africa, adding at least 35% to their value in materials or production costs, and shipping the finished products duty-free to the US and elsewhere in the world. The results of these studies were the planning of an industrial zone next to the city, although this has yet to be developed. As yet, the port of Eilat remains in its present State, and has yet to be developed to account for these proposed activities.

The increasing fortunes for Eilat also resulted in improvements in banking and also the development of a rail link with the rest of Israel to allow for the movement of both passengers and freight, especially linking the port of Eilat with Israel's Mediterranean ports. Freight would include containers and also the carriage of mineral resources, namely phosphates and potash from the Dead Sea and the Negev, to Eilat for shipment to Africa and the Far East instead of shipping these commodities through the port of Ashdod, close to the unstable area of Gaza, and Haifa, both on Israel's Mediterranean coast. The port of Eilat would also permit the offloading of coal from South Africa and Australia rather than shipping it through the Suez Canal to Israel's Mediterranean ports, a much further and costlier distance. This rail link is still in its planning stage.

A further initiative was to transfer Eilat's airport to a desert site eight miles to the north of the town, thus enabling the original airport, close to the town's centre, to be converted into a site for several hotels and a convention centre. The new airport, designated Ramon International Airport, opened in 2019 and now handles all domestic and international flights in and out of Eilat.

It must be pointed out that taxation in Eilat has been reduced, not eliminated. Many taxes are still applicable, but overall the fiscal burden to the area has been significantly reduced. This has undoubtedly increased Eilat's fortunes and provided the area with greatly needed fiscal and economic advantages.

Mauritius

Mauritius Freeport

The Mauritius Freeport (Free-Trade Zone) was established in 1992 as a Customs-Free Zone for goods destined for re-export. The government's objective is to promote the country as a regional warehousing, distribution, marketing, and logistics centre for Eastern and Southern Africa and the Indian Ocean rim. Through its membership in the Common Market for Eastern and Southern Africa (COMESA), the Southern African Development Community (SADC), and the Indian Ocean Commission (IOC), Mauritius offers preferential access to a market of 380 million consumers, representing an import potential of US$90 billion.

Situated on 52 hectares of land adjacent to port facilities and a modern container terminal, the Freeport offers 120,000 square metres of world-class infrastructure, including cold rooms, dry storage, an international trade exhibition centre, processing units, and office space for transshipment, consolidation, storage and processing activities. Freeport facilities are also available at the airport. Port Louis is increasingly used by major shipping lines (i.e. Maersk/Sealand, P&O Nedloyd, and MSC) as a regional container transshipment hub.

Adjacent to the seaport of Port Louis, Mauritius Freeport Development (MFD) has developed the largest logistics centre in the Indian Ocean. MFD offers world-class, cost-effective supply chain solutions through a comprehensive range of equipment and facilities which comply with the highest Standards in the industry: EU, HACCP, ISO.

MFD has refined the supply chain management concept to a single platform and offers a secured logistics package for a wide variety of products and services with a full private web traceability interface. International operators are provided with worldwide cargo service under the Freeport regime.

The Freeport legislation provides for a comprehensive package of liberal incentives for companies looking for a cost-effective storage, assembly and redistribution platform. As a result, Freeport-based companies in Mauritius benefit from many advantages, namely the following:

- Efficient Customs clearance process;
- Duty-free and VAT free goods and equipment;

- Exemption from Corporate Tax;
- 100% foreign ownership is possible;
- Free repatriation of profits;
- No foreign exchange control;
- 50% of reduction on port handling charges;
- 50% of turnover can be realised from local market sales;
- Access to offshore banking facilities.

Activities that can be carried out in the Freeport include the following:

- Warehousing and storage;
- Breaking bulk and deconsolidation;
- Sorting, grading, cleaning and mixing;
- Labelling, packing and repacking;
- Minor processing;
- Transshipment;
- Cash and carry sales;
- Export-oriented port-based activities;
- Export-oriented airport-based activities;
- Freight forwarding, express courier services;
- Mail order;
- Simple assembly;
- Reshipment; and
- Quality control and inspection services.

By the end of 2008, about 470 Freeport companies were engaged in activities such as re-export, transshipment, minor processing and assembly. In 2007, the Freeport imported US$188 million and re-exported US$335 million worth of goods. Main products re-exported include: machinery and telecommunication equipment (28%); apparel and accessories (26%); seafood (19%); textile yarns and fabrics (9%); chemical and pharmaceutical products (6%); and beverages and tobacco (3%). In 2007, the principal export markets for the Freeport were the United Arab Emirates, Madagascar, France, Reunion Island and Italy.

The Freeport sources its imports from a wide range of countries, including Hungary, China, India, Finland, Taiwan, France, Spain and South Africa. The main products imported include fish, chemicals and pharmaceuticals, telecommunication equipment, textile fabrics and accessories, ready-made garments, electrical goods and general consumer goods.

The Freeport facilities for warehousing, breaking bulk and re-export should be of particular interest to American companies. These services enable businesses to ship containerised goods to Mauritius, warehouse them in secure, low-cost facilities, then break bulk and re-export them in an efficient and timely manner to African and Indian Ocean rim destinations. Modern computerised warehouse/logistics facilities, including cold rooms and processing centres, are provided by the private developers. These include Freeport operations (Mauritius) Ltd, Mauritius Freeport Development Co. Ltd and Froid des Mascareignes. Goods can also be assembled in the Freeport for export to the African and Indian Ocean markets. Current assembly and processing activities in the Freeport include:

- Jewellery and precious stones;
- PET plastic bottles;

- Transformation of fish into fillets;
- Construction of aluminium frames and fittings;
- Repackaging of pharmaceuticals; and
- Reconditioning of second-hand vehicles.

Three US companies are present in the Mauritius Freeport. Expeditors International (Mauritius) Ltd, a subsidiary of Expeditors International of Washington Inc., is a freight logistics company providing freight forwarding services, supplier consolidation, and quality control. Boxmore Plastics (Mauritius) Ltd., which started operations in Mauritius in 2002, is 100% owned by Chesapeake Corporation, headquartered in Richmond, VA. It manufactures PET (polyethylene teraphthalate) pre-forms for the soft drink bottling companies in Mauritius, Reunion, Madagascar and Seychelles. Casamar (Mauritius) Ltd, a subsidiary of US-based Casamar Holdings, Inc., which specialises in the assembly and repair of nylon-braided tuna purse seine nets, opened an office in Mauritius which provides marketing support for its fishing net repair and assembly operations in the Seychelles.

The Government of Mauritius, in collaboration with the private sector, is actively promoting the Freeport as a seafood hub, in particular focusing on the transshipment, processing, storage, distribution and re-exportation of high value-added seafood products using the modern port and Freeport facilities and logistics. A one-stop shop has been established in the port area to help facilitate administrative clearances related to the seafood industry. Thon des Mascareignes Ltd (TDM), a leading Mauritian company in partnership with Spanish investors, is operating a tuna loin processing plant with a daily processing capacity of 300 tonnes for export to Europe and the US for final processing and packaging. US company Bumble Bee Foods has a tuna supply and processing agreement with TDM.

The Board of Investment, in collaboration with Airports of Mauritius Ltd, plans to develop a dedicated air cargo logistics centre at the country's main international airport. In December 2008, the government announced that it was granting the necessary clearance for the implementation of this project. The main activities targeted include re-export of high value/low volume products, light assembly operations, warehousing, labelling and repackaging, sea-air/air-sea and transshipment cargo, express courier and freight forwarding services.

SECTION 4

European Union

Shannon Free zone

Shannon Free Zone is today a 2.43 km^2 (600 acres) international business park adjacent to Shannon International Airport, County Clare, Ireland, 18 kilometres from Ennis and 20 kilometres from Limerick city. Although the site lost its Free Zone status in 2017, businesses based on the site can still enjoy a very attractive tax package on their profits, and this has served to attract a large number of multinational companies. Currently there are over 100 international firms and 6,500 people employed at Shannon Free Zone in a diverse range of activities. Companies who have invested at Shannon include Avocent, GE Capital, Ingersoll Rand, Intel, Lufthansa Technik, Mentor Graphics, Molex, Shannon Engine Support, SYKES, RSA Security and Zimmer.

The history of Shannon since its beginning in the 1940s has been a series of challenges and triumphs. Shannon Airport is located on the west coast of Ireland, on the north side of the Shannon Estuary. Shannon was selected in the mid-1930s as a site for a transatlantic airport. A group that included the pioneering aviator Charles Lindbergh visited the site in the late 1930s and endorsed its selection as the basis for a land-based international airport. Foynes, on the south side of the Shannon Estuary, was, in the late 1930s, the landing port for the Pan Am Boeing Clipper flying boats crossing the Atlantic. This traffic continued through the war years of 1939–1945, but faded out quickly when land-based aircraft such as the Douglas DC-4 and Lockheed Constellation started flying across the Atlantic in 1946 and landed at the new Shannon International Airport, on the north side of the Shannon Estuary.

The runway at Shannon Airport was completed in 1940 and flights from the airport commenced in 1942. The first scheduled transatlantic flight from Shannon Airport was in October 1945, after which the volume of transatlantic flights grew rapidly. About 50% of the aircraft flying the Atlantic used Shannon for refuelling in the 1950s, and a major business developed at the airport to service these flights, including in 1947 the world's first duty-free shop. The Shannon area is reputed to be where the world-famous alcohol-laced 'Irish Coffee' was first created, when the Pan Am Clipper flying boats were operating from Foynes, on the south side of the river, across the Atlantic Ocean.

The first challenge was to overcome the psychological trauma resulting from the Irish famine and 100 years of economic decline and emigration. Through the 1950s, 2,000 jobs were created directly at the airport, and another 5,000 indirect jobs in the Region, especially close to Shannon itself and Limerick, and elsewhere in the country. Given

DOI: 10.4324/9781003232025-23

Ireland's economic development since its independence from the UK, this was a major triumph at the time, especially given the sudden foreign investment in the region.

However, Shannon faced a new challenge with the introduction of the jet aircraft, particularly the longer range Boeing 707 Intercontinental jetliner, as the reason for its very existence was threatened, and with it the jobs of thousands of people. The national government, working with the management of the airport, reacted decisively. In 1959 the Shannon Free Airport Development Company Limited was formed as a development agency. Its mandate was to generate alternative sources of business and traffic through the airport, and it acted on three fronts:

- It established the world's first industrial Free Zone on a site adjoining the airport;
- It developed a number of tourist products within the Shannon Region and promoted tourist traffic through the airport;
- It also marketed the airport among the airlines of the world as a training base, refuelling stop, maintenance and repair centre and a destination stop.

The Shannon Free Zone was established by Shannon Development in 1959, specifically to ensure the survival and development of Shannon Airport, and to build on the new opportunities for foreign investment and tourism then emerging as an important economic sector. It was fortunate that all of these developments coincided with the opening of the country to external investment and the birth of the modern Irish economy as we know it today. In subsequent years the Zone went on to become a model for industrial development and foreign investment in other regions throughout the world, with the Shannon Development enterprise being a major driving force in the development of several of the world's Free Zones.

The Shannon Free Zone, administered by the Shannon Free Airport Development Company Ltd, was one of Ireland's earliest tax reduction initiatives. In order to establish an operation in the Free Zone, a licence was required under the Customs Free Airport (Amendment) Act 1958; this was issued by the Minister for Enterprise and Employment. A certificate entitling a company to the tax benefits of the Free Zone (10% Corporation Tax rate, VAT and Customs Duty exemptions, etc., although see below for implications of the 12.5% tax regime) was issued by the Minister for Finance. A wide range of activities could qualify for licences and certificates, including:

- The repair and maintenance of aircraft; or
- Trading activities in regard to which the Minister for Finance is of the opinion, after consultation with the Minister for Transport, that they contribute to the use or development of the Shannon Free Zone; or
- Trading activities which are ancillary to either of the above or to any operation consisting of the manufacture of goods; or
- Activities relating to the acquisition, disposal, licence, sub-licence and exploitation generally of intellectual property rights.

It is important to remember that the Free Zone, like the Financial Services-based International Financial Services Centre (IFSC) in Dublin, was primarily a job-creating measure as well as being a Customs-controlled enclave.

Existing companies in the Free Zone had certificates giving tax benefits until the end of 2005. After that, the tax rate increased to the 12.5% mainstream rate of Corporation Tax agreed by the Irish Government with the EU, which came into force generally from 1st January 2003. Companies which obtained certificates during 1999 had the 10% rate only until the end of 2002. However, unlike entry into the IFSC, which was quota-limited during 1998 and 1999, no quota was set for entry into the Free Zone, which will continue to operate fully other than in respect of the special Corporation Tax rate.

From the outset, Shannon Development, the enterprise which developed and controlled the Free Zone, was an immediate and dramatic success, and indeed became the model for various other global Free Zones. The Free Zone attracted some major international companies, for example De Beers Corporation, Jonathan Logan, Elsevier, Standard Pressed Steel and General Electric. So successful was the zone that Russian enterprises used it as a stopping-off point for cargoes destined for Cuba, and indeed there were regular scheduled flights from Russia to Cuba stopping at Shannon on the way. Presently, Volga-Dnepr air freighters are regularly seen at the airport. Major international airlines used Shannon as a training and Supply Base, and the tourist attractions such as Bunratty Castle, near Ennis, and Blarney Castle, just outside Cork, quickly developed an international reputation and contributed significantly to the growth of the Irish tourist and commercial sectors in Western Ireland. Again, the response to the second challenge was a major triumph, and in 1968 the government extended Shannon Development's mandate to cover development in the wider Shannon region. Over the last 40 years, the Shannon region has continued to grow and develop in common with other parts of the country.

However, the Region now faces a third challenge which is more complex and multi-faceted than any of the previous challenges. Shannon is now moving to a post-industrial society in common with the rest of Ireland. Environmental and lifestyle issues are critical, and the Free Zone concept in its present format is moving to the end of its lifecycle. The task now is to create conditions to attract investors in the research and advanced service activity sectors, which means creating conditions including access transport and communications facilities of a suitable standard. In typical Shannon tradition, these issues are now being addressed and a series or imaginative new initiatives are under way. Furthermore, the zone's automatic Customs-based duty suspension allowances were curtailed when the zone lost its Free Zone status in 2017, following the implementation of the EU's Union Customs Code the previous year.

Shannon Development is an Irish government agency whose aims are to establish Foreign Direct Investment on the Shannon Free Zone and to support existing foreign enterprises in expanding their businesses in the region. It assists with:

- Comprehensive information on business opportunities at Shannon;
- Advice and assistance when setting up a business at Shannon;
- Introductions to local industry, utility providers, lawyers, accountants, recruitment companies etc.;
- Assistance in arranging visiting programs;
- Identifying suitable property solutions.

When the multinational business community compares investment locations in the EU, Shannon Free Zone regularly emerges as the superior option. Shannon has been chosen by leading international corporations across a wide range of sectors. The Free Zone covers

240 hectares (600 acres) adjacent to Shannon International Airport, and is home to 100 companies with an employment level of 7,000 people employed. These companies generated €3.3 billion in sales, with over 90% in exports. Overseas companies, attracted by a positive pro-business environment, low Corporation Tax and a well-educated, skilled workforce, use Shannon to serve global markets. Internationally traded service activities now account for over 60% of enterprises and approximately 40% of employment.

Key sectors at Shannon include:

- Aerospace;
- Technology;
- Engineering;
- Pharmaceuticals;
- Healthcare.

Key business activities carried out at Shannon include:

- Customer support and Contact Centres;
- Financial Services;
- Supply Chain Management;
- Shared Services;
- Production;
- Headquarters.

Today, the Shannon Free Zone is still a critically important regional economic hub. It is home to 110 companies employing over 7,000 workers and generates over a 3.5 billion in export sales annually across an impressive range of internationally traded services and high-end manufacturing sectors.

With some of the leading names in world aviation, such as GE Commercial Aviation Services, Shannon Aerospace, Lufthansa Technik, Hamilton Sundstrand, and others based in Shannon, aviation is now one of the strongest activity clusters. Over 30 companies are currently engaged in various aspects of the industry, and Shannon can justly claim to be Ireland's premier aviation investment location. Existing companies provide a critical mix of aviation activities and services in one location, generating spin-off opportunities including training, education and a strong local talent pool of aeronautical skills and expertise.

The proposed Rosslare Free Zone

The port of Rosslare in south-east Ireland has for many years been an important ferry port serving West Wales, but more recently, especially with the exit of the UK from the European Union, it has increased its importance with the addition of ferry sailings direct to the European continent in order to avoid trailers having to exit the EU from Ireland into the UK, cross the UK and then re-enter the EU via a Channel/North Sea port. Furthermore, the development of offshore wind farms as part of international energy renewables projects has meant that there is an increasing need for the creation of onshore Supply Bases to service such projects by handling and assembling the wind turbine units destined for such offshore projects. These Supply Bases are designed to facilitate the storage, assembly and transportation of these units to their offshore destinations, including the accommodation of supply vessels at their quaysides. This usually means the construction of the Supply Base adjacent to an existing port in order to facilitate the swift and efficient movement for materials from incoming cargo vessels arriving at the port to the Supply Base for incorporation in the offshore projects. Because of the offshore nature of the project, such facilities must be Customs-controlled because they are not part of the national domestic regime, and therefore are not subject to the entry of such materials into domestic Free Circulation on a duty and tax-paid basis. This means that the whole offshore supply facility becomes by nature a Free Zone, outside domestic Customs and Tax jurisdiction. This issue has been discussed in Part One of this text, but in this section, the concept is applied to the Rosslare Offshore venture.

Following the announcement by Iarnród Éireann (Irish Rail) in July 2020 that Rosslare Europort, in which Irish Rail has an interest, is to undergo a major transformation with a €30m investment, the Dutch Project Logistics company XELLZ stated its intention to secure the port's position as a competitive offshore wind farm hub by developing a Free Zone, a secured Customs area adjacent to the port where non-Union goods can be imported and stored under suspension from import duties, charges (i.e. taxes such as VAT) and commercial policy measures. These goods may, following an undetermined time in the Free Zones, be released to the domestic market, subject to payment of import duties and other taxes, although it is envisaged that the vast majority of the materials stored or assembled in the Supply Base will be installed and used offshore as part of the offshore renewable energy projects. Indeed, it is envisaged that very little material will touch the domestic Irish market, as the very nature of these projects means that the entire activity of the Supply Base will serve the offshore renewables sector around the Irish coast, and that little, if any, of the materials stored on the Supply Base will be used for onshore activities. Any material destined for onshore projects, should they be initiated, would therefore be subject to Import Duty and VAT liability upon release from the Free Zone into Irish national Free Circulation.

This facility will give companies who locate in the Rosslare Europort Business Park Free Zone (EBP-FZ) the ability to operate and install offshore wind farms (OWF) in a cost-effective and competitive manner. There are many OWFs to be installed and operated in Ireland, UK, and across the continent and having a Free Zone will help ease the flow of goods and keep projects moving.

Through its offshore services subsidiary 24SHORE SBS (Supply Base Services) and XELLZ Ireland, XELLZ will establish an offshore wind Supply Base to serve and support future offshore wind farms, bringing new energy to the region. The EBP will become a major activity where businesses directly related to and engaged in the upcoming OWFs project can establish themselves. The EBP will offer storage and assembly areas that will be capable of handling wind turbines, transition pieces and mobilisation equipment.

The EBP offers a large amount of storage and assembly areas to manage the wind turbines, transition pieces and mobilisation equipment. There will be areas for companies providing maintenance, operational, and repair services to this budding renewable energy market. The space will also house a new training facility for the renewable industry where young potentials (YP) can undertake professional training for the offshore wind energy industry.

The individuality of this kind of Free Zone is that it is dedicated to the storage and assembly of offshore wind turbine units, a specific form of activity that is only now becoming more prevalent. The main body of this text detailed the advantages of Free Zones for the accommodation, storage and assembly of units for the offshore renewables sector, in particular wind turbines, and the use of these Zones as custom-designed areas specifically of these types of activities. Given the development of the offshore renewables sector, such a venture is seen as an activity designed to be economically beneficial to the region, especially considering that in this case, the need to develop the regional economy of south-east Ireland, coupled with the need to develop a regional hub for the supply and support of offshore renewable activities, is vital for the area. The loss of Free Zone status at the Shannon Zone is therefore being compensated to a degree by the new envisaged Free Zone at Rosslare. Its primary difference from other Free Zones is that it serves the offshore renewables sector rather than accommodating companies involved in general manufacturing. Given the nature of assembly and storage of materials for the offshore renewables sector, coupled with the need to handle and accommodate major project cargoes, the Rosslare Free Zone is an ideal opportunity to renew the basic Free Zone principle and adapt it for this sector. Offshore renewables, like offshore Oil & Gas projects, are based on long-term strategies, and therefore require long-term logistics solutions, especially where the import of materials for offshore use is concerned. The main condition of such operations is that the offshore projects must be located outside the national maritime territorial 12-mile limit, but given that with the exit of the UK from the EU, the Irish and Celtic seas are considered to be international waters, this condition applies as far as international maritime rules laid down by the UN Convention of the Law of the Seas (UNCLOS) are concerned.

Behind this venture lies an inherent issue concerning offshore project management and the role of the Free Zone in that materials destined for offshore projects in general, be they offshore Oil & Gas or offshore renewables, are generally imported from overseas. The major energy renewables companies purchase materials from a variety of global sources and have them shipped to the Supply Bases where they will be assembled into complete finished units ready for transport to the designated offshore field. By nature of the project concerned, these units are not destined for onshore use but for offshore use, and are therefore by nature to be located outside national territorial jurisdiction, that is, outside the 12-mile maritime limit of national control. On this basis, any material imported into the Supply Base for use in the offshore field should therefore be outside Customs jurisdiction and should therefore be suspended from all Customs Duties and Taxes while it is onshore awaiting shipment to the offshore location where it will be installed. On this basis alone, the Free Zone functions as a Customs-controlled base where preparatory activities may take place for this project to be fulfilled. Because of the nature of the project, Customs Duties and Taxes such as VAT on the materials concerned do not apply and must therefore be suspended while the material is stored in the Supply Base. This is why the Rosslare venture is a vital element to the economy of the south-east Ireland region, as it promotes economic development not only of the region itself but also of the niche market which it serves, as well as benefitting the community at large by the generation of offshore renewable energy. It is a win-win scenario for everyone, and removes unnecessary duty and tax burdens on the sector.

This type of Free Zone may be the first of its kind in Ireland, but is part of an increasing global trend, namely the conversion of existing Free Zones to such use or the creation of new Free Zones dedicated to this kind of operation. The need for the supply, support and servicing of offshore wind farms is becoming increasingly important, and, as such, the introduction and establishment of Free Zones dedicated to this activity is becoming paramount. The advantage of incorporating this kind of Free Zone within or adjacent to an overall port facility adds overall value to the project. The principle of this venture is that materials can be brought to the port by breakbulk project cargo vessels, unloaded into the port, transferred into the Free Zone, stored and assembled into full wind turbine units, and transported to the offshore renewables wind farm by dedicated supply vessels, also from the port. One of the main considerations is that there may be the need to construct a dedicated quayside where such vessels may be berthed in readiness for the loading of the turbine units and transported out to the offshore installations. This facility operates in the same way as a conventional offshore Oil & Gas Supply Base, with the same kind of storage areas, assembly facilities and loading/unloading facilities. The other advantage is that such projects are designed to generate regional employment, including training and education facilities, warehousing and administration centres. Overall, the facilities incorporated in such Free Zones are:

- Vessel berthing facilities;
- Enclosed warehousing facilities;
- Open storage facilities;
- Assembly areas;
- Office facilities;
- Canteen facilities;
- Car parking facilities;
- Equipment handing facilities, e.g. static and mobile cranes.

The layout of the zone depends upon the space available, but given that the company concerned had already acquired 200,000 square metres of land as part of its Europort Business Park (EBP) facility, and has subsequently acquired a further 100,000 square metres for the purposes of establishing the Free Zone, the overall capacity for the Free Zone will be substantial and will easily accommodate all the facilities required to operate the zone on an efficient and cost-effective basis. Its location will also increase the capacity of the port of Rosslare and will increase the port's capacity and throughput by a significant level, as well as diversifying the port's operations to include general breakbulk cargo traffic and dedicated offshore supply traffic.

The Madeira Free Trade Zone

The **International Business Centre of Madeira (IBCM** or **MIBC)**, formally known as the **Madeira Free Trade Zone**, is a set of tax benefits authorised by Decree-Law **500/80** in 1980, legislated in 1986, and amended throughout the years by the Portuguese government to favour the Autonomous Region of the island of Madeira. Its objectives are to attract foreign investment to the region and internationalise Portuguese companies by allowing them to benefit one of the lowest corporate taxation rates in Europe and in the OECD member countries. However, it is not a Free-Trade Zone in the sense of Import Duty and VAT incentives, as normal Import Duty rates apply given that the island is still part of Portuguese Duty regimes. However, VAT is reduced from the standard Portuguese rate of 20% to 14%.

Since 1987, the MIBC has been managed and promoted by a private company, Sociedade de Desenvolvimento da Madeira S.A. (known as SDM), in which the Regional Government of Madeira currently holds of 48.86% the shares. The other main shareholder is Pestana Group, holding 51.14% of the shares. As of January 2020, the Vice-Presidency of the Madeira Regional Government announced its intention of acquiring 51% of the shares of SDM.

The **International Shipping Registry of Madeira** (locally known as **MAR**), created by the Portuguese government to develop its so-called 'blue economy', that is, the preservation of the maritime environment, is closely associated with the MIBC. As one of Europe's largest ship and yacht registries, MAR accepts the registration of all types of commercial vehicles. In 2016, MAR had a total of 516 registered vessels. The registry offers benefits to shipping companies and ships, oil rigs and yachts, including a mortgage system and access to European continental and island cabotage. Other EU island registries include Malta and the Isle of Man, although the Isle of Man is not actually within the European Union, but has a Customs Union with the EU, as well as the same VAT rates as the UK.

The MIBC was created in 1986, the year that Portugal became a Member State of the European Union. The tax benefits approved for Madeira would be considered State aid under EU law, and subject to approval by the European Commission.

Approval of such tax benefits by the European Commission is covered by Article 349 of the Treaty on the Functioning of the European Union, which states that specific measures are to be implemented in the EU's outermost regions to offset structural, social and economic situations compounded by 'remoteness, insularity, small size, difficult topography and climate, economic dependence on a few products, the permanence and combination of which severely restrain their development'. Among the measures foreseen in the treaty is the creation of Free-Trade Zones.

The MIBC is regulated and supervised by Portuguese (the Regional Government of Madeira, the Portuguese Tax and Customs Authority, and the Portuguese Social Security System) and EU authorities (primarily the Directorate General for Competition). Through the MIBC, Madeira became the only jurisdiction in Portugal to allow the incorporation of trusts (a common law fiduciary relationship which is non-existent in Portuguese law). In a Madeiran trust, the settlor designates the law regulating the trust.

Corporation Tax

In 2007 the European Commission approved extension of Madeira's preferential tax regime until the year 2020. The new regime applies to new companies which are licensed and established in Madeira's International Business Centre during the years 2007 to 2013.

Details of the new regime

Under the new regime, companies will benefit from a reduced corporate tax rate as follows:

2007–2009	– 3%
2010–2012	– 4%
2013–2020	– 5%

The appropriate corporate tax rate is limited to a maximum of a particular organisation's annual taxable income dependent upon the number of jobs created in Madeira. Details of these figures are listed in the table below:

Job creation	*Reduced Tax Rate applies to the following taxable income*
1–2	€ 2 million
3–5	€ 2.6 million
6–30	€ 16 million
31–50	€ 26 million
51–100	€ 40 million
over 100	€ 150 million

Additional tax benefits

In addition to reduced corporate tax rates, new companies will continue to enjoy the following tax benefits until the end of the year 2020:

- Exemption from withholding taxes on the distribution of dividends, royalty and interest payments;
- Exemption from capital duty, notary and registration fees.

Existing companies licensed before 2001

Existing companies licensed before the year 2001 will continue to enjoy full exemption from corporate tax until the end of the year 2011. From the year 2012 onwards the new tax regime will apply to these companies.

Forms of offshore operation

Offshore operations may take place within the following forms:

- Private Limited Liability Company;
- Stock Corporation;
- Holding Company;
- Trust;
- Shipping Company.

Tax treatment of offshore operations

See Domestic Corporate Taxes for the general principles of Madeiran corporate taxation, which also apply to offshore entities when they pay tax. Also see Withholding Taxes for a simplified description of the Madeiran withholding tax regime.

Manufacturing companies in the Free-Trade Zone, if registered before 2001, receive exemption from income tax and capital gains tax, except in respect of transactions carried out in mainland Portugal, or with Portuguese residents. These exemptions apply until 2011, and an extension is not unlikely.

Under the Tax Reform Act of 2000, which was finally approved by the EU in late 2002, companies which register under the new regime are able to enjoy a reduced rate of tax of 1% in 2003–2004, 2% in 2005–2006 and 3% in 2007–2011 (instead of the normal rate, currently 25%).

In June 2007, the EU permitted an extension of the preferential tax regime for companies setting up in the Free-Trade Zone. This allows new companies licensed to carry on business there between 1 January 2007 and 31 December 2013 to benefit from a reduced tax rate of 3% in 2007–2009, 4% in 2010–2012 and 5% in 2013–2020.

Access to the scheme is restricted to companies which meet specific eligibility criteria, based on the number of permanent jobs created. The tax benefits are limited by a ceiling placed on the taxable base per company which ranges from €2m (where less than three new jobs are created) to €150m (where more than 100 new jobs are created). The companies involved have to start business within a fixed time limit (six months in the case of international services, and one year in the case of industrial or shipping activities), beyond which they will lose their licences.

Admission to the Free-Trade Zone is also restricted to the activities included in a list drawn up by the Portuguese authorities on the basis of the statistical classification of economic activities in the EU. As under the previous scheme, authorised by the Commission on 11 December 2002, financial and insurance intermediary activities, financial and insurance auxiliary activities and 'intra-group services' (coordination, accounting and distribution centres) are explicitly excluded.

In January 2008, the Portuguese government published Decree-Law No. 13/2008 which adds Article 34-A to the Statute of Tax Benefits. This article regulates the extension of the preferential tax regime of the International Business Centre of Madeira until the year 2020.

Non-exempt Portuguese transactions are taxed at normal rates under the Corporate Tax Code.

Service or financial companies in the International Services Centre and the Offshore Financial Centre, including offshore banks and insurance companies, can could be constituted as Private Limited Liability Companies or as Stock Companies. Such institutions licensed before 2001 receive tax exemption until 2011 on revenues derived from other companies within the various sectors of the International Business Centre (i.e. manufacturing, services etc.), and on revenue derived from non-residents on Portuguese territory.

However, the regime approved by the EU in late 2002 does not allow for new formations of financial services companies.

Companies setting up in the International Business Centre pay an 'Installation' fee of €1,000. Annual operating fees for a Holding Company were as follows:

- 1st year – €1,800;
- Subsequent years – €1,800 plus 0.5% of the previous year's profit, the first million euros being exempt.

Ships and vessels owned by companies licensed to operate under the Free-Trade Zone legislation are eligible for a number of tax incentives, namely:

- Until the year 2011 no Corporation Tax is payable on profits made from ships flying the Portuguese flag that operate in international waters. The same applies to corporate profits made by ships owned by companies licensed to operate under the Free-Trade Zone legislation but flying a foreign flag. However, Corporation Tax is levied on income earned carrying cargo and passengers between national ports;
- No capital gains tax is payable on profits made on the sale of a ship; nor is any capital gains tax payable on the sale of a ship by way of the sale of the shares in the company which owns the ship provided the shares sold are owned by a non-resident;
- Neither income tax nor Portuguese social security is payable by the officers or crew of ship operating in international waters.

A number of VAT advantages flow from having a vessel owned by a corporate entity licensed to operate under the Free-Trade Zone Legislation:

- Since 1993 a leisure boat cannot remain in European Union waters for more than six months in any one year unless it can prove that VAT has been paid on the yacht in one Member State. A boat purchased by a company licensed to operate under the Free-Trade Zone Legislation of Madeira company would automatically pay VAT so would not fall foul of the six months rule;
- A company licensed to operate under the Free-Trade Zone Legislation of Madeira pays 15% VAT on the purchase of a vessel as from 1st July, 2005 (subsequently reduced to 14%). The comparable rate in most other European Union jurisdictions is 17.5%;
- With a Madeira company VAT is paid on purchase and thereafter a vessel can move within the European Union free from VAT. In a number of other EU Member States and dependent territories, tax-privileged companies which own vessels cannot register for VAT in the EU with resulting disadvantages when it comes to subsequent re-sale or transfer of the vessel within the EU.

Fees for ship registration are €1,800 initially plus a variable amount based on tonnage, and €1,400 annually plus a variable amount based on tonnage.

Holding Companies and Mixed Holding Companies in Madeira receive a 95% deduction from taxable income received from their holdings, so that they are taxed at 25% of 5% of income, equals 1.25%.

If a Holding Company is established under Free-Trade Zone Legislation then income received from its holdings in the EU is taxable but income from non-EU sources is exempt from tax. Dividends distributed by such companies to non-resident shareholders are free of withholding tax.

Income earned by a Mixed Holding Company licensed under the Free-Trade Zone Legislation from trading activities (other than through the holding of shares) is exempt from Corporation Tax until the year 2011. However, income earned from trading activities carried out in mainland Portugal or with Portuguese residents is taxed at the Portuguese Corporation Tax rate.

It should be noted however that most EU Member States consider that Madeiran Mixed Holding Companies fall outside the ambit of the EU Parent/Subsidiary Directive, so that participation exemption is not given in respect of payments made to such companies.

Capital gains tax is payable by a Madeira Holding Company on the profitable sale of shares in a company in which it has a participating shareholding. Until 2000 these gains were not taxed where they are re-invested in the purchase of shareholdings in other companies ('roll over relief'), but the Tax Reform Act 2000 made them subject to Portuguese capital gains tax, payable in five equal annual instalments after the gain occurs.

Holding companies registered under Free-Trade Zone Legislation pay an application fee and continuing annual fees.

Mixed Holding Companies: Where a Madeira Mixed Holding Company receives dividends from a corporate entity in which it holds a participating shareholding and the participating company is a European Union entity then only 5% of these dividends will be taxed at a Corporation Tax rate of 25% meaning that the effective tax rate is 1.25%. If the participating entity is a non-European Union company then no Corporation Tax is payable on the dividends received by the Mixed Holding Company.

Mixed Holding Companies registered under the Free-Trade Zone Legislation pay an application fee of US$1,500, then US$1,500 annually plus 0.5% of the previous year's profits in excess of US$1m, with a ceiling of US$30,000.

Withholding taxes

All types of company in the International Business Centre (i.e. licensed under the Free-Trade Zone Legislation) are exempt until 2011 from charging withholding tax on remittances of dividends, interest or other payments to non-residents (whether on Portuguese territory or not) or to other companies within the Centre.

Broadly speaking, the shareholders of companies in the International Business Centre (other than Portuguese residents) are exempt from tax until 2011 on dividends and other payments received from them.

NB: The Tax Reform Act 2000 made some changes to the withholding tax regime applying to Holding and Mixed Holding Companies, particularly for Portuguese residents. The Act also made the non-resident status of MISC companies subject to documentary evidence that all transactions are with non-Portuguese residents.

Death Duties: No death duties are payable in Madeira on the transfer of a shareholding in a company licensed to operate under the Free-Trade Zone Legislation unless the shareholder was resident in Portugal.

Stamp Duty: No stamp duties are levied on the documents or transactions of companies incorporated under the Free-Trade Zone Legislation.

Capital Transfer Tax applies to real estate purchases made by Free-Trade Zone companies, except that the purchase of land or buildings for use as a head office is exempt. Standard rates apply: 8% for urban properties and 10% for rural ones.

VAT

VAT applies in Madeira at the rate of 15% as from 1 July 2005, subsequently reduced to 14%. The VAT rate is 20% in Portugal.

Offshore Trusts established in the International Business Centre under Free-Trade Zone Legislation have Madeiran-resident trustees. All income earned by a trust and all income distributed in favour of a beneficiary is free of tax in Madeira unless the source of that investment income is Portugal in which case it is taxed in the hands of the trustee.

For a further review of recent changes to the offshore regime in Madeira see a Briefing Paper by Corporate & Treasury and Barros, Sobral, G Gomes & Associados.

Madeira taxation of foreign employees of offshore operations

This section refers to the taxation of foreign employees of the various types of offshore entity; see Domestic Personal Taxes for the general principles of individual taxation in Madeira, which also apply to the resident employees of non-resident entities.

There is in fact no distinction between the employees of resident or non-resident operations. It is a question of individual status; residents and non-residents are treated differently of course. Most types of compensation and benefit paid to employees are taxable; there are no special privileges or exemptions for expatriate workers, except that the officers and crew of ships registered under the Madeiran Shipping Registry are exempt from income and social security taxes.

Madeira exchange control

Although under EU legislation capital and exchange controls have been abolished, some rules remain.

Significant capital transactions are reported to the Bank of Portugal 'for statistical purposes'. Again, 'for statistical purposes', foreign investment operations are reported to the Institute of Foreign Trade of Portugal after the event. These reports are made by the banks involved.

Foreign investments in the banking and finance industries are subject to Bank of Portugal approval.

Madeira offshore activities

The International Business Centre is a concept applying to the whole of Madeira rather than a particular physical location, except for the manufacturing Free-Trade Zone itself. Manufacturing entities, light and heavy industry can only be licensed to operate under the Free-Trade Zone Legislation if they locate within the physical confines of the Industrial Free-Trade Zone. By contrast, service entities such as banks, insurance companies and trust managers can locate anywhere on the islands and still be licensed to operate under the Free-Trade Zone Legislation (although new formations of financial services companies have not been possible for several years now).

The question often asked is whether residents of Portugal can avail themselves of the Free-Trade Zone Legislation. Although the answer is formally yes, the purpose of the legislation was to develop the economy of Madeira, and not to reduce the tax which could be levied by the Portuguese Treasury on its own citizens.

Thus the general rule (which is subject to exceptions) is that tax exemptions which apply to entities licensed to operate under the Free-Trade Zone Legislation will only apply in so far as the income relates to activities carried out abroad, within the Free-Trade Zone area or with other entities licensed to trade under the legislation. Likewise, unless an exception applies income from Free-Trade Zone companies distributed to Portuguese residents is taxed in the hands of the same under normal Portuguese tax rules.

Holding Companies are limited to holding participations in other companies. A Holding Company is not permitted by law to buy its own shares, purchase debentures in companies in which it does not hold a participating shareholding (subject to certain exceptions), make loans other than to companies in which it holds part of the share capital or engage in any commercial activities other than holding shares in other companies.

Mixed Holding Companies can hold shares in other companies and trade in their own right. They cannot engage in the type of trading activities which are carried on by banks and financial institutions and which require licensing and authorisation from the Bank of Portugal.

A Mixed Holding Company must combine its activities. Its trading activity cannot be exclusively limited to the holding of shares; nor can it be a pure trading company which does not hold shareholdings in any other company.

The property of Offshore Trusts must be outside Portugal, and income derived from outside the country.

SECTION 5

Russian Free-Trade Zones

Russia has numerous Special Economic Zones and Free Trade Ports, and is continuing to consider investing in more, especially nearer to the borders with China in both the Russian Far East and Siberia. Russia's recent history in such Zones has tended to place them with access to servicing the domestic, rather than export, markets, in ways similar to the US FTZ network. Therefore, many of the Zones listed are ideal for accessing Russia's heartland. However, doing this also requires knowledge of and access to shipping – Russia is bisected by several massive rivers that are used for transportation, as well as its highly developed Trans-Siberian rail system and its spin-offs. Consequently, understanding the significance of these Zones requires an understanding of Russian market dynamics and transportation modes. However, Zones such as Vladivostok to the East, and the cluster of Zones around Moscow and Western Russia also service markets in Eastern Europe and beyond. The list of these Zones, although not completely exclusive, roughly running from east to west, is as follows:

Vladivostok free port

Vladivostok is a Free Port, and offers reduced 5% Corporate Tax for the first five years of operations and 12% over the next five years (national corporate tax rate is 20%), zero land and property tax exemptions, reduced social insurance payments and tariff-free imports. The Free-Trade Zone has become popular with light manufacturing industries, and also houses the Eurasian Diamond Exchange, a trading platform for Siberian diamonds, with additional processing facilities. It is possible to obtain eight-day electronic visas for the region (check for qualifications). Vladivostok is the main terminus for the Trans-Siberian railway and is well connected to China, Japan and Korea.

Sovetskaya Gavan

Sovetskaya Gavan is a Port city on Russia's Far East Coast in Khabarovsk Krai, opening out onto the Sea of Japan. Sovetskaya Gavan's economy is largely dependent on the harbour and related activities; the town has a deep-water port for cargo and fishing vessels, as well as ship repair facilities. There is also some foodstuffs production, such as fish processing. The SEZ serves the logistics industry mainly in shipping.

DOI: 10.4324/9781003232025-24

Irkutsk Gate of Baikal SEZ

This SEZ covers 757 hectares and offers incentives for investors in the regional tourism industry. It provides 0% land and property taxes.

Tomsk Industrial SEZ

Tomsk is in Siberia and is connected to the Trans-Siberian railway. The SEZ comprises two parts, a northern area dedicated to petrochemicals and chemicals, and a southern section designed to attract hi-tech industries. It provides discounts on profits tax and social security in addition to zero duties on tariffs, property taxes and so on. There are no Customs Duties for goods imported into the zone, and corporate tax is reduced to 14.5%. Property tax is reduced to 0%, and social security fees are reduced to 21% instead of the national rate of 30%.

Sverdlovsk Titanium Valley SEZ

Sverdlovsk is in the Urals region of Russia, with the important regional capital city of Yekaterinburg. The Titanium Valley SEZ is engaged primarily in the metallurgy industry, including Titanium production, and related industries requiring usage of hi-tech metals such as aviation, medical equipment, engineering and so on. It offers reduced profits taxes to 2% in addition to discounts on social insurance, and zero rates for property and land taxes.

Alabuga SEZ, Yelabaluga

The Alabuga SEZ is in Tatarstan and specialises in industrial and production services, in a 20-km^2 area in the Kama Innovative Territorial Production Cluster. It is thus far one of the most successful SEZ in Russia, with varying reductions for profits taxes in addition to zero-rated land and property taxes and discounts on social insurances. It handles a large number of automotive works, including cars as well as industrial vehicles such as tractors and other agricultural machinery. The SEZ is connected to the main M7 auto highway as well as the Unified Deepwater Russian Rive network and the regional rail network, giving market access to much of Central and Southern Russia.

Samara Togliatti SEZ

Samara Togliatti SEZ is the gateway to the Volga region of Russia and is connected by road, rail and navigable river to Russia's heartland and most major cities. The SEZ specialises in mechanical engineering for aerospace, automotive and other machinery, food processing and light industrial products. It offers 2% profits tax rates, zero land and property taxes, reductions in social insurance and duty-free imports.

Innopolis SEZ

The Innopolis SEZ is based near to Kazan in Tatarstan and is a technology park with aims to become the IT centre of Russia, covering 1,200 hectares. It houses Russia's first IT university and provides discounts on corporate taxes, social insurance and land, property and other related taxes.

Astrakhan Lotus SEZ

The Astrakhan Lotus SEZ is based on the Caspian Sea and is connected to the Eurasian Land Bridge and ports from Kazakhstan such as Aktau, where another SEZ is located. Much of the zone's incentives relate to the Caspian Oil & Gas sector, as well as shipbuilding.

The Lotus SEZ provides Oil & Gas processing, other chemical and raw materials processing facilities, shipbuilding and other engineering facilities. It provides 2% Corporation Tax rates for the initial ten years, reduced social insurance, zero land and property taxes and import free tariffs, as well as 0% Import VAT.

Ulyanovsk SEZ

Ulyanovsk is sited next to the Volga River and as such has deep-water navigable port infrastructure. It is a major, diversified, industrial hub for the aviation and auto industries, and is a de facto industrial cluster comprising all elements of production in these fields. It covers 426 hectares, and offers 2% income tax for the first ten years in addition to the usual deductions in social insurance, land and property taxes.

SECTION 6

ASEAN

Singapore Free Zones

The State of Singapore is, to all intents and purposes, an integrated Free Trae Zone in its own right, owing to the encouragement by the Singapore government of an extensive regime of tax incentives within the State. However, within this overall regime, there is a regime of Free-Trade Zones designed to enhance and encourage tax incentives in terms of the suspension of Customs Duties and Sales Tax by way of individual Free-Trade Zones in the State.

The Singapore Free-Trade Zones are areas through which companies can import, sell or export goods without Customs Duties, Excise Duties or Goods and Services Tax (GST). Singapore also has Free-Trade Zones which enables companies in the trading sector to benefit from transportation facilities. These special areas are regulated by the Free-Trade Zones Act enacted in 1966 and more recently amended in 2014. Singapore's FTZs allow companies to store their merchandise temporarily until they are loaded onto a ship or an aircraft without the need for Customs clearance.

All Singapore Free Zones fall under the Free-Trade Zones Law which was enacted in 1966 and last amended in 2014. The law provides for the following:

- The authorities in charge with verifying the activities of companies operating in the Free Zones;
- The activities which can be undertaken by Free Zones companies in Singapore;
- The types of licences and permits required to manufacture and sell goods in the Free Zones;
- The penalties for not respecting the regulations imposed by the Free Zone authorities.

The main authorities which supervise the activities of Free Zone companies in Singapore are the Free Zone Advisory Committee, the Director of the Singapore Customs and the Ministry for Trade and Industry.

At present, Singapore has nine Free-Trade Zones, namely:

- Brani Terminal;
- Keppel District Park;
- Tanjong Pagar Terminal and Keppel Terminal;
- Jurong Port;
- Sembawang Wharves;

DOI: 10.4324/9781003232025-25

- Pasir Panjang Wharves;
- Changi Airport Group;
- Changi Airport Cargo Terminal Complex;
- Singapore FreePort, located in the Airport Logistics Park.

Singapore companies operating in one of these FTZs are not required to pay Customs Duties until their goods exit the Free Zones, as the whole of Singapore is subject to Customs-free tariffs. These companies also benefit from streamlined Customs procedures when importing goods in the city-state.

In order to operate in one of Singapore's Free Zones, local companies must obtain a permit from TradeNet which allows them to import, export and transport their goods overseas. Local companies must also obtain permission from the Customs Authorities in order to keep their goods in the FTZs. Foreign companies operating in Singapore must work with local transporters and traders in order to obtain a licence.

The main advantage of all Free Zones created in Singapore is related to the extensive storage facilities which can be accessed by both local and foreign companies. Apart from these, Singapore companies can also benefit from:

- The transshipment of non-controllable goods requires no permits or licenses within the Free Zone;
- There are no Customs Duties for goods transiting or being stored in the Free Zones;
- The products imported into the Singapore Free-Trade Zones are not subject to the GST;
- Companies operating in the Free Zones will benefit from simplifies Customs procedures.

All Singapore Free Zones are located close to some of the largest waterways transiting the city-state, which represents a great advantage for shipping companies.

Two of the largest Free Zones in Singapore are Jurong Port and Changi Airport. The first one offers access to one of the largest rivers in Singapore, while the second one to the largest airport in the city.

Jurong Port can accommodate up to 15,000 vessels per year and represents one of the world's largest multi-purpose ports with facilities which include a great number of warehouses and a cement terminal.

Changi Airport is dedicated to companies transporting goods by air and the **Free Zone** attached to the airport hosts both warehouses for the storage of goods, as well as office spaces for the Singapore companies operating at the location.

Keppel District Park (Distripark) is one of the most important Free Zones in Singapore which has undergone modernisation in order to offer large warehousing and office spaces, as well as cargo distribution systems which are connected to other Singapore Free Zones, among which Brani Terminal, Tanjong Pagar and Pasir Panjang. Keppel Distripark is also known for having quick access to some of the most important roads and highways in Singapore. Its services include:

- Cargo consolidation, trans-loading and storage;
- Cargo sampling, packing, surveying, marking and repacking;
- A central distribution and a regional distribution centre;

- Freight forwarding;
- Container operations.

Common carriers can also benefit from co-loading services even if they do not operate vessels.

Malaysia Free Zones

Across the Johor Strait, Malaysia operates a Free Zone at Tanjung Pelepas, as well as other Free Zones in the country, including Port Klang, further north up the Malacca Strait.

The Tanjung Pelepas Free Zone land comprises five development phases with a total area of 1,583 acres. Phase 1 and Phase 2 account for approximately 635 acres, and have been developed with basic infrastructure, namely electricity supply, water supply, telecommunications facilities, roads and drainage. To date, more than 80% of the developed land in phase 1 and 2 has been subleased to various local and global companies. Phases 3, 4 and 5 which constitute 948 acres, can be potentially developed to expand the current Free Zone development.

The Pelabuhan Tanjung Pelepas (PTP) Free Zone was accorded with Free Zone status in 1998 and the Free Zone Authority in 1999 to administer, manage and operate its Free Zone area. The Free Zone laws are governed by the Malaysian Free Zone Act 1990 which is enforced by the Malaysian Ministry of Finance. The Free Zone in PTP incorporates the local container trade volumes of the port and forms part of the hinterland cargo catchment area.

The Free Zone area allows for the development of the following activities which are synergised with PTP's container-driven port business. These activities are clean and environmentally friendly, and comply with all national laws and regulations. Warehousing and logistics comprise of regional procurement, consolidation, distribution and trading centres. Export-driven light-to-medium scaled manufacturing industries are located in the zone, such as food processing, packaging and other value-added activities.

Free Zone Tenants include the following:

- Volkswagen
- DAMCO
- DB Schenker
- Karcher
- DHL
- Johor Port Logistics
- Panalpina
- Naigai Nitto
- Pan Asia Logistics
- Nippon Express
- CJ Century
- MIDF
- Kontena Nasional
- TASCO
- Tiong Nam
- Goodman

- Jibri Logistics
- PAR International
- Nadi Fitri
- AME
- Axis REIT
- Wintelco
- Rancak Beta
- Integrated Supply Chain (ISC)
- Trinity Bliss (Mapletree)
- THAB (Boustead)
- CIBA Vision (Alcon)
- Flextronics
- Olam International
- JB Cocoa
- SMC Food21
- GCB Specialty Chocolates
- Japan Solderless Terminal (JST)
- Material Service Complex Malaysia (part of JX Nippon Mining & Metals Corp Group)
- OneSubsea
- Indochine Bio Plastiques (ICBP)
- Greenpen
- JB Distripark.

The **Bayan Lepas Free Industrial Zone** is a high-tech manufacturing area in Bayan Lepas, near the south-eastern tip of Penang Island in Penang, Malaysia. Created in 1972, the area is Malaysia's first Free-Trade Zone and was instrumental in alleviating an economic crisis in Penang. The zone is now home to various multinational firms, including Bosch, Osram Opto Semiconductors, Bosch, Motorola, Dell, Intel and Hewlett-Packard, and has been regarded as the Silicon Valley of the East.

The 1,400-acre (5.7 km^2) Bayan Lepas Free Industrial Zone was the brainchild of Lim Chong Eu, who served as the Chief Minister of Penang between 1969 and 1990, as a measure to alleviate Penang's economic downturn at the time. George Town, Penang's capital city, had its free port status revoked by the Malaysian Federal Government in 1969, leading to massive unemployment which peaked at 16.4%. Lim identified the electronics sector as having the best potential to absorb the State's excess semi-skilled workforce.

Nearly 1,000 acres (4.0 km^2) of land adjacent to Penang International Airport were acquired for the construction of Malaysia's first Free-Trade Zone, as well as the adjacent township of Bayan Baru. The Penang Development Corporation (PDC) was tasked with the construction of both the zone and the residential township. To attract multinational corporations to the zone, the Free-Trade Zones Act was enacted by the Malaysian Federal Government in 1971 and pioneer tax incentives were offered.

The first phase of the Bayan Lepas Free Industrial Zone, covering an area between the airport, Jalan Sultan Azlan Shah and the Kluang River, was opened in 1972. The zone has since been expanded and developed in phases. Phase 2 encompasses an area between Jalan

Sultan Azlan Shah, Bukit Gedung and the Snake Temple. Phase 3 was partially built on reclaimed land, while Phase 4, the largest and final phase, was completed by the 1990s.

The Bayan Lepas Free Industrial Zone proved successful in attracting multinational firms and its creation played a vital role in reversing Penang's economic crisis. Intel, AMD, Hewlett-Packard, Clarion, National Semiconductor, Hitachi, Osram and Bosch, collectively known as the *Samurai Eight*, were the first multinational companies to establish factories within the zone, followed by several other firms including Motorola and Dell. These companies are also supported by smaller, local-owned enterprises and start-ups, such as Piktochart. Consequently, the manufacturing sector became one of Penang's largest economic sectors, while the zone itself has been described by the international press as the 'Silicon Valley of the East'. Other tenants include Sanyo, Nippon Express, DHL Express, Schenker AG and Sony.

SECTION 7

China

China's Special International Trade Zones

China's special international trade Zones, officially called Special Customs Supervision Zones (SCSZs), are ideal locations for foreign investors engaged in export-oriented trade and production. These SCSZs are a type of economic Development Zone in China, which were first established in the 1990s as the country opened up to foreign investment and bonded processing trade.

Bonded processing trade is the business activity of importing raw and auxiliary materials and re-exporting the finished products after processing, where the materials and finished products can be exempted from import duties and taxes when taking place in specially regulated areas.

Upon approval by the Chinese State Council, SCSZs are set up under the supervision of the Chinese Customs Authorities. They are usually surrounded by an iron mesh enclosure, making them segregated areas. Thus, while the SCSZ is in the physical national territory of China, enterprises in the SCSZs are treated as 'overseas', in that they are subject to Chinese Customs controls. Goods entering SCSZs from abroad are not categorised as imports and are therefore subject to preferential bonded policies. Similarly, goods from domestic out-zone areas, that is, Chinese Free Circulation, which enter some SCSZs may enjoy export rebates.

SCSZs, therefore, tend to be the best-suited locations for foreign investors engaged in export-oriented trade and production in China. In fact, while SCSZs occupy only 1/20,000th of China's land, they generated around one-sixth of the country's total foreign trade in 2018.

This text introduces the different types of SCSZs in China and highlights the preferential policies and functions of comprehensive bonded Zones (CBZs), which may become the dominant type of SCSZ in the future owing to current Chinese policy trends.

Types of SCSZs in China

Currently, there are six types of SCSZs existing in China, as follows:

- Bonded Zones (BZs);
- Bonded Logistics Parks;
- Bonded Ports;
- Export Processing Zones (EPZs);
- Cross-Border Industrial Parks; and
- Comprehensive Bonded Zones (CBZs).

DOI: 10.4324/9781003232025-26

Chinese Economic Development Zones

China's Economic Development Zones (EDZs) are areas with preferential business policies that differ from those governing the country as a whole. First experimented with in the 1970s, China has created a range of EDZs to attract FDI and boost domestic growth.

EDZs provide a broad range of FDI incentives, which vary depending on the specific EDZ. Businesses operating in EDZs can expect, among other incentives, a higher level of autonomy over their operations, a variety of tax exemptions, land and building subsidies, and preferential employment policies.

Types of Economic Development Zones in China

There are at least 15 types of national-level EDZs. When considering investment into an EDZ, it is important to be aware of the subtle differences in the incentives that distinctive zone types provide.

The 15 EDZ types can be split into seven classes, with Zones falling in the first three being the most popular locations for FDI:

- Zones for specific economic activity;
- Zones for commercialising high-tech research;
- Zones for trade and exports;
- Zones for cross-border e-commerce business;
- Zones to attract investment for specific purposes;
- Zones for cooperation with specific countries; and
- New areas.

Zones for specific economic activity

SEZs and Economic and Technological Development Zones (ETDZ) fall into the first category. They are both heavily focused on attracting FDI and tend to provide incentives for manufacturing.

SEZs are only seven in number, cover much larger areas, and tend to have more generalised policies rather than incentives for specific sectors. For example, China's first SEZ was set up in Shenzhen, which now covers the whole city and primarily provides a preferential tax environment for manufacturers oriented towards export markets across a wide range of industries.

The respective types of SCSZs have different but partially overlapping functions.

However, as proposed in the plan to speed up the Integration and Optimisation of SCSZs Scheme, issued in 2015, all existing SCSZs will be integrated into two types in the future: Bonded Zones (BZs) and CBZs. Further, except for some BZs, many SCSZs will transition or are currently transitioning into becoming CBZs.

In Shanghai, for example, there are ten SCSZs that have received approval from the State Council on their integration and optimisation plans to become CBZs. In May 2019, the Caohejing and Fengxian EPZs were upgraded to CBZs.

The reason why CBZs are so favoured is because they integrate the functions of other SCSZs and provide the widest variety of services. They also offer businesses the most preferential policies and more convenient Customs clearance procedures, which is conducive to attracting more foreign investment. China is now promoting CBZs as the most advanced form of SCSZs.

The following table shows the various types of Chinese Economic Development Zones. Many of these are subject to Customs controls, but other Zones, designated purely for economic development, are also included.

Types of Chinese Economic Development Zones

Zone class	*Zone*	*Central purpose*	*Major preferential policies*
Zones for Economic Activities	Special Economic Zones (SEZs)	Increase Exports Improve Manufacturing	Tax exemptions for manufacturing and export companies
Zones for Economic Activities	Economic and Technological Development Zones (ETDZs)	Improve Manufacturing Attract FDI Increase Exports Located mainly in Coastal Cities	Tax exemptions for manufacturing companies Export Tax Rebates Financial Support for the Provision of some facilities/services Lower rental fees
Zones for commercialising High-Tech Research Findings	High-Tech Industrial Development Zones (HIDZs)	Take advantage in knowledge-intensive areas Commercialise High-Tech Research	Tax exemptions for High-Tech companies Exemptions from local Income tax and Property tax Export Tax Rebates Financial Support for the Provision of some facilities/services Lower rental fees
Zones for Trade/ Export purposes	Free-Trade Zones	Attract FDI Reduce storage cost of goods Act as testing ground for new policies	Import Duty exemptions and Export Tax rebates
Zones for Trade/ Export purposes	Export Processing Zones (EPZs)	Increase exports Provide concessions for manufacturing companies	Import Duty exemptions and Export Tax rebates VAT and Consumption Tax exemptions
Zones for Trade/ Export purposes	Bonded Port	Increase Exports Serve as logistics hub Located mostly in coastal cities	Same tax treatment as EPZs Tax-free transfer within Zones Concessions for manufacturing
Zones for Trade/ Export purposes	Bonded Logistics Park	Increase exports Serve as logistics hub Allows no advanced manufacturing	Same tax treatment as EPZs Tax-free transfer within Zones

Zone class	*Zone*	*Central purpose*	*Major preferential policies*
Zones for cross-border e-commerce business	Cross-Border E-Commerce Comprehensive Pilot Zones	Boost cross-border e-commerce business Increase exports Serve as entrepreneurship centre and logistics hub	VAT and Consumption tax exemptions New Corporate Income Tax policy for in-zone enterprises Preferential tax policies for SMEs
Zones to attract investment for specific purposes	National Tourism Resort Zones; Finance and Trade Zones	Develop tourism and finance industries	Preferential tax and subsidy policies for specific industries
Zones for cooperation with certain countries or regions	4 different zone types depending upon country	Build cross-border business relationships Incentives mainly for Taiwan, Macau, Russia	Preferential tax policies for companies from specific regions
New areas	Comprehensive Development Areas	Grant autonomous powers to municipalities	Higher level of decentralisation and autonomy

Source: Asia Briefing.

There are six types of SCSZs. These are shown and detailed in the following table.

Six types of SCSZs

SCSZs	*Features*	*Functions*
Bonded Zones (BZs)	Also called Bonded Warehouse Areas. Bonded goods can be stored here for a longer period. BZs offer preferential policies such as licence exemption, tax exemption, and bonded facilities.	Bonded Warehousing, Transit Trade, Export Processing etc.
Bonded Logistics Parks	Implement the policy of BZs, but mainly provide warehousing and logistics services.	Bonded warehousing, international transfer, international procurement, international distribution, product exhibition, international entrepôt trade etc.
Export Processing Zones (EPZs)	Special Zones for the manufacture, processing and assembly of commodities, components and products for export. EPZs offer various local tax relief and export rebate facilities.	Export Processing etc.

SCSZs	*Features*	*Functions*
Bonded Ports	Populated with and accommodating shipping centres and integrated port operations.	Bonded warehousing, logistics, international transfer and transit, international procurement and distribution, testing and after-sales maintenance services, product exhibition, R&D, processing, manufacturing, port operations, etc.
Cross-Border Industrial Parks	Established jointly by China and other countries or regions.	Manufacturing, logistics, transit trade, product exhibition, etc.
Comprehensive Bonded Zones (CBZs)	Integrated functions of other SCSZs and are generally the most advanced form of SCSZs.	Bonded warehousing, logistics, international transfer and transit, international procurement and distribution, testing and after-sales maintenance services, product exhibition, R&D, processing, manufacturing, etc.

Source: Asia Briefing.

Basic policies in CBZs

The Guidelines on Projects suitable for Entry into CBZs, issued by the General Administration of Customs China (GACC) in April 2019, offers a list of preferential policies in CBZs, the categories of enterprises highly encouraged to do business in CBZs, and sample cases of entry projects for reference for potential investors.

Here, we summarise the basic policies of CBZs.

Preferential tax policy

- Goods entering CBZs from abroad are bonded in the zone;
- Goods from Chinese non-zone areas entering CBZs can enjoy export rebates;
- In-zone goods sold to domestic markets can be declared to Customs, according to the relevant provisions on the import of goods, and be taxed, according to the actual State of the goods;
- Goods transactions between in-zone enterprises are exempted from VAT and consumption tax;
- Imported materials and equipment of capital construction will be exempted from tariffs and import-related taxes; and
- Other approved or authorised tax policies.

Trade control policy

No import and export quota or license administration shall be required for goods entering or leaving the country, unless specifically required.

Bonded supervision policy

- No storage period for bonded goods stored in the area; and
- Bonded goods can be transferred freely among enterprises in the zone.

Foreign exchange policy

Goods entering or leaving the zone (within the territory and outside the zone) may be settled in foreign currency or RMB.

Enterprises that are encouraged to do business in CBZs may include bonded processing enterprises, bonded logistics enterprises, and bonded service enterprises.

Policy trends in CBZs

In January 2019, the Chinese State Council issued the Opinions on promoting High-Level Opening and High-Quality Development of CBZs, aiming to promote CBZs to become 'five centres' – processing and manufacturing centres, R&D centres, logistics distribution centres, testing and maintenance centres, and sales and service centres.

The opinion announced 21 measures to facilitate in-zone enterprises to expand their business scope. The 21 measures include:

- Granting qualified in-zone enterprises the status of general VAT payers to better expand two markets;
- Allowing in-zone enterprises to import machinery and equipment for their own use and meanwhile allowing the imported machinery and equipment to enjoy related tax exemption in advance;
- Allowing in-zone enterprises to undertake domestic commissioned processing business;
- Exempting the automatic import licenses for mobile phones, auto parts, and other products for domestic sales;
- Simplifying Customs approval procedures; and
- Others.

As of January 2019, China has a total of 140 SCSZs and 96 CBZs.

SCSZs rank the first among all kinds of Economic Development Zones in China in terms of the intensity of investment per unit area and the industrial output, according to the GACC.

With further optimisation expected as a result of the latest policies, SCSZs are poised to continue to play an important role in promoting foreign trade, coordinating regional economic development, and expanding employment.

Understanding investment trends in China's bonded zones

The General Administration of Customs (GAC) announced in 2020 that all of China's SCSZs, which previously fell under six different categories, will be uniformly renamed as CBZs later this year. Not only will the SCSZs be changing names, but also their basic function. The new CBZs are expected to serve enterprises engaged in bonded processing, bonded logistics and bonded services.

Since 1990, 113 areas have been approved as SCSZs to meet the needs of economic development in China. These areas fall under six categories, namely bonded Zones, Export Processing Zones, Bonded Logistics Parks, cross-border industrial Zones, bonded port Zones and comprehensive bonded Zones – each serving different enterprises and business activities. However, a lack of readily-available information regarding the specific functions of each zone has made it difficult for foreign investors to choose the right location for their business operations. The GAC also stated that not all enterprises will be permitted to operate in the CBZs.

In the 'Guidelines on Projects Suitable for Entry into the Special Customs Supervision Zones (SCSZs) (*Shujiafa* [2012] No. 196)', three categories of enterprises are highly encouraged to do business in the CBZs:

1. Bonded processing enterprises conducting any of these major types of transactions:
   - Sourcing raw materials from Chinese non-bonded areas;
   - Sourcing raw materials from overseas;
   - Selling finished goods overseas; and
   - Selling finished goods to Chinese non-bonded areas.

The processing enterprise's target market will determine what kind of preferential policies apply. If the enterprise is selling to the domestic market, for example, the Customs Duty on the finished goods must be lower than the duty on the imported raw materials. This means that processing enterprises should avoid high consumption rate products such as tobacco, cosmetics and luxury goods.

2. Bonded logistics enterprises conducting any of these major types of transactions:
   - Importing goods stored in the bonded Zones without a time limit;
   - Importing goods to be transferred between CBZs;
   - Packaging and assembly of imported goods;
   - Transporting imported goods to Chinese non-bonded areas; and
   - Transporting imported goods to foreign countries after basic processing.
3. Bonded service enterprises providing any of these major services:
   - Research, testing and maintenance;
   - Exhibiting imported goods in special areas inside or outside of the bonded Zones approved by Customs; and
   - Outsourcing, including Information Technology Outsourcing (ITO) and Business Process Outsourcing (BPO).

Four categories of enterprises are not permitted for operations in the bonded Zones:

- Manufacturing and processing enterprises that (1) are oriented to the domestic market and (2) make products whose Import Duty is higher than the duty on the related raw materials. As a result, high consumption rate products such as tobacco and cosmetics cannot be processed in the Zones.
- Enterprises mainly operating a non-bonded business, which concerns goods sourced from the domestic market or imported via general trade.
- Manufacturing enterprises focused on domestic raw materials and high export duty products (or controlled export products).
- Manufacturing enterprises processing high energy consumption or high pollution products, or other products prohibited by the government.

The following preferential tax policies apply to enterprises operating in the Zones:

- Import tariff exemptions apply to machinery, equipment and other materials used in infrastructure construction, a reasonable quantity of office supplies and spare parts used for maintenance.
- Import goods brought into the Zones may be exempt from import tariffs.
- Goods traded between enterprises in the bonded Zones are exempt from VAT and consumption duties.

ETDZs, however, tend to focus on providing incentives for specific kinds of activities, such as international trade, utilising local resources or developing technological innovation. There are almost 200 national-level ETDZs, each of which covers a much smaller area than an SEZ.

To set up in the ETDZ, interested enterprises are recommended to check the official website or consult with the ETDZ to see whether they meet the requirements in terms of registration capital, operation period and professional qualifications of management personnel in advance (national-level ETDZs usually have the highest Standards).

Taking the Tianjin Economic-Technological Development Area (TEDA) as an example, if the eligible enterprise has already been registered in Tianjin, then it only needs to prepare all the required materials and physically submit them to the TEDA to be registered in the area.

Foreign-Invested Enterprises (FIE) newly setting up in the TEDA need to have their names pre-approved by the local Administration for Market Regulation (AMR). They will also need to check if their industry is on China's negative list for foreign investment. If it is, the FIE must seek approval from the examination and approval department; If not, the enterprise can just complete a record filing. The FIE will also need to go through registration procedures with taxation, foreign exchange and Customs. After successful registering with the AMR, the enterprise can submit the required materials to the zone authority for registration in the zone.

Zones for commercialising high-tech research findings

- High-Tech Industrial Development Zones (HIDZ) aim to use the technological resources of research institutions, universities and private companies to develop innovative high-tech products. Many HIDZs provide incentives for foreign tech firms with the aim of building collaboration between institutions to expedite the commercialisation of research and development.
- Innovation-focused ETDZs and HIDZs have similarities as they both focus on promoting innovation.
- ETDZs often have a specific industry focus, are located further away from city centres, and are more heavily linked to manufacturing. HIDZs are instead located inside city centres and tend to create clusters of high-tech research institutions to foster research collaboration rather than manufacturing capabilities.
- HIDZs usually welcomes foreign investment in industries that are encouraged by the State, such as high-end or smart manufacturing, green manufacturing, new materials, technical services, and so on. However, each HIDZ has its own

promoting industries. Interested FIEs are advised to check whether they fall under the wanted category.

- Similarly, newly established FIEs will need to get their enterprise names pre-approved. The FIE will need to consult with the HIDZ on the establishment procedures and prepare the required application materials for registration in the zone.

Zones for trade and export purposes

- There are four Zones in this category, namely Free-Trade Zones, EPZs, Bonded Logistic Parks, and Bonded Ports. Among other purposes, they collectively focus on attracting FDI to increase imports and exports through cost reductions.
- FTZs focus on developing trade and the internationalisation of the renminbi (RMB), while also acting as a testing ground for new policies before nationwide implementation. FTZs provide favourable environments for FDI primarily through less restrictive investment policies and administrative systems, as well as tax incentives for import and export.

The purpose of EPZs is similar, but they are primarily set up to develop export-oriented industries through export processing management. Bonded Ports, meanwhile, provide highly competitive trade-focused tax and subsidy policies, and Bonded Logistics Parks have a clear focus on the movement and storage of goods within the Zones.

To enter the FTZs, foreign investors must check whether their industry is listed on the Free-Trade Zone negative list for foreign investment. If it is in a restricted industry, they'll need to seek the approval in advance to enter the industry.

In addition, FTZs may also have various requirements in terms of registration capital, operation period, and professional qualifications of management personnel for different types of enterprises. For example, Shenzhen Qianhai FTZ requires FIEs to have registered capital of more than RMB 5 million (US$ 0.73 million), while wholly Hong Kong-invested enterprises don't need to meet this requirement. Qianhai FTZ also requires that the minimum registered capital of a finance leasing company is RMB 10 million (US$1.45 million).

Investors need to check the guidance on FIE establishment on the official website, prepare the application materials as required. They will have to file the application online and physically submit the required application materials as well.

Zones for cross-broader e-commerce business

China's Cross-Border E-Commerce Comprehensive Pilot Zones were set up to boost the development of cross-border e-commerce. These pilot Zones will try new technological Standards, business models and methods of supervision for cross-border e-commerce transactions, payments, logistics, Customs clearance, tax refund, foreign exchange settlement, and others. Successful practices will be replicated nationwide.

As of January 2020, China has set up 59 Cross-Border E-Commerce Comprehensive Pilot Zones in four batches, attracting a large number of e-commerce platforms, payment, logistics, warehousing, and financial service enterprises.

Eligible in-zone enterprises may enjoy tax exemptions on VAT and consumption tax for exported products, new corporate income tax policy, tax preferences for SMEs, and a more robust cross-border business chain.

The establishment procedures applying to Foreign-Invested Enterprises (FIEs) in any Cross-Border E-Commerce Comprehensive Pilot Zone vary between regions, as specific implementation plans are issued by provincial governments.

Taking the Hangzhou Cross-Border E-Commerce Comprehensive Pilot Zone as an example, to set up an FIE here, the enterprise needs to contact the administrative committee of the zone to determine the cooperation intention of both sides. The administrative committee may request a brief on the business operation mode, products, business performance, logistics operation mode, and so on of the FIE. Qualified enterprises will need to apply for some certificates as required and follow the registration rules of the zone. They may need to complete the relevant filing procedures at the Customs and the inspection and quarantine departments as well (if applicable).

Other Zones

The other seven zone types fall into the last three categories, namely:

- Zones to attract Investment for Specific Purposes;
- Zones for Cooperation with Specific Countries; and
- New areas.

These Zones collectively make up only a small proportion of all national-level EDZs.

Zones to Attract Investment for Specific Purposes have preferential tax and subsidy policies that focus specifically on either tourism or finance. They are worth investigating for businesses thinking of entering these sectors in China, as they are generally heavily restricted from FDI.

Zones for Cooperation with Certain Countries or Regions provide tax incentives for conducting trade and business with neighbouring regions, focusing mainly on Taiwan, Macau and Russia.

New Area Zones, such as the Shanghai Pudong New Area and Tianjin Binhai New Area, encompass some of the Zones mentioned in other categories. They have been established to grant autonomous regulatory power to the local governments that manage specific EDZs.

Investment in Chinese Zones

There are over 2,000 EDZs, each with unique investment incentives and accreditation at different levels of government. Even within Zones of the same type, the level of infrastructure, amount of autonomy and breadth of incentives vary widely, creating an extremely diverse investment environment.

Further complicating the business landscape, EDZs can have accreditation at the national, provincial, municipal and district levels. Accreditation at a higher level generally means larger tax exemptions and better infrastructure.

However, smaller companies are often better off locating in Zones with a lower level of accreditation because they may not be eligible for incentives in Zones with higher level accreditation.

The right EDZ for investment depends heavily on a company's specific business needs. Among many other factors, businesses need to take into account the location of Suppliers and resources, the quality of the surrounding transport network, the cost of land, and which tax exemptions they are eligible for.

The complicated and diverse nature of China's EDZs mean merely investing in any EDZ does not guarantee success. To ensure their investment pays off, businesses should consult experienced experts who understand the regulatory and business environment, and work with them throughout the investment process.

Shanghai Free-Trade Zone

The **Shanghai Free-Trade Zone** (Shanghai FTZ or SFTZ), officially **China (Shanghai) Pilot Free-Trade Zone**, is a Free-Trade Zone in Shanghai, China. On 22 August 2013, the State Council approved the establishment of the zone. Officially launched on 29 September 2013 with the backing of Chinese Premier Li Keqiang, it is the first Free-Trade Zone in mainland China and covers an area of 240.2 km^2 (92.7 miles squared). Shanghai FTZ integrates four existing bonded Zones in the district of Pudong, namely Waigaoqiao Free-Trade Zone, which was the first Free-Trade Zone to be established in China, Waigaoqiao Free Trade Logistics Park, Yangshan Free Trade Port Area and Pudong Airport Comprehensive Free-Trade Zone.

Since 21 April 2015, the zone's areas have been expanded to include Lujiazui Financial and Trade Zone, Shanghai Jinqiao Economic and Technological Development Zone (formerly Jinqiao Export Processing Zone) and Zhangjiang Hi-Tech Park. On 6 August 2019, Shanghai FTZ's areas were expanded again to include Nanhui New City (Lingang New City), Lingang Equipment Industry Area, Xiao Yangshan Island (Yangshan Port) and the south side of Pudong Airport.

The zone is being used as a testing ground for a number of economic and social reforms. For example, the sale of video game consoles, banned in China since 2000, will be allowed within the zone. While Microsoft had aimed at having its Xbox on the market by late April 2014, it ended up being delayed to 23 September 2014. While selling video game consoles was exclusive to the zone at the time, the ban on video game consoles was later lifted completely in 2015.

Although it was initially reported that the zone would also have unrestricted access to the Internet (with bans on sites such as Facebook lifted), the official Xinhua News Agency has stated that Internet restrictions would not be lifted.

Commodities entering the zone are not subject to duty and Customs clearance as would otherwise be the case. This has been a benefit to the wine industry in China, as it grants importers more flexibility in bringing wine into the country, as wine can be stored in the zone without any liability for import and excise duties at the time of import, as well as being suspended from any restrictions such as quotas and sanctions.

To give an idea of the Zone's efficiency and success, Shanghai Waigaoqiao data was reported at US$2.838 billion in December 2019. This records an increase from the previous figures of US$2.446 billion for November 2019.

SECTION 8

United Kingdom

New Freeport initiatives

As at 2021, the UK Freeport initiative allows for the creation of eight new Freeports as sanctioned by the UK Government's new Freeport initiative, embodied in the 2021 Finance Act. Some of the new Freeport initiatives are a renaissance of the original Freeports created as a result of the 1984 Finance Act. One of these is the new Freeport initiative adjacent to the Port of Liverpool.

The Port of Liverpool contains what used to be the United Kingdom's biggest Free Zone. The 383-hectare Liverpool Freeport at the Liverpool and Birkenhead Docks contained, at the time of its operation, almost 28 hectares of warehousing, which was later expanded by an additional 3.7 hectares. Liverpool Freeport was, at the time of the late 1980s and 1990s, the biggest and busiest Freeport in the UK, with cargoes from Felixstowe occupying much of the space in the Freeport. Operating from the Liverpool Intermodal Freeport Terminal, hundreds of large and small companies were either located in or used the Freeport's highly secured facilities. It encompassed much of the dock area adjacent to the main road alongside the port, in particular a large area located around Seaforth Dock, which was used for Customs-controlled warehousing and logistics facilities. Other, more isolated facilities, including the Rimrose estate, were located further down the Dock Road, and were accessible by different entrances. The Freeport handled a wide variety of products, from timber to automotive, as well as areas dedicated to minor processing activities.

The Freeport remained in existence until 2012, when the UK Government abolished all UK Free Zones on the basis that it was not going to renew the legislation originally enacted in 1984 with the UK Finance Act concerning the establishment of Freeports in the UK, a move that was condemned by many organisations as being against the incentives and spirit of international trade. For the same reasons, the Isle of Man Free Zone was also terminated, as the Isle of Man has a Customs Union with the UK. Whether the Isle of Man will decide to create a new Free Zone is an issue open to conjecture.

The new UK Government initiative to generate a consultation which led to legislation allowing for the creation of several Freeports, mainly in the North of England, is designed to allow for the creation of these Freeports in 2021, with the first Freeports envisaged to be up and running by late 2021.

As stated in its Freeport initiative, the UK Government has the following objectives for the UK Freeports:

- Establish Freeports as national hubs for global trade and investment across the UK – enhance trade and investment;

DOI: 10.4324/9781003232025-27

- Promote regeneration and job creation – create high-skilled jobs in ports and the surrounding areas around them;
- Create hotbeds for innovation – form dynamic environments that will attract new businesses, investors and innovations.

The stated aim of government policy concerning benefits generated by the UK Freeports is as follows:

- Customs;
- Tax. This includes measures on:
  - Stamp Duty Land Tax (SDLT) Relief
  - Enhanced Structures and Buildings Allowance
  - Enhanced Capital Allowances
  - Employer National Insurance Contributions Relief
  - Business rates.
- Planning;
- Regeneration and infrastructure: successful bidders will be able to access a share of £175 million of seed capital funding, depending on the submission of an outline business case (OBC);
- Innovation.

The government described the package of incentives as follows:

At the centre of the new Freeports policy is an ambitious new Customs model, drawing on international best practice, and building on the UK's existing Customs arrangements. A firm can import goods into a Freeport without paying tariffs, process them into a final good and then either pay a tariff on goods sold into the domestic market, or export the final goods without paying UK tariffs.

Areas given Freeport status will also benefit from a wide package of tax reliefs, including on purchasing land, constructing or renovating buildings, investing in new plant and machinery assets and on Employer National Insurance Contributions.

Streamlined planning processes and government funding will also boost redevelopment and promote regeneration and innovation.

The Freeports policy involves a number of UK Government departments. It was designed by the Treasury and the Ministry of Housing, Communities and Local Government (MHCLG). MHCLG took the lead in assessing Freeport bids with the decision signed off by the Treasury. The Department for International Trade, the Department for Business, Energy and Industrial Strategy and Border Force are also involved, as are the devolved administrations.

The government's Freeports policy will comply with various requirements on subsidy control:

- The UK's domestic subsidy control regime;
- The UK's subsidy control obligations at the WTO;
- State aid obligations in the Northern Ireland Protocol; and
- Subsidy control provisions negotiated in the UK's Free Trade Agreements including the Trade and Cooperation Agreement (TCA) with the EU.

On 3 March 2021, the UK Chancellor of the Exchequer, Rishi Sunak, announced in his Budget speech that eight Freeport bid submissions had been approved, all of which are located in England, and it was later announced that all eight submissions had been approved for development. These are:

- Plymouth
- Southampton Solent
- Thames (Tilbury and London Gateway)
- Felixstowe and Harwich
- Humber
- Teesport
- Liverpool
- East Midlands International Airport.

Four of these Freeports are located on the east coast of England, while Liverpool is a revival of the previous Freeport status. Tilbury was itself the location of a Freeport in the first UK Freeport initiative, but has been incorporated in the overall Thames Freeport initiative along with the London Gateway port complex. The only non-port Freeport is that to be located at East Midlands Airport, a major international airfreight logistics hub.

Teesport had been mooted for some time as a potential new Freeport location, adjacent to Teesport itself on the south bank of the River Tees to the east of Middlesbrough, and indeed the Tees Authority, supported by the Port, submitted a bid for Freeport status in January 2021, along with other bids submitted by London Gateway/Tilbury, Port of Tyne, Liverpool, Bristol and Plymouth. Of this tranche, only Bristol and the Port of Tyne were unsuccessful. It is presently claimed that the re-establishment of a Freeport at Liverpool could boost the local economy by £739m, with the creation of an additional 12,000 jobs in the area. However, other areas of the UK scheduled for development initiatives were also able to apply for Freeport status on the basis of the economic need and associated advantages to the region. These needs were reinforced by a combination of the need to develop regional ports and airports for cargo and freight purposes, as well as easy and convenient access to the regions concerned. What is recognised is that each Freeport bid is unique to the Freeport concerned, and therefore allows for specific trading activities pertinent to the region where the Freeport is to be located, including specific tax incentives likely to foster regional economic growth. The automotive sector may well have influenced the Freeport bids by Tilbury/London Gateway and Teesport. The large automotive facilities at Dagenham, on the River Thames, just outside East London, would have a major influence on the Thames bid, while the Teesport bid will no doubt have been influenced by the large Nissan automotive plant at Washington, Tyne & Wear, a few miles from Teesport, and which in any case uses the Teesport storage facilities to store imported parts for incorporation in its vehicle assembly facilities. Indeed, it was announced by the UK Government that the Teesport Freeport will be the first to become operational later in 2021. It is also claimed that the Teesport Freeport facility will create more than 18,000 skilled quality jobs over the next five years and will increase inward investment by £1.4 billion. You can view images of Teesport from this website: **www.pdports.co.uk**

Of course, the automotive sector is only part of the regional Freeport strategy. Other industries in both the manufacturing and logistics sector stand to benefit from these new Freeport initiatives, and time will tell concerning the long-term effects of the new strategy. However, given the economic and commercial influences behind these Freeport bids, it is likely that significant economic benefits will be gained by all the companies involved in the new Freeport initiatives. Indeed, it would appear that much of the driving force behind several of the successful Freeport bids has been their association with large manufacturing industries predominantly in the aviation and automotive sectors.

The East Midlands Freeport, close to East Midlands Airport, is also designed to be a conduit for materials destined for large companies in the automotive, aviation and transport industries. Based around the East Midlands Airport and Gateway Industrial Cluster (EMAGIC) in North-West Leicestershire, Uniper's Ratcliffe-on-Soar power station site in Rushcliffe in Nottinghamshire and the East Midlands Intermodal Park (EMIP) in South Derbyshire, it is envisaged that the Freeport will bring significant investment to develop and drive innovation, alternative energy sources and green technology supporting SME's and large regional employers, including Rolls-Royce, Toyota and Alstom (formerly Bombardier). An estimated 60,000 jobs are to be created in the region as a result of the Freeport.

The East Midlands Freeport bid was submitted by a consortium led by the Local Enterprise Partnerships representing Derby, Derbyshire, Nottingham, Nottinghamshire, Leicester, and Leicestershire. It included private sector businesses and local authorities, with support from universities, business groups, local MPs and the proposed East Midlands Development Corporation. Of all the successful Freeport bids, it is the only Freeport based close to an international airport, namely East Midlands Airport, which is also host to a major international air cargo centre. Its basis is far more established that any of its airport-based Freeport predecessors; the original Birmingham Freeport, based close to Birmingham airport, only enjoyed limited success, while the Prestwick Freeport, detailed earlier in this text, never achieved major success.

The Humber Freeport, to be located on land to the east of the city of Kingston-upon-Hull, is also intended to bring a large number of jobs to the region. The huge development site near Hull which has been given Freeport status is big enough to provide an estimated 6,500 jobs. Covering 453 acres, it stretches from the Saltend industrial complex to the outskirts of Paull village, close to the Humber estuary. The land is currently a greenfield site, straddling Hedon Haven which once formed a route for ships to the ancient port of Hedon, long since isolated from the river.

In the case of Harwich and Felixstowe, both ports will be included in the Freeport. The Port of Harwich currently handles a significant amount of wind turbines destined for offshore energy renewables projects in the North Sea. The port of Felixstowe is the UK's largest container port, and handles 40% of the UK's container traffic.

Perhaps the most ambitious Freeport project in the UK is that of the Thames area, encompassing the ports of London Gateway and Tilbury. The Thames Freeport project is designed to attract over 25,000 jobs, with significant investment in training and skills, as well as £400 million new port investment and the development of 1,700 acres of development land. Much of the driving force behind the project is the Dagenham engine plant, which is an integral part of the Ford company, also located at Dagenham, on the extremities of East London.

Thames Freeport is a digitally linked economic zone connecting Ford's Dagenham engine plant, the global ports at London Gateway and Tilbury and many communities in need of economic redevelopment in the Thames area. The respective Port Authorities of London Gateway, owned by DP World, and Tilbury, owned by Forth Ports, have stated that businesses seeking to expand are being urged to take advantage of the tax benefits of relocating to the Freeport and being part of a Customs-controlled Free Zone, which makes it easier and cheaper to move goods into and out of the country.

The other benefits of Thames Freeport include:

- £5.1 billion additional GVA;
- Over £4.5 billion in new public and private investment;
- 25,000+ new jobs with many more across supply chains, with significant investment in training and skills;
- 1,700 acres of development land – much with planning consent;
- £400 million port investment into some of the most deprived areas;
- 20% of the UK's most deprived communities are in London and the South-East;
- Freeports are part of the Thames Freeport strategy from a historic point of view – DP World began as a Free-Trade Zone in Jebel Ali, while Tilbury was a Freeport until 2012.

The last point is somewhat significant, as DP World, the operators of the London Gateway Port, also own and operate the large UAE Port and Free Zone of Jebel Ali, just outside Dubai, which commenced operations in 1985, and it is possible that the model that encompasses the Jebel Ali complex may also be used to influence the structure and operation of the new Thames Freeport.

Post-Brexit implications

The advantages of UK Freeports based on present and future economic conditions would be massive. The exit of the UK from the European Union Single Market on 1 January 2021 has had significant ramifications for border controls and the ability to process the perceived huge increase in the number of Customs Declarations processed by the UK Customs computer from then on. HM Revenue & Customs have already stated that they are looking to implement Simplified Procedures where possible to allow for what they class as frictionless cross-border activities. However, given the scale of the increase of cross-border Customs controls and the level of unpreparedness of many traders and freight operators to handle this increase, the risk of delays in Customs clearance is becoming far greater with the passing of each day following the UK's full exit from the EU.

Furthermore, the use of the Freeports for Customs-controlled storage and manufacturing activities means that any inference of the implementation of World Trade Organisation rules concerning the imposition of tariffs would be offset by in-zone storage and manufacturing activities. Although HMRC has not fully considered the use of Customs-controlled manufacturing facilities within the Zones, the impending relaxation of the rules concerning Customs-controlled manufacturing facilities, especially IP Relief, would mean that it would be much easier for Freeport tenants to obtain IP approval for manufacturing or processing activities, for either the re-export of finished goods or their release into Free Circulation.

However, there is a flip side to the coin. The HMRC Freeport Customs offer of mid-2021 requires what is defined as the Customs Site Operator, which is in itself responsible to the overall the Free Zone Authority, to be AEO(s) (Authorised Economic Operator – Safety and Security) or AEO(f) (AEO – Full, i.e. c+s (Customs + Safety/Security)) approved, as well as having an EORI (Economic Operator Registered Identification), for example a logistics operator such as a Port Operator or a 3PL (Third Party Logistics Operator). As a result, a UK Freeport will have three structural levels, namely:

- Freeport Authority;
- Customs Site Operator;
- Freeport Tenants/Businesses.

This means that, regardless of its overall structure, the Freeport Site Operator must obtain the status of a registered import/export organisation with a combination of an EORI Number and AEO authorisation, in the same way that freight forwarders, importers and exporters are EORI-registered.

Many of the UK's freight forwarders and shipping agents are already AEO-approved, which sets a high set of Standards concerning HMRC approvals. Indeed, the AEO standard is a global standard, and, given this AEO requirement, puts the UK Free Zone regime at levels somewhat above those of many existing global Free Zones, which may not necessarily be approved at AEO level. This set of Standards will also impose much higher HMRC approval Standards for any Freeport tenants, as they will be expected to adhere to the same Standards and levels of overall compliance as the Freeport authorities themselves.

UK Freeports and tax incentives

According to the UK Government, the UK Freeport model will require a primary Customs site (Primary Customs Zone) designated in or near a seaport, airport or rail port within which the Customs benefits will apply. Additional Freeport secondary subzones may also be permitted to enable multiple sites to benefit from the Freeports Customs model.

Freeports will also include a defined site within which Freeport tax reliefs will apply – operating in a similar way to existing Enterprise Zones. The purposes of the reliefs will be to encourage and foster business investment in capital assets and employment. However, clear eligibility criteria will apply to prevent tax evasion and avoidance.

Businesses operating within Freeport Customs sites will receive tariff benefits, including duty deferral and suspension while the goods remain on site, and duty inversion (Tariff Inversion/reversed cascading) if the finished goods exiting the Freeport attract a lower tariff than their component parts.

Businesses may also be able to take advantage of Customs Duty suspension on goods that are imported into a Freeport, processed into finished goods and subsequently re-exported, but this depends on the specific terms of the relevant UK trade agreements. This applies for the EU-UK Free Trade Agreement but that is not the case with all other countries: for some countries, companies based in Freeports may be excluded from benefitting from the agreement.

Companies will also be able to suspend Import VAT on goods entering the Freeport. In addition, businesses operating in Freeports will be authorised to use simplified import procedures. This model expands on existing Customs facilitations and procedures available to business.

Businesses located in UK Freeports will be able to claim reliefs from key business taxes within the bounds and confines of a Freeport. The current proposals include:

Stamp Duty Land Tax (SDLT) relief

The government intends to offer SDLT relief on land purchases within Freeport tax sites in England where that property is to be used for qualifying commercial activity. It is intended that this relief will apply from 1 April 2021 until 31 March 2026.

Enhanced Structures and Buildings Allowance (SBA)

The government intends to offer an Enhanced SBA rate, providing enhanced tax relief for companies constructing or renovating structures and buildings for non-residential use within Freeport tax sites.

Enhanced Capital Allowances (ECA)

The new ECA which the government intends to offer in Freeport tax sites will provide enhanced tax relief for companies investing in qualifying new plant and machinery assets. This accelerated relief is intended to allow firms to reduce their taxable profits by the full cost of the qualifying investment in the same tax period the cost was incurred. Firms investing in the Freeport tax site would be eligible to benefit from the relief where the qualifying investments are incurred on or after 1 October 2021 until 30 September 2026.

Employer National Insurance Contributions (NICs) rate relief

The government intends to enable employers operating in a Freeport tax site to pay 0% employer NICs on the salaries of any new employee working in the Freeport tax site. This 0% rate would be applicable for up to three years per employee on earnings up to a £25,000 per annum threshold. An employee will be deemed to be working in the Freeport tax site if they spend 60% or more of their working hours in that tax site. The relief is intended to be available for up to nine years from April 2022. Partway through, the government intends to review this relief and decide whether it should be continued up to its end date in 2031. The relief would end no earlier than April 2026 and would therefore be available for a minimum of four years.

Business rates relief

The government intends to offer up to 100% relief from business rates on certain business premises within Freeport tax sites. This relief is intended to be available to new and certain existing businesses in Freeport tax sites in England from 1 October 2021 and would apply for five years from the point at which the beneficiary first receives relief. The point at which a business first receives relief must be by 30 September 2026. The cost of the relief will be funded by central government. It is intended that newly formed businesses and businesses relocating to a Freeport will be eligible for the relief.

Local retention of business rates

It is intended that the council or councils in which the Freeport tax sites are located will retain the business rates growth for that area above an agreed baseline, following the example of Enterprise Zones. This will be guaranteed for 25 years, giving councils the certainty that they need to borrow to invest in regeneration and infrastructure that will support further growth.

Import and export declarations

Under the model, declaration requirements will be simplified to reduce the administrative burden of moving goods into a Freeport. A reduced amount of data would be provided using existing processes (Form C21) to allow goods to be cleared to leave a port and businesses would need to complete a declaration into their own commercial records (EIDR) recording information about the goods that will be brought into the UK. They would also need to provide adequate information to the Freeport operator's records management system so that a central record of all goods in the site can be maintained.

When businesses wish to remove goods from the site, they would need to complete normal import declarations if releasing the goods for sale on the domestic market or export declarations if exporting the goods for sale overseas. It will be possible for goods to be declared to another Customs procedure, such as transit, on leaving the Freeport site, if goods are to be transferred to another Customs-controlled regime in another company, for example Inward Processing or Customs Warehousing.

Businesses bringing goods into the UK via a UK port also need to submit Entry Summary Declarations (ENS) for safety and security purposes before arrival and submit cargo manifest information (IMO FAL 2 CUSCAR Customs Cargo Reporting equivalent) to notify the Customs Authority that the goods have arrived at the port. These formalities are generally carried out on behalf of importers by their appointed shipping and forwarding agents, and these processes for goods entering a port will not differ in respect of Freeports, as they are standard reporting requirements applied globally.

To this extent, there are therefore many advantages for the use of Freeports in the UK. These are:

- Customs-controlled storage of goods in the Freeports;
- Conglomeration of logistics and industrial activities within the zone;
- Simplified declaration procedures;
- Reduction in logistics costs;
- Adjacency of the Freeports to regional ports and airports;
- Storage and holding points for containers and trailers outside the port areas following entry into the UK;
- Storage of bulk commodities under Customs control;
- Duty-suspended storage and manufacturing activities within the Zones;
- Regional Distribution;
- Sources of employment;
- Economic benefits, including Duty and VAT Suspension;
- Other Tax reduction benefits;
- Re-export of goods free from Import Duty and VAT;
- Alleviation of port congestion, especially ports located on the Channel and North Sea;
- Customs-controlled maritime activities, including shipwork and offshore activities.

Overall appraisal for the UK

Although the Freeports introduced in the UK in 1984 were a major venture into Customs-controlled trading activities, they met with limited success, partly as a result of limited commercial awareness of the concept and partly because they were limited in terms of their use as a result of regulations imposed by HM Customs & Excise. The Liverpool Freeport became the most successful of all the UK Freeports at the time, mainly because of its strategic importance as a holding point for goods entering the country from several directions. Even the Isle of Man Free Zone, outside the jurisdiction of the UK Customs & Revenue Authorities, enjoyed significant success as a zone for both storage and light manufacturing. However, the government of 2012 allowed the Free Zone licences to expire for a variety of reasons, partly concerning the EU's dislike of Free Zones and partly because of a more liberalised Customs Warehousing regime that could be used by individual companies, both logistics providers and trading companies in the form of importers themselves.

The UK Government stated that it wanted bids for Freeports from across the UK, including Scotland, Wales and Northern Ireland. However, recent history suggests that provincial Freeports are less likely to succeed and are thus less viable, even from the planning and bid stage. The case in point is that of Prestwick Freeport, on the Clyde Coast, just north of Ayr, and located adjacent to Prestwick International Airport. Indeed, the authorities that were granted Freeport licences in early 2021 are all located in England, with nothing envisaged for either Scotland and Wales at this stage (May 2021).

In the UK, the Finance Act of 1984 established a Freeport regime, where goods could be stored under conditions similar to those of Customs warehouses, that is, Duty and VAT Suspension, but in designated areas adjacent to several seaports and airports, where several companies associated with port-centric storage activities could cluster and use such Customs-controlled facilities, either for the purposes of the release of goods from the Freeport into Free Circulation, or for re-export of these goods free from Customs Duties and VAT. The main success stories in the UK were Liverpool and Southampton, where the Freeports were located adjacent to the big seaports. Other ventures, such as Prestwick Freeport, were much less successful, and for much time there was significant doubt as to whether the Freeport at Prestwick had a long-term future as an operational Free Zone, which in the event proved to be correct, as the Freeport never achieved significant results, and duly closed well before the other Freeports. The Prestwick Freeport existed as a nominal venture, but, as at 2004, had no major companies operating from within its confines for Customs-controlled purposes, other than companies involved in aviation-related maintenance activities.

Part of the reason for a lack of initiative concerning the effectiveness of the Prestwick Freeport stems from the issue concerning the use of the airport itself. Prior to the late 1980s, Glasgow Prestwick Airport, located on the Clyde Coast just north of Ayr, was the main international airport serving the lucrative transatlantic markets, and was used by airlines such as Northwest Orient (based in Minneapolis-St. Paul, Minnesota, USA) and Air Canada (based in Montréal, Québec, Canada). The freight market was served by a variety of cargo airlines. One of the main justifications for these transatlantic services was the existence of the US nuclear Polaris ballistic-missile-carrying submarine base at the Holy Loch, further up the Firth of Clyde opposite Gourock, where the ferries transferred the submarine crews to the submarine base located in the loch occupied by a US submarine depot ship. This base had commenced operations in 1961, and remained active throughout the Cold War. However, as the Cold War threat from the erstwhile Soviet Union receded into the 1990s, the need for the base became less evident, to the point that it became surplus to US military strategic requirements, and it was finally closed in 1992.

Furthermore, the transatlantic flights to the US and Canada were transferred for a variety of reasons, largely political, to Glasgow's own more modern international airport at Abbotsinch, just outside Renfrew/Paisley, and a short distance out of Glasgow city centre, despite the latter airport having a less weather-friendly reliability than its Clyde Coast rival. The net result was that Prestwick Airport, by this time significantly dated in its appearance and function, lost out on much of Scottish commercial air traffic, until its renaissance as a regional airport courtesy of the Irish low-cost airline Ryanair. However, the air cargo business remained, although the large Temporary Storage area in the form of Prestwick International Bond prospered because of the need for Temporary Storage of freight for both outbound and inbound purposes, which also meant that the time that any cargo spent in the transit warehouses was limited, owing to the need for it to be cleared through Customs as quickly as possible and transported to its ultimate inland destination. In this respect, the Freeport had little justification, as it was limited to specific businesses such as aviation repair and maintenance, which in reality were activities which could be carried out by individual companies elsewhere in the vicinity of the airport using Customs-approved facilities, rather than having the need to be clustered on the site of the airport Freeport. Given that most of the industries served by Prestwick Airport were located further towards the major Scottish conurbations of Glasgow and Edinburgh, there was greater convenience in using the cargo facilities, albeit more limited, at the international airports serving these cities.

Prestwick Freeport, which had been established in South-West Scotland adjacent to Prestwick International Airport in the mid-1980s as part of the original national Freeport initiative, became less of a viable proposition, despite its proximity to the airport, as companies preferred to hold goods in limited Customs-controlled storage in the airport's Temporary Storage facilities for a short period of time and then release them into Free Circulation sooner rather than later. This they could easily accomplish using the Prestwick Cargo Centre bonded storage facilities, rather than using the longer-term Freeport facilities outside the airport confines, and indeed studies conducted at the Fraser of Allander Institute at the University of Strathclyde confirmed this, reaching the conclusion that there was significant doubt as to why the Freeport at Prestwick had been conceived and established in the first place. Besides which, the needs for dedicated air cargo and Free Zone activities were far lower than those for air cargo activities south of the border in England, where commercial activities have always been more dense and concentrated. Indeed, it was suggested by the Fraser of Allander Institute that the reasons for the establishment of Prestwick Freeport were more political than economic, partly based on the fact that a senior Minister in the government of Margaret Thatcher, the Prime Minister at the time, was MP for the local constituency.

During the 1990s, Customs-controlled warehousing facilities became less restricted and indeed were actively promoted by HM Customs & Excise for the purposes of use by individual companies located further away from the airport and closer to the main commercial centres and urban concentrations of the large cities, without the need to congregate international Customs-controlled activities within the confines of a single Free Zone. The use of electronic Customs Declaration facilities has further resulted in companies being able to operate Customs-controlled activities some distance from the airport (and seaports, for that matter), without the need to use the Freeport facilities, thus to a large extent rendering the original UK Freeport concept, for all its limitations, surplus to national and regional requirements. Today, Customs bonded facilities at Prestwick Airport are used primarily for the purposes of Temporary Storage, consolidation and breakbulk activities. In this respect, the airport's net gain has been the Freeport's net loss, even considering that there has been doubt of late as to whether Prestwick Airport itself has a future, given the short distance between itself and Glasgow International Airport, just outside the city of Glasgow. Its strategic location on the Firth of Clyde and its enviable weather record may suggest otherwise, as it is often the case that flights are diverted to Prestwick Airport owing to inclement weather conditions elsewhere in the UK. Besides which, it is used from time to time by overseas military authorities, particularly the Canadian Armed Forces, and it is often the case where Canadian military transport aircraft call at the Airport as part of military exercise programs.

Eight years after the original expiry of the licences for UK's Freeports, the present government initiated a project to revive the UK Freeport concept in the light of the withdrawal of the UK from the EU Single Market, and made the decision as of October 2020 to sanction the creation of ten Freeports throughout the country, this time with rather more flexible commercial activities allowable in the Free Zones under Customs control. Given the failure of the original Freeport at Prestwick, it is very unlikely that there will be a repeat initiative in the same location, as there is no economic justification for such a venture.

Despite various misgivings posed by academic researchers, there is no question of the advantages of the principle of Freeports for the UK economy, especially regional areas slated for economic development, that is, the South-West and the North of England. Even areas such as Kent, close to the Channel ports, and the East of England, would benefit hugely from the initiative, especially concerning the alleviation of potential delays cause by port congestion in the light of the implementation of full UK Customs border controls as from 1 January 2021. However, in the other areas such as Wales, Scotland and Northern Ireland, there is far less justification for the establishment of Freeports based on the arguments stated above, primarily for economic reasons.

Instead of port clearances of cargoes, the trailers or containers can be moved to the Freeport, where they can be held in Temporary Storage facilities pending Customs clearance, or even, as a better alternative, unloaded into Freeport warehouses, Customs-cleared into longer-term Customs-controlled facilities and distributed from the Freeports to their regional destinations using electronic Simplified Clearance Procedures which do not require full Customs Declarations at the point of import or export. If all these issues are taken into account, there are very few reasons against the concept, as the myths concerning duty exemption have proven unfounded, given that the notion of duty exemption does not exist and never has existed. Customs law in all countries states that duties apply for all goods released from a Free Zone into Free Circulation, except where the goods are to be re-exported. Goods held in Freeports are only held in the zone temporarily prior to being released either for entry into Free Circulation or for re-export, and do not remain there permanently. As the US FTZs were implemented to provide an answer to the US economic woes of the 1930s, Freeports can yet be the solution for the UK's present economic woes and challenges. It is anticipated that the UK Government's decision to facilitate the introduction of the first wave of ten Freeports at the end of 2020 will initiate a major incentive in the development of the UK's domestic and international economic prospects. However, it must be decided as to whether the Freeports will simply act as Zones for the relief of Import Duty and VAT, or whether other tax incentives such as relief from property and Corporation Tax will be implemented as a means of fiscal incentives and hence investment attraction for companies locating in the zone. Time will tell.

It should be noted that Free Zones do not happen or even succeed of their own accord. There is no magic wand conjuring up a massive Free Zone success. In order for Free Zones to be successful, there is need for commercial awareness and understanding of the Free Zone concept, as well as the understanding of the economic and fiscal benefits that the Free Zone regime can bring to commercial trading. Furthermore, there is a need for government support in the form of legislation and supportive regulations that facilitate the effectiveness and prosperity of Free Zones. Businesses themselves need to learn about the principle and concept of Freeports/Free Zones, and then understand the benefits of the use of these facilities. There is an overall need on the part of UK business as a whole for a greater understanding of international trade and Customs controls. Businesses also need to engage in effective duty and tax planning and management as part of their import and export activities, especially given the changes to Customs procedures and controls at the beginning of 2021. As it is said, pay no more tax than you legally owe (if, that is, you need to pay certain taxes at all). It would appear that in many cases, there is a distinct lack of knowledge of Customs and Tax Reliefs available for a variety of import and export activities, and these reliefs will become even more important from the start of 2021 in terms of fiscal management, especially in the event of greater Import Duty and VAT liabilities on imports into the UK.

As an additional issue, a dissertation written by Nicolas Spence in 2017 as part of a Master of Science degree at the World Maritime University in Malmö, Sweden, demonstrated that Free Zones can also contribute to the development of maritime ports. He used the case study of the port of Kingston, Jamaica, where there is also a Free Zone. He established by the use of appropriate data that Free Zone activities not only stimulate national economic growth and development, but also contribute to increased port activities in terms of vessel movements and cargo handling. This same phenomenon has also contributed to the development of other ports such as Jebel Ali, Dubai, and elsewhere in countries such as Malaysia and China. The Chinese port of Shanghai has greatly benefitted from the nearby Export Processing Zones in the Shanghai region, and Free Zone facilities have also contributed to the growth of the Russian port of Vladivostok, on Russia's Pacific coast.

The same arguments could therefore be proposed in favour of UK Freeport facilities at various selected ports, such as Teesport, Liverpool, Southampton, the Thames, the Humber and Plymouth. The ports of Tilbury and Liverpool are no strangers to the Freeport concept; Freeports were established at both these ports in 1984, and indeed both Freeports went on to enjoy significant success as conduits for Customs-controlled storage operations and the consequent enhancement of international trade which benefitted both the North-West of England and the Thames region. In the past, the Port of Liverpool benefitted significantly from the existence of the Freeport there between 1984 and 2012, when the

UK Freeport initiatives were allowed to expire. Given that both ports have been granted permission to operate Freeport facilities as part of the government's 2020/2021 Freeport initiative, then there is every chance that the existence of Freeports in these locations will stimulate port and overall international business development even further, especially given the UK's exit from the European Union. However, commitment and planning are required for each venture, and this equally requires significant organisation and compliance on the part of each Freeport project. Lessons learned from the 1984 initiative may go a long way to achieving this.

Challenges

The challenges faced are varied. There are significant start-up and investment costs associated with any Free Zone project, and much planning has to be executed before the initiation of the project itself. Blueprints and site plans need to be drawn up, applications need to be submitted to HMRC for authorisations to be granted, and a large budget is required to invest in the project on both short-term and long-term scales. Furthermore, extensive promotion of the zone projects is required on a national and international basis, as Free Zones per se do not generate their own business at the beginning of their operations. Communication with the local community is also vital, as there is a requirement for complete synergy between the zone authority and the local community. As most Freeports are located close to seaports, there is the need for operating synergy between the Freeport and the port itself. Sustainability as a prevalent factor is a foregone conclusion, as the Freeport has to be able to blend in with the local community and not cause any unnecessary pollution or inconvenience to the local community. And, above all, the Freeport must be a viable proposition. It must be capable of generating its own income without the need for State subsidies or governmental financial support. It must be able to attract a wide range of pertinent businesses, as well as cater for a variety of business needs in terms of international trade.

Although less than ten years have elapsed since the expiry of the origin Freeport concept, much has changed in the world of international trade. A series of global financial shocks plus the global COVID-19 have done much to destabilise the global economic community. The exit of the UK from the European Union has created significant economic uncertainty, although the UK is now free to pursue its own independent political and economic initiatives. Global Customs initiatives implemented by the WTO and the WCO in the form of the Trade Facilitation Agreement (TFA) and the SAFE (Safety and Accountability in the Freight Environment) Framework of Standards which resulted from the Revised Kyoto Convention have also contributed to the reshaping of international trade and global economics. This combination has led to a review of global trade policies, strategies and patterns, and has led more policymakers and governments to review their fiscal strategies. In this way, the role of global Free Zones has become more crucial and vital to the global economy. It is still a major consideration that tax incentives generate a dynamic and prosperous economy, especially where a country adopts a strategy of Free Zone incentives. The UAE, with all its Free Zones, is a classic case of how this initiative can work in a significant, influential and successful way.

Given the exit of the UK from the EU Single Market and Customs Union at the end of 2020, the need for a UK national Free Zone policy is greater than ever, as the UK vitally needs the Freeport/Free Zone initiative to develop the national economy to where it needs to be as a viable international competitor, free from many of the tax burdens which have enveloped it, especially those originally imposed by the EU. Despite a Trade and Cooperation Agreement between the UK and the EU which was concluded in late December 2020, allowing for duty-Free-Trade between the UK and the EU as long as the products and materials concerned originate in either the UK or the EU, much of the UK's trade is conducted with non-EU countries, and is therefore outside the scope of the UK-EU Trade Agreement. Indeed, many products imported from the EU into the UK do not originate in the EU owing to their non-EU content of components and raw materials, and are therefore subject to UK import tariffs. The new UK Freeports will be able to accommodate such materials on a duty-suspended basis until they are required by their respective importers.

However, what is primarily required in order to fully understand the importance and overall benefits of the Freeport/Free Zone concept to the UK is a far better understanding of the overall concept of Freeports and Free Zones on the part of UK industry, trade bodies and government, and how UK industry and commerce can use the Freeport/Free Zone initiative to its fullest advantage as a means of commercial and economic growth and prosperity. Location, of course, is a major influencing factor, and the initiative to create such Free Zones in areas considered by the UK Government to be economically disadvantaged, is seen as a major boost to these regional economies, especially where such Free Zones are also located close to or adjacent to regional seaports. However, serious thought must be given to the long-term viability of such ventures, as the UK history of the Freeport concept has not proven as successful as had been envisaged, based on its original concept back in the 1980s and 1990s, possibly due to operational limitations imposed on the Freeport concept by the government of the time through HM Customs & Excise.

Given the novelty of the concept at the time, and an inability on the part of most people to understand the concept of Free Zones, the concept never fully developed as envisaged and was never taken fully advantage of by many UK companies, let alone attracting Foreign Direct Investment into the various Freeport locations. Lessons learned from the existence of various UK Freeports based on the original initiative instigated and facilitated by the Finance Act of 1984 show that very few Freeport initiatives met with outstanding success. One of the comparative failures was the Prestwick Freeport in Scotland, which in reality was the only Scottish Freeport venture, and certain other Freeports located throughout England at the time were equally disadvantaged, with only a few enjoying comparative success such as Liverpool Freeport. It is perhaps ironic that Liverpool is set to revive its Freeport status with the new initiative of 2021. What is even more interesting is that there were no Freeport bids outside England included in the Freeport approvals of March 2021, and this may reflect in the inability of locations in Scotland and Wales to justify Freeport operations there.

Consequently, there needs to be a solid economic justification for the Freeport concept in the UK, especially concerning the economic development of the regional economies, with a much wider and varied remit in terms of fiscal advantages than its predecessor. This would include, as mooted by HM Government, Direct Tax incentives such as relief from corporate and property taxes, as well as indirect tax incentives from the suspension of Import Duty and VAT for all goods located within the Freeports. This strategy would therefore create a series of hybrid Zones offering a combination of Direct and Indirect

Tax incentives, a strategy envisaged by the UK Government from the very outset. Indeed, the Freeport concept extends to the concept of a service-based Free Zone in the UK as well, dedicated to international financial and IT services. The suggestion of London becoming a 'Singapore-on-Thames' would infer the creation of a Financial Services Free Zone, similar to the Financial Free Zone in Dubai, in the financial district of London, should the concept be considered viable and achievable. However, this is at present only a concept, and would require a great deal of consideration and discussion, as this concept would be radically different from the existing Freeport concept, and would possibly be based upon the Dubai Financial Free Zone model.

It is to be hoped that lessons have indeed been learned from the past, and that they will be seriously heeded in terms of the latest UK Freeport initiative, if this initiative is to succeed as hoped. Furthermore, significant awareness on the part of government and business is required, as several myths have been promulgated for some time concerning fiscal status in the zones (duty exemption, which does not exist), and the business and political community needs to be made aware of the true nature of the ventures, including social value benefits such as employment incentives and the revival of deprived or marginalised economic areas throughout the UK. It is to be hoped that this book will go a long way in dispelling existing myths and suppositions but will also be a source of enlightenment concerning the concept, function and practice of Freeports and Free Zones.

APPENDIX 1

UK Free Zones: Proposed guidelines

Top level – Free Zone authority

- Site Definition
- Customs Authorisations – Relationship with HMRC and Border Force
- Risk Analysis and Management
- Site Security and Controls
- Operation Controls – Tenants
- Links and Relationship with Port Authority and Port Facilities
- Relationship with local Authorities
- Permitted Activities – Tax, Customs
- Due Diligence
- Environmental Controls
- Phytosanitary Controls.

Site definition

The Site designated for the Freeport must be shown on appropriate maps and illustrations for official purposes, including HMRC approvals.

Customs authorisations

There is the need for official authorisations for Freeport status from HMRC, including authorisation for Simplified Procedures. These authorisations will become a requirement once the full HMRC guidelines have been published.

Risk analysis and management

Risk Analysis exercises must be conducted on the project at various stages during the planning and execution phases, in order to ensure that all parts of the project are planned carefully and are carried out accordingly. Any variance analysis must also be conducted concerning timescales and costs of the project, in order to ensure that budgets do not overrun and the project is carried out within all budgetary constraints.

Site security

All measures necessary must be taken to ensure that appropriate security measures are put in place from the outset of the project's initiation.

Operation controls

All tenants must be vetted and approved in accordance with HMRC requirements prior to the project being implemented. There is the need for an established and documented set of controls and procedures to ensure compliance with HMRC requirements.

Links with port authority and port facilities

Because of the structure of the Primary Customs Zone (PCZ), there will be the need for an electronic management system allowing for interface with the Port Community System (PCS) and Port Management systems in terms of the movement of vessels and cargoes.

Relationship with local authorities

Given that the Freeport is being supported by the local authorities, there is the need for close communication and accountability concerning the Freeport's activities. There will be the need for a reporting mechanism to be linked to the local authorities to ensure that all information relating to the Freeport and its activities is relayed to the local authorities as required.

Permitted activities – Tax, Customs

The Freeport Authority must ensure that all activities permitted by HMRC are documented and adhered to in line with HMRC requirements, and that any anomalies in such activities must be reported to HMRC as and when required.

Due diligence

In accordance with HMRC requirements, due diligence must be exercised by the Freeport Authority at all times to ensure compliance with HMRC-designated procedures and activities of Freeport tenants.

Environmental controls

In accordance with environmental legislation and regulations, the Freeport must adhere to all such environmental requirements as determined by the government.

Phytosanitary controls

In accordance with phytosanitary regulations, controls must be exercised over the import of plants and associated species in order to ensure that there are no breaches of such requirements as defined by the Authorities.

Middle level – zone tenants/operators

- Individual Tenants – Relationship with HMRC
- Authorisations – Storage, Manufacturing
- Compliances
- Financial Status
- Risk Status
- IT Status
- Staff Competence and Awareness
- Customs Import/Export Procedures
- Quality Management of Systems
- Record-keeping.

Many of these Guidelines can also be found on the HMRC Self-Assessment Questionnaires.

Low level – operations and procedures

- Customs Controls
- Imports
- Exports
- Releases into Free Circulation
- Logistics & Transport
- IT/Electronic Systems/Software
- Storage Facilities
- Transaction Records
- Import/Export SOPs
- Inventory Controls.

Customs controls

HMRC maintains full control over Customs Import and Export activities. It is therefore important that both the Free Zone Authority and the Free Zone tenants ensure that all Customs Import and Export requirements and compliances are adhered to at all times. HMRC reserves the right to examine all trader and authority records at any times and to conduct any necessary audits and investigations concerning Free Zone activities when required.

Imports

All Imports must be declared and recorded by the Free Zone tenants according to HMRC requirements.

Exports

All exports must be declared and recorded by the Free Zone tenants according to HMRC requirements.

Releases into Free Circulation

All releases into Free Circulation from the Free Zone must be declared and recorded by the Free Zone tenants according to HMRC requirements.

Logistics and transport

All logistics and transport operations must be carried out according to HMRC requirements concerning Free Zone activities. All inward and outward movements must be recorded and declared as per HMRC requirements.

IT/electronic systems/software

The Free Zone Authority and its tenants must use IT software solutions approved by HMRC to manage all aspects of Free Zone activities, including accounting, imports, exports, inventory and all other Customs-controlled activities.

Storage facilities

All Free Zone storage facilities must be supervised by the Free Zone authority in accordance with HMRC requirements. However, storage facilities pertaining to each Free Zone tenant are also the responsibility of each tenant, and must be governed and managed by specific approved inventory control systems.

Transaction records

In accordance with HMRC requirements, all import, export and release into Free Circulation transactions must be maintained by each Free Zone tenant, with such information and records made available to the Free Zone Authority for scrutiny wherever deemed necessary.

Import/export SOPs

In accordance with HMRC requirements, all Free Zone tenants must create and maintain Documented Import and Export Procedures as part of their Customs Free Zone approval.

Inventory controls

In accordance with HMRC and Free Zone requirements, all Free Zone tenants must maintain sufficient comprehensive electronic Inventory Controls and Warehouse Management Systems concerning all materials kept under their supervision in the confines of the Free Zone. These controls must be maintained on a regular basis in accordance with HMRC requirements.

APPENDIX 2

Original Freeport operations applicant questionnaire

This questionnaire is based on previous self-assessment questionnaires concerning applications for other HMRC Special Procedures, and has now been replaced by a more updated questionnaire by HMRC as at September 2021 requiring more specific information. However, the essence of the basic information required remains the same. It would be useful to point out that readers can access the new HMRC Guidance through Google or via the GOV.UK portal concerning Freeport operations.

The purpose of this document is for the Freeport applicant tenant to supply the information necessary to assess whether they meet the criteria for operation in a Freeport. Please complete this questionnaire honestly, as HMRC will test the information supplied.

Name of Company	
Address of business	
EORI	
Date of completion	

Questions	*Answer*
1. Company **a)** If you are a limited company or a limited liability partnership, enter your incorporation number (which can be found on your Certificate of Incorporation) opposite.	
b) If you are an incorporated company please list directors' details opposite (name, home address and date of birth) and provide a management structure/ personnel chart as an attachment. If you are a sole proprietor or partnership please provide the details opposite (name(s), home address(es) and date(s) of birth).	

Questions	*Answer*
c) List the names of senior personnel (name, position and responsibility) involved in the international trade supply chain and their experience in Customs matters.	
d) How many staff are employed in the business for each area (directors/office/warehouse/ transport)?	
2. Business activities **a)** What are the main and any subsidiary business activities i.e. shipping, manufacturing, warehousing etc.?	
b) What are your usual business opening hours, this should include separate hours if the main business and warehouse operate different work patterns?	
c) Do you have any special facilities, such as a cold store?	
3. Goods to be stored **a)** Who owns the goods that you intend to store, e.g. yourselves, an associated company(ies) or 3rd party clients?	
b) Are any of your goods liable to Excise Duty? If so detail opposite the plain language descriptions, eight-digit Commodity Code(s) and quantity.	
e) Are there any goods that are subject to licences, such as controlled goods, textiles or agricultural goods? If yes, detail opposite which apply and to which goods.	
f) If you store goods that are subject to licences briefly describe what procedures are in place to ensure licences/documents are obtained?	
g) Are there any goods on which preference will be claimed? If so, detail opposite how you will monitor this procedure (correct country of origin etc.). Note: All preference documents and usage have to be fully traceable through your system(s).	

Questions	*Answer*
h) Will you be claiming any tariff quotas? If yes, briefly detail opposite how you will identify which goods are applicable to the quota and at which stage in the process you will be claiming the quota.	
i) Do you deal in goods subject to anti-dumping duty or countervailing duties? If so, detail opposite the plain language description, eight-digit Commodity Code(s) and estimated quantity imported in a year.	
j) By what process and by whom is the tariff classification of goods decided?	
k) What quality assurance measures do you take to make sure that the tariff classifications are correct?	
l) How and by whom is the Customs value of goods established? If this is by your depositor please State opposite.	
m) What quality assurance measures do you take to make sure that the Customs value is properly established?	
n) Have you applied to use common storage (now known as equivalence)? If so, briefly detail the goods being stored under common storage, i.e. goods in UK Free Circulation. Note: For common storage/ equivalence of goods subject to a tariff preference, the goods must have been obtained from the same supplier in the same country of origin. The details of the certificate must be entered in the records before its expiry date and be fully traceable through your system. Equivalence cannot be used for any goods which are subject to anti-dumping duty.	

Questions	*Answer*
o) How will you monitor the use of equivalence, will this be through accounting segregation? Briefly detail opposite.	
p) Are all your of goods subject to VAT only (i.e. have a nil rate of Customs Duty)?	
4. Goods to be entered to the Manufacturing Procedure **a)** Describe the goods to be entered into the manufacturing procedure.	
b) Are the goods you intend to import liable to Excise Duty? If so, detail opposite the plain language descriptions, eight-digit Commodity Codes and quantities.	
c) Do you intend to import any goods that are subject to licences? If yes, detail opposite which apply and to which goods.	
d) If you intend to import goods that are subject to licences briefly describe what procedures are in place to ensure that licences/ documents are obtained.	
e) Are there any goods on which preference will be claimed? If so, detail opposite how you will monitor this procedure (correct country of origin etc.) Note: All preference documents have to be fully traceable through your system(s).	
f) Do you deal in goods subject to Anti-Dumping Duty or Countervailing Duties? If so, detail opposite the plain language description, eight-digit Commodity Code(s) and estimated quantities imported in a year.	
g) Do you import goods subject to tariff quotas? If yes, what procedures do you have to check eligibility for tariff quotas?	
h) By what process and by whom is the tariff classification of goods decided?	

Questions	*Answer*
i) What quality assurance measures do you take to make sure that the tariff classifications are correct?	
j) How and by whom is the Customs Value of Goods established?	
k) What quality assurance measures do you take to make sure that the Customs value is properly established?	
l) Please provide a detailed overview of the process together with the time needed to process and dispose of the imported goods.	
m) Are you aware of the procedures required if you need to destroy goods imported for processing?	
n) Have you applied to use equivalence? If so, briefly detail the goods being processed under equivalent goods to show they meet the conditions as per section 9.3 of Notice 3001. Are the equivalent goods subject to Anti-Dumping Duty?	
o) Do you require prior exportation? If yes, please provide details of when the replacement goods will be imported in months and if the importer will be someone other than you/your company.	
<u>5. Security of goods and premises</u> **a)** What measures are in place for protection of stock against theft and loss, e.g. locations of external and internal CCTV/alarms etc.? If multiple sites are applied for in the one authorisation, list each site separately. Attach pictures of the measures in situ (alternatively these can be e-mailed to HMRC when your application is accepted, if so State opposite and include the relevant e-mail address). CCTV cameras must be accessible and monitored, confirm opposite that this is the case.	

Questions	*Answer*
b) What are the documented procedures to control access through all gates/entrance points? State if there are any areas of damage and the timescale for repairs, for example holes in fences. If multiple sites are applied for in the one authorisation, list each site separately.	
c) How is access of persons controlled for office, shipping, loading and cargo areas (for incoming and outgoing goods)?	
d) Have there been any previous instances of unlawful entry/ tampering with security devices etc., and have these been addressed?	
e) Do you own or rent your premises? If you own your premises confirm when you bought the premises and if you rent attach a copy of the first page (this must show the address, leaser, lessee and term as a minimum) and signature page(s) to the application.	
f) What fire procedures do you have in place? Note: All fire exits must be kept clear at all times.	
g) Is there a Health & Safety Policy in place? If so, briefly describe opposite.	
h) Have you carried out a risk assessment to identify the risks and threats to your business? If so, what were the results and were any changes undertaken as a result?	
i) How will the goods be stored, for example in racking? Briefly detail opposite. If multiple sites are applied for in the one authorisation, list each site separately. Attach pictures of storage area (alternatively these can be e-mailed to HMRC when your application is accepted; if so, State opposite and include the relevant e-mail address).	

Questions	*Answer*
6. Customs procedures and authorisations **a)** Do you have any other Customs approvals, for example processing or Customs Freight Simplified Procedures (CFSP)? If so, State the authorisation number(s) (EORI number for CFSP) opposite.	
b) Will goods be moving from one special procedure to another? If so, briefly describe how your records will adequately show the audit trail.	
7. UK and non-UK goods **a)** Can UK goods stored along with goods under the Special Procedures be easily identified? If so, briefly detail how your system/stock control will differentiate.	
b) Can non-UK goods stored under Special Procedures be easily identified? If so, briefly detail how your system/stock control will differentiate.	
c) What are the procedures in place to prevent unlawful removal of goods from Customs supervision? Briefly detail opposite.	
8. Declaration procedures **a)** How will your declarations be lodged with HMRC, normal declarations, Customs Freight Simplified Procedure (CFSP) or Simplified Declaration Procedure (SDP)/Entry in Declarant's Records (EIDR) under the National Export System?	
b) Who will be declared as the consignee in box 8 of the Customs declaration into the Customs warehouse? Note: All consignees must be based in the EU and if applying for a private warehouse this must be same as the authorisation holder.	

Questions	*Answer*
c) What is or will be the duty point of releases from the Customs warehouse and when will be stock records be updated?	
d) Who is or will be responsible for submitting the declarations for or on behalf of the business?	
e) Will you be using a direct representative to submit your declarations into and or out of the Freeport warehouse? If so, who?	
f) If using a third party do you have written documented procedures for each party's responsibilities, management checks and record retention policy? If yes, briefly describe opposite. Note: This is a mandatory requirement and HMRC may ask for this document; if you do not have this in place, ensure that this is completed before application.	
g) If CFSP is used, which procedure(s) are you wishing to use (Simplified Declaration Procedure (SDP) or Entry in Declarant's Records (EIDR))? Include how declarations will be made upon entry and discharge from the Freeport warehouse. If only normal procedures are to be used go to question 9.	
h) Who is the authorised party(ies) for CFSP, for example, your business or a depositor?	
i) What system is used/intended to be used to submit declarations?	
j) If you are the authorised CFSP party, from where will the declaration information be drawn?	
k) If you are going to use EIDR what is the agreed tax point (what constitutes entry in the EIDR record) and dwell time? Note: This must match with the authorised party's CFSP authorisation.	

Questions	*Answer*
l) If a third party is involved State how the holder of the EIDR record has agreed to transfer the information to the third party and to HMRC.	
m) How will the accuracy of the declarations be assured, e.g. for valuation build up and classification purposes?	
n) If Simplified National Export System is being used, detail the procedure(s) that will be used opposite.	
9. Duty management system (DMS) **a)** Do you intend to use a duty management system in support of the commercial stock records? If so, detail the proposed DMS system. If you do not wish to use a DMS go to question 10.	
b) What interface will exist between the stock systems and DMS and how it will operate? Briefly detail opposite.	
c) How do you intend to reconcile stock between the different systems and its frequency (monthly as a minimum)?	
d) If the DMS forms part of the stock records will the system ensure that the stock records are updated daily? Note: This should include bank holidays and weekends.	
10. Records **a)** Confirm opposite that your stock records contain the minimum information required and will be kept up to date at all times. See paragraph 5.1 in Notice 3001 for further information.	
b) When are the goods entered into the stock account?	

Questions	*Answer*
c) Where are the records kept, who maintains them and for what period they are kept? Briefly detail opposite, including archive schedules.	
d) How does your system(s) provide an adequate audit trail between goods, commercial documents, Customs Declarations and authorisation reference numbers? Briefly detail opposite and attach evidence (e.g. screenshots) to your application (alternatively these can be e-mailed to HMRC when your application is accepted, if so State opposite and include the relevant e-mail address).	
e) Do you use a third party to complete/store your records? If so, briefly detail the procedures opposite and how the responsibilities are divided. Note: You must have at least read only access and all records must be made available to HMRC on request. You remain liable for any debt should errors be found.	
f) Are you applying for a multi-site authorisation (where multiple premises are authorised under one authorisation)? If so, briefly detail how your system will differentiate between different locations.	
g) If you are applying for a multi-site where are the main Customs warehouse records kept? Note: This must be the main storage facility and all records must be viewable at the main storage facility.	
11. Premises controls **a)** What are the procedures for selecting goods, dealing with mis-picks and any required flags on goods (such as licences or any other administrative requirement)? Briefly detail opposite.	

Questions	*Answer*
b) What procedures do you have in place to ensure that all goods removed from the Freeport warehousing procedure are assigned in a proper manner and at the proper time, for example, after a declaration has been accepted and that the required documentation is present prior to removal (e.g. C88, entry in EIDR record, Form A, Licences, Quota, preference certificates etc.)? Briefly detail opposite.	
c) How frequently will you conduct stock checks and how will these be evidenced?	
d) How will you notify HMRC of any stock discrepancies? Note: Any discrepancies which will result in a debt must be notified to your Supervising Office, a declaration to CHIEF must not be submitted for these goods.	
e) What procedures exist for dealing with damaged goods in warehouse?	
f) How will you deal with any goods that need to be destroyed within the warehousing procedure? Note: currently this must be competed under another procedure such as processing.	
g) What procedures are in place to ensure these goods are not released from Customs supervision until all admissibility and regulatory controls have been completed satisfactorily (such as licences)?	
<u>12. Sales and temporary removals</u> **a)** Do you wish to conduct sales within the Freeport regime? If so, briefly describe opposite. Note: There are only limited circumstances where this is allowed, Internet sales, travellers to/from third countries, diplomatic/consular arrangements etc. You may not conduct	

Questions	*Answer*
retail sales unless the goods are delivered to the buyer or consignee at a location different from the Customs warehouse.	
b) Do you intend to temporarily remove goods? If so, detail how you will maintain your records and how you will monitor the removals (including ensuring that it is returned within the set timescales).	
c) Do you intend to temporarily remove goods to another country? Describe how you intend to do the movement.	
d) Do you intend to use the Transfer of Rights and Obligations (TORO) procedure?	
e) If you intend to use TORO, who will you be transferring your right and/or obligations to? Note: include their name, address and EORI.	
f) Which rights and/or obligations will you be transferring? For example, a full TORO transfers all rights and obligations, whereas a partial can just move some of the obligations to another party. HMRC will decide whether this is acceptable.	
g) In the case of a partial TORO, what will the transferee be doing to the goods? For example, are they undertaking a usual form of handling on your behalf or temporarily storing the goods?	
h) In the case of a full TORO, detail the guarantee that will be used to secure the procedure and who this belongs to opposite. In the case of a partial TORO will your guarantee continue to be used in relation to these goods?	
13. Moving goods and Usual Forms of Handling (UFH) **a)** Will you be moving goods between premises/locations within the same authorisation? If so, briefly detail how you will control this procedure.	

Questions	*Answer*
b) Will you be using the Freeport regime to move goods to the office of exit for re-exportation? Note: You are liable for the goods until proper evidence of discharge is obtained.	
c) Do you envisage using New Community Transit System normal procedures or Simplified Procedures to move goods? If so, briefly detail how this will be completed and any authorisation number used. Note: The UCC has changed the way that Special Procedures can be discharged, so your intended procedures may not be allowed.	
d) Do you intend to undertake a UFH? If so, briefly detail what you intend to do.	
E-mail **HMRC takes the security of personal information very seriously**. If you are happy to correspond via e-mail can you please provide a list of e-mail addresses that you authorise us to correspond with in the box opposite. **By providing an e-mail address(es) you are confirming that you are content for us to send information concerning your business details, including financial information and using attachments. This is relation to all matters concerning CITEX (for example, Customs Warehousing, processing, end use, guarantees etc.)**. The main risks of using e-mail that concern HMRC are as follows. Confidentiality/privacy – there is a risk that e-mail sent over the Internet may be intercepted. Confirming your identity – it is crucial that we only communicate with established business contacts at their correct e-mail addresses. There is no guarantee that an e-mail received over an insecure network, like the Internet, has not been altered during transit.	

Questions	*Answer*
Financial information could be misused. Attachments could contain a virus or malicious code. We will desensitise information wherever possible, for example by only quoting part of any unique reference numbers. We are happy to discuss how you may do the same but still provide the information we need. **By providing your e-mail address(es) opposite you are confirming that you understand and accept these risks. This confirmation will be held on file and will apply to all future e-mail correspondence until we are notified otherwise.** If you would prefer us not to respond to your enquiry by e-mail, for example because other people may have access to your e-mail account, we are happy to respond by an alternative method which will need to be agreed. For more information, see HMRC's privacy policy (web).	
If there is anything about your health or personal circumstances that may make it difficult for you to deal with this matter, please tell me so that I can help you in the most appropriate way. For more details go to www.gov.uk/dealing-hmrc-additional-needs.	

I declare that the information provided above is a true and accurate representation of my business and I have disclosed any irregularities or matters which could affect HMRC's assessment of my ability to meet the criteria. If it is found that the data given above is false, HMRC may revoke any authorisation given. Anyone who gives false information about goods imported under these arrangements may be liable to penalties under the Customs and Excise Management Act 1979. I understand the above.

Signed

Full Name

Position in the company

Date

GLOSSARY OF TERMS

3PL – Third Party Logistics Provider
ASF – Alternative Site Framework (US)
BEPS – Base Erosion and Profit Shifting (OECD project aimed at combatting Tax Avoidance)
BZ – Bonded Zone (China)
CBP – (US) Customs & Border Protection (Agency)
CBI – Confederation of British Industry
CBZ – Comprehensive Bonded Zone (China)
CFSP – Customs Freight Simplified Procedures
CPC – Customs Procedure Code
CW – Customs Warehouse
DIFC – Dubai International Financial Centre
DMS – Duty Management System
DSO – Dubai Silicon Oasis
DTEC – Dubai Technology Entrepreneur Campus
DUCR – Declaration Unique Consignment Reference
EBP – Europort Business Park, Rosslare (Ireland)
EIDR – Entry in Declarant's Records
EPZ – Export Processing Zone
ETDZ – Economic and Technical Development Zone (China)
EU – European Union
FDI – Foreign Direct Investment
FFZ – Financial Free Zone (Dubai)
FIE – Foreign-Invested Enterprise (China)
FTZ – Foreign-Trade Zone (US)
FZ – Free Zone
FZA – Free Zone Authority
GBER – General Block Exemption Regulation
GST – Goods and Services Tax (Canada)
HIDZ – High-Tech Industrial Development Zone (China)
HMRC – HM Revenue & Customs
IFSC – International Financial Services Centre
IP – Inward Processing Relief
IPR – Intellectual Property Rights

JAFZ – Jebel Ali Free Zone
JAFZA – Jebel Ali Free Zone Authority
Magnet Site – General Purpose (Foreign Trade) Zone (US)
MAXNOM – Maximum allowed level of Non-originating Material
MFTZ – Manaus Free Trade Zone (English version of ZFM – Zona Franca de Manaus)
MPF – Merchandise Processing Fee (US)
OECD – Organisation for Economic Co-operation and Development
Offshore Supply Base – A Supply Base located next to a seaport which is designed to service the offshore Oil & Gas or Energy Renewables sectors
RKC – Revised Kyoto Convention
SAFE – Safety and Accountability in the Freight Environment (The SAFE Framework of Standards)
SCSZ – Special Customs Supervision Zone (China)
SD – Supplementary Declaration
SDG – Sustainable Development Goals
SDI – Supplementary Declaration Imports (Bonded Receipt)
SEZ – Special Economic Zone
SME – Small to Medium Enterprise
Tariff Inversion – Also known as 'Reversed Cascading': Where the finished product has a lower *Ad Valorem* Import Duty rate than those of its constituent Components
TFA – World Trade Organization Trade Facilitation Agreement
UAE – United Arab Emirates
UK – United Kingdom
UKTPO – UK Trade Policy Observatory
UN – United Nations
UNCLOS – United Nations Convention of the Law of the Sea
UNCTAD – United Nations Conference on Trade and Development
UNIDO – United Nations Industrial Development Organization
US – United States
VAT – Value Added Tax
WCO – World Customs Organization
WEPZA – World Export Processing Zone Authority
WFZO – World Free Zones Organization
WMS – Warehouse Management System
ZFM – Zona Franca de Madeira (Portugal); Zona Franca de Manaus (Brazil)

BIBLIOGRAPHY

Baissac, C. (1996). *A Critique of Cost-Benefit Analysis in the Evaluation of Export Processing Zones*. WEPZA, 15 April 1996.

Bolin, R. (1999). *The Changing World of Free Zones*. Flagstaff, AZ: Flagstaff Institute, p. 233.

Bolin, R. (1998). *The Global Network of Free Zones in the 21st Century*. WEPZA, p. 117.

Bost, F. (2016). The World of Free Zones. *World Free Zones Organization Bulletin*, pp. 21–25. Accessible at www.worldfzo.org/Portals/0/OpenContent/Files/446/World_FZO_Bulletin01.pdf; www.worldfzo.org.

Bost, F. (2011). *Are Economic Free Zones Good for Development*? West Africa Challenges, Sahel and West-Africa Club, OECD, p. 19. Accessible at www.oecd.org/dataoecd/24/39/49814045.pdf.

Bost, F. (2010). *Atlas mondial des zones franches*. Paris: La Documentation Française/CNRS.

Chen, X. (2019). Change and Continuity in Special Economic Zones: A Reassessment and Lessons from China. *Transnational Corporations*, 26(2).

Farole, T. and Akinci, G. (2011). *Special Economic Zones: Progress, Emerging Challenges, and Future Directions*. Washington DC: The International Bank for Reconstruction and Development/The World Bank, p. 319.

HM Government – Freeports Consultation (Feb 2020). www.gov.uk/government/consultations/freeports-consultation

HM Government – Response to Freeports Consultation (Oct 2020).

HMRC – Special Economic Procedures; Notice on GOV.UK website.

Holmes, P. and Serwicka, I. (Feb 2019). *What is the Extra Mileage in the Re-Introduction of Free Zones in the UK*? blogs.sussex.ac.uk/uktpo/files/2019/02/BP28print.pdf

Institute for Government – Trade: Freeports and Free Zones (Feb 2020). www.instituteforgovernment.org.uk/explainers/trade-freeports-free-zones

National Association of Foreign-Trade Zones (NAFTZ) (2019). *The US Foreign-Trade Zones Program*. www.naftz.org

OECD (2014). *Special Economic Zones: Helping Resource-rich Countries Diversify*. Working Paper, Paris, p. 100.

OECD (2007). *Export Processing Zones: Past and Future Role in Trade and Development*. OECD Trade Policy Working Paper No. 53.

Rowbotham, M. (2004). *Comparison of the Prestwick Freeport and the Montréal Mirabel Free-Trade Zone*. University of Glasgow. UK Government Policy on Freeports – April 2021.

UN (1985). *Export Processing Zones in Developing Countries*. (Kreye O., Heinrichs J, Fröbel F., UN/ILO, 1987).

UNCTAD (1999). *The Dynamics of Export-Processing Zones* (Wei Ge, 1999). www.unctad.org/system/files/official-document/dp_144.en.pdf

UNCTAD (2019). *World Investment Report 2019*: *Special Economic Zones*. New York and Geneva: United Nations, pp. 126–206.

UNCTAD (2002). Export Processing Zones. *World Investment Report: Transnational Corporations and Export Competitiveness*. Geneva: United Nations, pp. 214–220.

WFZO (2016). *Global Value Chain: Opportunities for the Free Zone of the Future*, p. 127.

WFZO (2015). *The World of Free Zones*. Dubai, p. 194.

World Bank (2019). *Eco-Industrial Park Handbook*. Title Page Photo: Teesport (courtesy of gazette-live.co.uk).

INDEX

Note: Page numbers in *italic* indicate a figure on the corresponding page.